Lecture Notes in Computer Science 15026

Founding Editors

Gerhard Goos
Juris Hartmanis

Editorial Board Members

Elisa Bertino, *Purdue University, West Lafayette, IN, USA*
Wen Gao, *Peking University, Beijing, China*
Bernhard Steffen, *TU Dortmund University, Dortmund, Germany*
Moti Yung, *Columbia University, New York, NY, USA*

The series Lecture Notes in Computer Science (LNCS), including its subseries Lecture Notes in Artificial Intelligence (LNAI) and Lecture Notes in Bioinformatics (LNBI), has established itself as a medium for the publication of new developments in computer science and information technology research, teaching, and education.

LNCS enjoys close cooperation with the computer science R & D community, the series counts many renowned academics among its volume editors and paper authors, and collaborates with prestigious societies. Its mission is to serve this international community by providing an invaluable service, mainly focused on the publication of conference and workshop proceedings and postproceedings. LNCS commenced publication in 1973.

Quentin Bramas · Arnaud Casteigts · Kitty Meeks
Editors

Algorithmics of Wireless Networks

20th International Symposium, ALGOWIN 2024
Egham, UK, September 5–6, 2024
Proceedings

Springer

Editors
Quentin Bramas
Université de Strasbourg
ILLKIRCH CEDEX, France

Kitty Meeks
University of Glasgow
Glasgow, UK

Arnaud Casteigts
CS Department
University of Geneva
Geneva, Switzerland

ISSN 0302-9743　　　　　　ISSN 1611-3349　(electronic)
Lecture Notes in Computer Science
ISBN 978-3-031-74579-9　　　ISBN 978-3-031-74580-5　(eBook)
https://doi.org/10.1007/978-3-031-74580-5

© The Editor(s) (if applicable) and The Author(s), under exclusive license
to Springer Nature Switzerland AG 2025

This work is subject to copyright. All rights are solely and exclusively licensed by the Publisher, whether the whole or part of the material is concerned, specifically the rights of translation, reprinting, reuse of illustrations, recitation, broadcasting, reproduction on microfilms or in any other physical way, and transmission or information storage and retrieval, electronic adaptation, computer software, or by similar or dissimilar methodology now known or hereafter developed.
The use of general descriptive names, registered names, trademarks, service marks, etc. in this publication does not imply, even in the absence of a specific statement, that such names are exempt from the relevant protective laws and regulations and therefore free for general use.
The publisher, the authors and the editors are safe to assume that the advice and information in this book are believed to be true and accurate at the date of publication. Neither the publisher nor the authors or the editors give a warranty, expressed or implied, with respect to the material contained herein or for any errors or omissions that may have been made. The publisher remains neutral with regard to jurisdictional claims in published maps and institutional affiliations.

This Springer imprint is published by the registered company Springer Nature Switzerland AG
The registered company address is: Gewerbestrasse 11, 6330 Cham, Switzerland

If disposing of this product, please recycle the paper.

Preface

This volume contains the papers presented at ALGOWIN 2024: the 20th International Symposium on Algorithmics of Wireless Networks, held during September 5–6, 2024, at Royal Holloway, University of London in Egham, UK, as part of ALGO 2024.

ALGOWIN is an international symposium dedicated to algorithmic aspects of wireless networks. Founded in 2004, it originally focused on sensor networks. It was formerly known as ALGOSENSORS and now covers algorithmic issues arising in wireless networks of all types of computational entities, static or mobile, including sensor networks, sensor-actuator networks and systems of autonomous robots. The focus is on the design and analysis of algorithms, models of computation and experimental analysis. The new title of the conference, the International Symposium on Algorithmics of Wireless Networks, reflects this broader scope.

In response to the Call for Papers, 26 submissions were received. Each submission was reviewed by at least three Program Committee members and some trusted external reviewers, and evaluated on its quality, originality and relevance to the symposium. The committee decided to accept 14 papers for presentation at ALGOWIN 2024 and inclusion in these proceedings. The program of ALGOWIN 2024 also included an invited talk by Petra Berenbrink, Universität Hamburg, entitled, "The Population Model as Model for Sensor Networks".

The Program Committee selected the following contribution for the Best Paper and Best Student Paper Award, both kindly sponsored by Springer:

- **Best paper:** Bike Assisted Evacuation on a Line of Robots with Communication Faults, by Khaled Jawhar and Evangelos Kranakis
- **Best student paper:** On the Exponential Growth of Geometric Shapes, by Nada Almalki, Siddharth Gupta and Othon Michail

We would like to thank the Steering Committee, chaired by Sotiris Nikoletseas, for giving us the opportunity to serve as Program Chairs of ALGOWIN 2024. Furthermore, we would like to thank all the authors who responded to the Call for Papers, the invited speaker for enriching the program of the event, and the Program Committee members and external reviewers for their fundamental contributions to the paper selection process, resulting in a strong program. We would also like to warmly thank the ALGO 2024 organizing committee, chaired by Argyrios Deligkas and Eduard Eiben, for enabling us to hold ALGOWIN as part of the ALGO symposium and taking care of all organizational matters. We would like to thank Springer for publishing the proceedings of ALGOWIN 2024 in the LNCS series and for their support and sponsorship.

Finally, we would like to acknowledge the use of EasyChair for handling the submission of papers and managing the review process.

September 2024

Quentin Bramas
Arnaud Casteigts
Kitty Meeks

Organization

Program Committee Chairs

Quentin Bramas — University of Strasbourg, France
Arnaud Casteigts — University of Geneva, Switzerland
Kitty Meeks — University of Glasgow, UK

Steering Committee

Jie Gao — Rutgers University, USA
Magnus M. Halldorsson — Reykjavik U., Iceland
Bhaskar Krishnamachari — U. of Southern California, USA
P.R. Kumar — Texas A&M U., USA
Sotiris Nikoletseas (Chair) — U. of Patras and CTI, Greece
Jose Rolim — U. of Geneva
Christian Scheideler — Paderborn University, Germany
Paul Spirakis — U. of Liverpool, UK

Organization Chairs

Argyrios Deligkas — Royal Holloway, University of London, UK
Eduard Eiben — Royal Holloway, University of London, UK

Program Committee

Eleni C. Akrida — Durham University, UK
Petra Berenbrink — University of Hamburg, Germany
Binh-Minh Bui-Xuan — LIP6 (CNRS — SU UPMC), France
Christelle Caillouet — Université Côte d'Azur, France
Monika Csikos — IRIF Université Paris Cité, France
Fabien Dufoulon — Lancaster University, UK
Thomas Erlebach — Durham University, UK
Paola Flocchini — University of Ottawa, Canada
Francesca Fossati — Sorbonne University, France
Jie Gao — Rutgers University, USA

Oana Iova   INSA Lyon, France
Sayaka Kamei   Hiroshima University, Japan
Ralf Klasing   CNRS and University of Bordeaux, France
Danny Krizanc   Wesleyan University, USA
Pierre Leone   University of Geneva, Switzerland
Andrea Marino   University of Florence, Italy
Hendrik Molter   Ben-Gurion University of the Negev, Israel
Jason Schoeters   University of Cambridge, UK
Ana Silva   Universidade Federal do Ceará, Brazil
George Skretas   Hasso Plattner Institute, University of Potsdam, Germany
Paul Spirakis   University of Liverpool, UK
Yuichi Sudo   Hosei University, Japan

Additional Reviewers

Duncan Adamson   University of St Andrews, UK
Michelle Döring   Hasso Plattner Institute, Germany
Nathan Flaherty   University of Liverpool, UK
Matthias Gehnen   RWTH Aachen University, Germany
Guilherme de Castro Mendes Gomes   Federal University of Minas Gerais, Brazil
Allen Ibiapina   Federal University of Ceará, Brazil
Anissa Lamani   University of Strasbourg, France
Raul Lopes   Federal University of Ceará, Brazil
Walner Mendonça   University of Warwick, UK
Minh Hang Nguyen   Université Paris Cité, France
Fukuhito Ooshita   Fukui University of Technology, Japan
Louise Penz   Université Le Havre Normandie, France
Gokarna Sharma   Kent State University, USA
Grzegorz Stachowiak   University of Wrocław, Poland
Antoine Toullalan   Université Le Havre Normandie, France
Daniel Vaz   Université Paris Dauphine, PSL, France
Katsuhisa Yamanaka   Iwate University, Japan

Contents

Collision-Free Robot Scheduling 1
   Duncan Adamson, Nathan Flaherty, Igor Potapov, and Paul G. Spirakis

On the Exponential Growth of Geometric Shapes 16
   Nada Almalki, Siddharth Gupta, and Othon Michail

Optimizing Robot Dispersion on Unoriented Grids: With and Without
Fault Tolerance 31
   Rik Banerjee, Manish Kumar, and Anisur Rahaman Molla

Channel Allocation Revisited Through 1-Extendability of Graphs 46
   Anthony Busson, Malory Marin, and Rémi Watrigant

On the Min-Max Star Partitioning Number 61
   Sarah Feldmann and Torben Schürenberg

Collision Detection for Modular Robots - It Is Easy to Cause Collisions
and Hard to Avoid Them 76
   Siddharth Gupta, Marc van Kreveld, Othon Michail,
   and Andreas Padalkin

Bike Assisted Evacuation on a Line of Robots with S/R Communication
Faults 91
   Khaled Jawhar and Evangelos Kranakis

On Permutation Selectors and their Applications in Ad-Hoc Radio
Networks Protocols 106
   Jordan Kuschner, Yugarshi Shashwat, Sarthak Yadav, and Marek Chrobak

Reconfigurable Routing in Data Center Networks 117
   David C. Kutner and Iain A. Stewart

The Threshold of Existence of δ-Temporal Cliques in Random Simple
Temporal Graphs 131
   George B. Mertzios, Sotiris Nikoletseas, Christoforos Raptopoulos,
   and Paul G. Spirakis

The Exact Spanning Ratio of the Parallelogram Delaunay Graph 144
   Prosenjit Bose, Jean-Lou De Carufel, and Sandrine Njoo

A 1.5-Approximation Algorithm for Activating Two Disjoint st-Paths 159
Zeev Nutov and Dawod Kahba

Modular Population Protocols 173
Michael Raskin

Decreasing Verification Radius in Local Certification 188
*Laurent Feuilloley, Jan Janoušek, Jan Matyáš Křišťan,
and Josef Erik Sedláček*

Author Index 203

Collision-Free Robot Scheduling

Duncan Adamson[1], Nathan Flaherty[2,3](✉), Igor Potapov[3],
and Paul G. Spirakis[3]

[1] School of Computer Science, University of St Andrews, St Andrews, UK
duncan.adamson@st-andrews.ac.uk
[2] Leverhulme Research Centre for Functional Materials Design, University of Liverpool, Liverpool, UK
[3] Department of Computer Science, University of Liverpool, Liverpool, UK
{n.flaherty,potapov,p.spirakis}@liverpool.ac.uk

Abstract. In this paper, we investigate the problem of designing *schedules* for completing a set of tasks at fixed locations with multiple robots in a laboratory. We represent the laboratory as a graph with tasks placed on fixed vertices and robots represented as agents, with the constraint that no two robots may occupy the same vertex at any given timestep. Each schedule is partitioned into a set of timesteps, corresponding to a walk through the graph (allowing for a robot to wait at a vertex to complete a task), with each timestep taking time equal to the time for a robot to move from one vertex to another and each task taking some given number of timesteps during the completion of which a robot must stay at the vertex containing the task. The goal is to determine a set of schedules, with one schedule for each robot, minimising the number of timesteps taken by the schedule taking the greatest number of timesteps within the set of schedules. We show that this problem is NP-complete for both star graphs (for $k \geq 2$ robots), and planar graphs (for any number of robots). Finally, we provide positive results for path, cycle, and tadpole graphs, showing that we can find an optimal set of schedules for k robots completing m tasks of equal duration of a path of length n in $O(kmn)$, $O(kmn^2)$ time, and $O(k^3m^4n)$ time respectively.

1 Introduction

Across a wide range of industries, there is an increase in the use of automation. This has led to a wide range of problems relating to the scheduling of autonomous agents within workplaces. This includes spacecraft manufacturing [20], Unmanned Aerial Vehicle [23], and vehicle routing [25].

In this paper, we are particularly interested in the scheduling of robots within chemistry labs. This is motivated by a significant and expanding body of work concerning robotic chemists. Initial work on these systems focused on building robots performing reactions within fixed environments [16–19,21], however recently Burger et al. [7] have presented a robot capable of moving within a laboratory and completing tasks throughout the space. The works of Burger et al. [7] and Liu et al. [20] provide the main motivation for this work, namely

© The Author(s), under exclusive license to Springer Nature Switzerland AG 2025
Q. Bramas et al. (Eds.): ALGOWIN 2024, LNCS 15026, pp. 1–15, 2025.
https://doi.org/10.1007/978-3-031-74580-5_1

the problem of moving robots within a laboratory environment (as presented by Burger et al. [7]) while avoiding collisions (as investigated in the manufacturing context by Liu et al. [20]).

In addition to physical science motivation, our model and algorithmic results are strongly based on graph theory, in particular, graph exploration. Informally, we model our problem as a graph problem, where robots are represented as agents in the graph, with the goal of finding a set of walks for each robot, allowing every task to be completed without any collisions. Our model of movement for robots within the graph matches the exploration model given by Czyzowicz et al. [8], where agents (robots) start at fixed points within the graph, then can move provided that no pair of agents occupy the same vertex in the same timesteps. The primary difference between our model and that of [8] is that in our setting, the agents are given a schedule from some central system rather than each having to determine the best route separately.

More general exploration problems have been considered in a variety of settings. Of particular interest to us are the works regarding the efficient exploration of temporal graphs. As in our setting, exploration is, in most cases, centrally controlled, with the primary goal of minimising the number of timesteps required to complete the exploration, corresponding to the length of the longest walk taken by any agent in the graph. Further, having the edge set of the graph change over time is similar to, and indeed can be closely mimicked by, the collision-avoiding condition in our problem, in the sense that the available moves for a given agent change throughout the lifetime of the graph.

There is a large number of results across many settings and variations of the temporal graph exploration problem, including when the number of vertices an agent can visit in one timestep is unbounded [4,14], bounded [10,11,22], and for specific graph classes [2,3,5,6,9,12,13,24]. Particularly relevant to us is the work of Michail and Spirakis [22], who showed that the problem of determining the fastest exploration of a temporal graph is NP-hard, and, furthermore, no constant factor approximation algorithm exists of the shortest exploration (in terms of the length of the path found by the algorithm, compared to the shortest path exploring the graph) unless $P = NP$. As noted, the change in the structure of temporal graphs is close to the challenges implemented in our graph by agents blocking potential moves from each other. In terms of positive results, the work of Erlebach et al. [10] provided a substantial set of results that have formed the basis for much of the subsequent work on algorithmic results for temporal graph exploration. Of particular interest to us are the results that show that, for temporal graphs that are connected in every timestep, an agent can visit any subset of m vertices in at most $O(nm)$ time, and provide constructions for faster explorations of graphs with b agents and an (r, b)-division ($O(n^2b/r + nrb^2)$ time), and $2 \times n$ grids with $4 \log n$ agents ($O(n \log n)$ time).

Our Contributions. In this paper, we present a set of results for the k-ROBOT SCHEDULING problem. A short summary is provided in Table 1. Informally, we define the k-ROBOT SCHEDULING scheduling problem as the problem of assigning schedules (walks on the graph with robots completing every task from a given set), minimising the time needed to complete the schedule.

We lay out the remainder of this paper as follows. In Sect. 2 we provide the definitions and notation used in the rest of the paper, with the k-ROBOT SCHEDULING problem fully presented in Problem 1. In Sect. 3 we show that k-ROBOT SCHEDULING is NP-complete for a large number of graph classes, explicitly Complete Graphs, Bipartite Graphs, Star graphs (Theorem 1), and Planar graphs (Theorem 2). Finally, Sect. 4 provides the algorithmic results for this paper, namely an optimal algorithm for constructing a schedule for k robots on a path, cycle and tadpole graphs for tasks with equal duration (Theorems 4, 6 and 7 respectively), and a k-approximation algorithm for creating a schedule with k robots on a path graph (Theorem 5).

Table 1. Our results for k-Robot Scheduling for different graph classes and values of $k \in \mathbb{N}$.

Setting	Result
General graphs, $k \in \mathbb{N}$	NP-complete (Theorem 3)
Star graphs (and trees), $k \geq 2$	NP-complete (Theorem 1)
Planar graphs, $k \in \mathbb{N}$	NP-complete (Theorem 2)
Path graphs, with m tasks of equal duration,	Optimal $O(kmn)$ time algorithm (Theorem 4)
Cycle graphs, with m tasks of equal duration	Optimal $O(kmn^2)$ time algorithm (Theorem 6)
Tadpole graph, with m tasks of equal duration	Optimal $O(k^3 m^4, n)$ time algorithm (Theorem 7)
Path graphs, $k \in \mathbb{N}$	k-approximation Algorithm (Theorem 5)

2 Preliminaries

For the remainder of this paper, we define graphs as a tuple containing a set of vertices V and a set of edges $E \subseteq V \times V$. A *walk* in a graph G of length ℓ is a sequence of ℓ edges such that the second vertex in the ith edge is the first vertex in the $(i+1)^{th}$ edge, i.e. a sequence of the form $(v_1, v_2), (v_2, v_3), \ldots, (v_{\ell-1}, v_\ell)$. Any walk w can visit the same vertex multiple times and may use the same edge multiple times. Given a walk $w = (v_1, v_2), (v_2, v_3), \ldots, (v_{\ell-1}, v_\ell)$, we denote by $|w|$ the total number of edges in w, and by $w[i]$ the ith edge in w. In this paper, we also allow walks to contain self-adjacent moves, i.e. moves of the form (v_i, v_i)

for every vertex in the graph. We do so to represent remaining at a fixed position for some length of time. Given a pair of naturals $i, j \in \mathbb{N}$ where $i \leq j$, we denote by $[i, j]$ the set $\{i, i+1, \ldots, j\}$. For a given walk w, we denote by $w[i, j]$ the walk $w[i], w[i+1], \ldots, w[j]$.

In this problem, we consider a set of agents, which we call *robots*, moving on a given graph $G = (V, E)$ and completing a set of tasks $\mathcal{T} = \{t_1, t_2, \ldots, t_m\}$. As mentioned in our introduction, this problem originates in the setting of lab spaces, particularly in the chemistry setting. As such, our definitions of robots and tasks are designed to mimic those found in real-world problems. We associate each task with a vertex on which it is located and the duration required to complete the task. We do not allow tasks to be moved by a robot, a task can only be completed by a single robot remaining at the station for the entire task duration, and any robot may complete any number of tasks, with no restrictions on which task a robot can complete. This requirement reflects the motivation from chemistry, where tasks reflect reactions that must be done within an exact time frame and at a fixed workstation.

Formally, we define a task t_i as a tuple (v_i, d_i) where d_i is the *duration* of the task, and v_i is the vertex at which the task is located. We use $|t_i|$ to denote the duration of the task t_i. In general, the reader may assume that for a graph $G = (V, E)$ containing the vertex set $V = \{v_1, v_2, \ldots, v_n\}$, the notation i_t is used to denote the index of the vertex at which task $t = (v_{i_t}, d)$ is located. This will be specified throughout the paper where relevant.

To complete tasks, we assign each robot a *schedule*, composed of an alternating sequence of walks and tasks. We note that each schedule can begin and end with either a walk and a walk, a walk and a task, a task and a walk, or a task and a task. We treat each schedule as a set of commands to the robot, directing it within a given time frame. In this way, we partition the schedule into a set of timesteps, with each timestep allowing a robot to move along one edge or complete some fraction of a task, with a task t requiring exactly $|t|$ timesteps to complete. We call the time span of a schedule the total number of timesteps required to complete it. The *time span* of the schedule C containing the walks $w_1, w_2, \ldots, w_p$ and tasks $t_1, t_2, \ldots, t_m$ is given by $|C| = \left(\sum_{i \in [1,p]} |w_i|\right) + \left(\sum_{j \in [1,m]} |t_j|\right)$. For a set of schedules $\mathcal{C}$ the time span is given by the maximum time span of all schedules in $\mathcal{C}$. Given a walk w directly following the task t in the schedule C, we require that the first edge traversed in w begins at the vertex v_{i_t} on which t is located. Similarly, we require that the task t' following the walk w' in the schedule C is located on the last vertex in the last edge in w'. We additionally assume that the robot remains on the vertex containing the last vertex visited in the schedule.

The *walk representation* $\mathcal{W}(C)$ of a schedule C is an ordered sequence of edges formed by replacing the task $t_i = (d, v_i)$ in C with a walk of length $|t_i| = d$ consisting only of the edge (v_i, v_i), then concatenate the walks together in order. Note that $|\mathcal{W}(C)| = |C|$. For a given robot R assigned schedule C, in timestep i R is located on the vertex $v \in V$ that is the end vertex of the ith edge in $\mathcal{W}(C)$, i.e., the vertex v such that $\mathcal{W}(C)[i] = (u, v)$. We require the first vertex in the walk representation of any schedule C assigned to robot R to be the *starting vertex* of R, i.e. some predetermined vertex representing where R starts on the graph. If the schedule C containing the task t is assigned to robot R, we say that t is *assigned* to R.

Given a set of schedules $\mathcal{C} = (C_1, C_2, \ldots, C_k)$ for a set of k robots $R_1, R_2, \ldots, R_k$, and set of tasks $\mathcal{T} = (t_1, t_2, \ldots, t_m)$. We say that $\mathcal{C}$ is *task completing* if for every task $t \in \mathcal{T}$ there exists exactly one schedule C_i such that $t \in C_i$. We call $\mathcal{C}$ *collision-free* if there is no timestep where any pair of robots occupy the same vertex or traverse the same edge. Formally, $\mathcal{C}$ is collision-free if, for every C_i, C_j where $i \neq j$ and time-step $s \in [1, |C_i|]$, $\mathcal{W}(C_i)[s] = (v, u)$ and $\mathcal{W}(C_j)[s] = (v', u')$ satisfies $u \neq u'$, $v \neq v'$ and $(v, u) \neq (u', v')$.

For the remainder of this paper, we assume every robot in the graph is assigned exactly 1 schedule. Given 2 sets of schedules $\mathcal{C}$ and $\mathcal{C}'$, we say $\mathcal{C}$ is *faster* than $\mathcal{C}'$ if $\max_{C_i \in \mathcal{C}} |C_i| < \max_{C'_j \in \mathcal{C}'} |C'_j|$. Given a graph $G = (V, E)$, set of k robots $R_1, R_2, \ldots, R_k$ starting on vertices $sv_1, sv_2, \ldots, sv_k$, and set of tasks $\mathcal{T}$, a *fastest* task-completing, collision-free set of k-schedules is the set of schedules $\mathcal{C}$ such that any other set of task-completing, collision-free schedules is no faster than $\mathcal{C}$. Note that there may be multiple such schedules.

Problem 1 (k-ROBOT SCHEDULING). Given a graph $G = (V, E)$, set of k robots $R_1, R_2, \ldots, R_k$ starting on vertices $sv_1, sv_2, \ldots, sv_k$, and set of tasks $\mathcal{T}$, what is the fastest task-completing, collision-free set of k-schedules $\mathcal{C} = (C_1, C_2, \ldots, C_k)$ such that C_i can be assigned to R_i, for all $i \in [1, k]$?

We can rephrase k-ROBOT SCHEDULING as a decision problem by asking, for a given time-limit L, if there exists some task-completing, collision-free set of k-schedules $\mathcal{C} = (C_1, C_2, \ldots, C_k)$ such that C_i can be assigned to R_i and $|C_i| \leq L$, for all $i \in [1, k]$.

Example 1. An example of a task-fulfilling set of schedules for the graph shown in Fig. 1 is

$$\mathcal{C} = \{([(v_7, v_8), (v_8, v_5)], (v_5, 5)),$$
$$([(v_9, v_6), (v_6, v_3), (v_3, v_2)], (v_2, 3), [(v_2, v_1), (v_1, v_4)], (v_4, 2))\}$$

which has a time span of 10 . Which is not optimal, since if the robot starting on v_9 was the one to complete v_5 then we have the following faster set of schedules,

$$\{[(v_7, v_4)], (v_4, 2), [(v_4, v_1), (v_1, v_2)], (v_2, 3), ([(v_9, v_6), (v_6, v_5)], (v_5, 5))\}$$

which has a time span of 8.

2.1 Problems Used for NP-Hardness Reductions

Before providing our results, we provide a quick overview of the problems that are used in Sect. 3 as a basis for the hardness. As these are well-known problems, this may primarily be thought of as an overview of the notation used for the remainder of the paper. For more details on this problem, we turn the reader to the textbook of Garey and Johnson [15].

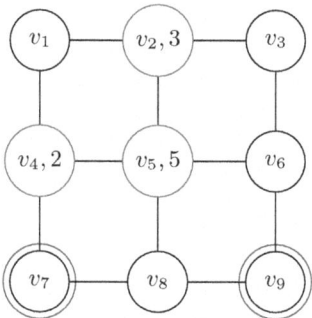

Fig. 1. A graph with tasks and robots. Blue vertices indicate the positions of robots, red vertices the locations of tasks, and red numbers the durations of the tasks. (Color figure online)

k-Set Partition. Given a set of integers $\mathcal{S} = (s_1, s_2, \ldots, s_m)$, we define a *partition* of $\mathcal{S}$ into k sets as a set of k-sets $S_1, S_2, \ldots, S_k$ such that $\bigcup_{i \in [1,k]} S_i = \mathcal{S}$ and for any $i, j \in [1, k], i \neq j, S_i \cap S_j = \emptyset$. In the case of multiple integers with the same value, we assume that each entry in the set has a unique identifier, allowing this definition to hold. An *exact partition* of $\mathcal{S}$ into k sets $S_1, S_2, \ldots, S_k$ is a partition such that $\sum_{s \in S_i} s = \sum_{s' \in S_j} s = \sum_{s'' \in \mathcal{S}} s''/k$, for every $i, j \in [1, k]$. The k-set partition problem asks if an exact partition exists for a given set $\mathcal{S}$ and integer k.

Hamiltonian Path. A *Hamiltonian path* for a given graph G is a walk w in G such that each vertex is visited *exactly* once. The Hamiltonian path problem asks if such a path exists for a given graph. For our reduction we consider the more restricted case of finding a Hamiltonian Path starting at a given vertex $v \in G$.

3 Hardness Results

In this section, we show that the k-ROBOT SCHEDULING problem is NP-complete, even for highly restricted graph classes. Explicitly, we prove NP-hardness results for complete graphs, bipartite graphs, trees and planar graphs. We note that our hardness result for complete graphs, bipartite graphs, and trees hold for at least 2 robots, while that for planar graphs holds even for 1 robot. As such, the result for trees does not imply the result for planar graphs. The proof of Theorem 3 follows from these proofs. In order to claim NP-completeness however, we must first prove that the problem is in NP.

Lemma 1. *k-ROBOT SCHEDULING is in NP, for any $k \in \mathbb{N}$.*

Proof. Observe that given any solution to k-ROBOT SCHEDULING, we can verify the correctness in polynomial time (relative to the size of input) by simulating the solution. Hence, the problem is in NP. □

Theorem 1. k-ROBOT SCHEDULING *is NP-complete on star graphs for* $k \geq 2$.

Proof. Recall that a star graph is a tree where all but one vertex has degree 1.

We prove this statement by a reduction from the set partition problem. Assume we are given a set partition instance where $\mathcal{S} = \{s_1, s_2, \ldots, s_m\}$. We assume, without loss of generality, that $s \geq 2$, for all $s \in \mathcal{S}$. From this instance, we construct the 2-ROBOT SCHEDULING instance as follows. Let $G = (V, E)$ be a graph containing the set $V = \{v_s\} \cup V^T \cup V^R = \{v_s\} \cup \{v_1^t, v_2^t, \ldots, v_m^t\} \cup \{v_1^r, v_2^r\}$ of $m+3$ vertices. We call the subset $V^T = \{v_1^t, v_2^t, \ldots, v_m^t\}$ the *task vertices*, the subset $V^R = \{v_1^r, v_2^r\}$ the *robot vertices* and vertex v_s, the *star vertex*. As the names imply, the task vertices contain the tasks, the robot vertices are the start position of the robots, and the star vertex is the central vertex of the graph. The edge set E is defined as $\{(v_s, v_i) \mid v_i \in V \setminus \{v_s\}\}$. We add 2 robots, R_1 and R_2, placing R_1 on v_1^r and R_2 on v_2^r.

We construct the set of tasks $\mathcal{T} = \{t_1, t_2, \ldots, t_m\}$, defining the task t_i as having a duration of $2 \cdot s_i - 2$, and is located on v_i^t. We highlight now that the even length of each task is key to the remainder of our reduction. In brief, we ensure that there exists some schedule where R_1 will complete tasks only on even timesteps and R_2 only on odd timesteps (in general for k robots, robot R_i completes tasks on timesteps $t+1$ for $t \equiv i \mod k$ for $i \in [k]$). In this way, we avoid collision as R_1 will only occupy the star vertex on odd timesteps and R_2 on even timesteps.

Now, we claim there exists a schedule $\mathcal{C}$ taking $1 + \sum_{s \in \mathcal{S}} s$ time if and only if there exists a perfect partition of $\mathcal{S}$ into 2 sets.

First, we show that given a schedule $\mathcal{C} = \{C_1, C_2\}$ taking $1 + \sum_{s \in \mathcal{S}} s$ time, we can construct 2 subsets of $\mathcal{S}, S_1, S_2$ such that $\sum_{s \in S_1} s = \sum_{s' \in S_2} s'$. We do so by adding to S_i the entry in $\mathcal{S}$ corresponding to each task completed in C_i. As the task t_i requires $s_i - 2$ time to complete, and the robot assigned to it requires 2 timesteps to reach v_i from the previous vertex, if the schedule C containing t_i is completed in either $\sum_{s \in \mathcal{S}} s$ or $1 + \sum_{s \in \mathcal{S}} s$ timesteps, then the size of the set S_1 must be $\sum_{s \in \mathcal{S}} s/2$, and hence S_1 and S_2 are a perfect partition of $\mathcal{S}$. In the other direction, given any perfect partition S_1, S_2 of $\mathcal{S}$, we can construct a schedule $\mathcal{C} = \{C_1, C_2\}$ taking $1 + \sum_{s \in \mathcal{S}} s$ timesteps by having r_1 complete the tasks $\{t_i \mid \forall s_i \in S_1\}$, and r_2 complete the tasks $\{t_j \mid \forall s_j \in S_2\}$, after waiting on the starting vertex for 1 timestep. As the time to travel between each task is 2, and as each task has an even length, r_1 will move only on odd timesteps and r_2 on even ones, thus this schedule is collision-free and requires $1 + \sum_{s \in \mathcal{S}} s$ timesteps to complete.

Now, assume that no schedule taking $1 + \sum_{s \in \mathcal{S}} s$ timesteps exists. Then, by the same arguments as above, it must not be possible to form any perfect partition of $\mathcal{S}$ as such a partition would give a schedule taking $1 + \sum_{s \in \mathcal{S}} s$ time. Hence, this statement holds. Similarly, if no perfect partition of $\mathcal{S}$ exists, then no schedule taking $1 + \sum_{s \in \mathcal{S}} s$ timesteps exists, completing the proof. □

Despite being NP-hard for $k \geq 2$, when we have only one robot the problem becomes trivial.

Observation 1. *1-Robot Scheduling can be solved in polynomial time for star graphs.*

Corollary 1. *k-Robot Scheduling is NP-complete for trees.*

Theorem 2. *1-Robot Scheduling on planar graphs is NP-complete, even when all tasks are of equal duration.*

For space reasons the full proof is in the full version on arXiv [1]. The high-level idea is to take as input an instance of the Hamiltonian path problem for a planar graph, and construct a 1-Robot Scheduling instance using the same graph, placing a task of duration 1 on each vertex. The fastest task-completing schedule to this new instance will correspond to the fastest walk over the graph visiting every vertex, and thus a Hamiltonian path if one exists.

Theorem 3. *k-Robot Scheduling is NP-complete for any $k \in \mathbb{N}$.*

4 Algorithmic Results for Path Graphs

In this section, we present a set of algorithmic results for path graphs. Recall that a graph G is a path if and only if every vertex has a degree at most 2, and there exist exactly 2 vertices with degree 1. Formally, a path P of length n contains the set of vertices $V = \{v_1, v_2, \ldots, v_n\}$, and the set of edges $E = \{(v_1, v_2), (v_2, v_3), \ldots, (v_{n-1}, v_n)\}$. For the remainder of this section for a given pair of vertices v_i, v_j on a path graph, we say that v_i is *left* of v_j if $i < j$, and that v_i is *right* of v_j if $i > j$.

In Sect. 4.1, we provide an algorithm for finding an optimal schedule for 1-Robot Scheduling on a line. In Sect. 4.2, we generalise this to give an optimal algorithm for k robots with equal-length tasks and a k-approximation in the general setting.

4.1 1-Robot Scheduling on Path Graphs

In this section, we provide an algorithm for finding the optimal schedule for a single robot on a path. We first provide a sketch of the algorithm, then prove in Lemma 2 that this algorithm is optimal. Corollary 2 shows that the time needed to complete the fastest schedule can be computed via a closed-form expression.

1-Robot Scheduling Algorithm. Let P be a path graph of length n, let $T = (t_1, t_2, \ldots, t_m)$ be a set of tasks, and let R be the single robot starting on vertex $sv = v_{i_s}$. We assume, without loss of generality, that t_j is located on v_{i_j} such that v_{i_j} is left of $v_{i_{j+1}}$, i.e. $\forall j \in [1, m-1], i_j < i_{j+1}$. Note that there may exist some task t_i located on sv without contradiction. Using this notation, the optimal schedule $\mathcal{C} = \{C\}$ is:

- $C = \{(v_{i_s}, v_{i_s+1}), \ldots, (v_{i_m-1}, v_{i_m}), t_m, (v_{i_m}, v_{i_m-1}), \ldots, (v_{i_{m+1}+1}, v+i_{m+1}), t_{m-1}, \ldots, (v_{i_1+1}, v_{i_1}), t_1\ \}$ if $|i_s - i_m| \leq |i_s - i_1|$.

- $C = \{\ (v_{i_s}, v_{i_s-1}),\ (v_{i_s-1}, v_{i_s-2}),\ \ldots,\ (v_{i_1+1}, v_{i_1}),\ t_1,\ (v_{i_1}, v_{i_1+1}),\ (v_{i_1+1}, v_{i_2+2}), \ldots, (v_{i_2-1}, v_{i_2}), t_2, \ldots, (v_{i_m-1}, v_{i_m}), t_m\ \}$ if $|i_s - i_m| > |i_s - i_1|$.

Lemma 2. *The fastest task-completing schedule for* 1-ROBOT SCHEDULING *on a path graph P of length n with m tasks $T = (t_1, \ldots, t_m)$ located on vertices $v_{i_1}, \ldots, v_{i_m}$, and a robot R starting on vertex v_{i_s} can be constructed in $O(n)$ time.*

Proof. We prove this statement by showing that the construction above is correct. Note that if T is not ordered, then we can sort the list by position of the tasks in $O(n)$ using a radix sort. Observe that any task-completing schedule must have the robot completing every task. Therefore, the fastest schedule will correspond to the shortest walk visiting every vertex containing a task. We further assume, without loss of generality, that $i_1 \leq s \leq i_m$, as the fastest schedule for any 1-ROBOT SCHEDULING instance where $s < i_1$ (respectively, $s > i_m$) must start with the robot moving from v_{i_s} to v_{i_1}, and thus this path can be appended to the final solution.

Observe that if v_{i_s} is neither v_{i_1} nor v_{i_m}, R must visit some subset of vertices more than once. Further, any task-completing schedule must visit both v_{i_1} and v_{i_m} at least once. Therefore, there must exist some subsequence F of the edges in the optimal schedule C corresponding to a walk between v_{i_1} and v_{i_m}. Additionally, there must be some subsequence F' corresponding to a walk in the optimal schedule C ending before the first edge in F and corresponding to a walk from v_s to either v_{i_1}, or v_{i_m}. Therefore, as the above construction only contains these walks, one must be minimal. Now, note that if $|i_s - i_m| \leq |i_s - i_1|$, then the shortest walk from v_{i_s} to v_{i_m} is shorter than the shortest walk from v_{i_s} to v_{i_1}, and thus the schedule starting with the walk from v_{i_s} to v_{i_m} is shorter than the schedule starting with the walk from v_{i_s} to v_{i_1}. Otherwise, the schedule starting with the walk from v_{i_s} to v_{i_1} is shorter than the schedule starting with the walk from v_{i_s} to v_{i_m}. □

Corollary 2. *The time span of the fastest task-completing schedule for* 1-ROBOT SCHEDULING *on a path graph P of length n with m tasks $T = (t_1, \ldots, t_m)$ located on vertices $v_{i_1}, \ldots, v_{i_m}$ and a robot R starting on vertex v_s is*

$$\min(|s - i_1|, |s - i_m|) + i_m - i_1 + \sum_{t \in T} t.$$

4.2 k-Robot Scheduling on Paths

Now, we generalise the 1 robot path instance to the k robot case. To do so, we build a dynamic programming algorithm based on the same principles as the previous partition algorithm. As in the previous sections, we first provide an overview of the algorithm, then the main results. In Theorem 4, we show that this algorithm is optimal when all tasks are of equal duration. Finally, in Theorem 5, we show that this algorithm produces a schedule that is at most a factor of k slower than the fastest schedule for a given k-ROBOT SCHEDULING instance.

The k-Partition Algorithm. Let P be a path of length n, $T = \{t_1, t_2, \ldots, t_m\}$ be a set of tasks, and let $sv_1, sv_2, \ldots, sv_k$ be the starting vertices of the robots $R_1, R_2, \ldots, R_k$ respectively, with the assumption that R_i starts left of R_{i+1}, for every $i \in [1, k-1]$. Further, we denote by i_t the index such that v_{i_t} contains task t, and assume that $i_{t_j} < i_{t_{j+1}}$ (i.e. task t_j is left of t_{j+1}) for every $j \in [1, m-1]$. We construct a $k \times m$ table S, with $S[c, \ell]$ containing the time required to complete the fastest collision-free schedule completing tasks $t_1, t_2, \ldots, t_\ell$ with robots $R_1, R_2, \ldots, R_c$. Let $C_1(P, T, sv)$ return the optimal schedule for a single robot starting at sv on the path P for completing the task set T, for ease of notation the starting vertex of the robot is often omitted as a parameter.

First, observe that $S[1, \ell]$ can be computed, for every $\ell \in [1, m]$, in $O(m)$ time. Now, assuming the value of $S[c-1, \ell]$ has been computed for every $\ell \in [1, m]$, the value of $S[c, r]$ is computed by finding the value r' minimising the larger of $|C_1(P, (t_{r'+1}, t_{r'+2}, \ldots, t_r))|$ and $S[c-1, r']$, formally

$$S[c, r] = \min_{r' \in [1, r]} \max(|C_1(P, (t_{r'+1}, t_{r'+2}, \ldots, t_r))|, S[c-1, r']).$$

Letting $\mathcal{S}$ be an auxiliary table such that $\mathcal{S}[c, \ell]$ contains the schedule corresponding to the time given in $S[c, \ell]$. A task-completing collision-free schedule for the k-ROBOT SCHEDULING instance is given in $\mathcal{S}[k, m]$. For the remainder of this section, let $S_k(P, T, (sv_1, sv_2, \ldots, sv_k))$ return the schedule determined by this table. Note that for $S_1(P, T, (sv_1))$, this becomes equivalent to $C_1(P, T)$

Example 2. An example of execution of the partition algorithm is shown in Fig. 2. For this example, the left robot (starting on vertex 5) will be assigned the schedule $([(5, 4), (4, 3)], 3, [(3, 2), (2, 1)], 1)$ and the right robot has the schedule $(6, [(6, 5), (5, 4)], 4)$.

Theorem 4. *Given an instance of k-ROBOT SCHEDULING on a path $P = (V, E)$ with equal duration tasks $T = (t_1, t_2, \ldots, t_m)$ on vertices $v_{i_1}, v_{i_2}, \ldots, v_{i_m}$ and k robots $R_1, R_2, \ldots, R_k$ starting at $sv_1, sv_2, \ldots, sv_k = v_{j_1}, v_{j_2}, \ldots, v_{j_k}$, there is no collision-free task-completing schedule for this instance taking less time than the schedule returned by $S_k(P, T, (sv_1, sv_2, \ldots, sv_k))$. Further, this schedule can be found in $O(kmn)$ time.*

Proof. We prove this in an inductive manner, using $S_1(P, T, (sv_1, sv_2))$ as a base case. Assume that, for every $c \in [1, k-1]$, $S_c(P, T, (sv_1, sv_2, \ldots, sv_c))$ returns such a schedule. Now, consider the schedule given by $\mathcal{C} = (C_1, C_2, \ldots, C_k) = S_k(P, T, (sv_1, sv_2, \ldots, sv_k))$. Let t_q be the leftmost task completed by R_k. Note that by construction, the schedule $S_{k-1}(P, (t_1, t_2, \ldots, t_{q-1}), (sv_1, sv_2, \ldots, sv_{k-1}))$ must be the fastest collision-free schedule completing the tasks $t_1, t_2, \ldots, t_{q-1}$ with the robots $R_1, R_2, \ldots, R_{k-1}$ on P.

Assume, for the sake of contradiction, that there exists some schedule $\mathcal{C}'$ such that $\mathcal{C}' = (C_1', C_2', \ldots, C_k')$ completes all tasks faster than $\mathcal{C}$. If $C_k = C_k'$ then we have a contradiction, as $(C_1', C_2', \ldots, C_{k-1}')$ must then complete

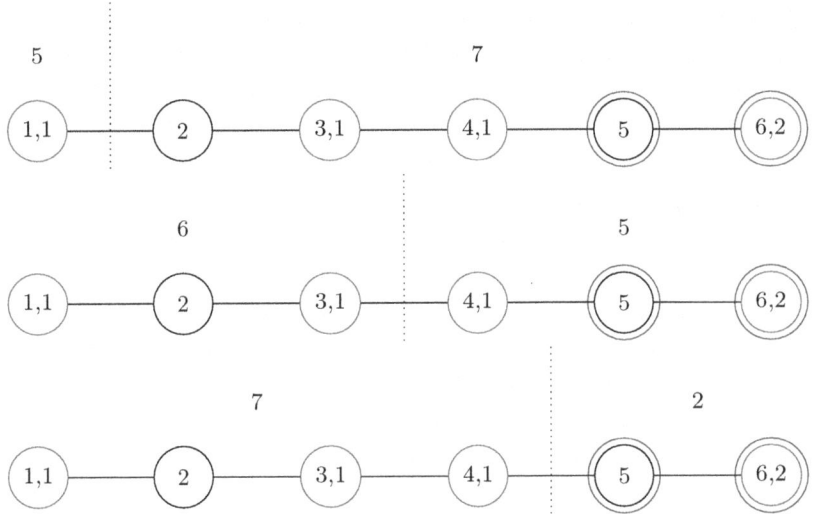

Fig. 2. An example of the partition algorithm deciding where to split the graph shown on a path P_6 with tasks in red and starting vertices of robots being circled in blue. The time span of the schedule C_1 is shown above each subgraph. (Color figure online)

$t_1, t_2, \ldots, t_{q-1}$ faster than $(C_1, C_2, \ldots, C_{k-1})$, contradicting the assumption that $S_{k-1}(P, (t_1, t_2, \ldots, t_{q-1}), (sv_1, sv_2, \ldots, sv_{k-1}))$ is optimal.

Now, assume that R_k does not solve t_m. Then, either every task is solved by some other robot, or there exists some task t' left of t_m that is solved by R_k. Now, if the robot currently assigned to t_m (which we shall call R_j) were to now complete t' - the leftmost task assigned to R_k (and similarly R_k to complete t_m) the new schedule takes at most as long as before, since the tasks are of equal duration and the travel time can only decrease since R_k is the rightmost robot and now completes the rightmost task. Following this argument for each task assigned to R_k from left to right gives a schedule in which R_k solves tasks $t_m, t_{m-1}, \ldots, t_r$ for some $r \in [1, m]$. And since the fastest schedule for R_k completing these tasks is given by $C_1(P, (\ t_{r'}, t_{r'+1}, \ldots, t_m\ ), sv_k)$, and the fastest task-completing schedule for the remaining tasks is given by $S_{k-1}(P, (t_1, t_2, \ldots, t_{r'-1}), (sv_1, sv_2, \ldots, sv_{k-1}))$, the schedule given by $S_k(P, T, (sv_1, sv_2, \ldots, sv_k))$ is therefore optimal.

For the time complexity, note that computing the table $\mathcal{S}$ requires $k \cdot m$ entries to be added, each needing $O(m)$ computations corresponding to each partition of the robots (the time span of the fastest schedule for one robot can be calculated in constant time by the formula in Corollary 2) and an additional $O(n)$ time to write the updated schedule. As there are $k \cdot m$ entries, the total time complexity of this process is $O(km^2 + kmn) = O(kmn)$. □

Despite being optimal for tasks of equal duration, the partition algorithm does not always return an optimal scheduling. See Fig. 3 for an example where this algorithm fails.

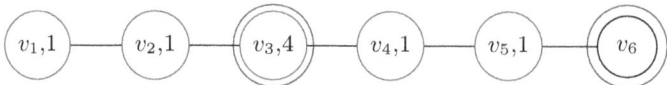

Fig. 3. Counter-Example to the optimality of the partition algorithm. The optimal solution would be the left robot completing the schedule $((v_3, 4), [(v_3, v_2), (v_2, v_1)], (v_1, 1))$ and the other robot doing $([(v_6, v_5)], (v_5, 1), [(v_5, v_4)], (v_4, 1), [(v_4, v_3), (v_3, v_2)], (v_2, 1))$ with a total time span of 7. Whereas the partition algorithm would return the schedules $((v_3, 4), [(v_3, v_2)], (v_2, 1), [(v_2, v_1)], (v_1, 1))$ and $([(v_6, v_5)], (v_5, 1), [(v_5, v_4)], (v_4, 1))$ with a total time span of 8.

Theorem 5. *Given an instance of k-ROBOT SCHEDULING on a path $P = (V, E)$ with tasks $T = (t_1, t_2, \ldots, t_m)$ on vertices $v_{i_1}, v_{i_2}, \ldots, v_{i_m}$ and robots $R_1, R_2, \ldots, R_k$ starting at $sv_1, sv_2, \ldots, sv_k = v_{j_1}, v_{j_2}, \ldots, v_{j_k}$, the schedule returned by $S_k(P, T, (sv_1, sv_2, \ldots, sv_k))$ takes time at most a factor of k of the fastest collision-free task-completing schedule for this instance.*

Proof. Let $\mathcal{C} = (C_1, C_2, \ldots, C_k)$ be the fastest schedule solving the k-ROBOT SCHEDULING instance, and let $\mathcal{C}' = (C'_1, C'_2, \ldots, C'_k)$ be the schedule returned by $S_k(P, T, (sv_1, sv_2, \ldots, sv_k))$. Further, let a be the number of timesteps required to complete $\mathcal{C}$. Observe that in a timesteps, there is sufficient time for each robot to complete all tasks assigned to it, as well as relevant movement, including having every robot move between the leftmost and rightmost tasks assigned to it. Therefore, R_1 can complete all tasks between the leftmost and rightmost tasks completed in C_1 in at most $k \cdot a$ time. Repeating this argument gives the k approximation. □

4.3 Extension to Cycles and Tadpoles

Full proofs of all statements in this section are found in the full version [1]. We provide a brief extension to k-ROBOT SCHEDULING on cycles. In short, we apply the above algorithm to at most $O(n)$ instances of k-ROBOT SCHEDULING on a path, each formed by removing some distinct edge from the cycle. To prove the correctness of this approach, we provide the following key observation.

Lemma 3. *Given an instance of k-ROBOT SCHEDULING on a cycle $G = (V, E)$ with a set of equal duration tasks $T = \{t_1, \ldots, t_m\}$ and robots $r_1, \ldots, r_k$, there exists a fastest collision-free task-completing schedule C such that there exists some edge $e \in E$ that is not traversed by any robot in C.*

With Lemma 3, we can solve the problem of k-ROBOT SCHEDULING on a cycle by checking each of the path graphs formed by removing exactly one edge from the cycle and choosing the best solution.

Theorem 6. *Given an instance of k-ROBOT SCHEDULING on a cycle $G = (V, E)$ containing n vertices and the set of tasks $T = \{t_1, t_2, \ldots, t_m\}$, a fastest collision-free task-completing schedule can be found in $O(kmn^2)$ time.*

Finally, we look at *tadpole graphs*. A graph $G = (V, E)$ is a (m, n)-tadpole graph if there exists a pair $V_1, V_2 \subseteq V$ such that $V_1 \cap V_2 = \emptyset$, $V_1 \cup V_2 = V$, $|V_1| = m$, where the subgraph $(V_1, V_1 \times V_1 \cap E)$ is a cycle, $|V_2| = n$, and the subgraph $(V_2, V_2 \times V_2 \cap E)$ is a path, and $|V_1 \times V_2 \cap E| = 1$. An example of this is given in Fig. 4. We provide two key tools that are used to solve the full problem. First, we show that we can solve the 2-ROBOT SCHEDULING problem on a tree with a single vertex of degree 3, and every other vertex having degree 2 or 1. Secondly, we show that for any instance of k-ROBOT SCHEDULING on a tadpole graph with equal-length tasks, there is an optimal, collision-free schedule where, at most, two robots complete tasks located on both the cycle and the path.

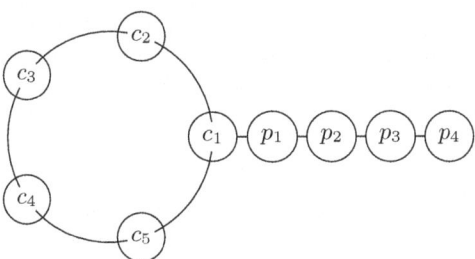

Fig. 4. (5,4)-Tadpole graph

Lemma 4. *Given an instance of 2-ROBOT SCHEDULING with m tasks on a tree T where T contains at most one vertex of degree 3, and every other vertex has degree one or two, we can determine a fastest collision-free task-completing schedule in $O(m^2)$ time.*

Lemma 5. *Given an instance of k-ROBOT SCHEDULING on a (m, n)-tadpole graph with the set of tasks T, there exists a fastest collision-free task-completing schedule C, where at most two robots r_a and r_b complete a task on both the cycle and the path in G. Further, there exists some tree $\mathcal{T}$ spanning all the tasks completed by either r_a or r_b, without containing any other node in which a task not completed by either robot is located.*

At a high level, the idea is to partition the set of robots into three subsets, those completing tasks on the cycle, those completing tasks on the path, and those completing tasks on both. Using Lemma 5, we show that we can find a fastest task completing schedule where at most two robots complete a task both on the cycle and on the path. Thus, we end up with at most $O(k^2)$ such sets, noting that any robot between the two robots that are completing tasks on both the cycle and the path must only complete tasks on the path. For each such set, we partition the set of tasks on the cycle (resp. on the path) between the robots completing tasks only on the cycle (resp. on the path), and those completing tasks on both, with $O(m^2)$ possible partitions in the worst case. For each of these partitions, we use Theorems 4 and 6 along with Lemma 4 to find an optimal solution to this partition. Finally, we choose the fastest such partition as our solution.

Theorem 7. *Given an instance of k-ROBOT SCHEDULING on a tadpole graph G with n vertices with m tasks, a fastest collision-free task-completing schedule can be found in $O(k^3 m^4 n)$ time.*

5 Conclusion

We have shown that our definition of k-ROBOT SCHEDULING is hard even on highly constrained classes of graphs while being solvable, with equal duration tasks, for path, cycle, and tadpole graphs as well as k-approximable for tasks of any length on path graphs. While these results paint a strong picture of the complexity of this problem, we are left with several open questions. The most direct is as to whether our approximation algorithm for path graphs can be improved or if an optimal algorithm can be found. We conjecture that a polynomial time algorithm exists for this setting; however, at present, no such algorithm has been found. The second natural direction is to look at the remaining classes of graphs that have not been covered by our existing results. The most interesting of these would be lattice graphs, starting with $n \times m$ grids. Such graphs can be used to simulate a wide variety of settings, while still not fitting into any of the classes that are known to be NP-hard. On the other hand, these still provide more complexity than our existing problems due to an exponentially greater number of paths that each robot can take without collision.

References

1. Adamson, D., Flaherty, N., Potapov, I., Spirakis, P.G.: Collision-free robot scheduling. arXiv:2402.12019 2024
2. Adamson, D., Gusev, V.V., Malyshev, D., Zamaraev, V.: Faster exploration of some temporal graphs. In: 1st Symposium on Algorithmic Foundations of Dynamic Networks (SAND 2022). Schloss Dagstuhl-Leibniz-Zentrum für Informatik (2022)
3. Akrida, E.C., Mertzios, G.B., Spirakis, P.G., Raptopoulos, C.: The temporal explorer who returns to the base. J. Comput. Syst. Sci. **120**, 179–193 (2021)
4. Arrighi, E., Fomin, F.V., Golovach, P., Wolf, P.: Kernelizing temporal exploration problems. arXiv preprint arXiv:2302.10110 (2023)

5. Bodlaender, H.L., van der Zanden, T.C.: On exploring always-connected temporal graphs of small pathwidth. Inf. Process. Lett. **142**, 68–71 (2019)
6. Bumpus, B.M., Meeks, K.: Edge exploration of temporal graphs. Algorithmica **85**(3), 688–716 (2023)
7. Burger, B., et al.: A mobile robotic chemist. Nature **583**(7815), 237–241 (2020)
8. Czyzowicz, J., Dereniowski, D., Gasieniec, L., Klasing, R., Kosowski, A., Pajak, D.: Collision-free network exploration. J. Comput. Syst. Sci. **86**, 70–81 (2017)
9. Deligkas, A., Potapov, I.: Optimizing reachability sets in temporal graphs by delaying. Inf. Comput. **285**, 104890 (2022)
10. Erlebach, T., Hoffmann, M., Kammer, F.: On temporal graph exploration. J. Comput. Syst. Sci. **119**, 1–18 (2021)
11. Erlebach, T., Kammer, F., Luo, K., Sajenko, A., Spooner, J.T.: Two moves per time step make a difference. In: 46th International Colloquium on Automata, Languages, and Programming (ICALP: volume 132 of Leibniz International Proceedings in Informatics (LIPIcs), pp. 1–14. Dagstuhl, Germany (2019)
12. Erlebach, T., Spooner, J.T.: Faster exploration of degree-bounded temporal graphs. In: 43rd International Symposium on Mathematical Foundations of Computer Science (MFCS 2018). Schloss Dagstuhl-Leibniz-Zentrum fuer Informatik (2018)
13. Erlebach, T., Spooner, J.T.: Exploration of k-edge-deficient temporal graphs. Acta Informatica **59**(4), 387–407 (2022)
14. Erlebach, T., Spooner, J.T.: Parameterized temporal exploration problems. In: 1st Symposium on Algorithmic Foundations of Dynamic Networks (SAND 2022). Schloss Dagstuhl-Leibniz-Zentrum für Informatik (2022)
15. Garey, M.R., Johnson, D.S.: Computers and Intractability. W. H. Freeman and Company (1979)
16. Granda, J.M., Donina, L., Dragone, V., Long, D., Cronin, L.: Controlling an organic synthesis robot with machine learning to search for new reactivity. Nature **559**(7714), 377–381 (2018)
17. King, R.D.: Rise of the robo scientists. Sci. Am. **304**(1), 72–77 (2011)
18. Langner, S., et al.: Beyond ternary OPV: high-throughput experimentation and self-driving laboratories optimize multi-component systems. arXiv:1909.03511 (2019)
19. Li, J., et al.: Synthesis of many different types of organic small molecules using one automated process. Science **347**(6227), 1221–1226 (2015)
20. Liu, S., Shen, J., Tian, W., Lin, J., Li, P., Li, B.: Balanced task allocation and collision-free scheduling of multi-robot systems in large spacecraft structure manufacturing. Robot. Auton. Syst. **159**, 104289 (2023)
21. MacLeod, B.P., et al.: Self-driving laboratory for accelerated discovery of thin-film materials. arXiv:1906.05398 (2020)
22. Michail, O., Spirakis, P.G.: Traveling salesman problems in temporal graphs. Theoret. Comput. Sci. **634**, 1–23 (2016)
23. Qamar, R.A., Sarfraz, M., Ghauri, S.A., Mahmood, A.: TRMaxAlloc: maximum task allocation using reassignment algorithm in multi-UAV system. Comput. Commun. **206**, 110–123 (2023)
24. Taghian Alamouti, S.: Exploring temporal cycles and grids. Ph. D. thesis, Concordia University (2020)
25. Zhang, L., Yang, C., Yan, Y., Cai, Z., Hu, Y.: Automated guided vehicle dispatching and routing integration via digital twin with deep reinforcement learning. J. Manuf. Syst. **72**, 492–503 (2024)

On the Exponential Growth of Geometric Shapes

Nada Almalki[1]($^{\boxtimes}$), Siddharth Gupta[2], and Othon Michail[1]

[1] Department of Computer Science, University of Liverpool, Liverpool, UK
{N.Almalki,Othon.Michail}@liverpool.ac.uk
[2] Department of Computer Science and Information Systems, BITS Pilani,
K K Birla Goa Campus, Goa, India
siddharthg@goa.bits-pilani.ac.in

Abstract. In this paper, we explore the exponential growth of geometric structures starting from a single node, focusing on centralized growth operations. We identify a parameter k, representing the number of turning points within specific parts of a shape. We prove that, if edges can only be formed when generating new nodes and cannot be deleted, trees having at most k turning points on every root-to-leaf path can be grown in $O(k \log n)$ time steps and spirals with $O(\log n)$ turning points can be grown in $O(\log n)$ time steps, n being the size of the final shape. For this model, we also show that the maximum number of turning points in a root-to-leaf path of a tree is a lower bound on the number of time steps to grow the tree and that there exists a class of paths such that any path in the class with k turning points requires $\Omega(k \log k)$ time steps to be grown. If nodes can additionally be connected as soon as they become adjacent, we prove that if a shape S has a spanning tree with at most k turning points on every root-to-leaf path, then the adjacency closure of S can be grown in $O(k \log n)$ time steps. In the strongest version of the model, where, additionally, edges can be deleted and neighbors handed over to new nodes, we present a universal algorithm for growing any shape S exponentially fast.

Keywords: Centralized algorithm · Growth process · Collision · Programmable matter

1 Introduction

In this work, we explore two interrelated questions: *"What are the structural properties associated with exponential growth of geometric shapes?"* and *"How can some of these properties be exploited and others avoided in order to design algorithms that can grow desired shapes exponentially fast?"*

Consider, for example, the question asking if a robot, whose n modules — called *nodes* hereafter— are arranged in a tree shape T, can be grown from a single node u_0 exponentially fast. One possible approach is to use breadth-first search on the line segments of T. Starting from u_0, the algorithm proceeds in phases of increasing line-segment distance, measured by the number of maximal line segments from u_0. In each phase i, the algorithm grows in parallel all maximal line segments at a line-segment distance i from u_0. Each line segment can be grown exponentially fast by doubling the length of the line in each time step. If T is sparse (informally meaning its branches are sufficiently far from each other) and has k line segments, where k is the number of turning points on every root-to-leaf path, then this algorithm would grow T in $O(k \log n)$ time steps, which gives a logarithmic number of time steps if k is a constant but can be as slow as linear for $k = \Omega(n/\log n)$. A less obvious observation is that, when T is not sparse, we need to specify how the efficiency or the feasibility of growing a branch depends on the nearby branches.

These observations prompt further questions that we explore in the present paper, such as: Is there an algorithmic approach that can grow any tree or any general shape of n nodes in $O(\log n)$ time steps? What other classes of shapes can be identified for which (poly)logarithmic upper bounds or super-logarithmic lower bounds can be proved? What are the relevant parameters of the geometry of a shape that affect the complexity of growth? What are the right modeling assumptions to represent, for example, how parallel local growth affects global growth, the different types of collisions that should be avoided, or properties related to the connectivity of the shape?

During the early stages of an organism's development, cells undergo exponential growth, beginning with a single cell and successively doubling their total number. Mathematical models of human embryonic growth have been proposed [11]. Though our model takes inspiration from natural growth processes, it also shares features with existing theoretical models of computation and robotics. The abstract Tile Assembly Model [16,17] is a mathematical model of self-assembly. The process starts from an initial assembly of tiles and the system grows, much like crystals in nature, by passive attachment of new tiles, which bind on existing tiles through glues on their edges. *Passive* means that interactions between the tiles are controlled by the environment. In practice, tiles are typically DNA molecules; see [8,15] for surveys of work on the theory of algorithmic self-assembly. Though growth is a defining property of both our model and self-assembly models, most self-assembly models grow passively on the external layer, including internal cavities. In contrast, algorithms in our model can actively control the structure's growth and can do so without an *a priori* limitation on where to apply the growth operations. As a result of this, growth in passive self-assembly is a relatively slow process both in theory and in practice, whereas the algorithms we develop use a number of time steps which is typically sub-linear and often (poly)logarithmic in the size of the final structure.

An example of a self-assembly model incorporating active molecular dynamics is the *Nubot* model [18]. The authors explore how to grow connected two-dimensional geometric shapes and patterns in time (poly)logarithmic in their size, an objective that is broadly similar to ours. For example, they show how to grow a chain and a square of monomers in time and number of monomer states which is logarithmic in the total number of monomers in the final structure. They use these constructions as a basis for constructing arbitrary shapes exponentially fast, combining further growth and other forms of reconfiguration. A difference between our model and [18] is that our processes are only allowed to update instances through growth. As is also the case in [18], most of our algorithms use the fast process of growing a chain as a sub-routine. Recently, there has been growing interest in studying the algorithmic foundations of *Programmable matter* systems, focusing on their ability to alter their shape through local reconfiguration [1,3,7,13]. Control can be either centralized or decentralized and the focus is typically on the feasibility of a given reconfiguration task, as most of these models share a natural quadratic lower bound on worst-case moves based on reconfiguration distance (translating to a linear lower bound if parallel moves are allowed) [13]. An exception is a recent line of work on models for fast parallel reconfiguration [5,9,14], extending the Amoebot model of Derakhshandeh *et al.* [6]. The growth processes studied in this paper could deploy programmable matter fast, either in its exact initial configuration or in a rough version of it that can be then refined through other types of operations.

An assumption of our model is that individual operations have *linear strength*, meaning that they can move any part of the structure. This has been a common simplifying assumption in the relevant literature and can sometimes be dropped, e.g., when multiple operations can be applied in parallel to collaboratively provide the required "force". Examples of other linear-strength models are [3,4,18].

Other studies close to our work are [2], which considered simpler forms of the growth models and operations we study, [10], which explored the complexity of deciding whether collisions will occur or can be avoided for a given set of growth and contraction operations, and [12], where the authors studied related growth problems on abstract (not necessarily geometric) graphs. The difference between the models of [2] and those in this paper is that growth operations in [2] affect specific parts of the shape (e.g., whole columns) and are defined to ensure no collision can happen. In contrast, the growth operations in this paper can be applied to any part of the shape, and it is the responsibility of the algorithm designer to ensure that no structural violation occurs. Our model also relates to von Neumann's concept of self-replicating machines.

1.1 Contribution

Our aim is to understand how geometric structures can be grown exponentially fast. Though this question is also relevant to distributed algorithms, our study focuses on the centralized case, as both are largely unexplored. The distributed case remains a direction for future research. Nevertheless, our centralized lower bounds also apply to distributed algorithms, and it might be possible to translate our centralized algorithms into —potentially less efficient— distributed algorithms.

In this paper, we represent geometric structures as shapes drawn on a two-dimensional square grid. Though three-dimensional space and other coordinate systems (including continuous) can be more suitable for some applications, the considered model is theoretically simpler and the techniques developed for it are likely to generalize. A shape is a geometric graph that is formed by nodes occupying distinct points on the grid and edges between pairs of adjacent nodes (i.e., nodes at a unit orthogonal distance from each other on the grid). We naturally restrict attention to connected shapes.

Intuitively, a *growth process* is a sequence of sets of growth operations that are applied starting from an initial shape S_0 —often a single node— to grow a final shape S of n nodes. We restrict attention to discrete time, which we measure in *time steps*. In all problems we study, we want to determine a bound τ such that for all shapes S_0 and S from given initial and final classes of shapes, respectively, there is a growth process σ that grows S from S_0 in τ time steps. For an upper bound to establish exponential growth, τ should be at most (poly)logarithmic in the size of S. Non-trivial lower bounds should be super-logarithmic in the size of S.

When the initial shape is a single node, it is probably plausible to assume that there might be a straightforward solution to this problem. One could try to grow a small compressed version T' of a spanning tree T of shape S, decompress T' through parallel growth to get T exponentially fast, and add any missing edges in order to get S. However, under reasonable assumptions, this generic approach fails to be exponentially fast in the worst case. One reason for this is that there might be no meaningful compression of S. The second reason is that even when there is a satisfactory compression, fast decompression might not be possible if self-intersection must be avoided. We call all structural violations of the shape *collisions* and are only interested in growth processes that are free from collisions.

In Sect. 2, we define a general model of growth and distinguish some of its variants. One distinction is drawn between those processes that can only form edges when generating new nodes (*connectivity graph*) and those that can additionally connect nodes as soon as they become adjacent (*adjacency graph*). Another is based on whether structural violations of cycles are to be avoided by preserving the affected cycles (*cycle-preserving* processes) or by breaking them (*cycle-breaking* processes). In Sect. 3, we study the connectivity graph model. We identify a parameter k, representing the number of turning points within specific parts of a shape, and show that, when starting from a single node, trees having at most k turning points on every root-to-leaf path can be grown in $O(k \log n)$ time steps through BFS on line segments and spirals with $O(\log n)$ turning points can be grown in $O(\log n)$ time steps through a pipelined variant of BFS. We also establish two lower bounds for trees and paths. For trees, we show that the maximum number of turning points in a root-to-leaf path of the tree is a lower bound on the number of time steps to grow the tree from a single node. For paths, we show that there exists a class of incompressible paths such that any path in the class with k turning points requires $\Omega(k \log k)$ time steps to be grown from a single node.

In Sect. 4, we discuss the cycle-preserving and cycle-breaking types of processes within the adjacency graph model, in which every pair of adjacent nodes is also connected in the shape. Note that this distinction is not meaningful in the connectivity graph model for processes starting from a single node, because the shapes grown by these processes are acyclic. For cycle-preserving processes, we prove that if a shape S has a spanning tree with at most k turning points on every root-to-leaf path, then the adjacency closure of S can be grown from a single node in $O(k \log n)$ time steps. For cycle-breaking processes with the additional assumption that neighbors can be handed over to newly generated nodes (*neighbor handover*), we show that there exists a universal algorithm: for any shape S it gives a process that grows S from a single node exponentially fast. Even though the combination of cycle-breaking and neighbor handover is a rather strong one, it shows that there is at least one reasonable model variant which can give a universal algorithm for exponential growth. To what extent neighbor handover can help increase the class of shapes that can be grown exponentially fast by cycle-preserving processes is an open question. In Sect. 5, we discuss this and other intriguing questions raised by this model and its variants.

2 Models and Problem

We consider a two-dimensional square grid, each point of which is identified by its $x \geq 0$ and $y \geq 0$ integer coordinates, x indicating the column and y the row. A *shape* is defined as a graph $S = (V, E)$ drawn on the grid. V is a set of n nodes, where each node u occupies a distinct point (u_x, u_y) of the grid. $E \subseteq \{uv \mid u, v \in V \text{ and } u, v \text{ are adjacent}\}$ is a set of edges between pairs of adjacent nodes, where two nodes $u = (u_x, u_y)$ and $v = (v_x, v_y)$ are *adjacent* if $u_x \in \{v_x - 1, v_x + 1\}$ and $u_y = v_y$ or $u_y \in \{v_y - 1, v_y + 1\}$ and $u_x = v_x$, that is, their orthogonal distance on the grid is one. We illustrate nodes as small circles drawn on the points they occupy; however, our results hold for any geometry of individual nodes that does not trivially make nearby nodes intersect. A shape is *connected* if the graph that defines it is a connected graph. Throughout the paper, we restrict attention to connected shapes. We define the *adjacency closure* of a shape $S = (V, E)$ as the shape $AC(S) = (V, E')$, where $E' = E \cup \{uv \mid u, v \in V, u, v \text{ are adjacent, and } uv \notin E\}$.

A *growth operation* (also called *doubling* [2] or *expansion* [10]) applied on a node u generates a new node in one of the points adjacent to u and possibly translates some part of the shape. One or more growth operations applied in parallel to nodes of a shape S either cause a *collision* or yield a new shape S'. There are two types of collisions: *node collisions* and *cycle collisions*. When describing the outcome of growth operations, we will be assuming that there is an *anchor* node which is stationary and other nodes move relative to it. This is without loss of generality under the assumption that the constructed shapes are equivalent up to translations.

Temporarily disregarding collisions, we begin by defining the effect of a single growth operation on a tree shape; we will add collisions to the definition of one or more operations applied in parallel. Let $T = (V, E)$ be a tree and $u_0 \in V$ its anchor. We set u_0 to be the root of T. A single growth operation is applied on a node $u \in V$ toward a point (x, y) adjacent to u. There are two cases, which are free from collisions: (i) there is no edge between u and (x, y), (ii) (x, y) is occupied by a node v and $uv \in E$. We first define the effect in each of these cases when *neighbor handover* is not allowed. In case (i), the growth operation generates a node u' at point (x, y) and connects it to u. In case (ii), assume without loss of generality that u is closer to u_0 in T than v. Let $T(v)$ denote the subtree of T rooted at v. Then, the operation generates a node u' between u and v, connected to both, which translates $T(v)$ by one unit away from u along the axis parallel to uv. After this, u' occupies (x, y) and uv has been replaced by $\{uu', u'v\}$. If neighbor handover is allowed, then any neighbor w of u perpendicular to uu' can be handed over to u'. This happens by a unit translation of $T(w)$ or $T(u)$ along the axis parallel to uu', depending on which of u, w, respectively, is closer to u_0 in T.

Let Q be a set of operations to be applied *in parallel* to a connected shape S, each operation on a distinct pair of nodes or a node and an unoccupied point. We assume that all operations in such a set are applied *concurrently*, have the same *constant execution speed*, and their *duration* is equal to one *time step*. A *node collision* occurs if the trajectories of any two nodes meet (see Fig. 1(a)). A *cycle collision* occurs when two parts of a cycle grow unequally (see Fig. 1(b)). A set of operations is said to be *collision free* if it does not cause any node or cycle collisions.

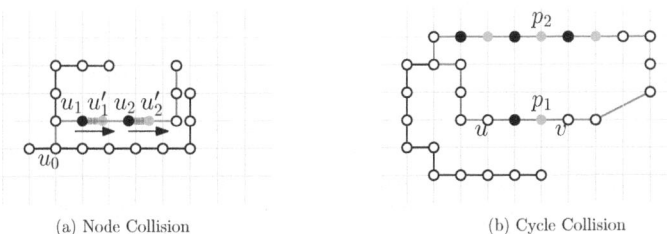

(a) Node Collision (b) Cycle Collision

Fig. 1. (a) An example of a node collision where u_1 and u_2 simultaneously grow east and generate u'_1 and u'_2, though u'_1 and u'_2 do not collide directly, their growth pushes their branch into an adjacent branch, causing a node collision. (b) An example of a cycle collision caused by the irregular growth of its sides occurs when the number of growth operations on one side of the cycle does not equal the number of growth operations on the other side.

A growth process σ starts from an initial shape S_0 —often a single node— and, in each time step $t \geq 1$, applies a set of parallel growth operations — possibly a single operation— on the current shape S_{t-1} to give the next shape S_t, until a final shape S is reached at a time step t_f. We say that σ *grows* S *from* S_0 in t_f time steps. We also assume that parallel operations have the same cardinal direction and that a node gets at most one operation per time step. These assumptions simplify algorithm descriptions and can be easily dropped.

A distinction can be drawn between processes that can only form edges when generating new nodes and processes that can additionally connect nodes as soon as they become adjacent. We further distinguish between processes that avoid cycle collisions by preserving cycles and those that can also do so by breaking them. These are defined as follows.

Definition 1. *Let S_t^b and S_t^e denote the shapes formed by the beginning and by the end of time step t, respectively, and assume that $S_1^b = S_0$. A cycle-preserving growth process applies a collision free set of parallel growth operations Q_t to S_t^b, for all time steps $t \geq 1$. A cycle-breaking growth process additionally removes a —possibly empty— subset of the edges of S_t^b, whose removal does not disconnect the shape, before applying Q_t to it. If* neighbor handover *is allowed, growth of a node u generating a new node u' in direction d can hand any neighbor w of u perpendicular to d over to u'. In the* connectivity graph *model, for all $t \geq 1$, $S_{t+1}^b = S_t^e$ holds. In the* adjacency graph *model, for all $t \geq 1$, $S_{t+1}^b = AC(S_t^e)$ holds.*

Intuitively, the additional assumption in the adjacency graph model is that, at the end of every time step, the graph model updates the shape by connecting all adjacent nodes that are not connected. Combining the adjacency graph model with cycle-breaking processes captures the less extreme case, in which the process can choose any spanning connected sub-shape of the adjacency closure.

Proposition 1. *For the models of Definition 1, the following properties hold:*

1. *Under the connectivity model, the growth processes never increase the number of cycles.*
2. *Under the connectivity model, if S_0 is a single node, the processes can only grow trees.*
3. *The cycle-preserving process never decreases the number of cycles.*
4. *Under the connectivity model, the cycle-preserving process preserves the number of cycles.*

We study a reachability problem between classes of shapes through growth, the problem definition is the same for all growth models in Definition 1.

Problem 1. Let $\mathcal{I}$ be a class of initial shapes and $\mathcal{F}$ a class of final shapes. We want to determine a bound τ such that for all $S_0 \in \mathcal{I}$ and all $S \in \mathcal{F}$ there is a growth process σ that grows S from S_0 in τ time steps.

Given our focus is on exponential growth, upper bounds must be of the form $\tau = O(\log n)$ or $\tau = (poly) \log n$. As there is a straightforward $\Omega(\log n)$ lower bound, non-trivial lower bounds should be at least $\omega(\log n)$. In all instances of the problem studied in this paper, at least one of $\mathcal{I}$ and $\mathcal{F}$ is a singleton, the initial shape typically being a single node. Our upper bounds are constructive: for each instance of the problem an algorithm is presented, which for every (S_0, S) from the respective classes gives a process that grows S from S_0 in τ time steps.

A node u of a shape S is called a *turning point* if either u is a leaf or there are a two neighbors v_1 and v_2 of u such that $v_1 u$ is perpendicular to uv_2. For uniformity of our arguments, we add the endpoints of a path to the set of its turning points. The nodes between any two consecutive turning points of a path form a line segment. Note that when a path P is a sub-shape of a shape S, there might be turning points of S in P which are not turning points of P. We use the terms *turning points* and *turning points of P* to distinguish between the two when ambiguity can arise.

A *column* or *row of a shape S* is a column or row of the grid occupied by nodes of S. We call a column or row of a shape S *compressible* if it contains no turning points and *incompressible* otherwise. A compressible column contains no vertical line segments and intersects one or more horizontal line segments. Similarly for rows. Let $(C_l, C_{l+1}, \ldots, C_r)$ be a maximal sequence of consecutive compressible columns of S. A *compression operation* on the sequence deletes the columns $C_l, C_{l+1}, \ldots, C_r$ and for every horizontal segment s intersected by these columns it connects $u_{l-1}(s)$ to $u_{r+1}(s)$. Compression on rows is defined analogously. A shape is called *incompressible* if it has no compressible columns or rows. We denote by $i(S)$ the incompressible shape obtained after compressing all compressible columns and rows of a shape S.

A *(single) spiral* is, intuitively, a path whose turning points, when ordered from one endpoint to the other, follow a continuous and unidirectional sequence of consecutive cardinal directions in either a clockwise or counterclockwise manner (see Fig. 2a in Sect. 3.2.2 for an illustration). Let $(tp_1, tp_2, \ldots, tp_k)$ be the order of the k turning points of a spiral, tp_1 being its internal and tp_k its external endpoint, respectively. The consecutive turning points tp_i, tp_{i+1}, for $i \in \{1, 2, \ldots, k-1\}$, define the ith line segment s_i of the spiral. We denote by $l(s_i)$ the length of segment s_i in edges.

Proposition 2. *A spiral satisfies $l(s_i) > l(s_{i-2})$, for all $i \in \{3, 4, \ldots, k-1\}$. An incompressible spiral satisfies $l(s_1) = l(s_2) = 1$ and $l(s_i) = l(s_{i-2}) + 1$, for all $i \in \{3, 4, \ldots, k-1\}$.*[1]

We call *double spiral* a path that consists of two intertwined single spirals: the first half of the path follows a unidirectional sequence of consecutive cardinal directions (either clockwise or counterclockwise), and at a midpoint, the path reverses direction, forming a second spiral in the opposite direction (see Fig. 3 in Sect. 3.2.2 for an illustration).

We denote by $\mathcal{C}_k$ the class of all shapes having a rooted spanning tree T such that every root-to-leaf path in T has at most k turns.

A *fast line growth process* begins from a single node and by successively doubling all nodes grows a line segment of length n in $O(\log n)$ time steps. Fast line growth is used as a sub-process in most of our constructions to efficiently grow line segments.

---

[1] Note that there is an exception to this definition of incompressible spirals: the spirals in which the compression of a single row or column is blocked by the presence of the external endpoint in it. We disregard this case for clarity and it is straightforward to extend our results to include it.

3 Connectivity Graph Model

By Proposition 1 when growth starts from a single node, the class of shapes that can be grown in the connectivity graph model is limited to tree structures. In this case, there is no difference between cycle-breaking and cycle-preserving growth, as there are no cycles.

3.1 Upper Bounds

Lemma 1. *In the connectivity model, any shape S can be grown from $i(S)$ in $O(\log n)$ time steps, n being the number of nodes in S.*

Corollary 1. *In the connectivity model, any shape S on n nodes can be grown from a single node in $\tau_{min}(i(S)) + O(\log n)$ time steps, where $\tau_{min}(i(S))$ is the minimum in which $i(S)$ can be grown from a single node.*

Let T be any tree shape having at most k turning points on every root-to-leaf path. We can combine BFS on line segments with fast line growth to grow T in $O(k \log n)$ time steps. Every root-to-leaf path of T is an alternating sequence of turning points and line segments $(u_0, s_1, u_1, s_2, u_2, \ldots, u_{j-1}, s_j, u_j)$, where $j \leq k - 1$. We refer to u_{i-1} and u_i as the *endpoints* of segment s_i closer to, and further from u_0, even though we do not formally include them in s_i.

Theorem 1. *Let T be any tree with at most k turns on every root-to-leaf path. BFS on line segments can grow T from a single node in $O(k \log n)$ time steps.*

The above bound can be rather crude in some cases; for example, on a path consisting of one line segment of length $\Theta(n)$ and $O(\log n)$ segments of constant length each, the BFS on line segments yields an actual $O(\log n)$ time steps compared to the $O(\log^2 n)$ of the above analysis. However, this cannot be improved by a better analysis in the worst case, even for paths.

Theorem 2. *Let P be any path with $\Theta(\log n)$ turning points, such that each of the line segments of P has length $\Theta(n/\log n)$. The process returned by BFS on line segments for P uses $\Theta(\log^2 n)$ time steps.*

For paths with a logarithmic number of turning points, we can grow some paths in this class in a logarithmic number of time steps using a pipelined variant of the BFS approach. Let us assume P is a spiral path in this class with n nodes and $k = O(\log n)$ turning points. P has a uniform growth property such that the lengths of its $k - 1$ segments follow a regular pattern (see Proposition 2). The following approach efficiently grows such spiral paths, using two iterative phases and continues until no new turning points can be added and all segments reach their final length.

Pipelined BFS
Input: any spiral path P with $k = O(\log n)$
Output: growth process σ for P

- **Construction and Waiting Phase**: during this phase, builds up to three turning points tp_i (where i ranges from 1 to 3) following P's geometry.
 - **Parallel Growing Phase**: grows the partially formed structure in parallel, except for segments that have reached their full length.

Theorem 3. *Let P be a spiral path with $k = O(\log n)$ turning points and $(tp_1, tp_2, \ldots, tp_k)$ the order of turning points, with tp_k being the external endpoint. Starting from tp_k, Pipelined BFS can grow P in $O(\log n)$ time steps.*

3.2 Lower Bounds

There is a generic lower bound which follows immediately due to the limit on the rate at which nodes can generate new nodes; a limit inherent to all the models we consider.

Proposition 3. *Let S be any shape on n nodes. In any of the considered models, any growth process for S starting from a single node, requires $\Omega(\log n)$ time steps.*

Refined lower bounds can be obtained as a function of a parameter of the final shape or by restricting attention to special classes of final shapes. In Theorem 4, we prove that the number of turning points of root-to-leaf paths of trees gives a lower bound on the number of time steps of any process for them. By focusing on path shapes, in Theorem 5 we obtain an $\Omega(k \log k)$ lower bound on the number of time steps of any process for a specific worst-case type of path, k being the total number of turning points of the path.

3.2.1 Trees

Let $S = (V, E)$ be a shape. Any growth process σ for S induces a relation $\to_\sigma$ on V, where $u \xrightarrow{t}_\sigma v$ iff node u *generates* node v at time step t. We also write $u \to_\sigma v$ to mean $u \xrightarrow{t}_\sigma v$ for some $t \geq 1$ and $u \rightsquigarrow_\sigma v$ iff $u = u_1 \to_\sigma u_2 \to_\sigma \cdots \to_\sigma u_l = v$, for some $l \geq 2$. We omit σ, writing just $u \xrightarrow{t} v$, $u \to v$, or $u \rightsquigarrow v$ when the growth process is clear from context. The relation $\to_\sigma$ defines a graph $G_{\to_\sigma} = (V, E_{\to_\sigma})$. The following proposition gives some properties of this graph.

Proposition 4. *$G_{\to_\sigma}$ is an out-tree spanning V, rooted at the initial node u_0.*

We now define a relation $\mapsto_\sigma$ induced by $\to_\sigma$ on the turning points of tree shapes. In particular, given a tree T and a growth process σ for T, for any two turning points u, v of T we write $u \xmapsto{t}_\sigma v$ iff (i) $u \xrightarrow{t}_\sigma v$ or (ii) $u \rightsquigarrow u' \xrightarrow{t}_\sigma v$ and u, u', v are on the same line segment at the end of time step t. We again write $u \mapsto_\sigma v$ to mean $u \xmapsto{t}_\sigma v$ for some $t \geq 1$, and will often omit σ. The relation $\mapsto_\sigma$ defines a graph $G_{\mapsto_\sigma}$ on turning points whose structure has a quite strong dependence on the structure of T.

Lemma 2. *Let $T = (V, E)$ be a tree and σ a growth process for T starting from $u_0 \in V$. For any root-to-leaf path $(u_0, u_1, \ldots, u_l)$ of T, where the u_is are restricted to the turning points of the path, $u_0 \mapsto u_1 \mapsto \cdots \mapsto u_l$ holds.*

Lemma 2 says that the turning points of any tree T that is constructed in the connectivity model, can only be generated in their root-to-leaf order in a rooted version of T. Note that this does not necessarily hold for non-turning points of T. The construction of the latter can bypass their actual order in T by, for example, growing line segments of such points through a fast line growth process.

Theorem 4. *Let $T = (V, E)$ be a tree and k any positive integer satisfying that for every root $u_0 \in V$ there is a root-to-leaf path in T containing at least k turning points. Then any growth process σ for T in the connectivity model requires at least $k - 1$ time steps. This lower bound is maximized for the maximum such k.*

3.2.2 Paths

Let P be a path with k turning points. Let σ be a process that grows P from a single node. Without loss of generality, we can assume that σ starts from a turning point of the path P. We now give a few observations and lemmas concerning some properties of σ. Recall that an edge, once generated, cannot be deleted in this model. This immediately implies the following observation.

Observation 1. *A node can grow in at most its degree many different directions. Moreover, once a node has its degree many neighbors in the path constructed by σ, it can only grow along one of its incident edges in the path.*

As there exists a unique subpath between any two vertices in a path, this fact, together with the above observation gives the following observation.

Observation 2. *Let x and z be any two vertices of P such that there exists a line segment between them in the path constructed so far by σ. Then, all the vertices on the subpath between x and z in P will lie on a line segment in the final path constructed by σ.*

The following lemma describes the order in which σ generates P's turning points.

Lemma 3. *Let P be a path between u and v with k turning points. Let $(tp_1, tp_2, \ldots, tp_k)$ be the order of turning points of P from u to v. Let σ be any process that grows P from a single node starting from the turning point tp_i. Then, the sets $\{tp_{i+1}, tp_{i+2}, \ldots, tp_k\}$ and $\{tp_1, tp_2, \ldots, tp_{i-1}\}$ of turning points are generated in the order $(tp_{i+1}, tp_{i+2}, \ldots, tp_k)$ and $(tp_{i-1}, tp_{i-2}, \ldots, tp_1)$, respectively by σ. Moreover, σ respects the direction of P at every node while generating the next node from it.*

Let P be an incompressible spiral path between u and v with k turning points (see Fig. 2a). Moreover, let u be the internal endpoint of P. We now give the following lemma about the lower bound on the number of time steps taken by any process that grows P from a single node starting from u.

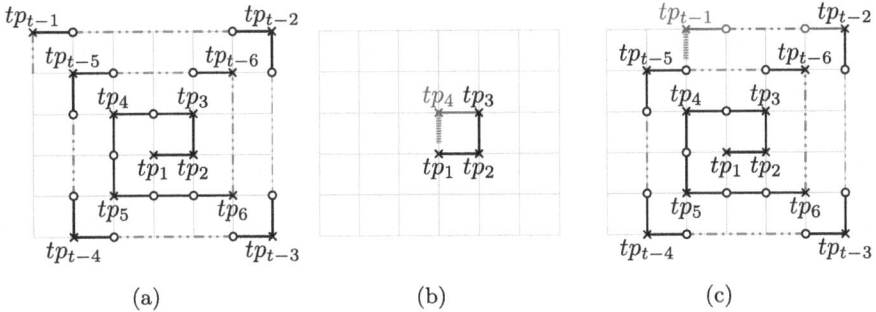

Fig. 2. (a) An illustration of turning points (drawn by cross points) of an incompressible spiral path P. (b) An illustration of the path $\widehat{P}$ constructed by σ in the Base Case in the proof of Lemma 5. The black (blue) part of $\widehat{P}$ shows the subpath, which is the same as (different from) P. The dotted green line shows the direction in which tp_5 will be generated. (c) An illustration of the path $\widehat{P}$ constructed by σ in the Inductive step in the proof of Lemma 5 for $t > 6$. The black (blue) part of $\widehat{P}$ shows the subpath, which is the same as (different from) P. The dotted green line shows the direction in which tp_t will be generated.

Lemma 4. *Let P be an incompressible spiral path between u and v with k turning points. Moreover, let u be the internal endpoint of P. Let σ be any process that grows P from a single node starting from u. Then, σ requires $\Omega(k \log k)$ time steps.*

Let $(tp_1 = u, tp_2, \ldots, tp_k = v)$ be the order of turning points of P from u to v. By Lemma 3, we know that σ generates the turning points in the order $(tp_1 = u, tp_2, \ldots, tp_k = v)$. Let GT_j be the time step when the turning point tp_j was generated by σ, for any $j \geq 2$. Let $\widehat{P}(t)$ be the path constructed by σ after time step t. Further, let a and b be two vertices of P. We denote by $P[a,b]$ the path between a and b (including both a and b) of P. Moreover, we denote by $|a - b|_P$ the number of edges in $P[a,b]$. Also, we denote by $X(a, P)$ the x-coordinate of the vertex a in P. To prove the above lemma, we first prove the following lemma about the path constructed by σ.

Lemma 5. *For any $j \geq 5$, the path $\widehat{P}(GT_j - 1)$ grown by σ till time step $GT_j - 1$ should be the same as the subpath $P[tp_1, tp_{j-1}]$ of P between $tp_1 = u$ and tp_{j-1}.*

We now give the proof of Lemma 4 using Lemma 5.
Proof of Lemma 4. Let ST_j be the time taken by σ to grow the path $P[tp_1, tp_j]$ starting from tp_1, for any $j \geq 2$. Then, by Lemma 5, we get that $GT_j \geq ST_{j-1} + 1$, for any $j \geq 5$. Moreover, by Lemma 5, we know when tp_j is generated, the subpath from tp_1 to tp_{j-1} is already generated by σ. So, the difference between $\widehat{P}(GT_j)$ and $P[tp_1, tp_j]$ is the length of the subpath between tp_{j-1} and tp_j in both the paths. As we know the subpath between tp_{j-1} and tp_j is a line segment in P, we can grow it in $\log(|tp_j - tp_{j-1}|_P)$ time steps. This implies that,

$ST_j = GT_j + \log(|tp_j - tp_{j-1}|_P)$. Combining the two equations, we get that $ST_j \geq ST_{j-1} + 1 + \log(|tp_j - tp_{j-1}|_P)$. It is easy to observe that $ST_4 = 4$. Thus, by solving the recursive relation, we get that $ST_j = \Omega(k \log k)$. This proves the lemma. □

We now give the main theorem of this section, which concerns a class of double spiral paths.

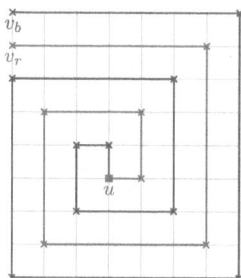

Fig. 3. An illustration of an incompressible path consisting of a red and a blue spiral (forming a double spiral) used in the proof of Theorem 5. The green square vertex u denotes the internal endpoint of both spirals. (Color figure online)

Theorem 5. *Let σ be a process that grows a path from a single node. Then, there exists a path for which σ takes $\Omega(k \log k)$ time steps.*

4 Adjacency Graph Model

Here we study two types of growth: one that avoids collisions by preserving cycles and another that does so by breaking them. Note that neighbor handover is only assumed in cycle-breaking growth. Since cycle-preserving growth is a special case of cycle-breaking growth, positive results for the former hold for the latter.

4.1 Cycle-Preserving Growth

BFS on line segments cannot be directly applied to cycle-preserving growth in the adjacency model due to the dependence between adjacent line segments. We give a modified BFS that overcomes this by growing adjacent line segments in different phases.

Theorem 6. *For any shape $S \in \mathcal{C}_k$, $AC(S)$ can be grown in $O(k \log n)$ time steps in the adjacency graph model.*

As an example application of Theorem 6, any compact shape whose perimeter has a bounded number of turns can be grown in $O(\log n)$ time steps.

4.2 Cycle-Breaking Growth with Neighbor Handover

This growth process breaks cycles within a shape to avoid collisions while maintaining global connectivity. Our main result is a universal algorithm that efficiently provides an $O(\log n)$ time steps *growth process* for any connected shape S. The algorithm specifies an elimination order of the nodes within the shape and then inverts this order to produce the *growth process*. This algorithm utilizes the *neighbor handover* property, which is crucial in breaking edges and transforming neighboring nodes. Given that a shape S has C columns and R rows, the *elimination* algorithm consists of two sets: vertical and horizontal phases. Without loss of generality, let us assume that we start with the vertical phases:

- In the first vertical phase, count rows starting from the bottom-most row and identify odd and even rows.
- For every node u in an odd row that has a neighbor v in an even row connected by the edge uv, eliminate v by contracting the edge uv toward u. Then, register the eliminated or translated nodes (i.e., if there is no neighbor, a node moves down one row) in a process σ to maintain their order.
- At the end of this phase, add all edges between nodes. Then, start the next vertical phase, recount rows from the bottom-most row, and repeat the steps.

After completing the vertical phases, we obtain a horizontal line with a length equal to the horizontal dimension of the shape (i.e., the number of columns in S). Then, we perform the same steps horizontally, eliminating the line through successive halving. Finally, we reverse the order of eliminated nodes and return the growth process.

Theorem 7. *Given any connected shape, S with dimensions $l \times w$, the elimination algorithm grows S from a single node in $O(\log l + \log w)$ time steps.*

5 Conclusion

We explored the exponential growth of geometric structures for different combinations of growth operations and graph models. A combination that we did not study is cycle-preserving growth with neighbor handover. It would be interesting to know what is the class of shapes that can be grown in this model and if the additional property can be used to improve efficiency. Distributed versions of the growth processes studied in this paper is another direction to be investigated. Studying optimality and growth processes whose initial shape is not necessarily a single node are other rich directions of further research.

References

1. Akitaya, H.A., et al.: Universal reconfiguration of facet-connected modular robots by pivots: the O(1) musketeers. Algorithmica **83**(5), 1316–1351 (2021)
2. Almalki, N., Michail, O.: On geometric shape construction via growth operations. Theoret. Comput. Sci. **984**, 114324 (2024)

3. Almethen, A., Michail, O., Potapov, I.: Pushing lines helps: efficient universal centralised transformations for programmable matter. Theoret. Comput. Sci. **830–831**, 43–59 (2020)
4. Aloupis, G., Collette, S., Demaine, E.D., Langerman, S., Sacristán, V., Wuhrer, S.: Reconfiguration of cube-style modular robots using O(log n) parallel moves. In: International Symposium on Algorithms and Computation (ISAAC), pp. 342–353 (2008)
5. Daymude, J.J., Richa, A.W., Scheideler, C.: The canonical amoebot model: algorithms and concurrency control. Distrib. Comput. **36**, 1–34 (2023)
6. Derakhshandeh, Z., Dolev, S., Gmyr, R., Richa, A.W., Scheideler, C., Strothmann, T.: Amoebot - a new model for programmable matter. In: Proceedings of the 26th ACM Symposium on Parallelism in Algorithms and Architectures (SPAA), pp. 220–222 (2014)
7. Derakhshandeh, Z., Gmyr, R., Richa, A.W., Scheideler, C., Strothmann, T.: Universal shape formation for programmable matter. In: Proceedings of the 28th ACM Symposium on Parallelism in Algorithms and Architectures (SPAA), pp. 289–299 (2016)
8. Doty, D.: Theory of algorithmic self-assembly. Commun. ACM **55**(12), 78–88 (2012)
9. Feldmann, M., Padalkin, A., Scheideler, C., Dolev, S.: Coordinating amoebots via reconfigurable circuits. J. Comput. Biol. **29**(4), 317–343 (2022)
10. Gupta, S., van Kreveld, M., Michail, O., Padalkin, A.: Collision detection for modular robots - it is easy to cause collisions and hard to avoid them. arXiv:2305.01015 (2023)
11. Luecke, R.H., Wosilait, W.D., Young, J.F.: Mathematical modeling of human embryonic and fetal growth rates. Growth Dev. Aging GDA **63**(1–2), 49–59 (1999)
12. Mertzios, G.B., Michail, O., Skretas, G., Spirakis, P.G., Theofilatos, M.: The complexity of growing a graph. In: International Symposium on Algorithms and Experiments for Wireless Sensor Networks (ALGOSENSORS), pp. 123–137 (2022)
13. Michail, O., Skretas, G., Spirakis, P.G.: On the transformation capability of feasible mechanisms for programmable matter. J. Comput. Syst. Sci. **102**, 18–39 (2019)
14. Padalkin, A., Kumar, M., Scheideler, C.: Shape formation and locomotion with joint movements in the amoebot model. arXiv:2305.06146 (2023)
15. Patitz, M.J.: An introduction to tile-based self-assembly and a survey of recent results. Nat. Comput. **13**, 195–224 (2014)
16. Winfree, E.: On the computational power of DNA annealing and ligation. DNA Comput. **27**, 119–221 (1996)
17. Winfree, E.: Algorithmic Self-assembly of DNA. California Institute of Technology (1998)
18. Woods, D., Chen, H.L., Goodfriend, S., Dabby, N., Winfree, E., Yin, P.: Active self-assembly of algorithmic shapes and patterns in polylogarithmic time. In: Proceedings of the 4th conference on Innovations in Theoretical Computer Science (ITCS), pp. 353–354 (2013)

Optimizing Robot Dispersion on Unoriented Grids: With and Without Fault Tolerance

Rik Banerjee[1], Manish Kumar[2(✉)] , and Anisur Rahaman Molla[1]

[1] Indian Statistical Institute, Kolkata, India
[2] Indian Institute of Technology Madras, Chennai, India
ic39275@imail.iitm.ac.in

Abstract. The introduction and study of dispersing mobile robots across the nodes of an anonymous graph have recently gained traction and have been explored within various graph classes and settings. While optimal dispersion solution was established for *oriented* grids [Kshemkalyani et al., WALCOM 2020], a significant unresolved question pertains to whether achieving optimal dispersion is feasible on an *unoriented* grid. This paper investigates the dispersion problem on unoriented grids, considering both non-faulty and faulty robots. The challenge posed by unoriented grids lies in the absence of a clear sense of direction for a single robot moving between nodes, as opposed to the straightforward navigation of oriented grids.

We present two deterministic algorithms tailored to our robot model. The first algorithm addresses non-faulty robots, ensuring both time and memory optimality, achieving dispersion in $O(\sqrt{n})$ rounds while requiring $O(\log n)$ bits of memory per robot. The second algorithm tackles faulty robots, which are prone to crashing at any time, causing permanent failure. In this scenario, our algorithm operates within $O(\sqrt{n} \log n)$ time and uses $O(\sqrt{n} \log n)$ bits of memory per robot. The robots need to know the value of n for termination.

Keywords: Mobile agents · Mobile robots · Grid graph · Mess network · Crash-fault robots · Robot's dispersion · Distributed algorithm

1 Introduction and Related Works

The distribution of autonomous mobile robots for achieving coverage across an area is a highly pertinent challenge within the field of distributed robotics, as highlighted in [6,7]. More recently, this issue has been framed in the context of graphs in the following manner: In a scenario where k robots are initially situated on the nodes of an n-node graph, the robots undertake autonomous repositioning to achieve a final configuration wherein each robot occupies a distinct graph node (referred to as the dispersion problem) [1]. This problem holds practical significance across various applications, such as the repositioning of self-driving electric cars (analogous to robots) to available charging stations (equivalent to nodes). This assumption involves the cars utilizing intelligent

---

M. Kumar—Part of the work was done while Manish Kumar was pursuing PhD at the Indian Statistical Institute, Kolkata, India.

communication methods to locate unoccupied charging stations [1,9]. Furthermore, the problem's importance stems from its interconnectedness with numerous other extensively researched challenges in autonomous robot coordination, including exploration, scattering, and load balancing [1,9].

The dispersion of mobile robots has garnered attention across various graph classes, including trees [1,9], rings [1,9,15], arbitrary graphs [1,10,12–14,16], dynamic graphs [11], directed graphs [8]. In the grid graph, the problem was explored by Kshemkalyani et al. [10], but they considered oriented grid (called planar grid) and non-faulty robots exclusively. Orientation plays a pivotal role in the symmetric graphs, Barrière et al. studied the scattering of autonomous mobile robots in the grid [3] and Becha et al. constructed a sense of direction on a torus by a mobile agent with the help of a token [4].

Oriented vs Unoriented Grid: In an oriented grid (see Fig. 1), the ports are organized in such a way that allows a single robot to traverse the grid along a path with a clear sense of direction. When a robot enters a node via an incoming port, it simply needs to select the second port (i.e., leave one port after the incoming port and select the next port) as its outgoing port to continue moving in the same direction. In Fig. 1, as a robot enters from port 1 at node u, it has the sense that the straight path leads from port 3 to node v. However, this straightforward approach is not applicable in an unoriented grid where the ports are interconnected arbitrarily, as depicted in Fig. 2. In such a scenario, robots cannot distinguish whether they are moving in the same direction (i.e., along a row or column) or traversing in a cycle or zigzag manner across the unoriented grid. In Fig. 2, a robot enters from the port 1 at node x. It is tough to decide based on the edges which path leads in the straight direction to y. In the grid, it appears that port 4 leads to the y unlike port 3. Consequently, it's not feasible to adapt the algorithm proposed in [10] to work in an unoriented grid.

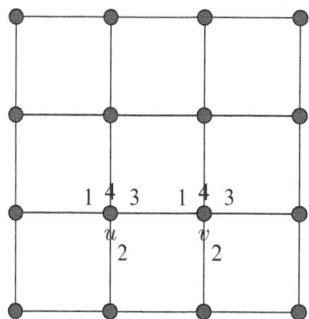

Fig. 1. 16 nodes oriented square grid.

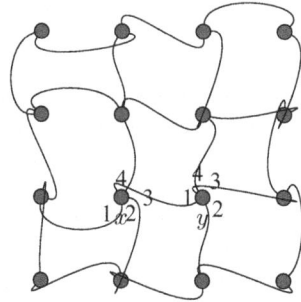

Fig. 2. 16 nodes unoriented square grid.

We provide two novel deterministic algorithms for dispersion on an unoriented grid graph. Our first algorithm works with non-faulty robots. Our second algorithm works with faulty robots, in which, a faulty robot can crash at any time during the execution of the protocol and never respond after crashing. Among the best-known results on dispersion [5,14], the paper [14] considered non-faulty robots and [5] considered faulty robots. However, applying the arbitrary graph results of [5,14] to grid graphs yields memory-optimal solutions but not time-optimal ones. The work in [14] resulted in a linear-time algorithm for grid-type graphs with non-faulty robots. In contrast, the approach in [5] may have quadratic complexity depending on the number of clusters and the presence of faulty robots in the grid. All of these results are summarized in the Table 1.

Table 1. Results for the dispersion of $k \leq n$ robots and up to $f \leq n$ faulty robots on an n-node, m-edge and Δ maximum degree graph having k robots out of which f are faulty. Here, l is the number of robot clusters in the initial configuration. Note that $m = O(n)$ and $\Delta = O(1)$ for a grid graph.

Algorithm	Graph Type	Faulty	Time	Memory (in bits)
Kshemkalyani et al. [10]	Oriented Grid	No	$O(\min(k, \sqrt{n}))$	$O(\log k)$
Kshemkalyani et al. [14]	Arbitrary Graph	No	$(\min\{m, k\Delta\})$	$O(\log(k + \Delta))$
Chand et al. [5]	Arbitrary Graph	Yes	$O((f + l) \cdot \min\{m, k\Delta, k^2\})$	$O(\log(k + \Delta))$
Algorithm in Sect. 3	Unoriented Grid	No	$O(\sqrt{n})$	$O(\log n)$
Algorithm in Sect. 4	Unoriented Grid	Yes	$O(\sqrt{n} \log n)$	$O(\sqrt{n} \log n)$

Challenges and Techniques. Recall that robots in the oriented grid possess a sense of direction. Firstly, a robot can reach the boundary nodes (nodes with degree 3) from the internal of the grid by moving in a straight direction. But if the grid is unoriented in that case the robots have no sense of the direction, therefore, a robot can not reach the boundary in optimal time. Secondly, a robot can reach the corner of the grid by following the boundary. In this way, robots can find each other by sending a single robot to find the appropriate corner to gather at a single corner. On the other hand, if the robots are faulty then gathering at a single corner becomes challenging due to the faulty nature of the robots. The single robot can crash and corner robots might wait for an indefinite time.

We overcome these challenges as follows. In the non-faulty unoriented setup, two or more robots ensure their direction of movement in a straight line. Firstly, the group of robots (2 or more) moves in the direction of the minimum port number. Now the challenge is to ensure the movement in a straight direction. In this, all robots except one remain stationary, and one robot r_u explores the shortest possible ways to reach its initial position in the grid where the rest of the robots are placed. The robot r_u reaches the initial position in two ways, using the shortest path. These two paths lie at 180° to each other. This helps to determine the direction of the robots in a straight line. The detailed description is given in Sect. 3. A similar problem is tackled in the faulty unoriented setup by sending half of the robots to explore the other two paths to reach their initial position (detailed description is given in Sect. 4). In this way, robots reach the corner with the help of the boundary. Secondly, the faulty corner robots find each other by sending half of their available corner robots in one direction and reach their initial position after a round trip of the grid. By using this strategy, either half of the robots crash or find the appropriate corner (based on ID) to move. In the worst case, every time half of the corner robots may crash which causes an overhead of $O(\log n)$ round trip of the grid and there would not be left any robot to disperse. Finding an appropriate node to settle in the unoriented grid is another challenge after gathering at the corner in a faulty setup since a singleton robot might be left in the internal grid. To tackle this challenge, we used some extra memory and discussed one of the approaches in Sect. 4.

The rest of the paper is organized as follows.

Paper Organization. Section 2 states our distributed computing model. In Sect. 3, the dispersion of non-faulty robots is presented on the unoriented grid. In Sect. 4, the dispersion of faulty robots on an unoriented grid is discussed. Finally, Sect. 5 concludes the paper with some interesting problems.

2 Distributed Computing Model

Graph: We consider an unweighted, undirected graph $G = (V, E)$ which is a square grid of $n = \sqrt{n} \times \sqrt{n}$ nodes embedded in 2-dimensional Euclidean plane such that $|V| = n$ and $|E| = m$, where V is the set of nodes and E is the set of edges. G is a connected graph having nodes with either degrees 2 or 3 or 4. Nodes with degrees 2, 3, and 4 are considered to be corner nodes, boundary nodes, and internal nodes, respectively. These nodes are memoryless and resourceless means, unable to store any information and perform computation on them. Furthermore, nodes are anonymous such that nodes do not have IDs (identifiers) but each incident edge is uniquely identified by a labeled port number from $[1, \delta]$ where δ is the degree of the node. The nodes connected via an edge are termed neighboring nodes and are considered to be one hop away from each other. There are two port numbers assigned to any edge (e) corresponding to two nodes $u, v \in G$, that connect these two nodes. Moreover, there is no relationship between any two port numbers of an edge.

Robots: The set of robots $R = \{r_1, r_2, \ldots, r_k\}$ represents a collection of $k \leq n$ robots that are located across the graph G at one or more nodes. Robots do not stay at the edge and stay only on the nodes of the graph G. Two or more robots situated at a node are termed as co-located robots and these co-located robots can communicate with each other. This model is known as *local communication model* [1,9]. Each robot contains a unique ID consisting of $O(\log k)$ bits. A robot can move from one node to another from the port if the nodes are connected to each other via an edge. Each robot consists of some memory to store information and computation. We considered the computation time to be negligible as compared to the movement time of the robots from one node to another. A robot performs the "Communicate-Compute-Move" operation which is defined below.

Cycle: We consider a synchronous setting, every robot is synchronized to a common clock and movement from one node to another is complete in a one-time cycle or round. A robot $r_i \in R$ remains active in the "Communicate-Compute-Move" (CCM) cycle in a synchronous setting. Following are the three operations carried out by the robots:

- **Communicate:** r_i can interact with the co-located robots and view the memory of a different robot, say $r_j \in R$.
- **Compute:** r_i can perform any required computation by using the data gathered during the "communicate" phase. This involves choosing a (potentially) port to leave v_i and selecting the data to be saved in the robot r_j.
- **Move:** r_i writes new information (if any) in the memory of a robot r_j at v_i, and exits v_i using the computed port to reach to a neighbor node of v_i.

Crash Faults: We consider the crash failure setup where a robot may fail by *crashing* at any time during the execution of the algorithm. The crashed robot is not recoverable and once a robot crashes it immediately loses all the information stored in itself, as if it was not present at all. Further, a crashed robot is not visible or sensible to other robots. We assume there are at most f faulty robots such that $f \leq k$.

Time and Memory Complexity: The time complexity conveys the number of discrete rounds or cycles taken before achieving DISPERSION. Memory complexity is the number of bits required to store each robot to successfully execute the algorithm.

Below, we formally define non-faulty and faulty robots' dispersion problems in a graph.

Definition 1 (NON-FAULTY ROBOTS DISPERSION). *Given $k \leq n$ robots, initially, placed arbitrarily over the nodes of an n-node graph, the robots re-position themselves autonomously such that each node has at most one robot on it and subsequently terminate.*

Definition 2 (FAULTY ROBOTS DISPERSION). *Given $k \leq n$ robots, up to $f \leq k$ of which are faulty, initially placed arbitrarily over the nodes of an n-node graph, the (non-faulty) robots re-position themselves autonomously such that each node has at most one non-faulty robot on it and subsequently terminate.*

3 Dispersion of Non-Faulty Robots on Unoriented Grid

In this section, we present a deterministic algorithm for dispersing $k \leq n$ robots initially placed arbitrarily on the nodes of an n-node unoriented square grid and avoided the pseudocode due to space constraints[1]. The algorithm is both time and memory optimal, achieving dispersion within $O(\sqrt{n})$ rounds while utilizing $O(\log n)$ bits of memory for each robot. Note that all robots considered in this algorithm are non-faulty.

---

[1] A complete pseudocode is available in the arXiv paper [2].

3.1 Algorithm

The dispersion algorithm designed for oriented grids [10] cannot be readily adapted for unoriented grids. For unoriented grids, one can employ the DFS (Depth First Search) traversal based algorithm [14] which works in an arbitrary graph and solves the dispersion problem in $O(\min(m, k\Delta))$ rounds, where m is the number of edges, Δ is the highest degree in the graph and $k \leq n$ is the number of robots. However, this algorithm takes $O(n)$ rounds, given that $m = O(n)$ and $\Delta = 4$ in a grid graph. Therefore, the challenge lies in reducing the time complexity from $O(n)$ to $O(\sqrt{n})$.

In the unoriented grid, the main challenge is the sense of direction as compared to the oriented grid as discussed before. Thus, a single robot situated at the internal nodes cannot move on a path in the same direction of the grid. However, we show that two or more robots working together can navigate along a path in the same direction. This ability to move along a path is crucial for achieving dispersion within $O(\sqrt{n})$ rounds since the length of a path in the square grid is $\sqrt{n}$. The outline of the algorithm is, first we gather the robots at a corner node of the grid. For this, a single robot at the node remains settled at its node. The robots in a group of two or more on the internal nodes (i.e., the node with degree four) move to the boundary nodes first and then move to a corner node. Then from the four corner nodes, the robots gathered at one corner node. Suppose the robots are gathered at the top-left corner of the grid. Notice that all the k robots may not be gathered as some singleton robots may be settled already. Then the algorithm sends some robots to each column in parallel to count the number of single robots settled at each row. The robots back and report the requirement of robots at each row to the gathered robots at the top-left corner. Then appropriate number of robots are sent to each column from the corner node. Then robots are dispersed along each row in parallel. Our approach takes $O(\sqrt{n})$ rounds to gather the non-singleton robots at a corner and another $O(\sqrt{n})$ rounds to disperse from the corner including counting the singleton robots. Below, we explain our algorithm in detail, breaking it into 3 stages.

Stage 1 - Gathering at Corners of the Grid: Initially, robots are arbitrarily placed in the unoriented square grid. Nodes with degree four (internal nodes) having two or more robots start moving in a straight line and reach the boundary node (node with degree three) of the grid – straight line movement of the internal robots is explained later. If robot r is already at the boundary node of the grid, then r moves across the boundary node of the grid and reaches the corner (node with degree two) – the movement of the robot across the boundary nodes of the grid is explained later. Robots at the corner (node with degree two) remain at the corner. As discussed in the straight line movement of the internal robots and movement of the robot across the boundary node of the grid takes $O(\log n)$ memory (in bits).

Stage 2 - Gathering at a Single Corner: After $59\sqrt{n}$ rounds (shown in Lemma 1), all the internal non-singleton robots, initially, placed at the node with degree four would gather at the corner. In between, all the robots at the boundary nodes would also gather at the corner. These robots would be distributed across the four corners (gathering might not be at a single corner). Now, we would gather them at, a single corner, the corner which has a minimum ID robot. All the corners that have more than one robot would send the highest ID robot available at that node across the boundary node of the grid and reach their initial corner after exploring the rest of the three corners. Notice that the minimum ID robot does not move from its position, therefore, each moving robot learns about the minimum ID robot and all the robots gather at that corner. These movements of the robots take place across the boundary nodes of the grid which take $3\sqrt{n}$ rounds to reach one corner to another (discussed in Lemma 1). In the gathering at a single corner, the robot needs to keep account of the boundary nodes' traversal and the minimum ID robot's hop distance. This takes $O(\log n)$ memory (in bits).

Stage 3 - Dispersion from the Single Corner: In $77\sqrt{n}$ rounds (from the Lemmas 1 and 2), all the internal non-singleton robots and non-internal robots on the grid gather at the single corner. If the number of robots at the corner is not more than $4\sqrt{n} - 4$ then disperse the robots along the boundary node and corner of the grid since there is no robot at the boundary nodes of the grid. On the other hand, if the number of robots at the corner is more than $4\sqrt{n} - 4$, then send a pair of robots to each column (except the boundary node of the grid) and count the number of robots required. The corner node considers the minimum port number at the boundary and other nodes in the direction as a column of the grid. The count can be done with the help of two robots by the straight movement of the robots in the column (explained in the straight line movement of the internal robots). These pairs of robots move in the column of the grid and know the number of robots required at each column. After having the round trip of their respective column, these pairs of robots consider the port number from where they entered their respective column to reach their initial corner position and move in a straight line across the boundary nodes. After knowing the required number of robots for each column, the required number of robots is sent to the corresponding column (if available) and dispersed. Notice that the first and last column requires $\sqrt{n}$ robots due to the unavailability of any robot on those columns. In this stage, pair robots keep the account of their column number and count of the required number of robots which takes $O(\log n)$ memory (in bits).

Straight Line Movement of the Internal Robots: Let us consider there exists an internal node with t number of robots such that $t > 1$ and the minimum ID robot is r_m. Now, all the robots move across the minimum port number, i.e., port 1, in a round. Now we want to make sure that the robots move in a straight line, therefore, these robots should not move across the same edge that they just crossed (say, backward port). This implies three ports' choices remain in which these robots can move. Now, the maximum ID robots (say, r) take the next minimum available port and explore it till four port distances away from the r_m in all the possible combinations (by giving priority to minimum port number) which are $3 * 3 * 3 = 27$ total different nodes. This round trip would take at most $2 * 27 = 54$ rounds from one hop away from the r_m while moving one hop away from the r_m takes 2 more rounds. Therefore, the total rounds in this round trip are 56. Notice that there exist precisely two ways for r to reach the initial position (position where r_m stays) of the robots. These two positions would be at $180°$ to each other. Further, let us consider two cases: (i) one of the ports from which the r reaches r_m is the backward port, then the other port would be the desired one in a straight line. Therefore, all the robots would proceed from that port in a straight line. (ii) None of the ports from which r reached r_m is the backward port, therefore, none of the ports among these two ports are at 180° of the backward port. As a consequence, one of the remaining ports is the backward port and the other one is at 180° of the backward port. In this way, we find the desired port to proceed in a straight line. Now, all the robots move in a straight line from the appropriate port and repeat the process till all of them reach the boundary node of the grid. Notice that some findings may take less than 56 rounds when the robot r explores the edge of the grid. Although we can consider that particular path to reach the boundary of the grid which is explored at 90° of our straight line direction, we would prefer to move in the straight line. Observe that it would not affect our overall round complexity but would keep the simple fact in consideration, i.e., the straight-line movement of the robots. Consequently, to move a single hop in a straight line takes at most 56 rounds. In the case of memory, the maximum ID robot keeps account of at most 28 ports to move one hop in a straight line and maximum ID and r_m, therefore, $O(\log k)$ (in bits) is used.

A similar straight-line movement idea was developed in [4], where an agent builds a sense of direction on a torus with the help of a token or pebble[2]. Note that the dispersion algorithm for oriented grids in [10] and this straight-line movement procedure together do not immediately give a solution for dispersion on an unoriented grid. The straight-line movement requires at least two robots (without a token) to work together. Thus the singleton robots need to be handled differently to achieve dispersion, which our algorithm addresses.

Movement of the Robot Across the Boundary Nodes of the Grid: Let us consider a robot r is placed at the boundary node of the grid. Robot r moves one hop from the minimum port then there arise two cases that do not lead to the corner node: (i) robot r reaches the boundary node of the grid or (ii) robot r reaches the node whose degree is four. In the first case, r explores the minimum port among the rest of the ports (excluding the port due to which r reached this boundary node of the grid) and finds the boundary node of the grid. In the second case, r comes back to the boundary node explores the next available minimum port (minimum unexplored port), and finds the boundary node. Similarly, r repeatedly explores the boundary nodes and reaches the corner of the grid. Notice that the boundary nodes' degree is three and only one port leads to the non-side node of the grid, therefore, r may select at most one non-side node of the grid before finding the correct boundary node of the grid. Therefore, robot r takes at most 3 rounds to move in a specific direction towards the corner of the grid. Also, the robot keeps an account of the last two traversed ports which takes constant memory.

Lemma 1. *Any boundary node robot takes at most $3\sqrt{n}$ rounds to reach the corner, while the group of robots (non-singleton robots) placed inside the grid reach the corner of the grid in at most $59\sqrt{n}$ rounds.*

---

[2] We devise the straight-line movement idea independently of the work in [4]. We thank the anonymous reviewer for bringing this paper to our attention.

Proof. Non-singleton robots first move from the internal node to the boundary node of the grid. Further, they move from the boundary node of the grid to the corner of the grid. As we have seen in *straight line movement of the internal robots,* that to move in a straight line there are at most 56 rounds required to move one hop. Also, there exists at most $\sqrt{n}$ such hop in a straight line of the grid. Therefore, any group of robots requires $56\sqrt{n}$ rounds to move from the internal node to the boundary node of the grid.

Further, *movement of the robot on the edge of the grid* takes 3 round to move one hop in a specific direction, and there exist at most $\sqrt{n} - 1$ such hop. Hence, the number of rounds required to move across the boundary nodes before reaching a corner node is at most $3\sqrt{n}$.

Therefore, overall rounds required to reach the corner node by non-singleton robots from the inside of the grid are $3\sqrt{n} + 56\sqrt{n} = 59\sqrt{n}$, i.e., $O(\sqrt{n})$ rounds. □

Lemma 2. *Gathering all the corner robots at a single corner node takes at most $18\sqrt{n}$ rounds.*

Proof. Firstly, the robots with the highest ID at their respective corner take a round of the whole grid via boundary nodes and corner edges. This takes four sides' exploration of the corner robots. It takes $3\sqrt{n}$ round for one boundary of the grid (shown in Lemma 1). Therefore, four sides take $12\sqrt{n}$ rounds. In this way, each node gets to know about the minimum ID robot present at the corner. Now, that minimum ID robot can be at most two sides ($2\sqrt{n}$ hops) away from any corner. Therefore, to reach that particular corner takes at most $6\sqrt{n}$ rounds. Hence, overall rounds required to gather at a single corner are at most $18\sqrt{n}$. □

Lemma 3. *Robots gathered at a corner node take at most $118\sqrt{n}$ rounds to disperse the robots on the square grid.*

Proof. Let us call that corner C_0 where all the robots gather. If the number of robots is not more than $4\sqrt{n} - 4$ then these robots would disperse across the boundary nodes which takes at most $12\sqrt{n}$ rounds, i.e., $O(\sqrt{n})$ rounds.

On the other hand, if the number of robots at C_0 is more than $4\sqrt{n}-4$ then the robots in pairs explore all the columns. To reach a particular column take $3\sqrt{n}$ (due to the movement of the robot across the boundary node of the grid) and then to take the round trip of a particular column take $2*56\sqrt{n}$ rounds. After that reporting about the required number of robots at a particular column to C_0 takes at most $3\sqrt{n}$ rounds. Now these robots reach a particular column in at most $3\sqrt{n}$ rounds and settle at their respective node in $56\sqrt{n}$. This implies the total number of rounds is $(3 + 112 + 3)\sqrt{n} = 118\sqrt{n}$. □

Lemma 4. *Our algorithm takes $195\sqrt{n}$ rounds and $O(\log n)$ bits of memory at each robot.*

Proof. From reaching the corner, gathering at a single corner, and dispersing all the robots in Lemmas 1, 2 and 3, respectively, take $59\sqrt{n} + 18\sqrt{n} + 118\sqrt{n} = 195\sqrt{n}$ rounds. Similarly, Stages 1, 2, and 3 show total memory required is $O(\log n)$ bits. □

From the above discussion, we conclude the following results.

Theorem 1. *Consider any unoriented square grid of n nodes having k robots such that $k \leq n$ where each robot has the memory $O(\log n)$ (in bits) then DISPERSION can be solved deterministically in $O(\sqrt{n})$ rounds.*

4 Dispersion of Faulty Robots on Unoriented Grids

In this section, we present a deterministic algorithm for the dispersion of faulty robots, arbitrarily placed on the nodes of a unoriented grid. The algorithm achieves dispersion within $O(\sqrt{n} \log n)$ rounds while utilizing $O(\sqrt{n} \log n)$ bits of memory for each robot.

4.1 Algorithm

In the presence of faulty robots, dispersion becomes more challenging. We can not adopt the procedure discussed in Sect. 3. The reason behind this is: Firstly, in the case of straight-line movement of the internal robots, there might be the case that there are $O(n)$ robots present at the internal node. After constant rounds, the highest ID robot crashes before deciding the direction of movement. This may happen $O(n)$ times, therefore, the round complexity's order becomes linear. Secondly, after reaching the corner, it would be costlier (in terms of rounds) to find the minimum ID robot at the corner of the grid. Since there might be the case that every robot that goes for the round trip via boundary nodes of the grid crashes every time. In the worst case, there might be $O(n)$ robots at the corner and each failure would cost $\Omega(\sqrt{n})$ rounds. Therefore, their consecutive failure would cost sub-quadratic round complexity. Thirdly, after gathering at a single corner (non-singleton internal robots and non-internal robots), it would be costlier to send a pair of robots to the columns and count the required number of robots in each column. If $O(n)$ robots are gathered at a single corner then sending them in pair and waiting for the $O(\sqrt{n})$ rounds would further take $O(\sqrt{n})$ rounds extra, in worst case. Each round would be $O(\sqrt{n})$ rounds costly. Consequently, round complexity would be linear.

Our approach for the faulty robots' dispersion is similar to the approach, in 3 stages, of the non-faulty robots' dispersion. We deal with the above-discussed challenges in detail and improve our algorithm stage-by-stage.

Stage 1 - Gathering at Corners of the Grid: Initially, robots are arbitrarily placed in the unoriented square grid. Node with degree four (internal node) having two or more robots start moving in a straight line and reach the boundary node (node with degree three) of the grid – straight line movement of the internal faulty robots is explained later. If the robot r is already at the boundary node of the grid, then r moves across the boundary edge of the grid and reaches the corner (node with degree two) as explained in the movement of the robot across the boundary edges of the grid (see Sect. 3). During the exploration of the boundary nodes and reaching the corner, faulty robots might crash and not reach the corner, unlike non-faulty robots. Robots at the corner (node with degree two) remain at the corner.

Stage 2 - Gathering at a Single Corner: After $56 \log n + 59\sqrt{n}$ rounds (shown in Lemma 5), all the internal non-singleton non-crashed robots, initially, placed at the node with degree four would gather at the corner. In between, all the robots at the boundary of the grid would also gather at the corner. These robots would be distributed across the four corners (gathering might not be at a single corner). After that, robots gather at a single corner that has a minimum ID robot known as whether crashed or non-crashed. All the corners which have more than two robots would send half of the higher ID robots (say, seeker robots) available at that node across the boundary edge of the grid from the minimum port number and reach their initial corner after exploring the rest of the three corners. The seeker robots and non-seeker robots of a corner node move at the corner which has/had the minimum ID robot according to both seeker and non-seeker robots. There might be a case that either all the seeker robots or non-seeker robots crashed, in that case, the remaining robots of a corner repeat the process to find the minimum ID robot on the boundary of the grid. This would be repeated until the seeker robots sent from the minimum port numbers meet the non-seeker robots after a round trip with the same known minimum ID robot, or at most one robot is remaining at the corner. These movements of the robots take place across the boundary edges of the grid. The boundary edge robots of the grid take $3\sqrt{n}$ rounds to reach the corner and there would be $O(\log n)$ round trip in the worst case. Therefore, round complexity for this stage is $O(\sqrt{n} \log n)$ (as shown in Lemma 6).

Stage 3 - Dispersion from the Single Corner: In $12\sqrt{n} \log n + 65\sqrt{n} + 56 \log n$ rounds (from Lemmas 5, and 6), all the internal non-singleton robots and non-internal robots on the grid would gather at the single corner. Let us consider C_{r_m} as the number of robots at the single corner and R_0 as the number of columns requiring no robots. Initially, R_0 is 0. If the number of robots at the corner is not more than $4\sqrt{n} - 4$ then disperse the robots along the boundary edges and corner of the grid based on their ID (smaller the ID nearer the position) since there is no robot on the boundary nodes of the grid. On the other hand, if the number of robots at the corner is more than $4\sqrt{n} - 4$, then send $\left\lfloor \frac{C_{r_m}}{\sqrt{n} - R_0 - 2} \right\rfloor$ robots to a column that requires robots (except the boundary edges of the grid) and disperse them in that column. The remaining robots report at the corner about the column which does not require robots and update C_{r_m} and R_0. This process is repeated until less than $4\sqrt{n} - 4$ robots are left, which would be dispersed across the boundary edges of the grid.

Straight Line Movement for the Internal Faulty Robots: We traverse similarly with the faulty robots as we did with the non-faulty robots. As discussed earlier there might be the case that maximum ID robots might crash every time before reporting the appropriate port number (port in the same direction at $180°$) for the traversal. It might increase the round complexity up to $O(n)$. Therefore, we consider half of the robots for finding the appropriate port number as compared to the maximum ID robot, and the other half stay at their place, waiting for the appropriate port number. If only one of the robots survived to report the appropriate port number then we know the appropriate port. Even if all the robots of a group crashed, then at most half of the robots would be left. Further, the remaining half of the robots partition themselves into two groups and repeat the process. Therefore, without moving on the right port (appropriate direction) these robots might crash $O(\log n)$ times, otherwise they will move in the appropriate direction (in a straight line). Consequently, round complexity would be $O(\sqrt{n} + \log n) = O(\sqrt{n})$. In other words, let us consider there exists an internal node with t number of robots such that $t > 1$ and the minimum ID robot known is r_m. Now, all the robots move across the minimum port number, i.e., port 1, and take one round. Now we want to make sure that the robots move in a straight line, therefore, these robots should not move across the same port which they just crossed (say, backward port). This implies there are three ports' choices remaining in which these robots can move. Now, $\lfloor t/2 \rfloor$ maximum ID robots take the next minimum available port and explore it till four port distances away from the group of r_m robots in all the possible combinations (by giving priority to minimum port number) which are $3*3*3 = 27$ total different nodes. This round trip would take at most $2*27 = 54$ rounds from one hop away from the r_m while moving one hop away from the r_m takes 2 more rounds. Therefore, the total rounds in this round trip are 56. Notice that there exist exactly two ways for the group of $t/2$ robots (even a single robot reporting would be enough to know the appropriate port number) to reach the initial position (position where other $t/2$ robots stay which may crash) of the robots. These two positions would be at $180°$ to each other. Further, let us consider two cases: (i) one of the ports from which the $t/2$ robots reached the initial position (where the other half of the robots are waiting for the appropriate port number) is the backward port, then the other port would be the desired one in a straight line. Therefore, all the non-crashed robots would proceed from that port in a straight line. (ii) None of the ports is the backward port, then none of the ports among these two ports are at $180°$ of the backward port. Therefore, one of the remaining ports is the backward port and the other one is at $180°$ of the backward port. In this way, we find the desired port to proceed in a straight line. Now, all the robots move in a straight line from the appropriate port and repeat the process till all of them reach the boundary edge of the grid. There might be two more possibilities with faulty robots based on the crash that $t/2$ robots crashed without reporting the port at $180°$ or the other half crashed, in that case, repeat the process by doing the partition of the remaining robots in two halves. There are only $\log n$ such partitions possible. Hence, to move a single hop in a straight line takes at most 56 rounds or at least half of the robots would crash. Therefore, it would take at most $56(\log n + \sqrt{n})$ rounds to reach the boundary edge of the grid.

Lemma 5. *In stage 1, the group of robots (non-singleton non-crashed robots) placed inside the grid reach corners of the grid in at most $56 \log n + 59\sqrt{n}$ rounds.*

Proof. There are $54\sqrt{n}$ rounds required if both the groups do not crash fully in the straight line movement for the internal faulty robots. But if one of the groups crashes fully, that might happen at most $\log n$ times. Hence, 56 rounds can be wasted without finding the appropriate direction $\log n$ times. Therefore, the total number of rounds required to reach the boundary edge of the grid is $56(\log n + \sqrt{n})$. In Sect. 3, we have seen that a non-faulty (robot which does not crash) single robot takes $3\sqrt{n}$ robot in the movement of the robot across the boundary edge of the grid. Therefore, non-singleton non-crashed robots reach at corners of the grid in at most $56 \log n + 59\sqrt{n}$ rounds from the internal node of the grid. □

Lemma 6. *In stage 2, corner robots gather at a single corner in $12\sqrt{n}\log n + 6\sqrt{n}$ rounds.*

Proof. Firstly, half of the robots with the highest ID at their respective corner takes a round of the whole grid via boundary edges and corner edges. This takes four boundary edge explorations for the corner robots. It takes $3\sqrt{n}$ round for one boundary of the grid (discussed in Lemma 5). Therefore, four boundaries take $12\sqrt{n}$ rounds. In this way, each robot gets to know about the minimum ID robot present at the corner. On the other hand, there might be the case that either half of the robots crash fully, and then the remaining half (at most) of the robots take another round trip across the boundary edges of the grid. There can be at most $\log n$ such incidents. Therefore, the overall round cost might be $12\sqrt{n}\log n$ to know the minimum ID robot's corner. Secondly, the minimum ID robot can be at most two boundaries ($2\sqrt{n}$ hops) away from any corner. Therefore, to reach the particular corner takes $6\sqrt{n}$ rounds. Hence, overall rounds required to gather at a single corner are $12\sqrt{n}\log n + 6\sqrt{n}$. □

Lemma 7. *In Lemma 6, all the non-crashed corner robots gather at the single corner.*

Proof. We prove the lemma by contradiction. Let us suppose there exist two corners, C_1 and C_2 in Lemma 6 such that C_2's corner ID was minimum then C_1. But the corner C_0 figures out the minimum ID robot at corner C_1 this implies that C_0's seeker robots neither crossed the C_2's non-seeker robots nor met in the middle with the seeker robots of the C_2. This implies there are no non-seeker robots at C_2. Additionally, seeker robots of C_2 did not cross the non-seeker robots of C_0. Consequently, there are no seeker robots from the corner C_2 exist in the grid. Therefore, there do not exist any C_2 robots with minimum ID. Hence, the lemma. □

Lemma 8. *In stage 3, dispersion from the single corner takes $O(\sqrt{n}\log n)$ rounds.*

Proof. In Stage 3, if the number of robots at the single corner is less than $4\sqrt{n} - 4$ then these robots are placed across the boundary nodes of the grid in $4 \cdot 3\sqrt{n}$ rounds based on their ID. On the other hand, if the number of robots at the single corner is more than $4\sqrt{n} - 4$ then an equal number of robots are sent in each column. There can be two cases: either half or more robots crash before reporting or not. If half or more robots report at their corner then half or more of the column does not require any robots further. Now, the number of columns left for the dispersion of the robots in the grid is less than or equal to half. This case can be repeated at most $\log n$ times, then there would be no column/node for the robots' dispersion. In another case, if less than half of the column reports to their corner then more than half of the robots are settled in the grid from the corner. This case also can be repeated at most $\log n$ times, after that, there would be no robot for dispersion. In the worst case, these two cases can arise alternatively, where this process can be repeated at most $2\log n$ times. As we know before reporting, there are rounds required $6\sqrt{n}$ rounds for moving on the boundary edge and $112\sqrt{n}$ for moving in the column of the grid. Therefore, dispersion from a single corner takes $236\sqrt{n}\log n$ rounds, i.e., $O(\sqrt{n}\log n)$. □

Lemma 9. *Our algorithm for faulty setup requires $O(\sqrt{n}\log n)$ memory at each robot.*

Proof. Each robot stores its own ID, therefore, $\log k$ bits are required. In stage 1 $O(\log k)$ memory is required to store the initial node's minimum ID and some constant memory to track the port number before deciding the appropriate straight direction for the internal robots. In the case of boundary edge movement, only port numbering is stored, therefore, constant memory is required.

In stage 2, traversal takes place along the boundary edges, therefore, the minimum ID corner and its position along with some constant port numbering require $O(\log n)$ memory.

In stage 3, the distance from the corner and the number of robots required should be stored at each robot, along with the traversal at the boundary edge and inside the grid. Therefore, $2\sqrt{n}\log n$ bits are required to store the position of the column and the required number of robots. Consequently, all these stages require the $O(\sqrt{n}\log n)$ bits memory. □

From the above discussion, we have the following results.

Theorem 2. *Consider any unoriented square grid of n nodes in the presence of any number of faulty robots where k is the number of robots, in which, each robot has memory access $O(\sqrt{n}\log n)$ bits then DISPERSION can be solved deterministically in $O(\sqrt{n}\log n)$ rounds.*

5 Conclusion and Future Work

In this paper, we studied dispersion for distinguishable mobile robots on a port-labeled unoriented square grid in an arbitrary configuration of the robots with and without fault. We presented $O(\sqrt{n})$ round algorithm for the setup of the non-faulty robot while $O(\sqrt{n}\log n)$ round algorithm for the setup of the faulty robot. In the non-faulty case, robots required $O(\log n)$ bits memory while the faulty case required $O(\sqrt{n}\log n)$ bits. Furthermore, both of our algorithms can be extended to solve the rectangular grid problem, which we did not discuss due to space constraints[3]. Some open questions that are raised by our work: i) What is the non-trivial lower bound, in terms of k when $k = o(\sqrt{n})$, for the round complexity in both the setup by keeping the memory $O(\log n)$? ii) Is it possible to improve the result in the faulty setup similar to the non-faulty setup? iii) Finally, whether similar bounds hold in the presence of Byzantine failures.

References

1. Augustine, J., Moses Jr., W.K.: Dispersion of mobile robots: a study of memory-time tradeoffs. In: ICDCN (2018)
2. Banerjee, R., Kumar, M., Molla, A.R.: Optimizing robot dispersion on grids: with and without fault tolerance. CoRR arXiv:2405.02002 (2024).
3. Barriere, L., Flocchini, P., Mesa-Barrameda, E., Santoro, N.: Uniform scattering of autonomous mobile robots in a grid. Int. J. Found. Comput. Sci. **22**(03), 679–697 (2011)

---

[3] An analysis of the rectangular grid is available in the arXiv paper [2].

4. Becha, H., Flocchini, P.: Optimal construction of sense of direction in a torus by a mobile agent. Int. J. Found. Comput. Sci. **18**(03), 529–546 (2007)
5. Chand, P.K., Kumar, M., Molla, A.R., Sivasubramaniam, S.: Fault-tolerant dispersion of mobile robots. In: CALDAM (2023)
6. Hsiang, T., Arkin, E.M., Bender, M.A., Fekete, S.P., Mitchell, J.S.B.: Algorithms for rapidly dispersing robot swarms in unknown environments. In: WAFR (2002)
7. Hsiang, T., Arkin, E.M., Bender, M.A., Fekete, S.P., Mitchell, J.S.B.: Online dispersion algorithms for swarms of robots. In: Fortune, S. (ed.) SCG (2003)
8. Italiano, G.F., Pattanayak, D., Sharma, G.: Dispersion of mobile robots on directed anonymous graphs. In: SIROCCO (2022)
9. Kshemkalyani, A.D., Ali, F.: Efficient dispersion of mobile robots on graphs. In: ICDCN (2019)
10. Kshemkalyani, A.D., Molla, A.R., Sharma, G.: Dispersion of mobile robots on grids. In: WALCOM (2020)
11. Kshemkalyani, A.D., Molla, A.R., Sharma, G.: Efficient dispersion of mobile robots on dynamic graphs. In: ICDCS (2020)
12. Kshemkalyani, A.D., Molla, A.R., Sharma, G.: Fast dispersion of mobile robots on arbitrary graphs. In: ALGOSENSORS (2019)
13. Kshemkalyani, A.D., Molla, A.R., Sharma, G.: Dispersion of mobile robots using global communication. J. Parallel Distrib. Comput. **161**, 100–117 (2022)
14. Kshemkalyani, A.D., Sharma, G.: Near-optimal dispersion on arbitrary anonymous graphs. In: OPODIS (2021)
15. Molla, A.R., Mondal, K., Moses Jr., W.K.: Byzantine dispersion on graphs. In: IPDPS (2021)
16. Shintaku, T., Sudo, Y., Kakugawa, H., Masuzawa, T.: Efficient dispersion of mobile agents without global knowledge. In: SSS (2020)

Channel Allocation Revisited Through 1-Extendability of Graphs

Anthony Busson, Malory Marin, and Rémi Watrigant[(✉)]

Univ Lyon, CNRS, ENS de Lyon, Université Claude Bernard Lyon 1, LIP UMR5668,
Lyon, France
remi.watrigant@univ-lyon1.fr

Abstract. We revisit the classical problem of channel allocation for Wi-Fi access points (AP). Using mechanisms such as the CSMA/CA protocol, Wi-Fi access points which are in conflict within a same channel are still able to communicate to terminals. In graph theoretical terms, it means that it is not mandatory for the channel allocation to correspond to a proper coloring of the conflict graph. However, recent studies suggest that the structure–rather than the number–of conflicts plays a crucial role in the performance of each AP. More precisely, the graph induced by each channel must satisfy the so-called 1-extendability property, which requires each vertex to be contained in an independent set of maximum cardinality. In this paper we introduce the 1-extendable chromatic number, which is the minimum size of a partition of the vertex set of a graph such that each part induces a 1-extendable graph. We study this parameter and the related optimization problem through different perspectives: algorithms and complexity, structure, and extremal properties. We first show how to compute this number using modular decompositions of graphs, and analyze the running time with respect to the modular width of the input graph. We also focus on the special case of cographs, and prove that the 1-extendable chromatic number can be computed in quasi-polynomial time in this class. Concerning extremal results, we show that the 1-extendable chromatic number of a graph with n vertices is at most $2\sqrt{n}$, whereas the classical chromatic number can be as large as n. We are also able to construct graphs whose 1-extendable chromatic number is at least logarithmic in the number of vertices.

1 Introduction

1.1 CSMA/CA Network and Channel

Wi-Fi Networks. Wi-Fi networks are one of the primary means of accessing the Internet today. A Wi-Fi network is composed of one or more access points (AP) giving Internet access to stations associated to them. Each access point uses exclusively a particular channel, which consists in a 20 MHz wide frequency band. There are currently 3 independent channels (with no common frequencies) in the 2.4 GHz band and around 23 in the 5 GHz band. These channels can be aggregated, enabling an AP to use a 40 Mhz frequency range, thus improving throughput. To arbitrate transmissions between access points and stations using the same channel, the CSMA/CA protocol is used. This is a listen-before-talk mechanism that enables time-sharing of the channel between stations and APs. Time-sharing is not static/predetermined, but opportunistic. For example, when two APs use the same channel, the number of transmissions is on average shared equally between the two APs (in an equivalent radio environment). The throughput is therefore approximately halved for each of the access points, compared with the case where they are alone on their channel. Such sharing is referred to as conflicts in the literature, and is represented by a conflict graph where the vertices are the APs and the edges indicate whether they share the channel. We consider only the DCF mode of Wi-Fi, which is the mode used in practice on commercial access points.

Channel Allocation. Channel allocation is the algorithm used to set channels on the various access points. There is then a conflict graph for each channel. The aim of the algorithm might be to minimize the number of edges in the conflict graphs, so as to have as little sharing as possible, or to distribute the network load over the different channels. The algorithms implemented on commercial Wi-Fi networks are variants of these two approaches. However, these approaches perform poorly when traffic on the access points become saturated (i.e. when an AP always has a frame to transmit). Depending on the topology of the conflict graph, some APs may starve and be unable to transmit any frames at all. Indeed, the performance of each AP depends on the structure of its conflict graph. More precisely, it appears that the structure of its *independent sets* plays a crucial role, where an independent set of a graph is a set of pairwise non-adjacent vertices.

A graph Theoretical Approach. The key metric describing the performance of a channel allocation is the proportion of accesses (number of transmissions) that each vertex of the conflict graph obtains. It is denoted by p_v for a vertex v. Hence, $p_v = 1$ if v has no neighbor in the conflict graph, and $0 \leqslant p_v < 1$ otherwise. If $p_v = 0$ the vertex is in starvation and cannot transmit any frame. The first formal study characterizing p_v was presented in [13], where it was demonstrated that under saturation conditions, p_v can be calculated as:

$$p_v = \frac{\sum_{S \in \mathcal{S}(G): v \in S} \theta^{|S|}}{\sum_{S \in \mathcal{S}(G)} \theta^{|S|}}$$

where θ is the ratio between transmission and listen phase durations, and $\mathcal{S}(G)$ is the set of independent sets of G. When θ tends to infinity, p_v tends to the ratio of the number of independent sets of maximum cardinality (maximum independent set, or MIS for short) that contains v ($\#_v \alpha(G)$) over the total number of MIS of G ($\#\alpha(G)$):

$$\lim_{\theta \to +\infty} p_v = \frac{\#_v \alpha(G)}{\#\alpha(G)}$$

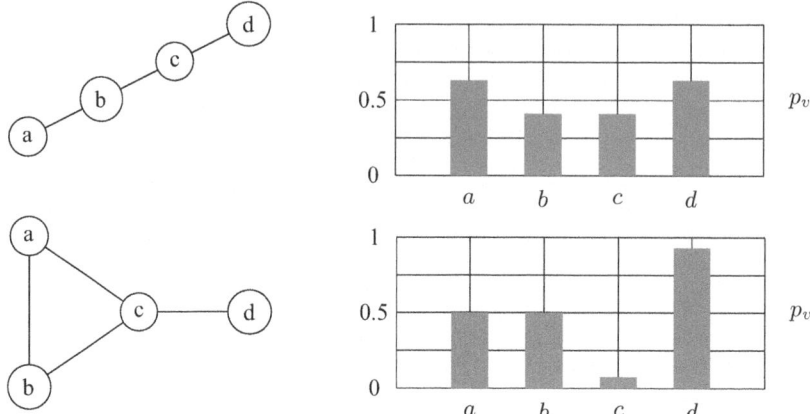

Fig. 1. Two graphs and the p_v value of each vertex, obtained with ns-3 simulations. ns-3 is a network simulator that implements the Wi-Fi protocol in the same way as the standards, and incorporates a realistic radio layer. The simulated Wi-Fi corresponds to the IEEE 802.11ax amendment with frame aggregation enabled and a physical transmission rate of 144.4Mbit/s. The top graph is 1-extendable and thus each vertex has a non-negligible throughput. The bottom graph is not 1-extendable, and the middle vertex has a very low throughput.

To ensure efficient channel utilization, θ is often set to a large value in practice. For example, in Wi-Fi networks, typical values of θ range from 20 to 100, depending on the transmission parameters. However, with such values, a node or vertex that does not belong to any MIS will experience a very low throughput. Figure 1 illustrates this phenomenon on two simple graphs.

To guarantee that every vertex has a fair share of the channel and to prevent any node from being deprived of transmission opportunities, it is essential that every vertex belongs to an MIS. In graph theoretical terms, each channel must induce a conflict graph that is 1-*extendable*. In the Wi-Fi context, this means that channel allocation must lead to 1-extendable conflict graphs. In this article, we investigate from a structural and algorithmic point of view whether such allocations are possible with a fixed number of channels.

1.2 Definitions and Related Work

A graph G is 1-*extendable* if each vertex belongs to at least one maximum independent set (MIS). This class was initially introduced by Berge [1] under the name of B-graphs in order to study *well-covered* graphs. The class of well-covered graphs was introduced by Plummer in 1970 [17], and is defined to be the graphs where every independent set that cannot be further extended is also an MIS. In other words, all (inclusion-wise) maximal independent sets have the same size. This property makes them particularly interesting as it guarantees that the greedy algorithm for constructing a large independent set always produces an optimal solution. In particular, a graph is well-covered if, and only if, for any $k \geqslant 1$ any independent set of size k is a subset of an MIS. This last property, when k is fixed, was called k-extendability by Dean and Zito [9]. More recently, the computational aspects of testing 1-extendability has been studied [2]. Specifically, it has been shown that recognizing 1-extendable graphs is NP-hard, even for unit disk graphs, which are a common model for wireless networks. A more involved computational complexity of recognizing 1-extendable graphs, well-covered graphs and generalizations was also conducted in [10], where in particular it was proved that deciding whether a given graph is 1-extendable is Θ_2^p-complete, and thus belong to a complexity class beyond NP.

For a graph G, we say that a partition $V_1, \ldots, V_k$ of its vertex set is a *1-extendable k-partition* if the subgraph induced by V_i is 1-extendable for every $i = 1, \ldots, k$. The *1-extendable chromatic number* of a graph G, denoted by $\chi_{\text{1-ext}}(G)$, is the smallest integer k such that G admits a 1-extendable k-partition. Observe that this number is bounded above by the "classical" chromatic number $\chi(G)$, which is the minimum integer k such that $V(G)$ has a partition into k independent sets (since an independent set is 1-extendable). The main objective of this paper is to study this new parameter both structurally and algorithmically. Given a graph G and an integer k, the 1-EXTENDABLE PARTITION problem asks whether $\chi_{\text{1-ext}}(G) \leqslant k$. In a nutshell, if G represents the conflict graph of a set of Wi-Fi access points, $\chi_{\text{1-ext}}(G)$ denotes the minimum number of channels in an assignment which guarantees that under saturation, no access point will be in starvation.

One classical way of attacking a graph optimization problem is to decompose the input into simpler pieces in a way that rearranging the pieces behaves well with the considered problem. As the 1-extendability deals with the structure of independent sets, it makes sense to consider a decomposition which preserves this structure. One such object is the so-called *modular decomposition*, which is a recursive representation of a graph in which each piece–a subset of vertices called *module*– has a homogeneous behavior with respect to the others (a formal definition will be given in Sect. 2). It is important to note that every graph admits a modular decomposition, and it can be obtained in linear time [14]. Moreover, it is worth noting that modular decompositions were also considered for studying well-covered graphs [15]. When dealing with the modular decomposition of a graph, a natural parameter measuring its complexity is the so-called *modular-width*, which informally represents the arity of the branching tree of the recursive decomposition. For a graph G, we denote its modular-width by $mw(G)$.

1.3 Contributions and Organization of the Paper

In this paper we conduct an analysis of the 1-extendable chromatic number through several different angles: complexity, algorithms, structure and extremal behavior.

In Sect. 3, we first study the computational complexity of deciding the exact value of this number for arbitrary graphs. It was recently shown that the problem of deciding whether a graph is 1-extendable belongs to a complexity class above

NP [10]. Namely, the problem is complete for Θ_2^p, which is the set of problems that can be solved in polynomial time with a logarithmic number of calls to a SAT oracle. It is natural to expect that computing the 1-extendable chromatic number is not easier by proving that 1-EXTENDABLE K-PARTITION is Θ_2^p-hard for every fixed $k \geqslant 1$.

We then turn to positive results. We first obtain an algorithm for deciding whether a graph is 1-extendable which runs in single exponential in the modular-width of the input graph, and linear time in its number of vertices. We then use this algorithm to compute the 1-extendable chromatic number is at most k in time $\alpha(G)^{O(mw(G)k)} \cdot n$, where $\alpha(G)$ is the *independence number* of a graph $\alpha(G)$, which corresponds to the size of an MIS of G.

A building block of these algorithms is the special case of *cographs*, which can be seen as the simplest graphs with respect to modular decomposition. In particular, cographs are exactly the graphs with modular-width 2, the smallest possible value. We are able to obtain an algorithm for deciding whether the 1-extendable chromatic number of a cograph G is at most k in time $k \cdot \alpha(G)^{O(k)}$. We also exhibit a number-theoretical formulation of the problem in the case of complete multipartite graphs, which is an even more restricted case of cographs, but seems to contain the main combinatorial complexity of the problem.

In Sect. 4, we investigate the extremal behavior of the 1-extendable chromatic number. We first show that this number is at most $2\sqrt{n}$ in general graphs with n vertices.

For the special case of cographs, we are even able to obtain a logarithmic bound, which appears to be tight, as there exist a cograph which requires a logarithmic bound. This result, together with the previously mentioned algorithm, implies an algorithm for deciding the 1-extendable chromatic number of a cograph G running in quasi-polynomial time, namely $k \cdot \alpha(G)^{O(\log_2(\alpha(G)))}$.

Finally, we conclude the paper in Sect. 5 with several open questions.

Due to space constraints, most of the proofs (those marked with a *) were omitted and are available in the long version of the paper [5]).

2 Preliminaries

Most definitions used in this paper are standard. We nevertheless recall those which are heavily used. For a non-negative integer n, let $[n] = \{1, \ldots n\}$. Given a graph G, $V(G)$ denotes its vertex set and $E(G)$ its edge set. Given $R \subseteq V(G)$, we use $G[R]$ to denote the subgraph of G induced by R, and $G - R = G[V(G) - R]$ to denote the subgraph of G induced by the complement of R. Unless otherwise stated, n always denotes the number of vertices of the considered graph. The *disjoint union* of two graphs G_1 and G_2 is the graph denoted by $G_1 \cup G_2$ whose vertex set is $V(G_1) \cup V(G_2)$ and edge set is $E(G_1) \cup E(G_2)$. The *complete sum* of two graphs G_1 and G_2 is the graph denoted by $G_1 + G_2$ whose vertex set is $V(G_1) \cup V(G_2)$ and edge set is $E(G_1) \cup E(G_2) \cup \{\{x, y\} : x \in V(G_1), y \in V(G_2)\}$. Given a graph H with $V(H) = \{v_1, \ldots, v_n\}$ and n graphs $G_1, \ldots, G_n$, the substitution operation of

$(G_1, \ldots, G_n)$ on H is the graph whose vertex set is $\cup_{i=1}^{n} V(G_i)$, and edge set $(\cup_{i=1}^{n} E(G_i)) \cup (\cup_{\{v_i, v_j\} \in E(H)} \{\{x, y\}, x \in V(G_i), y \in V(G_j)\})$. We say that H is the *representative graph* of this new graph. Notice that the disjoint union (resp. complete sum) operation corresponds to the substitution operation where H is the graph composed of two non-adjacent (resp. adjacent) vertices. Any graph can be recursively constructed from the graph with one vertex using only substitution operations, and the *width* of such a decomposition is the maximum order of the graphs H used along the process. The *modular-width* of a graph G, denoted by $mw(G)$ is the minimum width of such a decomposition. It is known that a decomposition of minimum width is unique. It is called the *modular decomposition* of G, and can be found in linear time [11]. The modular decomposition can naturally be represented as a rooted tree, where each leaf represents the introduction of a new single vertex, and each internal node is labeled by the graph H on which the substitution is done. Cographs are exactly the graphs of modular-width at most two, that is, graphs recursively obtained from a single vertex using only disjoint unions and complete sums. The corresponding tree representation of a cograph is called its *cotree*. A *module* of a graph G is a set of vertices M such that every vertex $v \in V(G) \setminus M$ is either adjacent to all vertices of M or not adjacent to any vertex of M, and it is a *strong module* if for any other module $M' \neq M$ the intersection $M \cap M'$ is either empty or equals M or M'. Observe that in the substitution of $(G_1, \ldots, G_n)$ on H, $V(G_i)$ forms a module in the new graph. In a modular decomposition, such modules are always strong modules. A graph G is a *complete multipartite graph* if there exists a partition of $V(G)$ into subsets $V_1, \cdots, V_q$ such that $\{x, y\}$ is an edge if and only if $x \in V_i$ and $x \in V_j$ with $i \neq j$. Observe that a complete multipartite graph is a cograph. A complete multipartite graph is called *balanced* if $|V_1| = \ldots = |V_q| = \ell$, and we call ℓ the *width* of G and q its *length*. A *Fixed Parameter Tractable* (FPT) algorithm is an algorithm deciding whether an instance of a decision problem is positive in time $f(k) \cdot n^c$, where c is some fixed constant, f is a computable function, n is the size of the instance, and k is some chosen parameter of it. If $c = 1$ (resp. $c = 2$) we say this is a *linear* (resp. *quadratic*) FPT algorithm For more details, see Cygan et al. [8].

3 Complexity and Algorithms

Deciding if a graph is 1-extendable was shown to be NP-hard in [2], even when restricted to subcubic planar graphs and unit disk graphs. Note that the problem is not in NP; it is, in fact, complete for the class $\Theta_2^p = P^{NP[\log]}$, which is the set of problems that can be solved in polynomial time with a logarithmic number of calls to a SAT oracle. This class is a subset of $\Delta_2^p = P^{NP}$ in the polynomial hierarchy. We exhibit a reduction from testing 1-extendability to 1-EXTENDABILITY PARTITION, and as a corollary, show that the problem is Θ_2^p-hard, which is stronger than simple NP-hardness.

Theorem 1. (⋆) *1-EXTENDABLE k-PARTITION is Θ_2^p-hard for every fixed $k \geqslant 1$.*

However, note that 1-EXTENDABLE PARTITION does not appear to be in Θ_2^p due to the additional complexity of the partition problem. The lowest class in the polynomial hierarchy where the problem seems to lie is $\Sigma_2^p = \text{NP}^{\text{NP}}$. It remains an open question whether the problem is complete for this class.

3.1 Cographs

We start with the simplest graphs in terms of modular decomposition: cographs. Due to the structure of their cliques and independent sets, cographs are a natural candidate for being easier instances of problems related to the notion of 1-extendability. Indeed, the recursive definition of cographs leads to a linear-time algorithm for determining the independence number. Similarly, we can also characterize 1-extendable cographs.

Proposition 1. *Let G_1 and G_2 be two cographs.*

- *$G_1 \cup G_2$ is 1-extendable if, and only if, G_1 and G_2 are 1-extendable.*
- *$G_1 + G_2$ is 1-extendable if, and only if, G_1 and G_2 are 1-extendable and $\alpha(G_1) = \alpha(G_2)$.*

This characterization also leads to a linear-time algorithm for determining whether a cograph is 1-extendable. We now focus on the complexity of determining the 1-extendable chromatic number of a cograph. We use this characterization in order to decide, in $k \cdot \alpha(G)^{O(k)}$ time, whether a cograph G has 1-extendable chromatic number at most k. Later, we will prove that this number is actually always bounded by $\log_2(\alpha(G)) + 1$, hence proving that it can be determined in quasi-polynomial time. We leave open the question whether the problem is polynomial-time solvable, and argue that this might be a more difficult question that it looks like, even in the very restricted case of complete multipartite graphs.

Theorem 2. *($\star$) Deciding whether a cograph G has 1-extendable chromatic number at most k can be done in time $k \cdot \alpha(G)^{O(k)}$.*

3.2 Generalization to Bounded Modular-Width

Here we show that the previous algorithm can be generalized to any graph class of bounded modular-width. In addition, we obtain an algorithm for testing whether a graph is 1-extendable which runs in single exponential time in the modular-width, and linear time in the number of vertices.

Testing 1-Extendablity. Given a graph G, the 1-EXTENDABILITY problem asks whether G is 1-extendable. In any class of graphs where computing the independence number is polynomial, one can test 1-extendability by verifying if $\alpha(G - N[v]) = \alpha(G) - 1$ for all $v \in V(G)$. Using this approach, testing 1-extendability is FPT in classical parameters such as clique-width or tree-width.

However, these algorithms are quadratic rather than linear. Here, we provide a linear FPT algorithm in modular-width, with a single exponential dependency on the parameter.

The following three results extend Proposition 1 to modular decomposition. Our approach is inspired by the algorithm for recognizing well-covered graphs which contain a few number of paths on four vertices [12]. The substitution case is of particular interest and is the main difference with the previous approach, where it is observed that if a graph is 1-extendable, then its representative graph, which is a vertex-weighted graph where the weights correspond to the independence number of each strong module, is also 1-extendable in a weighted sense. These results provide the foundation for developing a linear FPT algorithm based on the modular-width to effectively solve the 1-EXTENDABILITY problem.

Let G be a graph together with its modular decomposition, and let H be its representative graph (*i.e.* the first node of the modular decomposition). We define the weighted representative graph H_w [12] by assigning to each node t the weight $w(t) = \alpha(G[M_t])$, where M_t is the corresponding module of t in G. Observe that a weighted MIS of H_w has weight $\alpha(G)$. A weighted graph is 1-extendable if each vertex belongs to a maximum weighted independent set.

Lemma 1. *If G is 1-extendable, then for each module M of G, $G[M]$ is also 1-extendable.*

Proof. Suppose G is 1-extendable. Let v be a vertex in M and by 1-extendability of G, there exists an MIS I of G that contains v. Let $I_M = I \cap M$ and we show by contradiction that I_M is an MIS of $G[M]$.

If I_M is not an MIS of $G[M]$, let I'_M be such an MIS, and thus $|I'_M| > |I_M|$. By definition of a module, $I' = I \setminus I_M \cup I'_M$ is an independent set of G, and $|I'| > |I|$, contradicting the maximality of I. Therefore, I_M is an MIS of $G[M]$ that contains v and so $G[M]$ must be 1-extendable. □

Lemma 2. *If G is 1-extendable, then its weighted representative graph H_w is 1-extendable.*

Proof. Let t be a vertex of H_w and let M_t be the strong module of G represented by t. By Lemma 1, all strong modules of G are 1-extendable.

Let $v \in M_t$ and by 1-extendability of G, v is in an MIS I of G. Let $t_1, ..., t_k$ be the vertices of H_w such that $I \cap M_{t_i} \neq \emptyset$ for all $1 \leqslant i \leqslant k$. Note that $|I \cap M_{t_i}| = \alpha(G[M_{t_i}])$ for any $1 \leqslant i \leqslant k$, since otherwise we could swap $I \cap M_{t_i}$ with a maximum independent set of $G[M_{t_i}]$, contradicting the assumption that I is an MIS of G.

It follows that $T = \{t_1, ..., t_k\}$ is an independent set of H of weight $\alpha(G)$, and thus a weighted MIS of H_w. Finally, H_w is a weighted 1-extendable graph. □

Theorem 3. *A graph G is 1-extendable if and only if all its maximal strong modules are 1-extendable and if its weighted representative graph is 1-extendable.*

Proof. First, assume that G is 1-extendable, and let M_t be any strong module of G. By Lemma 1, $G[M_t]$ is also 1-extendable. Then, by Lemma 2, the weighted representative graph H_w of G is also 1-extendable.

Conversely, suppose that all its maximal strong modules and H_w are 1-extendable. Let v be any vertex in a strong module M_t of G. Since $G[M_t]$ is 1-extendable, there exists an MIS I_t of $G[M_t]$ that contains v. Moreover, since H_w is 1-extendable, there exists an MIS $t_1, \ldots, t_k$ of H_w that contains t. For each $i \in \{1, \ldots, k\}$ such that $t_i \neq t$, let I_{t_i} be any MIS of $G[M_{t_i}]$. Then, the set $I = I_t \cup I_{t_1} \cup \cdots \cup I_{t_k}$ is an MIS of G that contains v. Therefore, G is 1-extendable. □

Theorem 4. *($\star$) Deciding whether a graph G is 1-extendable can be done in time $2^{O(mw(G))} \cdot n$.*

1-Extendable Partition. We can use the modular decomposition to construct an algorithm that solves the 1-EXTENDABLE PARTITION problem in polynomial time when the number of parts and the modular-width of the input graph are fixed.

Theorem 5. *($\star$) Deciding whether a graph G with n vertices and independence number α has 1-extendable chromatic number at most k can be done in time $\alpha^{O(mw(G)k)} \cdot n$.*

3.3 Complete Multipartite Graphs

We continue our exploration of the partition into 1-extendable induced subgraphs by focusing on a specific class of cographs, namely the complete multipartite graphs. Although being a very restricted case, it appears that the problem within this graph class establishes connections with other fields, making it inherently interesting. We first begin with the following observation.

Proposition 2. *A complete multipartite graph is 1-extendable if, and only if, it is balanced.*

Proof. Let G be a complete multipartite graph with parts $V_1, \ldots, V_m$. G is a cograph obtained with m consecutive joins between independent sets. By Proposition 1, G is 1-extendable if and only if all parts have same cardinality. □

With that previous proposition, partitioning a complete multipartite graph into 1-extendable induced subgraphs is exactly the same as partitioning into balanced complete multipartite subgraphs. An example is illustrated in Fig. 2.

To avoid confusion, from now on the term *part* is reserved for the elements of the (initial) partition of the complete multipartite graph, while we will use the term *color* to refer to the elements of a 1-extendable partition.

In a complete multipartite graph G with partition $V_1, \ldots, V_q$, every vertex of a same part has the same neighborhood, hence a 1-extendable partition

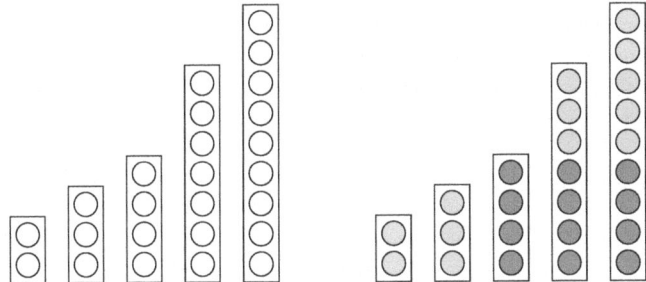

Fig. 2. A complete multipartite graph (left) and a 1-extendable 3-partition of it, represented as a coloring (right). For the sake of readability, the edges are not shown, the rectangles represent the partition into independent sets.

$(C_1, \ldots, C_k)$ in that case can actually be defined simply by giving, for each color C_i, its width together with the subset of parts of G it intersects. Alternatively, one can also give the way each part V_i is split by the 1-extendable partition. And since all vertices of a same part have the same neighborhood, it is actually sufficient to give the way $|V_i|$ is decomposed by the 1-extendable partition. This observation leads to an equivalent[1] reformulation of the problem as a numbers problem. In the usual sense, a set B of integers is a *generating set* of a set N of integers if every $p \in N$ can be written as a sum of elements in B. This problem is thus called GENERATING SET.

GENERATING SET
Input: m integers $n_1, \ldots, n_m$ and an integer k.
Question : Are there k integers $\alpha_1, \ldots, \alpha_k$ such that, for any $1 \leqslant i \leqslant m$, there exists $J \subset [k]$ such that $\sum_{j \in J} a_j = n_i$?

As observed previously, this problem is equivalent to the 1-EXTENDABLE PARTITION problem in complete multipartite graphs. It appears that we are able to obtain a much simpler quasi-polynomial algorithm than in the case of cographs. Consider an instance $n_1, \ldots, n_m, k$ of the GENERATING SET problem where the input is encoded in unary. We call $\alpha = \max_{1 \leqslant i \leqslant m} n_i$ and $n = \sum_{i=1}^{m} n_i$. The algorithm lists all the k-tuples $(\alpha_1, \ldots, \alpha_k) \in \{0, \ldots, \alpha\}^k$, and solves, for each $i \in [m]$, the SUBSET SUM problem with numbers $(\alpha_1, \ldots, \alpha_k)$ and target n_i in time $O(k^2 \alpha)$. The overall complexity of such an algorithm is thus $O(\alpha^{k+1} k^2)$. Now observe that we may always assume that $k \leqslant \lceil \log_2(\alpha) \rceil + 1$, since $\{2^i : 0 \leqslant i \leqslant \lceil \log_2(\alpha) \rceil\}$ is always a solution, by taking the binary representation of each integer n_i.

It turns out that a number-theoretic version of GENERATING SET was already studied in the context of cryptanalysis, called HIDDEN SUBSET SUM [3,7,16]. More precisely, a fast generator of random pairs $(x, g^x \mod p)$ was first presented [3], whose security relies on the potential hardness of HIDDEN SUBSET

---

[1] Naturally, in our graph-theoretical version, the integers are encoded in unary.

SUM. However, an efficient lattice-based attack was quickly presented [16], and further improved [7]. In [6], the problem was shown to be NP-complete. However, the existence of a (worst-case) polynomial-time algorithm for GENERATING SET is still open, the input being encoded in unary.

4 Extremal Results

In this section, we explore structural and extremal properties of 1-extendable partitions. Specifically, we show that $\chi_{\text{1-ext}}(G) = O(\sqrt{n})$ for any n-vertex graph G. Then, we focus once again on cographs and demonstrate that $\chi_{\text{1-ext}}$ is always logarithmic in the size of the independence number, and we provide two constructions that achieve this optimal bound. The first one is a complete multipartite graph and the second one is both an interval graph and a cograph. Together with the algorithm described in Sect. 3, it implies that 1-EXTENDABLE PARTITION can be solved in quasi-polynomial time in cographs.

4.1 General Case

Lemma 3. *For any graph G, $\chi_{\text{1-ext}}(G) \leqslant \alpha(G)$.*

Proof. We show that $\chi_{\text{1-ext}}(G) \leqslant \alpha(G)$ by induction on $\alpha(G)$. If $\alpha(G) = 1$, then G is a clique and thus G is 1-extendable. We assume that the result is true for any graph G such that $\alpha(G) \leqslant k$ for some $k \geqslant 1$. Let G be a graph such that $\alpha(G) = k+1$, and let V_{k+1} be the set of all vertices of G that are in an MIS. We notice that $G[V_{k+1}]$ is 1-extendable since each vertex is in an MIS by definition. In addition, $G[V(G) - S_{k+1}]$ has an independence number at most k since all independent sets of size $k+1$ have been removed. By applying the induction hypothesis, $V(G) - V_{k+1}$ can be partitioned into k subsets $V_1, ..., V_k$ (possibly empty) such that $G[V_i]$ is 1-extendable for any $1 \leqslant i \leqslant k$. By completing the partition with V_{k+1}, we obtain a desired partition for $V(G)$. □

The previous bound can be combined to obtain a square root upper bound in the order of a graph.

Theorem 6. *For any graph G with n vertices,*

$$\chi_{\text{1-ext}}(G) \leqslant 2\sqrt{n}$$

Proof. Let G be a graph. We consider the following greedy coloring of G. Select an MIS S_1 of G and repeat with $G - S_1$. We obtain a partition $S_1, ..., S_k$ of G where each $G[S_i]$ is an independent set. In addition, we notice that for any $1 \leqslant i < k$, $|S_i| \geqslant |S_{i+1}|$, and let k_0 be the largest integer i such that $|S_i| \geqslant \sqrt{n}$. We notice that $k_0 \leqslant \sqrt{n}$, otherwise we would obtain strictly more than n vertices in $S_1 \cup ... \cup S_{k_0}$. Let $V_1 = \bigcup_{i:|S_i| \geqslant \sqrt{n}} S_i$, and $V_2 = V \setminus V_1$. First, we have $\chi(G[V_1]) \leqslant k_0 \leqslant \sqrt{n}$. Then, we have $\alpha(G[V_2]) < \sqrt{n}$, since if there is a stable $S \subseteq V_2$ such that $|S| \geqslant \sqrt{n}$, it would have been selected instead of S_{k_0+1} in the greedy algorithm since $|S_{k_0+1}| < \sqrt{n}$.

By coloring separately $G[V_1]$ and $G[V_2]$, we obtain a 1-extendable coloring of G using at most $2\sqrt{n}$ colors. □

4.2 Cographs

Upper Bound. In this section, we prove that the 1-extendable chromatic number of a cograph is at most logarithmic in the size of its independence number. The general idea of the proof is to extract a 1-extendable induced subgraph while reducing the independence number of the remaining graph by a factor of 2.

The next lemma is the key ingredient of our upper bound.

Lemma 4. ($\star$) *For any cograph G and any $k \in \{0, ..., \alpha(G)\}$, there exists a partition of the vertices into two subsets V_1 and V_2 such that*

- *$G[V_1]$ is 1-extendable;*
- *$\alpha(G[V_1]) = k$;*
- *$\alpha(G[V_2]) \leq \max(k-1, \alpha(G) - k)$.*

Sketch of the proof. The result is proved by structural induction on the cographs. Given an integer k, we consider the two cases $G = G_1 \cup G_2$ and $G = G_1 + G_2$.

1. Case $G = G_1 + G_2$. If $k \leq \min(\alpha(G_1), \alpha(G_2))$, we apply the induction on (G_1, k) and (G_2, k) and we combine the two partitions. The other cases are straightforward.
2. Case $G = G_1 \cup G_2$. The key idea is to find two integers k_1 and k_2 to apply induction hypothesis on (G_1, k_1) and (G_2, k_2). Using the properties of k_1 and k_2, we construct the partition of G using both partitions. □

We derive the upper bound by recursively applying the previous lemma.

Theorem 7. ($\star$) *For any cograph G, $\chi_{1\text{-}ext}(G) \leq \log_2(\alpha(G)) + 1$.*

The bound in the previous theorem is obtained through recursive calls that halve the independence number, resulting in a logarithmic number of colors. However, this may not always be the optimal choice. For example, if G is an independent set, a better choice would be to use only one color for the entire graph. Nevertheless, as we will see in the next section, the bound obtained from Theorem 7 is structurally optimal, as there exist cographs for which at least a logarithmic number of colors is required.

Combining the previous result with the algorithm presented in Theorem 2 allows to obtain the following.

Corollary 1. ($\star$) *There exists an algorithm solving* 1-EXTENDABLE PARTITION *on cographs in quasi-polynomial time.*

Observe that Theorem 7 can be generalized to every graph whose vertex set can be partitioned into a bounded number of induced cographs. This is for instance the case of P_4-bipartite graphs which include distance-hereditary graphs, parity graphs, P_4-reducible graphs, and P_4-sparse graphs.

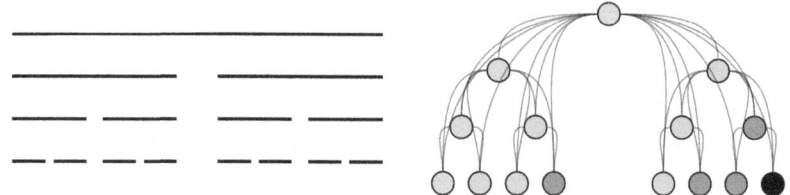

Fig. 3. An interval representation of G_4, and a 1-extendable 4-partition of it. In the partition, each color class induces a disjoint union of cliques, which is 1-extendable.

Lower Bound. We show that the previous logarithmic bound is essentially tight by constructing two different families of cographs that achieve this bound.

Complete Multipartite Graph. We consider the graph G_k, where $k \geqslant 0$, which is the complete multipartite graph with parts $V_0, ..., V_k$ and $|V_i| = 2^i$ for any $0 \leqslant i \leqslant k$.

Theorem 8. *($\star$) For any $k \geqslant 0$, G_k has $2^{k+1}-1$ vertices and $\chi_{1\text{-}ext}(G_k) \geqslant k+1$.*

Interval Graph. A pertinent question to consider is whether there exist cographs that require a logarithmic number of colors without being complete multipartite. In this context, we present an example that shows the existence of such cographs. The construction will be based on the creation of a specific interval graph denoted as G_k ($k \geqslant 1$), defined as follows:

- $G_1 = K_1$, i.e., the graph containing only a single vertex;
- For any $i \geqslant 1$, $G_{k+1} = K_1 + (G_k \cup G_k)$, where K_1 denotes a single vertex and $(G_k \cup G_k)$ represents the disjoint union of two copies of G_k.

It can be observed that for any $k \geqslant 1$, in addition of being a cograph, the graph G_k is an interval graph, as depicted in Fig. 3. By immediate induction, it may be shown that $\alpha(G_k) = 2^k - 1$ for any k.

Theorem 9. *($\star$) For any $k \geqslant 0$, $\chi_{1\text{-}ext}(G_k) \geqslant k$.*

Interestingly, this logarithmic lower bound is also tight for interval graphs, since every interval graph G satisfies $\chi_s(G) \leqslant \log_2(n) + 1$, *i.e.* we can partition its vertex set into a logarithmic number of parts, each of them inducing a disjoint union of cliques [4].

5 Conclusion and Open Questions

Motivated by practical applications in wireless networks, this study introduced the concept of the 1-extendable chromatic number and examined its structural and algorithmic properties.

Our primary contribution is a quasi-polynomial algorithm for determining this number in cographs, achieved by combining an algorithm exponential in the number of available colors with a logarithmic upper bound. The existence of a polynomial-time algorithm remains an open question, even in the very restricted case of complete multipartite graphs, where the problem intriguingly reformulates in number-theoretic terms. Additionally, we extended our algorithm to arbitrary graphs using modular decomposition, resulting in a polynomial-time algorithm when both the modular width and the number of parts are fixed. We also provided a linear FPT algorithm in terms of modular width to determine if an input graph is 1-extendable, with a single exponential dependency on the parameter.

On the structural side, we demonstrated the existence of n-vertex graphs that require a logarithmic number of 1-extendable parts. Moreover, we provided an upper bound of $O(\sqrt{n})$ colors, though closing the gap for the 1-extendable chromatic number remains a challenging task.

After examining arbitrary graphs through modular decomposition, the next logical step is to focus on restricted graph classes commonly used in wireless network contexts. Geometric graphs, such as (unit) disk graphs, present an intriguing class for further study of the 1-extendable chromatic number.

Acknowledgments. We thank Carl Feghali and Pierre Bergé for valuable discussions on the subject.

References

1. Berge, C.: Some common properties for regularizable graphs, edge-critical graphs and B-graphs. In: Peter, L.H., Alexander, R., Gert, S., Jean, T. (ed.) Theory and Practice of Combinatorics, volume 60 of North-Holland Mathematics Studies, pp. 31–44. North-Holland (1982)
2. Bergé, P., Busson, A., Feghali, C., Watrigant, R.: 1-extendability of independent sets. In: Bazgan, C., Fernau, H. (ed.) Combinatorial Algorithms, pp. 172–185. Springer International Publishing, Cham (2022)
3. Boyko, V., Peinado, M., Venkatesan, R.: Speeding up discrete log and factoring based schemes via precomputations. In: Nyberg, K. (ed.) EUROCRYPT 1998. LNCS, vol. 1403, pp. 221–235. Springer, Heidelberg (1998). https://doi.org/10.1007/BFb0054129
4. Broersma, H., Fomin, F.V., Nešetřil, J., Woeginger, G.J.: More about subcolorings. Computing **69**(3), 187–203 (2002)
5. Busson, A., Marin, M., Watrigant, R.: Aaachannel allocation revisited through 1-extendability of graphs. CoRR, abs/2408.14633 (2024). arXiv:2408.1463d3
6. Collins, M.J., Kempe, D., Saia, J., Young, M.: Nonnegative integral subset representations of integer sets. Inf. Process. Lett. **101**(3), 129–133 (2007)
7. Coron, J.-S., Gini, A.: A polynomial-time algorithm for solving the hidden subset sum problem. In: Advances in Cryptology - CRYPTO 2020, pp. 3–31. Springer (2020)
8. Cygan, M., et al.: Parameterized Algorithms, 1st edition. Springer Publishing Company, Berlin (2015). Incorporated

9. Dean, N., Zito, J.: Well-covered graphs and extendability. Discret. Math. **126**(1), 67–80 (1994)
10. Feghali, C., Marin, M., Watrigant, R.: Beyond recognizing well-covered graphs. In: 50th International Workshop on Graph-Theoretic Concepts in Computer Science (WG) (2024)
11. Habib, M., Paul, C.: A survey of the algorithmic aspects of modular decomposition. Comput. Sci. Rev. **4**(1), 41–59 (2010)
12. Klein, S., de Mello, C.P., Morgana, A.: Recognizing well covered graphs of families with special p_4-components. Graphs Combinatorics **29**(3), 553–567 (2013)
13. Liew, S.C., Kai, C., Leung, H.C., Wong, P.B.: Back-of-the-envelope computation of throughput distributions in CSMA wireless networks. In: 2009 IEEE International Conference on Communications, pp. 1–6 (2007)
14. McConnell, R.M., Spinrad, J.P.: Modular decomposition and transitive orientation. Discret. Math. **201**(1), 189–241 (1999)
15. Milanic, M., Pivac, N.: Computing well-covered vector spaces of graphs using modular decomposition. Comput. Appl. Math. **42**(8), 360 (2023)
16. Nguyen, P.Q., Stern, J.: The hardness of the hidden subset sum problem and its cryptographic implications. In: Proceedings of the 19th Annual International Cryptology Conference on Advances in Cryptology, CRYPTO 1999, pp. 31-46 (1999). Springer-Verlag, Berlin
17. Plummer, M.D.: Some covering concepts in graphs. J. Comb. Theory **8**(1), 91–98 (1970)

On the Min-Max Star Partitioning Number

Sarah Feldmann[1] and Torben Schürenberg[2](✉)

[1] Otto-von-Guericke University Magdeburg, Magdeburg, Germany
sarah.feldmann@ovgu.de
[2] University of Bremen, Bremen, Germany
torsch@uni-bremen.de

Abstract. In this paper, we introduce a novel star partitioning problem for simple connected graphs $G = (V, E)$. The goal is to find a partition of the edges into stars that minimizes the maximum number of stars a node is contained in while simultaneously satisfying node-specific capacities. We design and analyze an efficient polynomial time algorithm with a runtime of $\mathcal{O}(|E|^2)$ that determines an optimal partition. Moreover, we explicitly provide a closed form of an optimal value for some graph classes. We generalize our algorithm to find even an optimal star partition of linear hypergraphs, multigraphs, and graphs with self-loops. We use flow techniques to design an algorithm for the star partitioning problem with an improved runtime of $\mathcal{O}(\log(\Delta) \cdot |E| \cdot \min\{|V|^{\frac{2}{3}}, |E|^{\frac{1}{2}}\})$, where Δ is maximum node degree in G. In contrast to the unweighted setting, we show that a node-weighted decision variant of this problem is **strongly NP-complete** even without capacity constraints. Furthermore, we provide an extensive comparison to the problem of minimizing the minimum indegree satisfying node capacity constraints.

Keywords: Edge coloring · edge orientation · max-flow · min-max objective · star partitioning

1 Introduction

We introduce a novel graph problem that arises in static communication networks, the *min-max star partitioning problem* (MINMAXSTAR). The goal is to find a partition of the edges into stars that minimizes the maximum number of stars a node is contained in. A star is a tree, where at most one node has more than one neighbor. In our setting, a star is required to contain at least one edge. The *internal node* of a star containing more than one edge is defined as the node with at least two neighbors. For stars consisting of only one edge, we fix one of the incident nodes as the internal node. Additionally, each node can be the internal node of at most one star. The star partitioning problem can be seen as a new kind of edge coloring problem.

In this paper, we define a set of valid edge colorings and optimize a min-max objective function. We initially deal with simple connected graphs $G = (V, E)$,

© The Author(s), under exclusive license to Springer Nature Switzerland AG 2025
Q. Bramas et al. (Eds.): ALGOWIN 2024, LNCS 15026, pp. 61–75, 2025.
https://doi.org/10.1007/978-3-031-74580-5_5

where each edge contains two nodes. In Sect. 5 we extend the problem to graphs with self-loops, multigraphs, and linear hypergraphs. Every node v has a given capacity restriction, denoted by κ_v. We initially color every node in a distinct color. A valid edge coloring is achieved when each edge has a color identical to that of one of its incident nodes, and for every node v the number of different colors of incident edges to v is at most κ_v. It is possible that no valid edge coloring exists, that fulfills the capacity restrictions. Our goal is to minimize the maximum number of incident edge colors of a node in valid edge colorings. This graph coloring defines a partition of the edges of our graph into star graphs. That is why we refer to it as a *star coloring* or a *star partition*. Depending on the coloring, the maximum number of different edge colors to which a node in the graph is incident may vary. Our goal is to minimize this value among all valid star colorings, which we refer to as $x^*(G)$.

Our Results. We explicitly provide a closed form of an optimal value for some graph classes in Sect. 3 and construct a simple polynomial-time algorithm based on depth-first search, which finds an optimal star partition in $\mathcal{O}(|E|^2)$ time in Sect. 4. We apply this algorithm to linear hypergraphs. Given an integer x, we test if $x^*(G) \leq x$ holds by computing a maximum flow in a network with unit capacities constructed from G. This flow technique and a binary search allow us to improve the simple algorithm to a runtime of $\mathcal{O}(\log(\Delta) \cdot |E| \cdot \min\{|V|^{\frac{2}{3}}, |E|^{\frac{1}{2}}\})$ in Sect. 6. We apply both algorithms to graphs with multiple edges and self-loops in Sect. 5. We show similarities and differences between MINMAXSTAR and the problem of *minimizing the maximum indegree* (MINMAXIND), which was studied by Asahiro et al. in [3,4] and Venkateswaran in [25]. Additionally, we provide solutions that are optimal for both problems simultaneously when no capacity constraints are present in Sect. 7. As a separation, we show in Sect. 8 that the node-weighted decision variants W-MINMAXSTAR and W-MINMAXIND of these problems are `strongly NP-complete` even without capacity constraints and provide a 2-approximation algorithm for W-MINMAXIND and a 4-approximation algorithm for W-MINMAXSTAR in Sect. 9. All omitted proofs and details can be found in the online version of this paper [16].

Related Work. Various star coloring and star partitioning problems with different objective functions have been explored in the literature.

Graph colorings have been researched extensively in the past, for both edge and node colorings [9,20]. Feasible edge colorings are subject to different rules and various objective functions are studied in the literature. The most well-known edge coloring rule specifies that adjacent edges can not share the same color. The edge chromatic number is defined as the minimum number of different colors needed to color a graph according to this rule, researched for instance in [6,15,23,28]. In his seminal work [27], Vizing proved that the edge chromatic number of any simple graph G is either $\Delta(G)$ or $\Delta(G)+1$, where $\Delta(G)$ denotes the maximum degree of the graph.

Divya and Vijayakumar analyze the partition of nodes of split graphs into as few sets as possible, such that the induced subgraph of every set in the partition is a star [10]. The star chromatic number researched by Borodin [7] is the minimum number of colors needed for a vertex coloring in which every path on four vertices uses at least three distinct colors. Fertin et al. define a star coloring as a node coloring where incident nodes have different colors and no path of length three is bicolored [17]. Egawa et al. [12] and Shalu et al. [24] define a star partition as a partition of the nodes of a given graph such that for each node set of the partition, the induced subgraph is a star. In contrast to our definition, Egawa et al. and Shalu et al. color or partition the nodes and not the edges. Minimizing the total number of stars results in the vertex cover problem, for which Karp shows the NP-completeness of the decision variant in [21].

Given a star partitioning, we define the value of a node as the number of stars the node is contained in. Another natural utilitarian objective function is given by minimizing the sum of these values. This objective counts every edge and every star exactly once, and is thus a reformulation of the NP-complete vertex cover problem. On the other hand, if for every node v we do not count the star with internal node v, the problem gets easy to solve because the optimal objective value $|E|$ is independent of the edge partitioning.

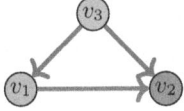 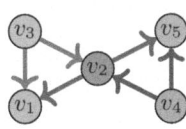

(a) An optimal solution of MinMaxStar which is not optimal for MinMaxInd

(b) An optimal solution of MinMaxInd which is not optimal for MinMaxStar

Fig. 1. Examples where optimal solutions of MinMaxInd and MinMaxStar do not coincide.

In a graph where each node has a distinct color, directing an edge is equivalent to assigning the color of its tail to the edge. Many papers discussing various edge orientation problems were recently published, for instance, by Asahiro et al. [2]. Other orientation problems have been studied by Ahadi and Dehghan [1], Asahiro et al. [3,4], Borradaile et al. [8] and Venkateswaran [25]. Borradaile et al. introduce an algorithm that minimizes the lexicographic order of the indegrees. Venkateswaran provides an algorithm with a runtime of $\mathcal{O}(|E|^2)$, that computes an edge orientation which minimizes the maximum indegree $k^*(G)$. This was further improved by Asahiro et al. [4] to a runtime of $\mathcal{O}(|E|^{\frac{3}{2}} \cdot \log(\Delta(G)))$ using flow techniques. Without node capacity constraints in contrast to our objective, Asahiro et al. and Venkateswaran direct the edges to minimize only the maximum number of outgoing and incoming edges, respectively, over all nodes. This corresponds to minimizing the maximum number of stars containing v that do not have v as an internal node. Thus, $k^*(G) \leq x^*(G) \leq k^*(G) + 1$. We will denote the problem of finding an orientation that achieves $k^*(G)$ while ensuring node capacity constraints by MINMAXIND. As evident in Fig. 1, optimal star colorings do not always coincide with optimal edge orientations. Therefore, our variant needs to be examined separately.

Application Example. We are given a set of players, represented by the nodes of a graph. For each player, the task is to communicate with all their neighboring players in this static communication network. Each player i has a secret communication key with the weight w_i. If two neighboring players want to communicate with each other, one of the two players must remember the key of the other. The sum of the weights of the communication keys that the players need to memorize is called the memory requirement of a player. What is the smallest maximum memory requirement over all players? If each person does not need to memorize their own communication key, we have W-MINMAXIND. If a player needs to memorize their own communication key if it is memorized by at least one other player, we have the problem W-MINMAXSTAR. If we set the weight of each key to 1, we obtain the unweighted problems MINMAXIND and MINMAXSTAR, for which we can construct a solution that is optimal for both cases simultaneously.

2 Problem Statement

We consider a non-empty undirected simple connected graph $G = (V, E)$. The terms *coloring* and *partitioning* are used interchangeably. For each node $v \in V$, we define the degree $\delta(v) := |\{e \in E \mid v \in e\}|$ as the number of edges incident to v. The degree of the graph $\Delta(G)$ is thus the maximum degree of all nodes $\Delta(G) := \max_{v \in V} \delta(v)$. A node capacity $\kappa_v \in \mathbb{N}_{\geq 0}$ and a unique color $C(v)$ are assigned to each node v. If no node capacities are given, they are assumed to be $\Delta(G)$. An edge coloring assigns a color $C(e)$ to each edge e. A star coloring is an edge coloring where each edge $e \in E$ has a node $v \in e$ with $C(e) = C(v)$. A *valid* star coloring on G is a star coloring where the number of distinct incident edge colors never exceeds the node capacity κ_v for all $v \in V$. A partial star coloring on G is a star coloring of $G' = (V, E')$ for some $E' \subseteq E$. The *set of all valid star colorings* on G is referred to as $\mathcal{C}(G)$, and the set of all valid partial star colorings on G as $\mathcal{C}'(G)$. We omit G if it is obvious. For each $C \in \mathcal{C}(G)$ and $v \in V$, we define $x(G, C, v) := |\{C(e) \mid e \in E, v \in e\}|$, the number of different edge colors that the node v is incident to. Additionally, we define the *star partitioning number* $x(G, C) := \max_{v \in V} x(G, C, v)$, the maximum value of $x(G, C, v)$ over all nodes $v \in V$. The *min-max star partitioning number* in the set of all valid star colorings is denoted by

$$x^*(G) := \min_{C \in \mathcal{C}(G)} x(G, C) = \min_{C \in \mathcal{C}(G)} \max_{v \in V} x(G, C, v).$$

If no valid star coloring exists, we set $x^*(G) := \infty$.

We define the *min-max star partitioning problem* (MINMAXSTAR) and similar to Asahiro et al. in [4] the *min-max indegree problem* (MINMAXIND) with node capacities as follows:

(MinMaxStar): Min-Max Star Partitioning Problem
   Input: A simple connected graph $G = (V, E)$ and $\kappa_v \in \mathbb{N}_{\geq 0}$ for all $v \in V$.
   Output: Compute a valid star coloring C with $x(G, C) = x^*(G)$ or state that none exists.

(MinMaxInd): Min-Max Indegree Problem
   Input: A simple connected graph $G = (V, E)$ and $\kappa_v \in \mathbb{N}_{\geq 0}$ for all $v \in V$.
   Output: Compute an orientation, which minimizes the maximum indegree such that $\delta^-(v) \leq \kappa_v$ for all $v \in V$ or state that none exists.

A partial coloring $C' \in \mathcal{C}'(G)$ is called x-satisfying if every node is incident to at most x different edge colors in every valid star coloring $C \in \mathcal{C}(G)$, which can be constructed from C' by assigning a color to each uncolored edge. Given a coloring $C \in \mathcal{C}(G)$, the only way to reduce the number of stars a node is contained in is to color more incident edges in its color. For a given x, a partial coloring C' is thus an x-satisfying partial coloring if for every node $v \in V$ it holds that every completion $C \in \mathcal{C}(G)$ assigns the color $C(v)$ to at least $l(v, x) := \max\{0, \delta(v) - \min\{\kappa_v, x\} + 1\}$ many edges incident to v if $l(v, x) > 1$ holds. In this setting $x^*(G)$ is the smallest x for which it is possible, that every node v with $l(v, x) > 1$ has at least $l(v, x)$ incident edges colored in its color.

A valid star coloring C can be transformed into an orientation $\Lambda(G, C)$ by directing each edge $\{v, w\}$ colored with $C(v)$ from v to w. Additionally, each orientation $\Lambda(G, C)$ can be transformed into a valid star coloring C by coloring each edge $\{v, w\}$, which is directed to w with the color $C(v)$. Thus, valid colorings and orientations are inverse to each other. So we can use these perspectives interchangeably.

3 Optimal Value for Special Graph Classes

For a few graph classes, we can state the optimal value $x^*(G)$ explicitly.

Lemma 1. *The following statements hold for simple graphs G.*

(a) $x^*(G) \geq 1$ iff G has at least one edge.
(b) $x^*(G) \leq 1$ iff G is a cycle free graph with a diameter at most two.
(c) If G is a pseudoforest, i.e., in each connected component there exists at most one cycle, then $x^*(G) \leq 2$.
(d) Let G be the fully connected bipartite graph $K_{n,n}$ with $1 < n \in \mathbb{N}$. Then $x^*(K_{n,n}) = \lceil \frac{n}{2} \rceil + 1$.

Due to space limitations, the proof can be found in the full online version of the paper [16].

4 Algorithm for MinMaxStar

In this section, we sketch the algorithm `MinimumStarColoring`, which computes a min-max star partition or states infeasibility in $\mathcal{O}(|E|^2)$ time. The pseudocode can be found in the full online version of the paper [16].

A valid partial star coloring C can be seen as a partially directed graph G_C, where edges $\{v,w\}$ with the color $C(v)$ are directed toward v. Note that $\Lambda(G,C)$ is the inverse orientation of G_C. We use this formulation for the algorithm.

We always know that $x^*(G) \leq \Delta(G)$ if the instance is feasible. Thus, we start with $x = \Delta(G)$. If we find an x-satisfying partial coloring C for some x, we decrease x by one and repeat the paragraph below using the partial coloring C until we find an integer x with $x^*(G) > x$. Completing C with random valid colors yields a min-max star partition of G.

We aim to find a star coloring C fulfilling $x(G,C) \leq x$ or determine $x^*(G) > x$ the following way. For each node v with $l(v,x) > 1$, we try to color incident edges with $C(v)$ until $l(v,x)$ edges are colored with $C(v)$. This coloring is done via a depth-first search in G_C for an uncolored edge. If we find such an edge, we insert it into the path and invert the direction of all edges on that path, such that the whole path points toward v. The coloring C is changed appropriately. For all nodes w along the path, except v, inverting the direction of the path does not change the number $|C(w)|$. Additionally, we enlarge $|C(v)|$ by one. If such a path does not exist, we return that $x^*(G) > x$ holds.

Figure 2 shows the last steps of the algorithm using an example, where it has already found a partial 3-satisfying coloring and tries to improve it to a partial 2-satisfying coloring. Note that the depth-first search fails even though there exists an uncolored edge in the graph.

Each depth-first search runs in $\mathcal{O}(|E|)$ time (see [13]) and either colors an additional edge or states infeasibility. During the algorithm, we store for each node v its degree and the number of edges colored with $C(v)$. Thus, we only need $\mathcal{O}(|E|^2)$ steps.

If the depth-first search fails at a node v, where less than $l(v,x) > 1$ edges are colored with $C(v)$, then there is no uncolored edge in G_C reachable from v. During the algorithm, we colored for each node w at most $l(w,x)$ edges with $C(w)$ iff $l(w,x) > 1$ holds. Let K be the set of nodes in G_C reachable from v. The number of edges incident to at least one node in K is strictly less than $\sum_{w \in K : l(w,x) > 1} l(w,x)$. The strict inequality results from $l(v,x) > 1$ and because we colored strictly less than $l(v,x)$ edges with $C(v)$. Therefore, it is not possible to color an additional edge incident to any node $u \in K$ with $C(u)$ without reducing the number of edges colored with $C(w)$ for another node $w \in K$. Each $u \in K$ is reachable from v and the set of nodes reachable from $u \in K$ is contained in K. Thus, we have $x^*(G) > x$. This results in the following theorem.

Theorem 1. *The* `MinimumStarColoring` *algorithm terminates after $\mathcal{O}(|E|^2)$ steps with the correct solution to* MinMaxStar.

5 Extension to Other Graph Classes

Self-loops. By definition, no self-loop can be part of a star. To include self-loops in the edge partitioning, we change the definition of star graphs and allow the internal node of a star to have a self-loop. If we define the degree of a node as

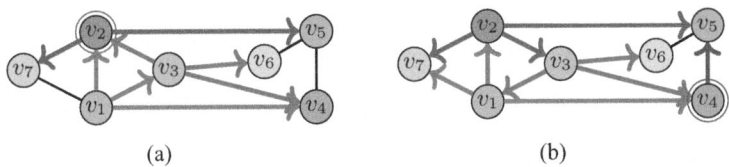

Fig. 2. The depicted graph is the reverse graph of G_C. For $x = 2$ the depth-first search starting at v_2 is successful along the path (v_2, v_3, v_1, v_7) in (a). In (b) the depth-first search starting at v_4 succeeds only once and then fails. This results in $x^*(G) = 3$. Note that there is still one uncolored edge in the graph.

the number of incident edges, then a self-loop only increases the degree of the node by one. The algorithms and correctness proofs can be applied directly to this case.

Multigraphs. Coloring parallel edges in a multigraph with the same color does not increase the objective value. Therefore, there are always optimal colorings that color all parallel edges with the same color. Thus, we transform each multigraph H_M into a simple graph $G = (V, E)$ by merging each set of parallel edges into one edge, searching for a coloring in G instead, and coloring every edge in H_M with the assigned color of its representative.

Hypergraphs. A hypergraph $H = (V, E)$ is called *linear* if for every edge pair $e_1 \neq e_2 \in E$ we have $|e_1 \cap e_2| \leq 1$. The depth-first search from the previous section can be applied directly to linear hypergraphs with a runtime of $\mathcal{O}(|E| \cdot \eta(H))$, where $\eta(H) := \max\{|e| : e \in E\}$ is the maximum cardinality of the edges. This is due to an edge e now visited not at most twice but at most $|e|$ times. Therefore, the total runtime of the MinimumStarColoring algorithm is $\mathcal{O}(\eta(H) \cdot |E|^2)$. If $\eta(H)$ is bounded by a constant, we get the runtime of $\mathcal{O}(|E|^2)$. As shown in the full online version of the paper [16], the MinimumStarColoring algorithm can not be applied directly to general hypergraphs.

6 Improved Algorithm

For simple connected graphs $G = (V, E)$ with node capacities, we use the flow techniques of Asahiro et al. [4] to improve the runtime from $\mathcal{O}(|E|^2)$ to $\mathcal{O}(\log(\Delta) \cdot |E| \cdot \min\{|V|^{\frac{2}{3}}, |E|^{\frac{1}{2}}\})$. As noted in Sect. 2, valid star colorings C and orientations $\Lambda(G, C)$ can be transformed naturally into each other such that the transformation is inverse. For a given $x \in \mathbb{N}_{\geq 0}$, we test if $x^*(G) \leq x$ holds, adapting the flow construction introduced by Asahiro et al. in [4]. For any orientation $\Lambda(G, C)$, any number $x \in \mathbb{N}_{\geq 0}$ and any capacity constraint κ_v we use the outdegree $\delta^+(v)$ of a node v to define its slackness as

$$s(G, \Lambda(G,C), v, x) := \begin{cases} \delta^+(v) & \text{if } l(v,x) \leq 1, \\ \delta^+(v) - l(v,x) \\ = \delta^+(v) - \max\{0, \delta(v) - \min\{\kappa_v, x\} + 1\} & \text{else.} \end{cases}$$

If the slackness at v is positive, then it is possible to change the orientation of $|s(G, \Lambda(G,C), v, x)|$ edges that are directed outward from v without violating $x(G, C, v) \leq x$ and the capacity constraint κ_v of the induced coloring. On the other hand, if the slackness of v is negative, then it is necessary to reverse the orientation of at least $|s(G, C, v, x)|$ edges, which are directed to v in order to satisfy $x(G, C, v) \leq x$ and the capacity constraint κ_v.

Using our graph with an arbitrary orientation Λ, we construct a flow multi-graph $\tilde{G} = (\tilde{V} = V \cup \{s, t\}, \tilde{E})$. Similar to Asahiro et al. [4], the edge set $\tilde{E}$ is constructed by adding the following edges to E. For each node v with $s(G, \Lambda(G,C), v, x) > 0$ we add $|s(G, \Lambda(G,C), v, x)|$ times the edge (s, v) and for each node v with $s(G, \Lambda(G,C), v, x) < 0$ we add $|s(G, \Lambda(G,C), v, x)|$ times the edge (v, t). Because the absolute value of the slackness is bounded by the degree of the node, we get $|\tilde{E}| \leq 3|E|$. Finding the maximum flow in the unit-capacity network $\tilde{G}$ can be done in $\mathcal{O}(|\tilde{E}| \cdot \min\{|\tilde{V}|^{\frac{2}{3}}, |\tilde{E}|^{\frac{1}{2}}\})$ time, as Even and Tarjan show in [14]. By construction, this flow has an integer value at each edge. Note that this maximum flow algorithm can be replaced by any other algorithm, where a solution has the same properties. The runtime has to be adapted accordingly.

The problem of increasing the slackness of all nodes with negative slackness to at least 0 is equivalent to asking if there exists an s-t flow in $\tilde{G}$ with a value of at least $\sum_{v \in V} \max\{0, -s(G, \Lambda(G,C), v, x)\}$. This is the case iff this flow fully uses every edge connected to t. If such an integer flow exists, we flip the orientation of every edge $e \in E$ with flow equal to one to get an induced x-satisfying coloring. Examples can be found in the full online version of the paper [16].

Using this construction and binary search, we find $x \in \{1, \cdots, \Delta(G), \infty\}$ with $x = x^*(G)$. We get a runtime of $\mathcal{O}(\log(\Delta) \cdot |E| \cdot \min\{|V|^{\frac{2}{3}}, |E|^{\frac{1}{2}}\})$. The correctness of this approach can be proved analogously to [4]. We call this algorithm MinimumStarColoringFlow. The key insight about the improved runtime is, that the slackness of all nodes with negative slackness is increased simultaneously. Note that this approach can not be applied to linear hypergraphs directly, due to the lack of the flow techniques for hypergraphs.

Theorem 2. MinimumStarColoringFlow *computes $x^*(G)$ for a simple connected non-empty graph G with a runtime of $\mathcal{O}(\log(\Delta) \cdot |E| \cdot \min\{|V|^{\frac{2}{3}}, |E|^{\frac{1}{2}}\})$.*

MinimumStarColoringFlow can also be used to compute an optimal solution of MinMaxInd in $\mathcal{O}(\log(\Delta) \cdot |E| \cdot \min\{|V|^{\frac{2}{3}}, |E|^{\frac{1}{2}}\})$ time by reducing it in linear time to MinMaxStar, as we show in Theorem 3. Therefore, this algorithm is a generalization of the algorithm which Asahiro et al. present in [4].

7 Comparing MinMaxStar and MinMaxInd

In this section, we show a linear reduction from MinMaxInd to MinMaxStar. Afterward, we prove, that there always exists an orientation of G that is optimal for MinMaxStar and MinMaxInd simultaneously when we consider the case without node capacities, i.e., $\kappa_v \geq \delta_v$ for all $v \in V$. Furthermore, we state explicitly how to compute such a solution.

Theorem 3. *There exists a linear-time reduction from MinMaxInd to MinMaxStar for simple graphs.*

Proof. (Sketch) Given a graph $G = (V, E)$ with node capacities κ, for which we want to solve MinMaxInd, we construct a graph G' with node capacities κ', on which we solve MinMaxStar instead. The graph $G' = (V \cup V', E \cup E')$ is constructed as follows: For each node v, we insert a copy v' into V' and insert the edge $\{v, v'\}$ into E'. The node v gets the capacity $\kappa'_v := \kappa_v + 1$ and v' has the capacity $\kappa'_{v'} = 1$. This construction is visualized in Fig. 3. Due to space limitations, the proof of $k^*(G) = x^*(G') - 1$ is given in the full online version of the paper [16]. □

Theorem 4. *For any given simple connected graph G without node capacity constraints, we can compute a solution that is optimal for MinMaxStar and MinMaxInd simultaneously in $\mathcal{O}(\log(\Delta) \cdot |E| \cdot \min\{|V|^{\frac{2}{3}}, |E|^{\frac{1}{2}}\})$.*

Proof. Using the algorithm of Theorem 2 we compute an optimal orientation Λ_1 for MinMaxStar with value $x^*(G)$. Combining Theorem 2 and the linear reduction of Theorem 3 we get an optimal orientation Λ_2 for MinMaxInd with value $k^*(G)$. On the one hand, if $x^*(G) = k^*(G) + 1$, then Λ_2 is also optimal for MinMaxStar. If on the other hand, $x^*(G) = k^*(G)$ then Λ_1 is also optimal for MinMaxInd, since in Λ_1 the indegree of any node is at most $x^*(G)$. □

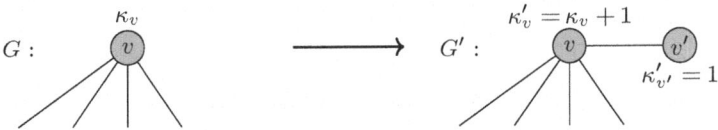

Fig. 3. A node v in G and its representation in G'

8 Hardness Results

In this section, we provide several reductions between the node-weighted decision versions of MINMAXSTAR, MINMAXIND and bin packing. For each node v, we introduce a positive node weight w_v. In contrast to the unweighted versions, we show that the weighted versions of both problems are `strongly NP-complete`. Note that this holds without any capacity constraints on the nodes.

For a valid star partition C, we redefine $x(G, C, v)$ for each node $v \in V$ as the sum of the weights of all stars v is contained in. The weight of a star is defined as the weight of the node coloring all edges in the star. This node is defined as the internal node. For a given orientation Λ, we define $k(G, \Lambda, v)$ for each node $v \in V$ as the sum of weights of nodes having a directed edge toward v. If the graph and the orientation are clear from context, we simply write $x(v)$ or $k(v)$.

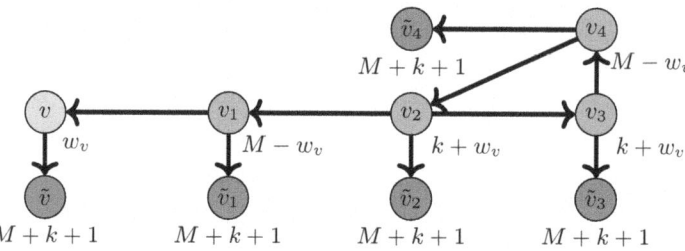

Fig. 4. Visualization of the gadget G_v with a valid orientation with the value of at most $M + k$. The gadget forces v to orientate $\{v, v_1\}$ toward v and $\{v, \tilde{v}\}$ toward $\tilde{v}$ in each star partition with the value of at most $M + k$. The weights of the nodes are visualized next to each node.

(W-MinMaxStar): Node-Weighted Min-Max Star Partitioning Problem
  Input: $k \in \mathbb{R}_{>0}$, a simple graph $G = (V, E)$, weights $w_v \in \mathbb{R}_{>0}$ $\forall v \in V$.
  Question: Does there exist a star partitioning such that $\max_{v \in V} x(v) \leq k$?

(W-MinMaxInd): Node-Weighted Min-Max Indegree Problem
  Input: $k \in \mathbb{R}_{>0}$, a simple graph $G = (V, E)$, weights $w_v \in \mathbb{R}_{>0}$ $\forall v \in V$.
  Question: Does there exist an orientation such that $\max_{v \in V} k(v) \leq k$?

8.1 Reduction from W-MINMAXIND to W-MINMAXSTAR

In this subsection, we will reduce W-MinMaxInd to W-MINMAXSTAR. We show that deciding W-MINMAXIND on G is equivalent to deciding W-MINMAXSTAR on a constructed graph G' with value at most $M+k$ with $M := k + 2\max_{v \in V} w_v$.

The graph G' is constructed by adding the gadget G_v to every node $v \in V$ where $G_v = (V_v \cup \tilde{V}_v, E_v)$ with the node sets $V_v = \{v, v_1, v_2, v_3, v_4\}$ and $\tilde{V}_v = \bigcup_{w \in V_v} \tilde{w}$ and the edge set $E_v = \{\{v, v_1\}, \{v_1, v_2\}, \{v_2, v_3\}, \{v_2, v_4\}, \{v_3, v_4\}\} \cup \bigcup_{w \in V_v} \{\{w, \tilde{w}\}\}$ as visualized in Fig. 4. The weights of the nodes in G_v are according to this figure.

Theorem 5. *There is a linear-time reduction from* W-MINMAXIND *to* W-MINMAXSTAR.

Due to space limitations, the proof can be in the full online version of the paper [16]. Note that because of the node weights, the reduction needs to be more evolved than Theorem 3.

8.2 Reduction from Bin Packing to W-MinMaxInd

In this subsection, we will reduce the strongly NP-complete bin packing problem to W-MINMAXIND. This shows together with Theorem 5 that W-MINMAX-IND and W-MINMAXSTAR are strongly NP-complete.

Theorem 6. W-MINMAXIND *is strongly NP-hard.*

Proof. We construct a reduction from the strongly NP-hard bin packing problem [18]. Let a bin packing problem $\mathcal{B}$ be given by a finite set $I = i_1, \ldots, i_n$ with size $s_i \in \mathbb{Z}^+$ for every element $i \in I$, which should be distributed into $K \geq 2$ bins with bin capacities c. We construct a graph $G_\mathcal{B} = (V = V_1 \dot\cup V_2, E)$, where we introduce for every element of $i_j \in I$ a node $v_j \in V_1$ and for every bin b_j a node $b_j \in V_2$. We construct an edge $\{v, b\}$ for every $v \in V_1, b \in V_2$. Additionally, we set the node weights $w_v = s_v$ for every $v \in V_1$ and $w_b = \frac{c}{K-1}$ for every $b \in V_2$. The graph $G_\mathcal{B}$ and its node weights have a size depending polynomial on the size of the bin packing problem $\mathcal{B}$.

Given a partition of the elements in I into K bins, which obeys the capacity restriction c of the bins, we construct an orientation of $G_\mathcal{B}$ with a maximum weighted indegree of at most c the following way. If $i_j \in b$, we orient the edge $\{v_j, b\}$ toward b and the edges $\{v_j, b'\}$ with $b' \in V_2 \setminus \{b\}$ toward v_j. Each node $v \in V_1$ has exactly $K-1$ incoming edges, which weights sum up to c. The weights of the elements in bin b sum up to at most c, and the only edges directed toward the corresponding node $b \in V_2$ are edges from nodes which are constructed from these elements.

Given an orientation Λ of $G_\mathcal{B}$ with a maximum weighted indegree of at most c, we construct a partition of I into K bins with capacity c, as visualized in Fig. 5. For every $v \in V_1$, there exists at least one edge that is directed away from v since otherwise $k(G, \Lambda, v) = K \cdot \frac{c}{K-1} > c$. For each node $v_j \in V_1$, let $b_l \in V_2$ be the node with the smallest index, where the edge $\{v_j, b_l\}$ is directed toward b_l. We put the element i_j into the bin b_j. The weight of the elements in the bin b is at most the sum of the weights of the incoming edges. This weight is at most c. □

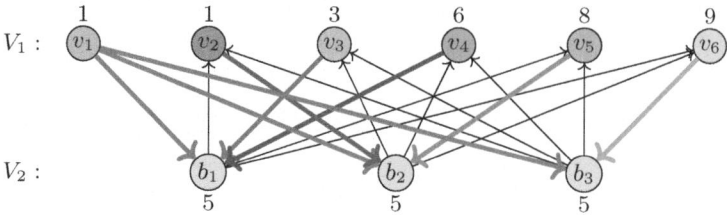

Fig. 5. Visualization of an orientation with value at most c of the constructed graph $G_\mathcal{B}$ for a given bin packing instance $\mathcal{B}$ with $K = 3$ and $c = 10$. Items are assigned to the leftmost bin in case the item has more than one outgoing edge.

Corollary 1. *Both W-MinMaxInd and W-MinMaxStar are **strongly NP-complete**.*

The **strong NP-hardness** of the problem is a consequence of the polynomial-time reductions from bin packing to W-MinMaxInd and from W-MinMaxInd to W-MinMaxStar. W-MinMaxInd and W-MinMaxStar are in NP, because given an orientation Λ or a valid coloring C, we can verify in polynomial time if $k(G, \Lambda, v) \leq x$ holds for every node v or if $x(G, C, v) \leq x$ holds for every node v.

9 Approximation Algorithms

We have seen that W-MinMaxInd and W-MinMaxStar are NP-complete. We construct approximation algorithms for finding minimal values k for which these problems are YES-instances for a given graph G.

Theorem 7. *Each algorithm that is an α-approximation for W-MinMaxInd is a 2α-approximation for W-MinMaxStar.*

Proof. Note that $k^* \leq x^*$ holds for optimal solutions k^* of W-MinMaxInd and x^* of W-MinMaxStar. Let Λ be an orientation with $k(G, \Lambda) \leq \alpha \cdot k^*$. For each node $v \in V$ we can distinguish two cases. If v has no incoming edges, then $x(G, \Lambda, v) = k(G, \Lambda, v)$. Else, we have $x(G, \Lambda, v) = k(G, \Lambda, v) + w_v$ and the value w_v contributes to $k(G, \Lambda, w)$ for at least one $w \in V \setminus \{v\}$. Therefore, we can deduce that if v has at least one outgoing edge then $w_v \leq k(G, \Lambda)$. Thus, it holds $x(G, \Lambda) \leq 2 \cdot k(G, \Lambda) \leq 2\alpha \cdot k^* \leq 2\alpha \cdot x^*$. □

In scheduling unrelated parallel machines there are m parallel machines and n independent jobs. The objective is to assign each job to exactly one machine in a manner that minimizes the makespan. Assigning a job i to a machine j contributes to the processing time of machine j with $p_{i,j}$. A special instance occurs when taking an W-MinMaxInd instance and interpreting each node as a machine and each edge $e = \{v_i, v_j\}$ as a job with processing times $p_{e,v_i} = w_{v_j}$, $p_{e,v_j} = w_{v_i}$ and $p_{e,v} = \infty$ for $v \notin e$.

Thus, W-MINMAXIND is a special case of scheduling unrelated parallel machines for which Lenstra et al. showed a 2-approximation in [22] and their approximation algorithm yields a 4-approximation for W-MINMAXSTAR.

10 Conclusion and Outlook

We introduced MINMAXSTAR and created two algorithms finding an optimal solution in $\mathcal{O}(|E|^2)$ and $\mathcal{O}(\log(\Delta)\cdot|E|\cdot\min\{|V|^{\frac{2}{3}},|E|^{\frac{1}{2}}\})$ time. We then extended MINMAXSTAR to multigraphs and linear hypergraphs. We showed the connection between MINMAXSTAR and MINMAXIND. Afterward, we introduced node-weighted variants W-MINMAXSTAR and W-MINMAXIND, which we proved to be **strongly NP-complete** in contrast to MINMAXSTAR and MINMAXIND. Furthermore, we provided approximation algorithms for W-MINMAXSTAR and W-MINMAXIND with approximation factors of 4 and 2, respectively.

In the future, one could investigate the problem of maximizing the minimum number of incident edge colors of nodes, also known as the Santa Claus problem in scheduling [5]. Further research can be done to find an algorithm that computes a star partition of hypergraphs, which are not linear. One may investigate if there exist even better approximation algorithms or approximation lower bounds for W-MINMAXSTAR and W-MINMAXIND. Furthermore, one can construct a star partitioning problem with weighted edges and different ways of incorporating the edge weights into the objective. This would be similar to graph balancing [11,19,26].

Acknowledgments. Constructive feedback by Tom Freudenberg, Volker Kaibel, Alexander Lindmayr, Elias Pitschmann, Sebastian Sager, Jens Schlöter, Daniel Schmand, Nicole Schröder and our anonymous reviewers is gratefully acknowledged. Sarah Feldmann is funded by the Deutsche Forschungsgemeinschaft (DFG, German Research Foundation) - 314838170, GRK 2297 MathCoRe. Torben Schürenberg acknowledges funding by the Deutsche Forschungsgemeinschaft (DFG) - Project number 281474342.

Disclosure of Interests. The authors have no competing interests to declare that are relevant to the content of this article.

References

1. Ahadi, A., Dehghan, A.: The complexity of the proper orientation number. Inf. Process. Lett. **113**(19–21), 799–803 (2013). https://doi.org/10.1016/j.ipl.2013.07.017
2. Asahiro, Y., et al.: Shortest longest-path graph orientations. In: Wu, W., Tong, G. (eds.) Computing and Combinatorics, pp. 141–154. Springer Nature Switzerland (2024). https://doi.org/10.1007/978-3-031-49190-0_10
3. Asahiro, Y., Jansson, J., Miyano, E., Ono, H.: Graph orientation to maximize the minimum weighted outdegree. Int. J. Found. Comput. Sci. **22**(3), 583–601 (2011). https://doi.org/10.1142/S0129054111008246

4. Asahiro, Y., Miyano, E., Ono, H., Zenmyo, K.: Graph orientation algorithms to minimize the maximum outdegree. Int. J. Found. Comput. Sci. **18**(2), 197–215 (2007). https://doi.org/10.1142/S0129054107004644
5. Bansal, N., Sviridenko, M.: The Santa Claus problem. In: Proceedings of the Thirty-Eighth Annual ACM Symposium on Theory of Computing, STOC 2006, pp. 31-40. Association for Computing Machinery, New York (2006). https://doi.org/10.1145/1132516.1132522
6. Beineke, L.W., Wilson, R.J.: On the edge-chromatic number of a graph. Discret. Math. **5**(1), 15–20 (1973). https://doi.org/10.1016/0012-365X(73)90023-X
7. Borodin, O.V.: On acyclic colorings of planar graphs. Discret. Math. **25**(3), 211–236 (1979). https://doi.org/10.1016/0012-365X(79)90077-3
8. Borradaile, G., Iglesias, J., Migler, T., Ochoa, A., Wilfong, G.T., Zhang, L.: Egalitarian graph orientations. J. Graph Algorithms Appl. **21**(4), 687–708 (2017). https://doi.org/10.7155/jgaa.00435
9. Chartrand, G., Zhang, P.: Chromatic Graph Theory, 1st edn. Chapman & Hall/CRC, Boca Raton (2008)
10. Divya, D., Vijayakumar, S.: On star partition of split graphs. In: Kalyanasundaram, S., Maheshwari, A. (eds.) Algorithms and Discrete Applied Mathematics, pp. 209–223. Springer Nature Switzerland (2024), https://doi.org/10.1007/978-3-031-52213-0_15
11. Ebenlendr, T., Krčál, M., Sgall, J.: Graph balancing: a special case of scheduling unrelated parallel machines. Algorithmica **68**, 62–80 (2014). https://doi.org/10.1007/s00453-012-9668-9
12. Egawa, Y., Kano, M., Kelmans, A.K.: Star partitions of graphs. J. Graph Theory **25**(3), 185–190 (1997). https://doi.org/10.1002/(SICI)1097-0118(199707)
13. Even, S.: Graph Algorithms. Cambridge University Press, Cambridge (2011)
14. Even, S., Tarjan, R.E.: Network flow and testing graph connectivity. SIAM J.Comput. **4**(4), 507–518 (1975). https://doi.org/10.1137/0204043
15. Faudree, R.J., Sheehan, J.: Regular graphs and edge chromatic number. Discret. Math. **48**(2–3), 197–204 (1984). https://doi.org/10.1016/0012-365X(84)90182-1
16. Feldmann, S., Schürenberg, T.: On the min-max star partitioning number (2024). https://arxiv.org/abs/2408.07370
17. Fertin, G., Raspaud, A., Reed, B.: Star coloring of graphs. J. theory **47**(3), 163–182 (2004). https://doi.org/10.1002/jgt.20029
18. Garey, M.R., Johnson, D.S.: Computers and Intractability; A Guide to the Theory of NP-Completeness. W. H. Freeman & Co., USA (1990)
19. Jansen, K., Rohwedder, L.: Local search breaks 1.75 for graph balancing. In: Baier, C., Chatzigiannakis, I., Flocchini, P., Leonardi, S. (eds.) 46th International Colloquium on Automata, Languages, and Programming, ICALP 2019, 9-12 July 2019, Patras, Greece. LIPIcs, vol. 132, pp. 1–14. Schloss Dagstuhl - Leibniz-Zentrum für Informatik (2019). https://doi.org/10.4230/LIPIcs.ICALP.2019.74
20. Jensen, T.R., Toft, B.: Graph coloring problems (1994). https://api.semanticscholar.org/CorpusID:118910784
21. Karp, R.M.: Reducibility Among Combinatorial Problems, pp. 219–241. Springer, Berlin (2010). https://doi.org/10.1007/978-3-540-68279-0_8
22. Lenstra, J.K., Shmoys, D.B., Tardos, É.: Approximation algorithms for scheduling unrelated parallel machines. Math. Program. **46**, 259–271 (1990). https://doi.org/10.1007/BF01585745
23. Melnikov, L.S., Vizing, V.G.: The edge chromatic number of a directed/mixed multigraph. J. Graph Theory **31**(4), 267–273 (1999). https://doi.org/10.1002/(SICI)1097-0118(199908)

24. Shalu, M., Vijayakumar, S., Sandhya, T., Mondal, J.: Induced star partition of graphs. Discr. Appl. Math. **319**, 81–91 (2022). https://doi.org/10.1016/j.dam.2021.04.015
25. Venkateswaran, V.: Minimizing maximum indegree. Discret. Appl. Math. **143**(1–3), 374–378 (2004). https://doi.org/10.1016/j.dam.2003.07.007
26. Verschae, J., Wiese, A.: On the configuration-LP for scheduling on unrelated machines. J. Sched. **17**(4), 371–383 (2014). https://doi.org/10.1007/s10951-013-0359-4
27. Vizing, V.G.: On an estimate of the chromatic class of a p-graph. Diskret analiz **3**, 25–30 (1964)
28. Zhang, X.: The edge chromatic number of outer-1-planar graphs. Discret. Math. **339**(4), 1393–1399 (2016). https://doi.org/10.1016/j.disc.2015.12.009

Collision Detection for Modular Robots - It Is Easy to Cause Collisions and Hard to Avoid Them

Siddharth Gupta[1], Marc van Kreveld[2], Othon Michail[3], and Andreas Padalkin[4](✉)

[1] BITS Pilani, K K Birla Goa Campus, Goa, India
siddharthg@goa.bits-pilani.ac.in
[2] Utrecht University, Utrecht, The Netherlands
m.j.vankreveld@uu.nl
[3] University of Liverpool, Liverpool, UK
othon.michail@liverpool.ac.uk
[4] Paderborn University, Paderborn, Germany
andreas.padalkin@upb.de

Abstract. We consider geometric collision-detection problems for modular reconfigurable robots. Assuming the nodes (modules) are connected squares on a grid, we investigate the complexity of deciding whether collisions may occur, or can be avoided, if a set of expansion and contraction operations is executed. We study both discrete- and continuous-time models, and allow operations to be coupled into a single parallel group. Our algorithms to decide if a collision may occur run in $O(n^2 \log^2 n)$ time, $O(n^2)$ time, or $O(n \log^2 n)$ time, depending on the presence and type of coupled operations, in a continuous-time model for a modular robot with n nodes. To decide if collisions can be avoided, we show that a very restricted version is already NP-complete in the discrete-time model, while the same problem is polynomial in the continuous-time model. A less restricted version is NP-hard in the continuous-time model.

Keywords: Modular robots · Collision detection · Computational geometry · Complexity

1 Introduction

Modular reconfigurable robotics and the related concept of programmable matter concern systems composed of interconnected elementary entities, called modules. The collection of modules can coordinate its limited communication, computation, sensing, and local actuation to accomplish nontrivial global tasks. Local actuation of modules is enabled through a set of one or more mechanical operations that they can perform. An operation typically involves the module that

---

Andreas Padalkin was supported by the DFG Project SCHE 1592/10-1.

applies it as well as modules in its local neighborhood. Examples of such operations are pushing, pulling, expanding, contracting, doubling, and rotating. Apart from their induced local changes, these operations are often capable of causing a more global effect on the robotic structure within a limited period of time. An example is when a large part of the structure moves due to the simultaneous application of one or more local operations.

The ability of local operations to globally affect the robotic structure is a double-edged sword. On one hand, it is a convenient form of parallelism, where global structural changes can happen faster. On the other hand, if not properly orchestrated, it could cause small violations of the structure or even complete structural failure, such as uneven cycle growth, global connectivity breaking, and self-intersection of the structure. We, hereafter, shall call all structural violations and failures *collisions*. Operations that—when applied on individual modules—can globally affect the structure, are sometimes called *linear-strength operations*.

The positive effect of such operations has been studied from a theoretical point of view in a number of papers, for different underlying models and types of operations. In a series of papers, Aloupis et al. [3–5] studied a model of a robotic system known as crystalline robots [19]. The 2D version of the crystalline model represents modules as squares on a 2D grid, forming a connected shape of modules attached to adjacent modules. Each individual module can expand and contract, by extending one of its faces one unit out and retracting it back at some later point. Due to modules being attached to each other, up to linear-size components can move due to a module's expansion or contraction. In [5], Aloupis et al. gave a universal centralized reconfiguration algorithm for the crystalline model that, for any pair of connected shapes S_I, S_F of the same number of modules n, can transform S_I into S_F within $O(\log n)$ parallel time steps by performing $\Theta(n \log n)$ individual operations.

In [21], Woods et al. proposed the nubot model, motivated by the programmable self-assembly of molecules, such as DNA strands. In this model, modules represent monomers on a 2D triangular grid. The model incorporates a number of different types of operations, such as insertion, deletion, and rotation of modules. The motion caused by operations is propagated to larger parts of the shape through its connections. Operations whose global effect would violate the rigidity of a connection are assumed to be canceled. Their main result is a distributed, asynchronous algorithm which, starting from a singleton, can form any connected 2D shape and pattern of size n, within a polylogarithmic (in n) number of parallel time steps in expectation.

Almalki and Michail [1], building on the insertion operations of [21] and the growth processes on graphs by Mertzios et al. [17], investigated what families of shapes can be grown in time polylogarithmic in their size by using only growth operations. They did this in a 2D square grid model, under different requirements on operation couplings that must be satisfied in each time step. Their operations were defined so that collisions can never occur. They gave centralized algorithms for growing a shape S_F from a shape S_I (possibly a singleton), which yield polylogarithmic parallel time-step schedules for large classes of shapes.

The amoebot model of Derakhshandeh et al. [12] –and its recent canonical extension [9]– is another model in which the main operations considered are expansions and contractions of modules. The modules operate on a 2D triangular grid and reconfiguration happens through expansions of the head of modules toward empty space, followed later by contraction of their tail toward their head. Shape formation algorithms in this model are usually designed in a way that operations are parallel but each is affecting only a local region around it and not larger parts of the shape. See [8], for a recent chapter covering the main algorithmic developments in this model. Recently, Feldmann et al. [14] have proposed to add linear-strength operations to the model, which were formalized by Padalkin et al. [18].

The necessity to avoid collisions between large moving parts of a shape is also present in programmable matter by folding [16] and the algorithmic questions related to it [11]. In those models, the goal is to fold a polyhedral complex starting from a sufficiently large surface, such as a piece of paper, without self-intersecting in the process. Coordinated motion planning is another line of research having some similarities to our work. There the goal is to reconfigure a swarm of robots to a target configuration as fast as possible while avoiding collisions of robots [10,20]. Another model in which individual operations can have up to a linear effect on the shape, is the line-pushing model of Almethen et al. [2].

It is evident that most studies have restricted attention to those operations that are safe to perform in parallel. These are either linear-strength operations that cannot collide or operations that affect only the local region around them. In this paper, we explicitly pose the algorithmic question of determining when a set of operations may cause a collision and when a collision can be avoided. In particular, given a shape and a set of linear-strength operations on that shape we aim to give centralized algorithms that can compute a schedule of these (sets of) operations that would (i) cause a collision or (ii) avoid collisions. The former subquestion is motivated by asynchronous distributed algorithms, in which any of the possible interleavings of operations might be the one that the modules will actually realize; the latter by the need to design efficient reconfiguration algorithms that avoid collisions, instead of having collision-avoidance built into the model. To the best of our knowledge, the present is the first study to be explicitly considering these types of questions.

Approach. We choose to study these questions in a 2D square grid model, where modules, called nodes hereafter, are unit squares occupying distinct cells of the grid. This choice makes the 2D crystalline model of Aloupis et al. [5] and the growth model of Almalki and Michail [1] to be the closest to our model. Nodes can be connected to some of their adjacent nodes, in a way that always forms an initial connected shape S. We do not allow new connections to be created between the nodes. The operations considered are expansion and contraction. These operations can also be viewed as a linear-strength extension of the expansions and contractions of the amoebot model [12]. The input to our problems is a connected shape S, an assignment of operations on S without multiplicities,

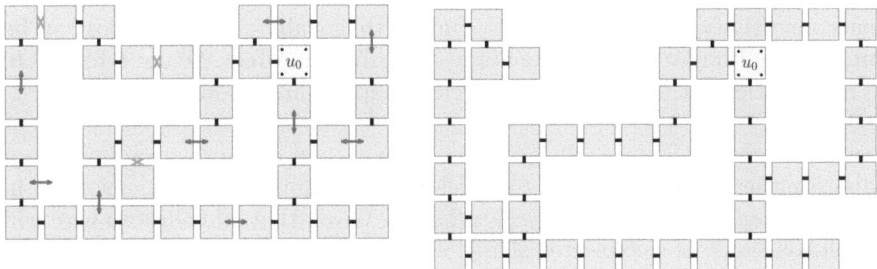

Fig. 1. Applying a collision-free set of parallel operations to a shape. In general, a shape's edge set is shown by the black edges between the nodes, and u_0 denotes the anchor. Red double arrows indicate an expansion and green X's indicate a contraction. Any operation applied between two nodes should be regarded as taking place over an edge, which is not drawn to keep the illustration clean. For the same reason, nodes will be drawn slightly smaller than their actual size. (Color figure online)

and a coupling partition of the operations. The coupling partition specifies which operations will be performed in parallel. See Fig. 1 for an example.

Results and Overview. Section 2 describes the model in which we study the collision problems. In particular, we specify the assumed input, the operations and their coupling, collisions, and time models. Then we give our problem definitions. Section 3 first presents algorithms for the problem of detecting whether collisions may occur in the continuous-time model, where operations may start any time. When there is no specified parallelity of operations, we give an $O(n \log^2 n)$ time algorithm. When certain operations are specified to be in parallel, we present algorithms that run in $O(n^2)$ time or $O(n^2 \log^2 n)$ time, depending on the degree of parallelity. We then give polynomial-time algorithms in the discrete-time model, where any operation or coupled group must complete its action before the next one begins. Section 4 addresses the problem of determining whether all operations can be performed while avoiding collisions. We show that a restricted version is already NP-complete in the discrete-time model, while it is polynomial-time solvable in the continuous-time model. A somewhat less restricted version is again NP-hard in the continuous-time model. The NP-hardness results require that certain operations be specified as parallel. Due to space constraints, we have to omit some proofs, which can be found in the full version [15].

2 Model

We assume a 2-dimensional square grid where each cell has integer coordinates (x, y). Nodes (modules) occupy cells, defining a set of occupied integer points such that no two nodes occupy the same cell. We represent every node $u = (u_x, u_y)$ as a square of size equal to and perfectly aligned with cell (u_x, u_y) of the grid. A *shape* $S = (V, E)$ is a configuration of nodes V together with their connectivity, represented by E. Only orthogonally adjacent nodes can be connected, but adjacent nodes are not necessarily connected. We use n to denote $|V|$ and restrict our attention to connected shapes, throughout.

Operations and Collisions. In general, applying one or more *operations* to a shape S either causes a *collision* or yields a new shape S'. Collisions come in two types: *node collisions* and *cycle collisions*. Given that all collisions here will be "self-collisions" of a connected shape, we can assume without loss of generality (abbreviated "w.l.o.g." throughout) that there is an *anchor* node $u_0 \in V$ that is stationary and other nodes move relative to it. We begin with the simpler case where the shape is a tree $T = (V, E)$, where cycle collisions do not exist, and then generalize to any connected shape S.

We start by defining single *expansion* and *contraction* operations;[1] see Fig. 1. An *expansion* operation is applied to a pair of adjacent integer points uv, where either (i) $u \in V$ and $v \notin V$, or (ii) $u, v \in V$ and $uv \in E$ holds. The remaining case where $u, v \in V$ but $uv \notin E$ immediately gives a collision. In case (i), the expansion generates a node at the empty cell v connected to u. In case (ii), assume w.l.o.g. that u is closer to u_0 in T than v. Let $T(v)$ denote the subtree of T rooted at v. Then, the expansion generates a node between u and v, connected to both, which translates $T(v)$ by one unit away from u along the axis parallel to uv. In both cases, the new node starts as a unit-length segment that widens into a unit square. A *contraction* operation is applied to a pair of nodes $uv \in E$, v being the furthest from the anchor. It merges v with u by translating $T(v)$ by one unit toward u while v narrows to a unit-length segment. In both types of operations, if after $T(v)$'s translation two nodes occupy the same cell then a collision has occurred. We call this type of collision a *node collision* and more generally define it as the non-empty intersection of the areas of any two nodes at any point in time. Otherwise, a new tree T' has been obtained.

When S has cycles, then any single operation, an expansion that adds a node to the cycle or a contraction of two adjacent nodes on the cycle, will force the cycle: it cannot generate a new proper cycle. We call this a *cycle collision*.

We assume that no node is ever adjacent to more than one operation.

Coupling. Let Q be a set of operations to be applied *in parallel* to a connected shape S, each operation on a distinct pair of nodes or a node and an unoccupied cell. We call such a set a *coupling*, and the operations it contains are *coupled* or *parallel*. We assume that all operations in Q are applied *concurrently*, have the same *constant execution speed*, and their *duration* is equal to one unit of time.

Let $T = (V, E)$ be a tree and $u_0 \in V$ its anchor. We set u_0 to be the root of T. We want to determine the displacement of every $v \in V \setminus \{u_0\}$ due to the parallel application of the operations in Q. As u_0 is stationary and each operation translates a subtree, only the operations on the unique $u_0 v$ path contribute to

---

[1] We believe that our definitions and techniques can be extended to alternative versions of expansion and contraction—including the case where the operations can be reversed—and to different geometries such as a triangular grid.

v's displacement. In particular, any such operation contributes one of the unit vectors $\langle -1, 0\rangle, \langle 0, -1\rangle, \langle +1, 0\rangle, \langle 0, +1\rangle$ to the motion vector $\boldsymbol{v}$ of v. Moreover, for any node $u \in V$ that expands toward an empty cell, we add a new node v with a corresponding unit motion vector $\boldsymbol{v}$. We can use the set of motion vectors to determine whether the trajectories of any two nodes will collide at any point.

Now, let S be any connected shape with at least one cycle and any node u_0 be its anchor. Then, a set of operations Q on S either causes a cycle collision or its effect is essentially equivalent to the application of Q on any spanning tree of S rooted at u_0. Let u, v be any two nodes on a cycle. If p_1 and p_2 are the two uv paths of the cycle, then $\boldsymbol{v}_{p_1} = \boldsymbol{v}_{p_2}$ must hold: the displacement vectors of v along the paths p_1 and p_2 are equal. Otherwise, we cannot maintain all nodes or edges of the cycle; such a violation is a cycle collision. We call a set of operations that does not cause any node or cycle collisions *collision free*.

Discrete and Continuous Time. We consider two different models for the scheduling of the operations. In the *discrete-time model*, each operation or coupling starts at a different integer time and takes one unique unit of time. In other words, no two operations are active at the same time unless they are coupled. In the *continuous-time model*, we do not make the integer starting-time assumption. Operations can start at any time and their active times can overlap. Coupled operations start and finish at the same time. Our assumption that each operation takes one unit of time to complete and has constant execution speed holds for both timing models. In the discrete-time model, only the order of the operations (individual or coupled) matters for having collisions or not. In the continuous-time model, the precise starting times of the operations matter.

Problem Definitions. We now define the problems considered. Given a shape S and an assignment of operations on S that involve any node at most once, a *coupling partition of operations on S* is a collection of sets $\{Q_1, Q_2, \ldots, Q_k\}$, where each Q_i (possibly a singleton) denotes a subset of the operations that should be performed in parallel.

COLLIDING SCHEDULE. Given a shape $S = (V, E)$ from a given family of shapes and a coupling partition of operations $\{Q_1, Q_2, \ldots, Q_k\}$ on S, decide if a starting time $t_0(Q_i) \in \mathbb{R}$ for each coupled set Q_i exists such that the application of the operations according to these starting times causes a collision.

COLLISION-FREE SCHEDULE. Given a shape $S = (V, E)$ from a given family of shapes and a coupling partition of operations $\{Q_1, Q_2, \ldots, Q_k\}$ on S, decide if a starting time $t_0(Q_i) \in \mathbb{R}$ for each coupled set Q_i exists such that the application of the operations according to these starting times is collision free.

The discrete special cases of these problems, DISCRETE COLLIDING SCHEDULE and DISCRETE COLLISION-FREE SCHEDULE, respectively, are obtained by requiring all $t_0(Q_i)$'s to be unique integers.

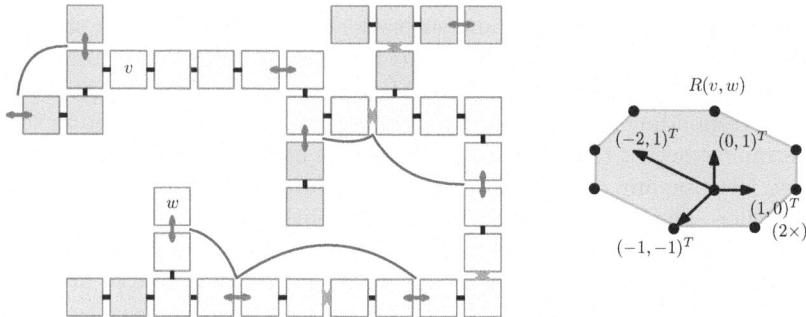

Fig. 2. A shape S with operations and v and w indicated. Only operations with both ends on the vw path influence how w can move with respect to v. The couplings are shown with blue arcs. There are five vectors in total implied by the path, of which two are the same. The corresponding region $R(v,w)$ for w with respect to v is the zonotope shown on the right. The $(2\times)$ label in the zonotope represents the fact that the vector $(1,0)^T$ is implied twice by the path. (Color figure online)

3 Algorithms for Colliding Schedule

In this section, we present algorithms to decide whether a connected shape can have collisions for some schedule of the operations. We distinguish in the case without couplings and cases with various forms of coupling. We first discuss the case where S is a tree; then we extend to solve COLLIDING SCHEDULE for general connected graphs.

3.1 Continuous and Discrete Colliding Schedule for Trees

We assume that the topology of S is that of a tree. We first present a general method to decide if collisions may occur which works when couplings may exist. The method is slightly more efficient when all couplings have constant size or each coupling is horizontal-only or vertical-only. Then we present an improved algorithm for the case when no couplings exist.

Let v be any node in S. We will give an algorithm to decide if v can collide with any other node w. Recall that there is exactly one path between v and w, and only the operations and couplings on this path determine whether v and w can collide. Assuming that v is stationary, coupled operations on this path allow w to translate over a vector $\langle i,j \rangle$ with integer coordinates. By letting all nodes take the role of v, we get a complete algorithm.

Starting at v, we perform a traversal of S and visit all other nodes. Whenever we visit and treat a node w', we have already visited the nodes on the path from v to w', in particular the neighbor w of w' on this path. The idea of the algorithm is to maintain the vectors made by the operations and couplings, with multiplicity, when traversing S from node to node.

Let $\mathrm{Vec}(v,w)$ be the multi-set of vectors describing the independent operations and couplings between v and w (see Fig. 2), and let $\mathcal{T}(v,w)$ be the tree storing Vec(v, w) sorted by angle in the leaves. We augment $\mathcal{T}(v, w)$ by storing at every internal and leaf node the sum vector of all vectors (with multiplicities) in the leaves below it.

One extra traversal step in S, going from w to w', means we must update $\mathcal{T}(v, w)$ to obtain $\mathcal{T}(v, w')$: (i) If the edge between w and w' is not an operation, then $\mathcal{T}(v, w') = \mathcal{T}(v, w)$. (ii) If the edge is an operation without coupling on the path so far, we get one new vector from $\langle -1, 0\rangle, \langle 0, -1\rangle, \langle +1, 0\rangle, \langle 0, +1\rangle$, which we insert into $\mathcal{T}(v, w)$ (possibly by increasing a multiplicity count instead of a leaf insertion) to create $\mathcal{T}(v, w')$. (iii) If the edge is an operation coupled with one or more operations between v and w, then a vector is modified by adding an extra operation to it. The corresponding vector changes by ± 1 in the x- or y-direction. The vector can become the zero vector, in which case we remove it. In the other case, we perform a deletion and an insertion to change the vector.

The tree $\mathcal{T}(v, w)$ is an implicit representation of the reachable region $R(v, w)$ of a node w with respect to v. In the continuous-time model, the reachable region is a convex region that contains the node w itself. It is the *zonotope* of the vectors Vec(v, w), and has twice as many edges as there are unique directions of vectors (we note that $R(v, w)$ is not convex if there are couplings and we use the discrete-time model). With a continuous-time model, w can always intersect any cell inside by starting the operations at suitable times.

The next lemma shows that we can query the search tree $\mathcal{T}(v, w)$ to find an extreme point of $R(v, w)$ in a given query direction efficiently, and test for intersection of nodes v and w.

Lemma 1. *We can find an extreme point of $R(v, w)$ in a given query direction ρ in $O(\log n)$ time, and test whether v and w can intersect in $O(\log^2 n)$ time.*

For the complete algorithm, we have n starting nodes v, and for each, we traverse S. Treating any encountered node w takes $O(\log^2 n)$ time for the search with v in the region of w, and $O(\log n)$ time for updating $\mathcal{T}(v, w)$ to prepare for the next node w' in the traversal of S. Hence the overall algorithm runs in $O(n^2 \log^2 n)$ time. The analysis of the algorithm for the case where all couplings have size $O(1)$ or all couplings are purely horizontal or purely vertical is easy: The region $R(v, w)$ and the tree $\mathcal{T}(v, w)$ have constant complexity, so the logarithmic factors vanish. The running times improve to $O(n^2)$.

When there are no couplings at all, we take a different approach that leads to a more efficient algorithm. Choose an anchor node v of the shape S whose removal creates subtrees (subshapes) each of which has size at most half of the original size. Such a central node always exists, and we obtain at most four subtrees. Observe that any operation in one subtree can influence the position of nodes in that subtree only, and not the positions of nodes in any other subtree.

We will determine for each subtree separately where all of its nodes can be. If these regions overlap for any two subtrees, then we have two nodes in different subtrees of S that can cause a collision and we have answered our question. We have also answered our question when one of the subtrees has a node that can occupy the location of the anchor v. Otherwise, we answer our question recursively in each subtree (note that the intersection of two regions of nodes in the same subtree does not tell us anything). In recursive steps, anchors are different and also the regions are different.

For each node w_1 in a subtree S_1, consider all operations on the path between v and w_1. These are horizontal and vertical contractions and expansions. These together specify all locations where w_1 can possibly be. These locations necessarily form a rectangle $R(v, w_1)$ because there is no coupling. We do this for all nodes in S_1, giving a set $\mathcal{R}$ of "red" rectangles, and we do the same for all nodes in another subtree S_2, giving a set $\mathcal{B}$ of "blue" rectangles. We can compute $\mathcal{R}$ and $\mathcal{B}$ in linear time by tree traversal from the anchor v and maintaining the operations on the path from v. With a standard plane sweep and segment trees, we can decide if any rectangle in $\mathcal{R}$ intersects any rectangle in $\mathcal{B}$ in $O(n \log n)$ time [7]. Due to recursion on the subtrees of S we spend $O(n \log^2 n)$ time overall.

Theorem 1. *Let S be a shape consisting of n unit square nodes with operations defined on the edges between adjacent nodes, and let the adjacency structure of S be a single tree. Then we can solve* COLLIDING SCHEDULE

- *in $O(n^2 \log^2 n)$ time if couplings exist;*
- *in $O(n^2)$ time if each coupling has constant size, or is horizontal-only or vertical-only;*
- *in $O(n \log^2 n)$ time if the operations are not coupled.*

We can also solve DISCRETE COLLIDING SCHEDULE in polynomial time. The algorithm without coupling is still correct, but with coupling we need a different approach. We now present an algorithm to decide whether w can be moved with respect to another node v such that they collide in the discrete-time model and when there are couplings. Recall that the couplings on the path between v and w imply a set of vectors $\text{Vec}(v, w)$. Unlike the continuous-time case, the reachable region $R(v, w)$ of w is no longer convex when there are couplings.

Our approach is an extension of the classical dynamic-programming method to solve subset sum in the case where the numbers are integers of bounded value. There are two main differences. Firstly, we do not have integers, but pairs of integers (vectors). Secondly, we need to handle the case where movement of the node w collides with v *during* the movement.

We put the vectors of $\text{Vec}(v, w)$ into an arbitrary order $\tau_1, \ldots, \tau_m$, and for all $1 \leq j \leq m$, we leave out vector τ_j and rename the others to become $\nu_1, \ldots, \nu_{m-1}$. We will show how to generate all cell locations that w can reach using all subsets of these ν vectors, and then test if moving w over vector τ_j causes a collision with v. Since every colliding schedule must end with some vector that causes the collision, we cover all possibilities.

We define a state (i, x, y) as a Boolean that should be set to $True$ by the algorithm if and only if some subset of $\nu_1, \ldots, \nu_i$ gives a sum of the first part that equals x and sum of the second part that equals y. We store the state in a 3-dimensional table which has size $O(n^3)$ as $m \leq n$ and the maximum values of x and y are n.

In dynamic-programming fashion, we define $(i+1, x, y)$ based on entries with smaller first index. We initialize the table with all entries set to $False$. Then we set $(0, 0, 0) := True$. Let $\nu_{i+1} = \langle \nu_{i+1}^x, \nu_{i+1}^y \rangle$.

- If $(i, x, y) = True$, then we set $(i+1, x, y) := True$.
- If $(i, x, y) = True$, then we set $(i+1, x + \nu_{i+1}^x, y + \nu_{i+1}^y) := True$.

When the table is filled, we know all possible starting locations of w before the final move over the vector τ_j. We test them all for a collision with v. In total, this algorithm takes $O(n^4)$ time. This basic algorithm can be improved with the following observation.

Lemma 2. *The set* $\text{Vec}(v, w)$ *has at most* $O(n^{2/3})$ *unique vectors.*

Since vector addition is commutative, we can assume that all vectors with the same direction are consecutive. This means that we can exclude not just one vector τ_j, but all equal vectors. At the end we test collision with the summed vector in that direction. Since there are only $O(n^{2/3})$ unique vectors, we run the dynamic programming method only $O(n^{2/3})$ times, giving an running time of $O(n^{11/3})$ to test if v and w can intersect.

Moreover, when couplings have size $O(1)$ or we have horizontal-only and vertical-only couplings, we have only $O(1)$ directions of vectors, leading to $O(n^3)$ running time. These running times are for each pair of nodes v, w, so we get:

Theorem 2. *Let S be a shape consisting of n unit square nodes with operations defined on the edges between adjacent nodes, and let the adjacency structure of S be a single tree. Then we can solve* DISCRETE COLLIDING SCHEDULE

- *in $O(n^{17/3})$ time if couplings exist;*
- *in $O(n^5)$ time if each coupling has constant size, or is horizontal-only or vertical-only;*
- *in $O(n \log^2 n)$ time if the operations are not coupled.*

For the last result we can use the continuous-time model result, since the reachable region $R(v, w)$ is the same in the discrete and continuous cases when no couplings exist.

Finally, we note that when there is just one single coupling of all operations, then COLLIDING SCHEDULE and COLLISION-FREE SCHEDULE are the same, as are the discrete-time and continuous-time models. We can model the problem by adding a third dimension. Each node is at its starting location in the plane $z = 0$ and at its destination—given some anchor—in the plane $z = 1$. We make a prism with square horizontal cross-section for each node by connecting the starting and destination squares. The question whether a node collision occurs then boils down to determining whether a proper intersection occurs among the prisms. We can solve this problem, for any constant $\epsilon > 0$, in $O(n^{3/2+\epsilon})$ time by ray shooting along all of the prism edges in the faces of the other prisms [13].

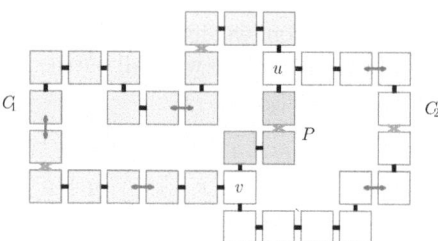

Fig. 3. A simple cycle $\mathcal{C}$ split into $\mathcal{C}_1$ and $\mathcal{C}_2$ at two nodes u and v, and an interior path $\mathcal{P}$ (of three nodes) connecting u and v.

3.2 Colliding Schedule for General Graphs

Recall that a cycle collision occurs between two nodes u and v on a cycle if the two paths between them do not agree on where one node moves to with respect to the other node. For any cycle that contains an individual operation in that cycle, it is easy to cause a cycle collision by performing that operation only. More generally, the horizontal operations must be in couplings that compensate for their effect on the cycle, and the same is true for the vertical operations. If this is not true for any cycle, then a cycle collision can be created. The possibility of a cycle collision is not dependent on the two nodes whose relative movement we check. Any pair of nodes on the cycle will give the same result.

We can show that if the couplings are such that in every *elementary cycle* of the graph, there is no cycle collision, then this is true for the whole graph. So we need to check the $O(n)$ elementary cycles only. We make this more precise.

Let $S = (V, E)$ be the connectivity graph of a connected shape. An *elementary cycle* is the outer boundary of a bounded face of a biconnected component. We obtain them by removing all nodes that are cut nodes of the graph. What remains are zero or more components each of which is biconnected. Each bounded face of the embedding is enclosed by a simple cycle of nodes. These are the elementary cycles.

Lemma 3. *For any connected shape S, the elementary cycles cannot cause a cycle collision if and only if all cycles cannot cause a cycle collision.*

Proof. We need to prove only that non-collision of elementary cycles implies non-collision of any cycle.

It is easy to see that in any simple cycle, a horizontal operation must be in a coupling with another horizontal operation in that cycle. By symmetry the same holds for vertical operations. It is also easy to see that operations incident to a cut node cannot cause a cycle collision, only a node collision. The latter observation leads to the fact that we can restrict ourselves to biconnected components.

Let $\mathcal{C}$ be any cycle in a biconnected component, and assume that all elementary cycles of that biconnected component cannot cause cycle collisions. We will show that $\mathcal{C}$ cannot have a cycle collision either, by induction on the number f of faces inside $\mathcal{C}$.

If $f = 1$, then $\mathcal{C}$ is elementary so the claim is true by assumption. Let $f > 1$ and assume that all cycles with $\leq f-1$ faces inside cannot cause a cycle collision. Take a simple path $\mathcal{P}$ in the biconnected component and inside $\mathcal{C}$; see Fig. 3. Let u, v be the two nodes on $\mathcal{C}$ that are adjacent to the first and last nodes of $\mathcal{P}$. We consider the three paths between u and v: two on $\mathcal{C}$, and $\mathcal{P}$ itself. We let u and v be the start and end of each of these paths, so that all operations on $\mathcal{C}$, on $\mathcal{P}$, and between $\mathcal{P}$ and u and v occur on exactly one of these paths. Call these three paths $\mathcal{C}_1$, $\mathcal{C}_2$, and $\mathcal{P}'$.

By induction we know that the cycles formed by $\mathcal{C}_1$ and $\mathcal{P}$ and by $\mathcal{C}_2$ and $\mathcal{P}$ cannot cause cycle collisions, since they have fewer than f faces inside. Treat u as an anchor, and consider how the operations on $\mathcal{C}_1$ move v. This is specified by a vector $\langle i, j \rangle$. Since the cycle formed by $\mathcal{C}_1$ and $\mathcal{P}$ cannot cause collisions, the path $\mathcal{P}'$ must also move v over the same vector $\langle i, j \rangle$. Repeating this argument on $\mathcal{C}_2$ and $\mathcal{P}$, we see that $\mathcal{C}_2$ must also move v by $\langle i, j \rangle$. Hence, the cycle $\mathcal{C}$ cannot cause a cycle collision either. The argument holds for any couplings that make sure that the smaller cycles do not cause cycle collisions. □

We now detect possible collisions as follows: First, we test if a cycle collision can be made in any elementary cycle. This is easy to do in linear time overall. If we found a collision, we are done. If not, we must check for node collisions. In Sect. 2 we observed:

Observation 1. *For a graph S with cycles which cannot cause cycle collisions, the occupied cells after any subset of the operations is the same as for any spanning tree of S.*

Hence, we compute any spanning tree T of S and use the algorithm of Sect. 3.1 on T to find node collisions. Pairs of nodes between which an edge in S was omitted in T cannot cause node collisions. This extends the results of Sect. 3.1 from trees to general connected graphs with the same time bounds.

4 Continuous and Discrete Collision-Free Schedule

So far we considered detecting whether collisions might occur for an input instance. In this section, we consider the problem of deciding if all operations can be performed without any collisions, for a suitable choice of operation order or starting times. We show that, even if there are only expansions that are w.l.o.g. horizontal and couplings have size $O(1)$, in the discrete-time model the problem is NP-complete. Interestingly, the same problem is solvable in polynomial time in the continuous-time model. When we add vertical expansions, the problem is NP-hard in the continuous-time model.

Theorem 3. DISCRETE COLLISION-FREE SCHEDULE *is NP-complete even if all operations are horizontal expansions and all couplings have size $O(1)$.*

Proof. In order to prove NP-hardness, we reduce the following problem to DISCRETE COLLISION-FREE SCHEDULE.

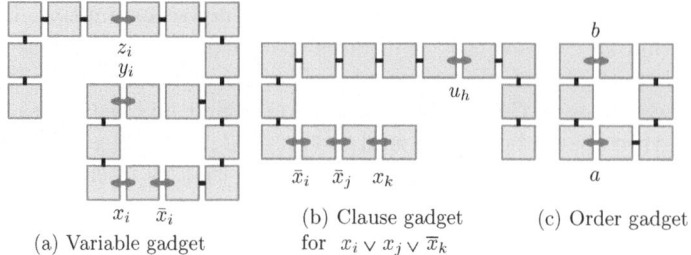

Fig. 4. Gadgets for the NP-hardness proof of Discrete Collision-free Schedule.

LSAT (Linear SAT). Given a CNF formula where each clause contains exactly three literals, each clause has common literals with at most one other clause, and two clauses have at most one common literal, decide if there is a satisfying assignment for the formula.

LSAT is NP-complete [6]. Let ϕ be a formula of LSAT with n variables $\{x_1, \ldots, x_n\}$ and m clauses. We construct an instance of Discrete Collision-free Schedule for formula ϕ such that there is a collision-free schedule for the instance if and only if ϕ is satisfiable.

For each variable x_i, we utilize the *variable gadget* shown in Fig. 4(a). We perform operation x_i or $\bar{x}_i$ to set variable x_i to true or false, respectively. The gadget causes a collision if we try to set variable x_i both to true and false. We use operation y_i to enforce that the variable is set, and later use operation z_i to make sure that the other operation, $\bar{x}_i$ or x_i, can also be performed.

For each clause, we utilize the *clause gadget* shown in Fig. 4(b). The gadget contains an operation for each literal that we couple with its inverse in the respective variable gadget, i.e., the operation is performed if and only if the literal is set to false. The gadget causes a collision if and only if all three operations are performed, i.e., all three literals are set to false; here we assume that operation u_h cannot be performed yet. Hence, a collision implies that the clause is not satisfied. We find a satisfying assignment for ϕ if and only if there are no collisions after setting all variables.

Two more ingredients are needed: First, we must make sure that all operations are eventually possible if ϕ can be satisfied, because Discrete Collision-free Schedule requires that we perform all operations. For that, we have included a release operation in each variable and clause gadget, namely z_i resp. u_h. By expanding those, we obtain enough space to expand all x_is and $\bar{x}_i$s.

Second, we must ensure that the release operations are not possible before all variables are set. For that, we introduce the *order gadget* shown in Fig. 4(c). The gadget causes a collision if and only if we perform operation b before a. Hence, it forces an order between a and b. Let $a \prec b$ denote that a has to be performed before b. We define the following order between the operations:

$$y_1 \prec y_2 \prec \cdots \prec y_n \prec z_1 \prec z_2 \prec \cdots \prec z_n \prec u_1 \prec u_2 \prec \ldots u_m.$$

We need a single order gadget for each relation in the chain, $2n + m - 1$ in total. At the time we perform y_n, each variable must have been set to either true or false. This is the moment when a truth assignment of ϕ is tested. Note that in the discrete-time model, each coupled set of operations must have completed before the next one starts, so we cannot start with any z or u before all y are completed, which requires that each variable has been set.

We have only utilized horizontal expansions in our gadgets. Furthermore, in LSAT, each literal occurs at most twice. Hence, each operation x_i and $\bar{x}_i$ occurs once in a variable gadget, and at most twice in clause gadgets. Each other operation occurs once in a variable or clause gadget, and at most twice in order gadgets. Thus, each coupling is of constant size. We can connect all gadgets into a single tree structure of linear size to produce a connected shape S.

Finally, note that DISCRETE COLLISION-FREE SCHEDULE is in NP since we can trivially check any schedule for collisions in polynomial time. □

Theorem 4. COLLISION-FREE SCHEDULE *is solvable in linear time if all operations are horizontal.*

Theorem 5. COLLISION-FREE SCHEDULE *is NP-hard.*

5 Conclusions and Open Problems

We have studied algorithmic questions associated with modular reconfigurable robot models which can be summarized as "Can collisions be caused?" and "Can collisions be avoided?", while performing all operations in the specification. All versions of causing collisions are polynomial-time solvable, but for avoiding collisions, this is not true.

The most intriguing open problem is whether the general version of avoiding collisions without coupling is NP-hard, or whether it can be solved in polynomial time. It would also be interesting to know if causing collisions can be solved in subquadratic time with couplings.

Acknowledgements. The authors thank all participants of the Bertinoro Workshop on Distributed Geometric Algorithms, in particular Peyman Afshani for suggesting the $O(n \log^2 n)$ time solution for detecting collisions without couplings, Irina Kostitsyna and Christian Scheideler for the organization, and the latter also for proposing the collision detection problem. Finally, we thank Jesper Nederlof for some useful observations.

References

1. Almalki, N., Michail, O.: On geometric shape construction via growth operations. Theor. Comput. Sci. **984**, 114324 (2024)
2. Almethen, A., Michail, O., Potapov, I.: Pushing lines helps: efficient universal centralised transformations for programmable matter. Theor. Comput. Sci. **830–831**, 43–59 (2020)

3. Aloupis, G., et al.: Realistic reconfiguration of crystalline (and Telecube) robots. In: WAFR. Springer Tracts in Adv. Robotics, vol. 57, pp. 433–447. Springer (2008)
4. Aloupis, G., et al.: Linear reconfiguration of cube-style modular robots. Comput. Geom. **42**(6–7), 652–663 (2009)
5. Aloupis, G., Collette, S., Demaine, E.D., Langerman, S., Adinolfi, V.S., Wuhrer, S.: Reconfiguration of cube-style modular robots using O(log n) parallel moves. In: ISAAC. LNCS, vol. 5369, pp. 342–353. Springer (2008)
6. Arkin, E.M., et al.: Selecting and covering colored points. Discr. Appl. Math. **250**, 75–86 (2018)
7. de Berg, M., Cheong, O., van Kreveld, M.J., Overmars, M.H.: Computational Geometry: Algorithms and Applications, 3rd edn. Springer, Berlin (2008)
8. Daymude, J.J., Hinnenthal, K., Richa, A.W., Scheideler, C.: Computing by programmable particles. In: Distributed Computing by Mobile Entities, LNCS, vol. 11340, pp. 615–681. Springer (2019)
9. Daymude, J.J., Richa, A.W., Scheideler, C.: The canonical amoebot model: algorithms and concurrency control. Distributed Comput. **36**(2), 159–192 (2023)
10. Demaine, E.D., Fekete, S.P., Keldenich, P., Meijer, H., Scheffer, C.: Coordinated motion planning: reconfiguring a swarm of labeled robots with bounded stretch. SIAM J. Comput. **48**(6), 1727–1762 (2019)
11. Demaine, E.D., Tachi, T.: Origamizer: a practical algorithm for folding any polyhedron. In: SoCG. LIPIcs, vol. 77, pp. 1–16. Dagstuhl Publishing (2017)
12. Derakhshandeh, Z., Dolev, S., Gmyr, R., Richa, A.W., Scheideler, C., Strothmann, T.: Brief announcement: amoebot - a new model for programmable matter. In: SPAA, pp. 220–222. ACM (2014)
13. Ezra, E., Sharir, M.: On ray shooting for triangles in 3-space and related problems. SIAM J. Comput. **51**(4), 1065–1095 (2022)
14. Feldmann, M., Padalkin, A., Scheideler, C., Dolev, S.: Coordinating amoebots via reconfigurable circuits. J. Comput. Biol. **29**(4), 317–343 (2022)
15. Gupta, S., van Kreveld, M.J., Michail, O., Padalkin, A.: Collision detection for modular robots - it is easy to cause collisions and hard to avoid them. CoRR, abs/2305.01015 (2023)
16. Hawkes, E., et al.: Programmable matter by folding. Proc. Natl. Acad. Sci. U.S.A. **107**(28), 12441–12445 (2010)
17. Mertzios, G.B., Michail, O., Skretas, G., Spirakis, P.G., Theofilatos, M.: The complexity of growing a graph. In: ALGOSENSORS. LNCS, vol. 13707, pp. 123–137. Springer (2022)
18. Padalkin, A., Kumar, M., Scheideler, C.: Reconfiguration and locomotion with joint movements in the amoebot model. In: SAND. LIPIcs, vol. 292, pp. 1–20. Dagstuhl Publishing (2024)
19. Rus, D., Vona, M.: Crystalline robots: self-reconfiguration with compressible unit modules. Auton. Robots **10**(1), 107–124 (2001)
20. Schwartz, J.T., Sharir, M.: On the piano movers' problem: III. coordinating the motion of several independent bodies: the special case of circular bodies moving amidst polygonal barriers. Int. J. Robot. Res. **2**(3), 46–75 (1983)
21. Woods, D., Chen, H., Goodfriend, S., Dabby, N., Winfree, E., Yin, P.: Active self-assembly of algorithmic shapes and patterns in polylogarithmic time. In: ITCS, pp. 353–354. ACM (2013)

Bike Assisted Evacuation on a Line of Robots with S/R Communication Faults

Khaled Jawhar[✉] and Evangelos Kranakis

School of Computer Science, Carleton University, Ottawa, ON, Canada
khaledjawhar@cmail.carleton.ca

Abstract. Two autonomous mobile robots and a non-autonomous one, also called bike, are placed at the origin of an infinite line. The autonomous robots can travel with maximum speed 1. When a robot rides the bike its speed increases to $v > 1$, however only exactly one robot at a time can ride the bike and the bike is non-autonomous in that it cannot move on its own. An Exit is placed on the line at an unknown location and at distance d from the origin. The robots have limited communication behavior; one robot is a sender (denoted by S) in that it can send information wirelessly at any distance and receive messages only in F2F (Face-to-Face), while the other robot is a receiver (denoted by R) in that it can receive information wirelessly but can send information only F2F. The bike has no communication capabilities of its own. We refer to the resulting communication model of the ensemble of the two autonomous robots and the bike as S/R.

Our general goal is to understand the impact of the non-autonomous robot in assisting the evacuation of the two autonomous faulty robots. Our main contribution is to provide a new evacuation algorithm that enables both robots to evacuate from the unknown Exit in the S/R model. We also analyze the resulting evacuation time as a function of the bike's speed v and give upper and lower bounds on the competitive ratio of the resulting algorithm for the entire range of possible values of v.

Keywords: Faults · Line · Robots · Search · Receiver · Sender · S/R Communication Model

1 Introduction

Evacuation (also known as group search) is similar to search except that it involves many entities which cooperate in order to find an unknown exit. There are plenty of applications related to search and evacuation in a distributed system such as data mining, crawling, and surveillance which makes it an area of interest. Many researchers have studied the linear search and evacuation problems with

---

E. Kranakis—Research supported in part by NSERC Discovery grant.

one or more robots moving at different speeds. Most investigations in this domain highlight algorithms that achieve the best possible upper and lower bounds. There are several factors that may affect the solution of the linear search and evacuation problems. For example, the robot(s) may know how far the exit is from the origin but may not be aware of the direction (to the left or right of the origin), the robot(s) may know the direction but not the distance from the origin to the exit, or in a more complicated case the distance and the direction are unknown to the robots. In our present study, the distance and the direction are unknown and there is a communication fault affecting both robots.

1.1 Preliminaries, Notation and Terminology

The system consists of two autonomous mobile agents (referred to as robots) and non-autonomous one (referred to as bike). The two robots and the bike together are sometimes referred to as the ensemble. The two robots have different identities and can see each other when they are situated at the same position. The search domain is the infinite line and it is bidirectional in that the robots can move in either direction on the line without this affecting their speeds. The two autonomous mobile agents can move around on their own with maximum speed 1 or ride the bike with speed $v > 1$. The robots can change direction at any time as specified by an algorithm; further, this change in direction of a robot is instantaneous, with or without the bike). An autonomous robot riding the bike is also referred to as *biker*, otherwise it also referred to as *hiker*.

An evacuation algorithm is given by the complete description of the trajectories traced by the two bikers until they both find the exit and evacuate. We are interested in evacuation algorithms which achieve the best competitive ratio which is defined as the optimal ratio of the evacuation time achieved by an algorithm which enables both autonomous robots to evacuate from the exit when its location is unknown divided by the evacuation time needed if all the robots know where the exit is.

The bike is not autonomous and cannot move and/or communicate on its own and thus plays only the role of assistant in order to speed up the search. The autonomous robot using the bike has an advantage in that it can move with speed $v > 1$ which is of course faster than its walking speed 1. Since the bike is a limited resource, in that it can be used by only one robot at a time, it must be shared by the robots in the sense that they must take turns using it. This is easily seen to be an advantage since it will ultimately improve the overall evacuation time and hence also the competitive ratio of the ensemble.

An important aspect in our algorithms will be "bike switching", by which we mean changing the rider of the bike. We will assume throughout the paper that bike switching between robots is instantaneous and at no time cost. Note that the robots may recognize the presence of the bike when they are at the same location as the bike.

We employ a communication model referred to as S/R model (this model was first proposed on the infinite line by [14] and on a unit disk by [18]) in which the robots have certain limited communication behavior and may communicate throughout the execution of the algorithms in the following way. Face-To-Face (F2F) (resp. Wireless) communication can take place only when the robots are co-located (resp. at any distance). The sender can only send information wirelessly and receive information F2F while the receiver can only receive information wirelessly and send information F2F. A typical communication exchange may involve, e.g., "exit is found", "bike released", "switch bike", etc. Note that the robots are endowed with pedometers and have computing abilities so that they can deduce the location of the other robot and/or the bike from relevant communications exchanged. Moreover, their ability to communicate F2F never fails. The bike itself has no communication capabilities on its own. In a way we think of the S/R model as describing a type of fault and in the sequel, we refer to the ensemble of the two robots and the bike as the S/R (communication) model.

Throughout the paper we will be using S and R to denote the sender and receiver respectively (which we often refer to as bikers) and B to denote the bike (non-autonomous robots). The robots are equipped with pedometers which can be used either when walking or riding the bike and are identical in all their capabilities (locomotion). The origin of the real line will be at the point $x = 0$ on the x-axis and this will also be the starting location of the robots and the bike. The adversary may place the exit at either of the points $\pm d$, where $d > 0$ will denote the unknown distance of the exit from the origin. In addition, $v > 1$ will denote the speed that a biker can attain when riding the bike.

The following lemma is shown in [20] can be proved easily using the standard analysis of bike-sharing and will be used extensively in the sequel.

Lemma 1. *Assume two robots of maximum speed* 1 *are sharing a bike of speed* $v > 1$. *Together the ensemble can cover a segment of length d in time* $\frac{d(v+1)}{2v}$. *In fact the ensemble travels with speed equal to* $\frac{2v}{v+1}$. *Moreover, these time and speed values are optimal.*

1.2 Related Work

The first search problems in the literature concerned a single robot and were proposed for a continuous infinite line by Beck [5] and Bellman [6] with the focus on stochastic search models and their analysis. Assuming that the distance and the direction to the exit are unknown, they proposed an optimal algorithm with competitive ratio 9. Additional research in that field can be found in [1,22]. There have been many variants of the search problem such as having static or moving targets, involving multiple robots with limited communication behavior, or robots with differing speeds, etc.

Search and evacuations problems were studied in environments with multiple distinct speed robots [4,13,16] as well as in various domains including disks, triangles, and circles [8,10,12]. Evacuation algorithms for two robots on a line without bike assistance are known for two robots without limited communication behavior and with different speeds v and 1 such that $v < 1$; for example, there is an evacuation algorithm in the F2F model with optimal competitive ratio of $\frac{1+3v}{1-v}$, for $v \leq \frac{1}{3}$, and 9 otherwise, see [4]. The same paper also considers the wireless communication model. Our work differs from [4] in two aspects: first we are using a mixed communication model S/R, and second a bike (non-autonomous robot) is present which is shared by the two autonomous robots and has the effect of increasing the overall evacuation time of the ensemble. The competitive ratio of evacuation for two robots without communication fault using the F2F model is known to be 9, see [12]. Additional studies on linear search can be found in the works of [2,3] and under various models of linear search concerning search cost and robot communication in [7,9,17].

An interesting variant of the original linear search problem is concerned with the case where some of the robots are faulty (crash or byzantine). There are several research works on this theme. The two main papers in this line of research are [16] for crash-faulty robots and [13] for Byzantine-faulty robots. Moreover, [15] studies search and evacuation with a near majority of faulty agents (e.g., three robots at most one of which is byzantine faulty)–which also exhibits the worst-case evacuation time. In addition, the S/R mixed communication model (also considered in our current paper) was considered as a way to model group search in the presence of robots with faulty communication capabilities and was first introduced for an infinite line by [14]; it was shown that there is an evacuation algorithm with competitive ratio of $3 + 2\sqrt{2}$ and this is optimal; however, this paper does not include the concept of the non-autonomous robot considered here.

We should also mention that the S/R faulty communication model considered in our present paper was also studied for a unit disk in the recent paper [18]. Additional research on evacuation from a unit disk in the presence of a (byzantine) faulty robot was first studied in [11] and further elaborated for crash and byzantine faults in [19].

Bike-assisted search and evacuation on a line was first considered for two robots without faults in [20] and soon thereafter [18] for a unit disk. To the best of our knowledge the present study of Bike-assisted search and evacuation on a line for two robots and a bike in the S/R model has not been considered in the search literature.

1.3 Outline and Results of the Paper

In the sequel, in Sect. 2 we give the main evacuation algorithm in three parts: Subsubsect. 2.1.1 includes the algorithm when $v \in [1, 3]$, Subsect. 2.1.2 the algorithm when $v \in [3, 10]$, and Subsect. 2.2 the algorithm when $v \in [10, \infty)$, while in Subsect. 2.3 we plot the evacuation time for the entire range of the bike's speed v so that we can gauge the performance of the main algorithm. Table 1 displays in detail the competitive ratios in each of the algorithms for the upper bound cases, respectively, based on the speed v of the biker.

We prove a lower bound in Sect. 3, and in Table 2 we display the competitive ratios in each of the algorithms for the lower bound cases, respectively, based on the interval to which the speed v of the biker belongs to Finally we conclude in Sect. 4 with a summary and a discussion of additional ideas for research. All proofs missing from the main text can be found in the appendix in [21].

Table 1. Upper bound on the competitive ratio for the three different algorithms; the first column gives the algorithm, the second column the speed v of the biker for which the respective upper bound on the competitive ratio in the third column is valid.

Algorithm	Bike Speed	Competitive Ratio
Algorithm 1	$v \in [1,3]$	$\frac{2v}{v+1}\left(\frac{2v+\frac{-(7v+v^2)+v\sqrt{v^2+30v+97}}{2v+6}}{v\frac{-(7v+v^2)+v\sqrt{v^2+30v+97}}{2v+6}}\right)$
Algorithm 2	$v \in [3,10]$	$\frac{2v}{v+1}\left(1+\frac{1}{v}+\frac{v^2-3v-2-\sqrt{v^4+18v^3-7v^2+4v+4}}{4v(1-v)}\right)$
Algorithm 3	$v \in [10,\infty]$	$\frac{2v}{v+1}\left(\frac{9}{v}+\frac{1}{2}-\frac{1}{2v^2}\right)$

Table 2. Lower bound on the competitive ratio for the evacuation of the two robots for the given range on the speed v of the biker.

Bike Speed v	Competitive Ratio
$v \leq 3$	$\frac{v^2+2v-3}{v^2-1}$
$v > 3$	$\frac{6}{v+1}$

2 Evacuation in the S/R Model

In this section we describe the algorithms in order to obtain upper bounds for two robots in the S/R model. We also analyze the resulting competitive ratios. Recall that the competitive ratio of an algorithm is defined as the evacuation time of the algorithm divided by the shortest time required by both robots to reach the exit if they know where the exit is.

In order to reach the exit in shortest time possible, there are two cases to consider. In the first case, the two robots choose to move in opposite direction and the one which finds the exit first will notify the other one (see Subsect. 2.1). In the second case, the sender takes the bike and uses a Zig-Zag strategy and the receiver imitates the sender using its maximum unit speed (see Subsect. 2.2). Let us study the algorithms proposed in each of the two cases.

2.1 Robots Move in Opposite Direction

Let us consider the case that the sender S and the receiver R are moving in opposite direction. To this end we will "reduce" the speeds of the sender and the receiver and our analysis will show the choice that will yield the shortest evacuation time. Let us assume that S moves with speed $0 \leq u_1 \leq 1$ and R takes the bike and moves with speed $0 \leq u_2 \leq v$. As already proposed, the objective is to find the optimal speeds u_1 and u_2 that should be used by S and R, respectively, in order for the resulting evacuation time to be minimal. There are two cases to take into account depending on which of the two autonomous robots finds the exit first:

Case 1: S finds the exit first.

As soon as S reaches the exit, it communicates with R which is on the other side to proceed to the exit. Based on Fig. 1, S needs time $\frac{d}{u_1}$ to reach the exit. When S reaches the exit, R would be at distance $\frac{du_2}{u_1}$ on the other side and it needs time $\frac{du_2}{vu_1}$ to go back to the origin and additional time $\frac{d}{v}$ to go from the origin to the exit. Thus taking this into account the total evacuation time will be as follows:

$$\mathcal{E}_1 = \frac{d}{u_1} + \frac{du_2}{vu_1} + \frac{d}{v} \qquad (1)$$

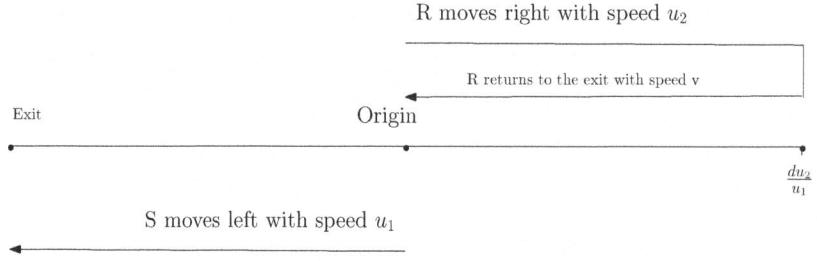

Fig. 1. Depicted is Case 1 where two robots S and R are moving in opposite direction such that S finds the exit first.

Case 2: R finds the exit first.

Based on Fig. 2, when R reaches the exit, then S is at distance $\frac{du_1}{u_2}$ to the left of the origin. In this case R needs to go back to the left to bring S toward the origin. When R reaches the origin, S will be at distance $\frac{du_1}{u_2} + \frac{du_1}{v}$ to the left

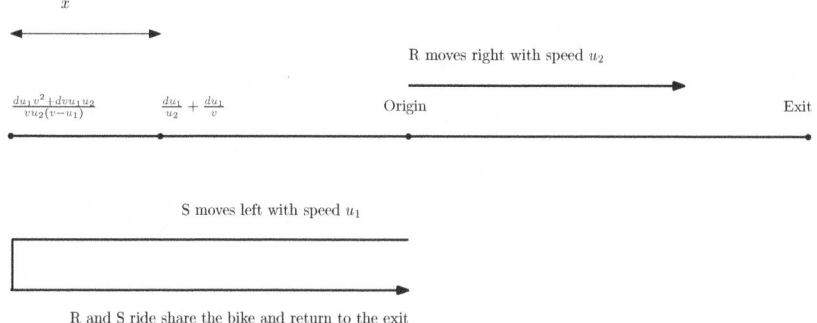

Fig. 2. Depicted is Case 2 where two robots S and R are moving in opposite direction and such that R finds the exit.

of the origin. At that point if S meets R at distance x from its current position, then we have the following:

$$\frac{x}{u_1} = \frac{du_1}{u_2v} + \frac{du_1}{v^2} + \frac{x}{v} \implies x\left(\frac{v-u_1}{u_1v}\right) = \frac{du_1v + du_1u_2}{u_2v^2}$$

$$\implies x = \frac{du_1^2v + du_1^2u_2}{(v-u_1)u_2v}$$

After S and R meet, they will be away from the origin by the following distance:

$$\frac{du_1}{u_2} + \frac{du_1}{v} + x = \frac{du_1}{u_2} + \frac{du_1}{v} + \frac{du_1^2v + du_1^2u_2}{(v-u_1)u_2v} = \frac{du_1v^2 + dvu_1u_2}{vu_2(v-u_1)}$$

Thus S and R will be away from the exit by

$$d + \frac{du_1v^2 + dvu_1u_2}{vu_2(v-u_1)} = \frac{du_1v + du_2v}{u_2(v-u_1)}.$$

Using Lemma 1, the time needed to share the bike at distance $\frac{du_1v+du_2v}{u_2(v-u_1)}$ from the exit will be as follows:

$$\frac{(du_1v + du_2v)(v+1)}{2vu_2(v-u_1)} = \frac{du_1v^2 + du_1v + du_2v^2 + du_2v}{2u_2v(v-u_1)}$$

Now we can find the evacuation time $\mathcal{E}_2$ as follows:

$$\mathcal{E}_2 = \frac{d}{u_2} + \frac{d}{v} + \frac{du_1}{u_2v} + \frac{du_1}{v^2} + \frac{du_1^2v + du_1^2u_2}{(v-u_1)u_2v^2} + \frac{du_1v^2 + du_1v + du_2v^2 + du_2v}{2u_2v(v-u_1)}$$

$$= \frac{2dv^2 + 2du_2v + du_1v^2 + du_1v + du_2v^2 + dvu_2}{2u_2v(v-u_1)}. \quad (2)$$

Since we do not know where the exit is situated, we should consider the worst case scenario of the evacuation time, denoted by $\mathcal{E}$, to be the maximum of $\mathcal{E}_1$ and $\mathcal{E}_2$, as given in Eqs. (1) and (2), as follows:

$$\mathcal{E} = \max\{\mathcal{E}_1, \mathcal{E}_2\} \quad (3)$$

In order to minimize the total evacuation time, we need to know for what value of v is each of $\mathcal{E}_1$ and $\mathcal{E}_2$ minimized.

Using Eq. (1), we see that $\mathcal{E}_1$ is minimized if $u_1 = 1$ and $u_2 = 0$ since we assume that the exit is on the side of the sender S. In this case $\mathcal{E}_1$ will be as follows: $\mathcal{E}_1 = d \cdot \frac{1+v}{v}$.

Using Eq. (2), we see that $\mathcal{E}_2$ is minimized if $u_2 = v$ and $u_1 = 0$ since we assume that the exit is on the side of the receiver R. In this case $\mathcal{E}_2$ will be as follows: $\mathcal{E}_2 = d \cdot \frac{v^3 + 5v^2}{2v^3} = d \cdot \frac{v+5}{2v}$. Thus

$$\mathcal{E}_1 - \mathcal{E}_2 = d \cdot \left(\frac{1+v}{v} - \frac{v+5}{2v}\right) = d \cdot \frac{v-3}{2v}.$$

We conclude that $\mathcal{E}_1 \leq \mathcal{E}_2$, if $v \leq 3$. Thus we have two cases to consider based on the speed of the biker.

Case 1: $v \leq 3$

We have $\mathcal{E}_1 < \mathcal{E}_2$ and thus the maximum evacuation time is $\mathcal{E} = \max\{\mathcal{E}_1, \mathcal{E}_2\} = \mathcal{E}_2$ and in this case $\mathcal{E}_2$ is minimized if we set $u_2 = v$.

Case 2: $3 \leq v \leq 10$

(Note that if $v > 10$, then the zig-zag algorithm discussed later in Sect. 2.2 performs better.) We have $\mathcal{E}_2 < \mathcal{E}_1$ and thus the maximum evacuation time is $\mathcal{E} = \max\{\mathcal{E}_1, \mathcal{E}_2\} = \mathcal{E}_1$ and in this case $\mathcal{E}_1$ is minimized when we set $u_1 = 1$.

2.1.1 Algorithm 1: $1 \leq v \leq 3$

In the first algorithm, the receiver takes the bike and moves in one direction with its maximum speed, while the sender moves with optimal speed $0 \leq u_1 \leq 1$ in the other direction. If the sender finds the exit first, then it informs the receiver and stays at the exit, while if the receiver finds the exit first, then it changes direction to catch up with the sender and then both robots ride-share the bike toward the exit. The first algorithm performs better when the speed of the bike satisfies $1 \leq v \leq 3$. If we assume the sender moves to the left with speed $0 \leq u_1 \leq 1$ and the receiver to the right with maximum speed v.

The algorithm will be as follows:

Algorithm 1. OppDirectionWithBikerMovingAtMaxSpeed (S source, D destination)

1: Sender moves to the left with speed u_1
2: Receiver takes the bike and moves to the right with speed v
3: **if** Receiver finds the Exit first **then**
4:     it changes direction and catches up to the Sender;
5:     The two robots change direction and ride-share the bike towards the Exit;
6: **else**
7:     **if** Sender finds the Exit first **then**
8:         it informs the Receiver that the Exit has been found but stays at the Exit;
9:         The Receiver rides the bike to the Exit;

We prove the following result.

Theorem 1. *The optimal competitive ratio of Algorithm 1 is*

$$\frac{2v}{v+1}\left(\frac{2v + \frac{-(7v+v^2)+v\sqrt{v^2+30v+97}}{2v+6}}{v\frac{-(7v+v^2)+v\sqrt{v^2+30v+97}}{2v+6}}\right)$$

Proof. We have that S moves in one direction with speed $0 \leq u_1 \leq 1$ and R moves in the other direction with speed v. Thus we will have the following equations $\mathcal{E}_1 = \frac{2d}{u_1} + \frac{d}{v}$ and $\mathcal{E}_2 = \frac{dv^2+5dv+du_1v+du_1}{2v(v-u_1)}$. In order to determine the optimal speed u_1 for the sender, we should set the evacuation times in both cases above to be equal, namely $\mathcal{E}_2 = \mathcal{E}_1$. This will give us the following:

$$\frac{d(v^2 + 5v + u_1 v + u_1)}{2v(v - u_1)} = \frac{2dv + du_1}{u_1 v} \implies (3+v)u_1^2 + (7v + v^2)u_1 - 4v^2 = 0$$

This is a quadratic equation of u_1 and it has two solutions. Keeping the positive root we get

$$u_1 = \frac{-(7v + v^2) + v\sqrt{v^2 + 30v + 97}}{2v + 6}.$$

We expect the optimal speed u_1 to be less than 1 when the speed v is between 1 and 3. If we substitute u_1 in the evacuation time, denoted by $\mathcal{E}$, calculated in any of the two cases we get the following

$$\mathcal{E} = d \left(\frac{2v + \frac{-(7v+v^2)+v\sqrt{v^2+30v+97}}{2v+6}}{v\frac{-(7v+v^2)+v\sqrt{v^2+30v+97}}{2v+6}} \right)$$

Thus, using Lemma 1, the competitive ratio will be

$$\frac{2v}{v+1} \left(\frac{2v + \frac{-(7v+v^2)+v\sqrt{v^2+30v+97}}{2v+6}}{v\frac{-(7v+v^2)+v\sqrt{v^2+30v+97}}{2v+6}} \right).$$

This completes the proof of Theorem 1. □

2.1.2 Algorithm 2: $3 \leq v \leq 10$
In the second algorithm, the sender moves in one direction with unit speed while the receiver takes the bike and moves in the other direction with optimal speed $1 < u_2 < v$. If the sender finds the exit first, then it informs the receiver and stays at the exit, while if the receiver finds the exit first, then it changes direction to catch up with the sender and then both robots ride-share the bike toward the exit. The second algorithm performs better when the speed $3 \leq v \leq 10$ as we will see later in Fig. 4. We assume the sender moves to the left with unit speed and the receiver to the right with speed $1 \leq u_2 \leq v$.

The main algorithm will be as follows:

Algorithm 2. OppDirectionWithWalkerMovingAtMaxSpeed (S source, D destination)

1: Sender moves to the left with unit speed
2: Receiver takes the bike and moves to the right with speed u_2
3: **if** Receiver finds the Exit first **then**
4:     it changes direction and catches up to the Sender;
5:     The two robots change direction and ride-share the bike towards the Exit;
6: **else**
7:     **if** Sender finds the Exit first **then**
8:         it informs the Receiver that the Exit has been found but stays at the Exit;
9:         The Receiver rides the bike to the Exit;

We prove the following result.

Theorem 2. *The optimal competitive ratio of Algorithm 2 is:*

$$\frac{2v}{v+1}\left(1+\frac{1}{v}+\frac{v^2-3v-2-\sqrt{v^4+18v^3-7v^2+4v+4}}{4v(1-v)}\right)$$

Proof. S moves in one direction with unit speed and R moves in the other direction with speed $3 \leq u_2 \leq v$. We will have the following:

$$\mathcal{E}_1 = \frac{dv+du_2+d}{v} \text{ and } \mathcal{E}_2 = \frac{3dv+du_2v+3du_2+d}{2u_2(v-1)}$$

The optimal speed u_2 is obtained by setting the evacuation time in the two cases above to be equal, namely $\mathcal{E}_2 = \mathcal{E}_1$. Thus we have the following:

$$\frac{u_2+v+1}{v} = \frac{3v^2+3u_2v+u_2v^2+v}{2u_2v(v-1)}$$

If we multiply out we will end up having the following quadratic equation in the variable u_2: $(2-2v)u_2^2 + (3v-v^2+2)u_2 + 3v^2 + v = 0$. Keeping the positive root gives:

$$u_2 = \frac{v^2-3v-2-\sqrt{v^4+18v^3-7v^2+4v+4}}{4(1-v)}$$

Thus the evacuation time will be

$$d\left(1+\frac{1}{v}+\frac{v^2-3v-2-\sqrt{v^4+18v^3-7v^2+4v+4}}{4v(1-v)}\right)$$

Using Lemma 1, it follows that the competitive ratio will be

$$\frac{2v}{v+1}\left(1+\frac{1}{v}+\frac{v^2-3v-2-\sqrt{v^4+18v^3-7v^2+4v+4}}{4v(1-v)}\right)$$

This completes the proof of Theorem 2. □

2.2 Algorithm 3: $10 < v$

In the next Algorithm 3, the sender takes the bike and uses a doubling strategy to search for the exit and moves a distance 2^k during the k-th iteration. The receiver also uses a doubling strategy but since it is moving with unit speed it will try to stay as close as possible to the biker. This can be achieved by having the receiver moves a distance $\frac{2^k}{v}$ during the kth iteration, since moving any further will cause the sender to be farther away from the receiver during the $(k+1)^{st}$ iteration.

In the third algorithm the Receiver imitates the Sender and as it will be seen in the sequel it performs better when the speed v satisfies $v > 10$. The main algorithm is as follows:

Algorithm 3. (ReceiverImitateSender)

1: **for** $k \leftarrow 1$ to ∞ **do**
2:     **if** k is odd (resp.even) **then**
3:         Sender takes the bike and moves right (resp. left) a distance 2^k unless the exit is found;
4:         Receiver moves right (resp. left) a distance $\frac{2^k}{v}$;
5:         **if** exit is found by sender **then**
6:             Communicate with receiver;
7:             Sender moves back $\frac{d}{2} - \frac{d}{2v}$ to leave the bike for the receiver and then returns to exit;
8:             Receiver continues toward the exit after picking up the bike;
9:             Quit;
10:         Sender turns; then moves left (resp. right), returns to the origin;
11:         Receiver turns; then moves left (resp. right), returns to the origin;

Theorem 3. *The competitive ratio for Algorithm 3 is* $\leq \left(\frac{2v}{v+1}\right)\left(\frac{9}{v} + \frac{1}{2} - \frac{1}{2v^2}\right)$.

Proof. In this algorithm the sender uses a doubling strategy with maximum speed v. The receiver will follow the sender but will move $\frac{2^k}{v}$ in each iteration instead of 2^k. The sender will reach the exit first then it will communicate with the receiver to proceed to the exit. The sender will go back distance $\frac{d}{2} - \frac{d}{2v}$ to drop off the bike so that the receiver can pick it up on its way to the exit. We will justify why the sender needs to move $\frac{d}{2} - \frac{d}{2v}$ after reaching the exit to leave the bike for the receiver. After the sender reaches the exit, there is no benefit to stay at the exit with the bike since the receiver which is moving with unit speed can benefit from the bike to reach the exit faster.

The key to finding the distance x which is the distance between the exit and the point where the bike is dropped off is to have the sender drop it off at a point such that when it goes back to the exit it will reach the exit at the same time as the receiver.

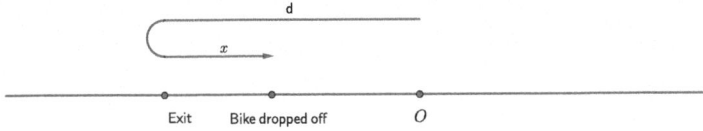

Fig. 3. Graph depicts the minimal distance x away from the origin at which the bike is dropped off by the sender and allows the receiver to take the bike and reach the exit sooner.

Based on Fig. 3, if we recall that d is the distance from the origin to the exit and x is the distance from the exit to the point where the sender drops off the bike, then we have the following:

$$d - x + \frac{x}{v} = \frac{d}{v} + \frac{x}{v} + x \implies x = \frac{d}{2} - \frac{d}{2v}$$

This will guarantee that when the sender drops off the bike at distance x, it will reach the exit at the same time as the receiver.

Assume that the exit is found during the kth iteration, then $2^{k-2} < d \leq 2^k$. We can calculate the evacuation time, denoted by $\mathcal{E}$, as follows:

$$\begin{aligned}\mathcal{E} &= \frac{2 \cdot 2^0}{v} + \frac{2 \cdot 2^1}{v} + \cdots + \frac{2 \cdot 2^{k-1}}{v} + d - x + \frac{x}{v} \\ &= \frac{2(2^k - 1)}{v} + d - x + \frac{x}{v} \\ &= \frac{2^{k+1}}{v} - \frac{2}{v} + d - \frac{d}{2} + \frac{d}{2v} + \frac{d}{2v} - \frac{d}{2v^2} \\ &= \frac{2^{k+1}}{v} - \frac{2}{v} + \frac{d}{2} + \frac{d}{v} - \frac{d}{2v^2}\end{aligned}$$

Combining similar terms above we obtain

$$\begin{aligned}\mathcal{E} &\leq 2^3 \cdot \frac{2^{k-2}}{v} - \frac{2}{v} + \frac{d}{2} + \frac{d}{v} - \frac{d}{2v^2} \\ &\leq \frac{8d}{v} - \frac{2}{v} + \frac{d}{2} + \frac{d}{v} - \frac{d}{2v^2} \\ &\leq \frac{9d}{v} + \frac{d}{2} - \frac{d}{2v^2} - \frac{2}{v} \\ &\leq \frac{9d}{v} + \frac{d}{2} - \frac{d}{2v^2}\end{aligned}$$

Thus, using Lemma 1, the resulting competitive ratio will be upper bounded by the quantity $\left(\frac{2v}{v+1}\right)\left(\frac{9}{v} + \frac{1}{2} - \frac{1}{2v^2}\right)$. This completes the proof of Theorem 3. □

2.3 Performance of the Upper Bound Algorithms

The performance of the three algorithms is compared in Fig. 4. As it can be seen in this figure, the performance of the algorithm depends on the speed v of the non-autonomous robot.

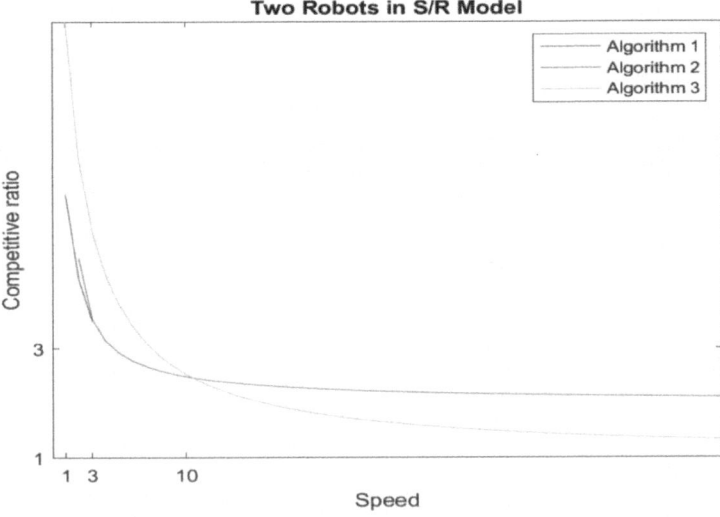

Fig. 4. Graph showing the performance of the 3 algorithms by showing how the competitive ratio fluctuates in terms of the speed. Note in the pictures above Algorithms 1 is depicted in the range $[1, 3]$ and Algorithms 2 and 3 are depicted in the range $[1, +\infty)$.

From the plots we can confirm that Algorithm 1 performs best if the speed is less than 3, while Algorithm 2 performs best if the speed is between 3 and 10. Finally, Algorithm 3 performs best if the speed is larger than 10 and in this case the competitive ratio converges to 1 as $v \to \infty$, which is also the best that could be achieved if both autonomous robots have full knowledge in that they know where the exit is.

3 Lower Bound

Finally, we prove a lower bound.

Theorem 4. *The lower bound for the competitive ratio is*

$$\begin{cases} \frac{6}{v+1} & \text{if } v \leq 3 \\ \frac{v^2+2v-3}{v^2-1} & \text{if } v > 3 \end{cases}$$

4 Conclusion

The purpose of our investigations was to study the limits of communication for robots with mixed faults. In particular, in this paper we gave evacuation algorithms and studied the upper and lower bounds for evacuation in the S/R communication model where the faults involve a sender and a receiver seeking to evacuate through an unknown exit situated on an infinite line. In particular, in Sect. 3 we presented a lower bound and in Subsect. 2.3 we presented the asymptotic behaviour of the main algorithm. However the possibility of improving the lower bound remains an open problem. An extension of the problem already analyzed could also be considered for the case of multiple (more than two) autonomous robots in a setting where the autonomous robots may suffer any of S/R, crash, and byzantine faults. One could also consider the case of multiple non-autonomous robots. The possibility of studying other search domains (geometric star graph, disk, polygon, etc.) would also be interesting.

References

1. Ahlswede, R., Wegener, I.: Search Problems. Wiley-Interscience (1987)
2. Baeza-Yates, R., Culberson, J., Rawlins, G.: Searching in the plane. Inf. Comput. **106**(2), 234–252 (1993)
3. Baeza-Yates, R., Schott, R.: Parallel searching in the plane. Comput. Geom. **5**(3), 143–154 (1995)
4. Bampas, E., et al.: Linear search by a pair of distinct-speed robots. Algorithmica **81**(1), 317–342 (2019)
5. Beck, A.: On the linear search problem. Israel J. Math. **2**(4), 221–228 (1964)
6. Bellman, R.: An optimal search. SIAM Rev. **5**(3), 274–274 (1963)
7. Bose, P., De Carufel, J.-L.: A general framework for searching on a line. Theor. Comput. Sci. **703**, 1–17 (2017)
8. Brandt, S., Laufenberg, F., Lv, Y., Stolz, D., Wattenhofer, R.: Collaboration without communication: evacuating two robots from a disk. In: Fotakis, D., Pagourtzis, A., Paschos, V.T. (eds.) CIAC 2017. LNCS, vol. 10236, pp. 104–115. Springer, Cham (2017). https://doi.org/10.1007/978-3-319-57586-5_10
9. Chrobak, M., Gasieniec, L., Gorry, T., Martin, R.: Group search on the line. In: SOFSEM, pp. 164–176. Springer, Heidelberg (2015)
10. Czyzowicz, J., Dobrev, S., Georgiou, K., Kranakis, E., MacQuarrie, F.: Evacuating two robots from multiple unknown exits in a circle. Theoret. Comput. Sci. **709**, 20–30 (2018)
11. Czyzowicz, J., et al.: Evacuation from a disc in the presence of a faulty robot. In: Das, S., Tixeuil, S. (eds.) SIROCCO 2017. LNCS, vol. 10641, pp. 158–173. Springer, Cham (2017). https://doi.org/10.1007/978-3-319-72050-0_10
12. Czyzowicz, J., Georgiou, K., Kranakis, E.: Group search and evacuation. In: Distributed Computing by Mobile Entities, pp. 335–370. Springer, Cham (2019)
13. Czyzowicz, J., et al.: Search on a line by byzantine robots. In: ISAAC, pp. 27:1–27:12 (2016)
14. Czyzowicz, J., et al.: Group evacuation on a line by agents with different communication abilities. In: ISAAC 2021, pp. 57:1–57:24 (2021)
15. Czyzowicz, J., Killick, R., Kranakis, E., Stachowiak, G.: Search and evacuation with a near majority of faulty agents. In: SIAM Conference on Applied and Computational Discrete Algorithms (ACDA 2021), pp. 217–227. SIAM (2021)
16. Czyzowicz, J., Kranakis, E., Krizanc, D., Narayanan, L., Opatrny, J.: Search on a line with faulty robots. Distrib. Comput. **32**(6), 493–504 (2019)
17. Demaine, E.D., Fekete, S.P., Gal, S.: Online searching with turn cost. Theoret. Comput. Sci. **361**(2), 342–355 (2006)

18. Georgiou, K., Giachoudis, N., Kranakis, E.: Evacuation from a disk for robots with asymmetric communication. In: 33rd International Symposium on Algorithms and Computation (ISAAC 2022). Schloss Dagstuhl-Leibniz-Zentrum für Informatik (2022)
19. Georgiou, K., Kranakis, E., Leonardos, N., Pagourtzis, A., Papaioannou, I.: Optimal circle search despite the presence of faulty robots. In: Dressler, F., Scheideler, C. (eds.) ALGOSENSORS 2019. LNCS, vol. 11931, pp. 192–205. Springer, Cham (2019). https://doi.org/10.1007/978-3-030-34405-4_11
20. Jawhar, K., Kranakis, E.: Bike assisted evacuation on a line. In: Bureš, T., et al. (eds.) SOFSEM 2021. LNCS, vol. 12607, pp. 104–118. Springer, Cham (2021). https://doi.org/10.1007/978-3-030-67731-2_8
21. Jawhar, K., Kranakis, E.: Bike assisted evacuation on a line of robots with communication faults (2024). arXiv:2307.15808
22. Stone, L.: Theory of Optimal Search. Academic Press, New York (1975)

On Permutation Selectors and their Applications in Ad-Hoc Radio Networks Protocols

Jordan Kuschner, Yugarshi Shashwat, Sarthak Yadav, and Marek Chrobak[✉]

University of California at Riverside, Riverside, USA
marek@cs.ucr.edu

Abstract. Selective families of sets, or selectors, are combinatorial tools used to "isolate" individual members of sets from some set family. Given a set X and an element $x \in X$, to isolate x from X, at least one of the sets in the selector must intersect X on exactly x. We study (k, N)-*permutation selectors* which have the property that they can isolate each element of each k-element subset of $\{0, 1, ..., N-1\}$ in each possible order. These selectors can be used in protocols for ad-hoc radio networks to more efficiently disseminate information along multiple hops. In 2004, Gasieniec, Radzik and Xin gave a construction of a (k, N)-permutation selector of size $O(k^2 \log^3 N)$. This paper improves this by providing a probabilistic construction of a (k, N)-permutation selector of size $O(k^2 \log N)$. Remarkably, this matches the asymptotic bound for standard strong (k, N)-selectors, that isolate each element of each set of size k, but with no restriction on the order. We then show that the use of our (k, N)-permutation selector improves the best running time for gossiping in ad-hoc radio networks by a poly-logarithmic factor.

1 Introduction

Selective families of sets, or selectors, are combinatorial tools used to "isolate" individual members of sets belonging to a given collection of sets. Given a set X and some element $x \in X$, to isolate x from X, at least one of the sets in the selector must intersect X on exactly x. Various types of selectors have been constructed in the literature and used in applications ranging from group testing to coding, bioinformatics, multiple-access channel protocols, and information dissemination in radio networks.

To illustrate this concept on a concrete example, consider the contention resolution problem in multiple-access channels (MACs) without feedback: N devices are connected to a shared broadcast channel (say, a radio frequency or ethernet), and each has a unique identifier from the set $U = \{0, 1, ..., N-1\}$. If exactly one device transmits in some time slot, then its message will be delivered through the channel to all other devices. However, if two or more devices transmit simultaneously, then a collision on the broadcast channel occurs. Channel collisions are indistinguishable from background noise, and the sender does not receive any feedback about the fate of its transmission.

Suppose that some unknown set of k devices initially activate and have messages to be transmitted. (See Fig. 1.) We seek a protocol that would allow these k active devices

---

Research supported by NSF grant CCF-2153723.

© The Author(s), under exclusive license to Springer Nature Switzerland AG 2025
Q. Bramas et al. (Eds.): ALGOWIN 2024, LNCS 15026, pp. 106–116, 2025.
https://doi.org/10.1007/978-3-031-74580-5_8

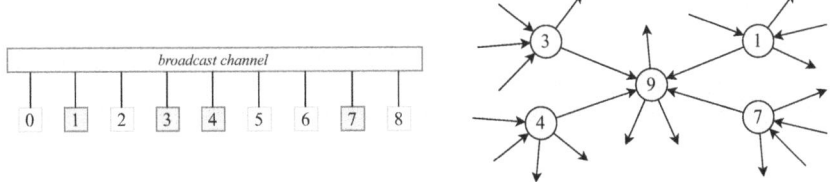

Fig. 1. On the left, an illustration of MAC contention resolution, with $N = 9$ and $k = 4$. Active devices are marked with darker colors. On the right, a node v in a radio network, with label 9 and four in-neighbors.

to transmit successfully, providing that the other devices remain idle. Without any feedback, each protocol for this model is non-adaptive, that is, it can be uniquely identified with the sequence of transmission sets $\bar{S} = S_0, S_1, ..., S_{m-1}$, where each S_t is the set of devices allowed to transmit at time slots t, if active. A trivial protocol would avoid collisions altogether by using singleton transmission sets $\{0\}, \{1\}, ..., \{N-1\}$, but this requires $m = N$ steps to complete k transmissions, which seems wasteful if k is small.

For an active device x to transmit successfully at a slot t of a transmission sequence $\bar{S}$, x must be the only active device in set S_t. Therefore $\bar{S}$ must satisfy the following property: for any set $X \subseteq U$ of cardinality k and any $x \in X$ there is $t \in \{0, 1, ..., m-1\}$ such that $S_t \cap X = \{x\}$. A family $\bar{S}$ that satisfies this condition is called a *strong (k, N)-selector*. In other words, a strong (k, N)-selector isolates each element of each subset of U of cardinality k. Optimizing the time to complete all transmissions in the above MAC model is equivalent to constructing a strong (k, N)-selector of minimum size m.

Very similar challenges arise in information dissemination protocols for ad-hoc radio networks. A radio network is a directed graph whose nodes represent radio transmitters/receivers and edges represent their transmission ranges. There are n nodes, each assigned a unique label from $U = \{0, 1, ..., N-1\}$. When a node transmits, its message is sent to all its out-neighbors; however, the possibility of collisions at the out-neighbors can result in the loss of transmitted messages. The ad-hoc property dictates that the nodes are oblivious to the network's topology at the beginning. In particular, in the scenario with a node v having k in-neighbors that attempt to transmit to v, the challenge is equivalent to the MAC contention resolution. (See Fig. 1.) A protocol that applies a strong (k, N)-selector will guarantee that in at most m steps all in-neighbors of v will successfully transmit their messages to it. This property is particularly useful in the problem of *gossiping* (full information exchange), where all nodes in the network have some information that needs to be delivered to all other nodes in the network. (The formal definition of the gossiping problem is given in Sect. 3.)

Strong (k, N)-selectors have been well studied in the literature (see the discussion at the end of this section). It is known that there are strong (k, N)-selectors of size $m = O(k^2 \log N)$, beating the earlier-mentioned trivial bound of N if k is small.

Our Contribution. We study a new type of selectors called (k, N)-*permutation selectors*. We earlier saw that a strong (k, N)-selector isolates all elements of each k-element set $X \subseteq U$. The (k, N)-permutation selector guarantees an extra property that for each possible permutation of X, it isolates all $x \in X$ in the order of this permutation.

The motivation comes from radio networks, where, unlike in the MAC contention resolution problem, a message may need to travel along a path of multiple nodes. At each node v along the path, the in-neighbors of v need to overcome contention to successfully transmit to v. Consider such a path $P = v_0 v_1 ... v_s$, and suppose that the in-neighborhood X of P (the set of nodes with edges going to P) has at most k nodes. (See Fig. 2 for illustration.) An s-fold repetition of a strong (k, N)-selector will deliver a message from v_0 to v_s in time $O(sk^2 \log N) = O(k^3 \log N)$. A (k, N)-permutation selector of size m can achieve this in time m, because it guarantees that in m steps the nodes $v_0, v_1, ..., v_{s-1}$ will successfully transmit, one by one, *in this order*.

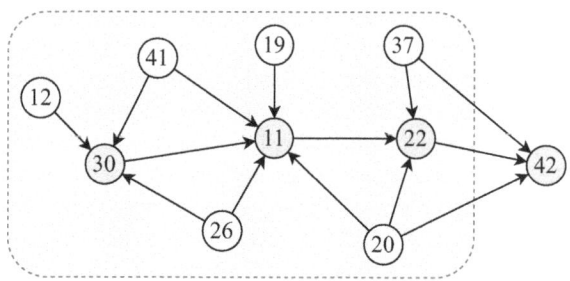

Fig. 2. An example of a path and its in-neighborhood, with nodes identified by their labels. The path is $P = 30, 11, 22, 42$ and its neighborhood (shaded) has 9 nodes.

The concept of (k, N)-permutation selectors is implicit in the work by Gasieniec, Radzik and Xin [10]. They show that a (k, N)-permutation selector can be constructed by interleaving other known types of selectors[1]. Their construction is called a *path selector* and it has size $O(k^2 \log N \log^2 k)$. Thus, assuming that N is polynomial in the network size n, a protocol based on their path selector will deliver a message along a path with in-neighborhood of size at most k in time $O(k^2 \log^3 n)$. They used this idea to give an $O(n^{4/3} \log^{10/3} n)$-time protocol for gossiping in ad-hoc radio networks. This is the best currently known upper bound for this problem.

The main result of our paper is an improved upper bound on the size of (k, N)-permutation selectors. Let $2 \leq k \leq N$. Using a probabilistic construction, we prove the following theorem in Sect. 2.

Theorem 1. *There is a (k, N)-permutation selector of size $m = O(k^2 \log N)$.*

This bound matches the best bound on strong (k, N)-selectors. This seems surprising, as (k, N)-permutation selectors offer more capability: they can isolate any k elements in any given order, while strong selectors will only do so in some unknown order. Theorem 1 leads to a poly-logarithmic improvement of the time complexity of

---

[1] We remark that in [10] the authors use a different style for specifying the parameters of selectors. The notation in our paper follows the convention from [7].

gossiping in ad-hoc radio networks. A further minor improvement can be achieved by using a faster procedure for broadcasting [6] inside the gossiping protocol. This leads to the following result:

Theorem 2. *If N is polynomial in n, then the gossiping problem in ad-hoc radio networks can be solved in time $O(n^{4/3} \log^2 n (\log \log n)^{2/3})$.*

In Sect. 4 we consider even more general structures that we named (k, q, N)-*permutation selectors*. These are defined by the following property: for each permutation of each k-element set X, the selector isolates some q-elements of X in the order of this permutation. This naturally extends the concept of (k, q, N)-selectors, which isolate q elements of a k-element set without restricting the order. (See the discussion below.) Extending the proof of Theorem 1, we show that there exists a (k, q, N)-permutation selector of size $O(kq \log N)$.

Related Work. Combinatorial structures closely related to selectors have been studied in different settings and under different terminology, with connections between these concepts not always obvious. Some of these structures are equivalent to strong (k, N)-selectors, while others are related to the concept of *weak (k, N)-selectors*, which only isolate any one element of each k-element set. Examples include superimposed codes used in information retrieval [12], cover-free set families [9], as well as protocols for non-adaptive group testing [11] and for MAC contention resolution [13]. The use of selectors in protocols for ad-hoc radio networks was initiated in [1,3], and various forms of selectors have been used in essentially all deterministic protocols for information dissemination in such networks.

One classical example of applications of selectors outside of networking is group testing, a method used in fields such as medical diagnostics, quality control, or bioinformatics. The goal in group testing is to efficiently identify individuals who test positive for a specific trait, such as a disease. Instead of testing these individuals separately, group testing works by pooling individuals into groups for collective testing. With this approach, selectors can be employed to minimize the number of required tests. For more thorough discussion of applications of selectors, see [7] and the references therein.

For strong (k, N)-selectors, the upper bound of $O(k^2 \log N)$ can be established by a problabistic construction [9,12,13]. An explicit construction matching this bound can be found in [16]. Note that such bounds are of interest only for $k = O(\sqrt{N/\log N})$, because for larger values of k a trivial construction using N singletons is better. This $O(k^2 \log N)$ bound is essentially tight, given a lower bound of $\Omega(k^2 \log^{-1} k \log N)$ (for $k = O(\sqrt{N})$) established in [2,5,8].

De Bonis et al. [7] introduced a more general model of selectors called (k, q, N)-*selectors*. A (k, q, N)-selector has the property that it can isolate at least q elements from each k-element subset of U. A strong (k, N)-selector is a special case when $q = k$, and a weak (k, N)-selector is a special case when $q = 1$. They proved that there are (k, q, N)-selectors of size $O(k^2/(k - q + 1) \log N)$.

2 Permutation Selectors

The objective in this section is to prove Theorem 1, namely to show that there is a (k, N)-permutation selector of size $m = O(k^2 \log N)$.

We start with a more formal definition of our permutation selectors. Recall that $U = \{0, 1, ..., N - 1\}$, and let $2 \le k \le N$. Consider a sequence $\bar{S} = S_0, S_1, ..., S_{m-1}$ of subsets of U. We call $\bar{S}$ a (k, N)-*permutation selector* if it has the following property:

(PS) For every $X \subseteq U$ with $|X| = k$ and for each permutation $\pi = x_1, x_2, ..., x_k$ of X, there exists an increasing sequence of indices $0 \le i_1 < i_2 < ... < i_k \le m - 1$ such that S_{i_l} isolates x_l from X for each $l = 1, 2, ..., k$.

If $\bar{S}$ satisfies this property for a set X and a permutation π, we will say that it *isolates X in order π*, or simply that $\bar{S}$ *isolates* π. Thus $\bar{S}$ is a (k, N)-permutation selector if it isolates each k-permutation of U.

The proof idea is to choose each set S_i randomly, by having each label in U, independently, add itself to S_i with probability $\frac{1}{k}$. This way, for any fixed set X of cardinality k, each S_i will isolate some element of X with probability $\gamma = (1 - 1/k)^{k-1}$, so γ is in the range $\frac{1}{e} < \gamma \le \frac{1}{2}$. (Recall that $k \ge 2$.) We then show that the probability that X is not isolated in order π is exponentially small with respect to m/k. This, using the union bound, will give us that the probability that $\bar{S}$ is *not* a (k, N)-permutation selector is less than 1 if $m = \Theta(k^2 \log N)$, with a sufficiently large constant hidden behind the big-Theta. Therefore, some sequence $\bar{S}$ of length $m = O(k^2 \log N)$ is a (k, N)-permutation selector.

We now proceed with the details. As in the first part of the proof we fix X and π, we can as well assume that $X = \{0, 1, ..., k - 1\}$ and that the desired permutation of X is $\pi = 0, 1, ..., k - 1$. Our first goal is to estimate the probability that $\bar{S}$ does not isolate X in order π.

To this end, we start by considering an auxiliary problem, which is basically a variant of coupon collection: Suppose that we generate uniformly a random sequence $\bar{r} = r_0, r_1, ..., r_{\ell-1}$ of elements of $\{0, 1, ..., k - 1\}$, where $\ell \ge k \ge 2$. We want to compute the probability $p_{\ell,k}$ of the event "$\bar{r}$ does not contain π as a subsequence". To compute $p_{\ell,k}$, we reason as follows. For a given $j \in \{0, 1, ..., k - 1\}$, if $\bar{r}$ contains $0, 1, .., j - 1$ as a sub-sequence, associate with $\bar{r}$ the unique *lexicographically-first appearance* of $0, 1, .., j - 1$, namely the increasing sequence $i_0, i_1, ..., i_{j-1}$ of positions in $\bar{r}$, where i_0 is the position of the first 0, i_1 is the first position of 1 after i_0, and so on. The number of $\bar{r}$'s that contain $0, 1, 2, ..., j - 1$ but not $0, 1, 2, ..., j$ can be computed by multiplying the number of choices, $\binom{\ell}{j}$, for the lexicographically-first appearance of $0, 1, ..., j - 1$, and the number of ways for filling the remaining $\ell - j$ positions, which is $(k - 1)^{\ell-j}$. This yields the formula for $p_{\ell,k}$, given below, for which we then derive an upper bound estimate.

$$\begin{aligned} p_{\ell,k} &= \frac{1}{k^\ell} \cdot \sum_{j=0}^{k-1} \binom{\ell}{j} (k-1)^{\ell-j} \\ &= (1 - 1/k)^\ell \cdot \sum_{j=0}^{k-1} \binom{\ell}{j} (k-1)^{-j} \\ &< e^{-\ell/k} \cdot \sum_{j=0}^{k-1} \left(\frac{\ell}{k-1}\right)^j \le e^{-\ell/k}(2\ell/k)^k, \end{aligned} \quad (1)$$

where the last step follows from $\ell/(k-1) \leq 2\ell/k$ and $\sum_{j=0}^{k-1}(2\ell/k)^j = (2\ell/k)^k/(2\ell/k - 1) \leq (2\ell/k)^k$, as $\ell \geq k$.

Next, still with X and π fixed as above, we estimate the probability that $\bar{S}$ does not isolate X in order π. Let h be the random variable representing the number of sets S_i that isolate some element of X (with repetitions counted). As stated earlier, the probability that some element of X is isolated by a given S_i is $\gamma \in (\frac{1}{e}, \frac{1}{2}]$. So h is a binomial random variable with success probability γ and mean $\mu = \gamma m$. Therefore, letting $\delta = 1 - 1/(4\gamma)$ (note that $\delta \in [\frac{1}{2}, 1 - e/4)$) and using the Chernoff bound for the lower tail of h's distribution, we get

$$\Pr[h \leq m/4] = \Pr[h \leq (1-\delta)\mu] \leq e^{-\delta^2\mu/2} = e^{-\delta^2\gamma m/2} = \alpha^m, \quad (2)$$

where $\alpha = e^{-\delta^2\gamma/2} \in (0, 1)$.

Consider now the length-h sequence consisting of elements of X (with repetitions) that are isolated by $\bar{S}$, in order in which they are isolated. For an integer $\ell \geq k$, let E_ℓ be the event that the first $\min(\ell, h)$ elements of this sequence do not contain our permutation π as a subsequence. Then $\Pr[E_\ell | h \geq \ell] = p_{\ell,k}$, so

$$\begin{aligned}
\Pr[\bar{S} \text{ does not isolate } X \text{ in order } \pi] &\leq \Pr[h \leq m/4] + \Pr[E_{m/4} | h \geq m/4] \\
&\leq \alpha^m + p_{m/4,k} \\
&\leq \alpha^m + e^{-m/4k}(m/2k)^k \\
&\leq \beta^{m/k}(m/k)^k, \quad (3)
\end{aligned}$$

for $\beta = \max(\alpha, e^{-1/4})$. (We can assume that $m \geq 2k$.) Clearly, $\beta \in (0, 1)$.

Let $m = ck^2 \log N$, for some constant c that will be specified later. To upper bound the probability that $\bar{S}$ is not a (k, N)-permutation selector, we apply the union bound. We have $\binom{N}{k}$ choices of k-element sets X, and each can be permuted in $k!$ ways. So, using the bound (3), we obtain

$$\begin{aligned}
\Pr[\bar{S} \text{ is not a } (k,N)\text{-permutation selector}] &\leq \binom{N}{k} \cdot k! \cdot [\beta^{m/k}(m/k)^k] \\
&\leq \binom{N}{k} \cdot k! \cdot \beta^{ck \log N} \cdot (ck \log N)^k \\
&\leq N^k \cdot N^k \cdot \beta^{ck \log N} \cdot c^{k \log N} \cdot N^k \cdot N^k \\
&= N^{4k} \cdot (c\beta^c)^{k \log N} < 1, \quad (4)
\end{aligned}$$

where the last inequality holds if c is large enough so that $c\beta^c < \frac{1}{16}$. This proves that for this c and $m = ck^2 \log N$ there exists a (k, N)-permutation selector $\bar{S}$ of length m.

3 Gossiping in Ad-Hoc Radio Networks

In this section we prove Theorem 2. We start by giving a formal description of the ad-hoc radio network model. The gossiping protocol we use is essentially identical to the one in [10], but we include its high-level description and sketch the analysis, for the sake of completeness.

Ad-Hoc Radio Network Model. A radio network can be naturally modeled as a directed graph $G = (V, E)$ whose nodes represent processing elements equipped with radio transmitters/receivers. Each node has a unique label from the set $U = \{0, 1, \ldots, N - 1\}$. The directed edges represent the nodes' transmission ranges, that is $(u, v) \in E$ iff v is in the range of the transmissions from u. If $(u, v) \in E$ then v is called an *out-neighbor* of u and u is an *in-neighbor* of v.

Initially, all nodes know only their own label and the upper bound N on the number of labels. They do not have any information about the network's topology. The time is discrete, divided into equal-length time steps. If a node u transmits a message, this message is sent to all its out-neighbors at the same time step. If v is one of these out-neighbors, and u is the only in-neighbor of v transmitting at this step, then v will receive u's message. But if some other in-neighbor of v transmits at the same step, a *collision* occurs. The model does not assume any collision detection capability, so u will not receive any collision notification and v will not know that u transmitted. There are no restrictions on message size or local computation.

The two most basic information dissemination primitives in this model are broadcasting and gossiping. In broadcasting (or one-to-all communication) the goal is to deliver a message from a designated *source* node to all other nodes. In gossiping (or all-to-all communication) each node starts with its own piece of information that we call a *rumor*, and the rumors from each node must be delivered to all other nodes. For these problems to be well defined, G must satisfy appropriate connectivity assumptions: in broadcasting all nodes must be reachable from the source node, and in gossiping the network must be strongly connected.

The Gossiping Protocol. We describe the protocol under the assumption that $N = n$, and later we will show how to extend it to the general case, when N is polynomial in n. With this assumption, a trivial gossiping protocol would broadcast the rumors from nodes labeled $0, 1, \ldots, n - 1$ one by one. Denoting by $B(n)$ the running time of a broadcasting protocol, this would take time $O(nB(n))$. To speed this up, the gossiping protocols in [4, 10, 14] work by grouping rumors in some nodes so that these nodes can broadcast the collected rumors in a single message.

To reduce the number of such broadcasts, the idea is to broadcast from nodes that have many rumors. We call a rumor *active* if it has not been broadcast yet, and a node is *active* if its rumor is active and *dormant* otherwise. We use procedure DISPERSE(μ), which repeatedly chooses a node with at least μ active rumors and then broadcasts from this node. Choosing such a node can be accomplished with broadcasting and binary search [4]. The number of chosen nodes will be $O(n/\mu)$, so the total running time of DISPERSE(μ) is $O((n/\mu)B(n)\log n)$.

One clever observation in [10] is that it is sufficient to give a protocol for a task called *quasi-gossiping*, where each node needs to either become dormant itself or have its rumor delivered to a dormant node. This is because a single repetition of the transmission sequence from the quasi-gossiping protocol will in fact complete full gossiping. The pseudo-code for the quasi-gossiping protocol is given in Algorithm 1. It uses a parameter κ whose value will be determined later.

The correctness of Protocol QUASIGOSSIP is justified by focussing on *active paths*, which are paths consisting only of active nodes. For any active path, define its *active in-*

Algorithm 1. QUASIGOSSIP

1: **for** $v = 0, 1, ..., n - 1$ **do**
2:     transmit from node v
3: DISPERSE(κ)
4: **repeat** $\log \kappa + 1$ **times**
5:     the active nodes transmit according to a (κ, n)-permutation selector
6:     DISPERSE($\kappa/2$)
---

neighborhood to be the set of active in-neighbors of the nodes on this path. Let ℓ be the largest number such that each active path with ℓ nodes has its active in-neighborhood size (strictly) smaller than κ. After the execution of DISPERSE(κ) in Line 3, each node will be left with fewer than κ active in-neighbors, so at this point we have $\ell \geq 1$. Each iteration of the **repeat** loop at least doubles the value of ℓ. Since all nodes (except possibly the last) on an active path belong to the active in-neighborhood, the value of ℓ cannot exceed κ. So after $\log \kappa$ iterations there cannot be any active paths left of length at least κ, and then the last iteration will complete the quasi-gossiping task.

In line 5 we use the (κ, n)-permutation selector from Theorem 1, so the total cost of these selectors will be $O(\kappa^2 \log^2 n)$. The cost of all calls to DISPERSE() is $O((n/\kappa + \log n)B(n) \log n)$. Thus the overall running time of Protocol QUASIGOSSIP is asymptotically bounded by:

$$(n/\kappa + \log n)B(n) \log n + \kappa^2 \log^2 n$$

Letting $\kappa = (nB(n)/\log n)^{1/3}$, and using the bound $B(n) = O(n \log n \log\log n)$ from [6,15] on the complexity of broadcasting, we obtain a gossiping protocol with running time $O(n^{4/3} \log^2 n (\log\log n)^{2/3})$.

To extend Protocol QUASIGOSSIP to the case when N is polynomial in n, we first replace n by N in all invocations of selectors. After this, the only problematic part of Protocol QUASIGOSSIP is the **for** loop in Lines 1–2 that reduces the active in-neighborhoods of the individual nodes. Instead of this loop, the protocol in [10] uses $(s, s/4, N)$-selectors for geometrically decreasing values of s, combined with operations DISPERSE($s/4$), to gradually reduce these in-neighborhoods. (This is similar to the method in [13].) The running time of this process amortizes to $O((n/\kappa)B(n) \log n)$—same time as for the case of small labels. So the overall running time also remains the same, completing the proof of Theorem 2.

4 (k, q, N)-Permutation Selectors

In Sect. 2 we defined (N, k)-permutation selectors, a family of sets that isolates all elements of any k-permutation π of the label set $U = \{0, 1, \ldots, N-1\}$, meaning that all elements in π are isolated in their listed order in π.

We now generalize this concept analogously to the way (k, q, N)-selectors generalize standard selectors, by requiring that some q elements of each k-permutation π are isolated in the order of π. Formally, let $\bar{S} = S_0, S_1, \ldots, S_{m-1}$ be a sequence of subsets of U. $\bar{S}$ is called a (k, q, N)-*permutation selector* if the following property holds:

(PS') For each $X \subseteq U$ with $|X| = k$, and for each permutation $\pi = x_1, x_2, ..., x_k$ of X, there are increasing sequences of indices $0 \leq i_1 < i_2 < ... < i_q \leq m - 1$ and $d_1 < d_2 < ... < d_q$ such that, for all $l = 1, 2, ..., q$, set S_{i_l} isolates x_{d_l} from X.

This section provides a probabilistic construction of a (k, q, N)-permutation selector, proving the following theorem. Let $2 \leq k \leq N$ and $1 \leq q \leq k$.

Theorem 3. *There exists a (k, q, N)-permutation selector $\bar{S} = S_0, S_1, \cdots, S_{m-1}$ of size $m = O(kq \log N)$.*

Proof. As in the proof of Theorem 1, we use a probabilistic argument. The construction is the same: for each $j = 0, 1, ..., m-1$, we let S_j be a random subset of U obtained by each element $x \in U$ adding itself to S_j, independently, with probability $\frac{1}{k}$. We then need to prove that if c is a sufficiently large constant and $m = c \cdot qk \log N$, then

$$\Pr[\bar{S} \text{ is not a } (k, q, N)\text{-permutation selector}] < 1. \tag{5}$$

The proof's high-level strategy is the same as in the proof of Theorem 1. We use the Chernoff bound to reduce the problem to a version of the coupon collection problem. We consider the following variant of the coupon collection problem: For a random sequence $\bar{r} = r_0, r_1, ..., r_{\ell-1}$ of coupons from $\{0, 1, ..., k - 1\}$, where $\ell \geq k \geq 2$, let $p'_{\ell,k,q}$ be the probability of the event "$\bar{r}$ does not contain an increasing subsequence of length q". To show (5), it is sufficient to prove that

$$p'_{\ell,k,q} \leq \gamma^{\ell/q}(2\ell/q)^q, \tag{6}$$

for some constant $\gamma \in (0, 1)$. Indeed, this is analogous to (1). We can then use the Chernoff-based bound (2), to obtain a bound of $\delta^{m/q}(m/q)^q$, for some $0 < \delta < 1$, on the probability that $\bar{S}$ does not isolate q elements of π in order, analogously to (3). For the union-bound estimate, we then take $m = ckq \log N$, with large enough c. Since then $\delta^{m/q}(m/q)^q = \delta^{ck \log N}(ck \log N)^q \leq \delta^{ck \log N}(ck \log N)^k$, the derivation for the union bound (4) will be essentially the same, with δ instead of β.

It remains to estimate $p'_{\ell,k,q}$. We reason as follows. First, to avoid clutter in the calculations below, we will assume that q is a divisor of k. (If it is not, the values of k/q in the calculations below need to be rounded up or down. This does not affect our asymptotic estimate.)

We now consider a special type of increasing sub-sequences that we refer to as *q-jump sub-sequences*. Partition the set of coupons $\{0, 1, ..., k - 1\}$ into q equal size blocks $B_0, B_1, ..., B_{q-1}$, each having k/q consecutive coupons. That is, the h-th block is $B_h = \left\{h\frac{k}{q}, h\frac{k}{q} + 1, ..., (h+1)\frac{k}{q} - 1\right\}$, for $h = 0, 1, ..., q - 1$. For $j \leq q$, a jump sub-sequence is a sequence of j coupons $a_0, a_1, ..., a_{j-1}$ such that $a_h \in B_h$ for each $h = 0, ..., j - 1$.

Define now $p''_{\ell,k,q}$ to be the probability of the event "$\bar{r}$ does not contain a jump sub-sequence of length q". Since $p''_{\ell,k,q} \geq p'_{\ell,k,q}$, it is sufficient to prove that the same inequality (6) holds for $p''_{\ell,k,q}$ instead of $p'_{\ell,k,q}$. We do this by refining the argument in the proof of Theorem 1. For a given $j \in \{0, 1, ..., q - 1\}$, if $\bar{r}$ contains a length-j jump sub-sequence then associate with $\bar{r}$ the unique *lexicographically-first appearance* of a length-j jump sub-sequence. The number of $\bar{r}$'s that contain a length-j jump sub-sequence but not a length-$(j+1)$ jump sub-sequence can be obtained by choosing the lexicographically first length-j jump sub-sequence in $\binom{\ell}{j} \cdot (k/q)^j$ ways and multiplying it by the number of ways of filling the remaining $\ell - j$ positions, which is $(k - k/q)^{\ell-j}$. We thus have

$$\begin{aligned} p'_{\ell,k,q} \leq p''_{\ell,k,q} &= \frac{1}{k^\ell} \sum_{j=0}^{q-1} \binom{\ell}{j} \cdot (k/q)^j \cdot (k - k/q)^{\ell-j} \\ &= (1 - 1/q)^\ell \sum_{j=0}^{q-1} \binom{\ell}{j} (q-1)^{-j} \\ &\leq (1 - 1/q)^\ell \sum_{j=0}^{q-1} (2\ell/q)^j \\ &\leq e^{-\ell/q} (2\ell/q)^q. \end{aligned}$$

This proves (6) (with $\gamma = 1/e$), completing the proof.

For $q = k$, the bound in Theorem 3 matches the bound from Theorem 1 and the best bound for strong (k, N)-selectors. For $q = 1$, it also matches the $O(k \log N)$ bound for weak (k, N)-selectors. We are not sure about the optimum size of (k, q, N)-permutation selectors for intermediate values of q. The case when $q = \sqrt{k}$ is particularly interesting. From the bound in [7], $(k, \sqrt{k}, N)$-selectors have size $O(k \log N)$. Can some probabilistic construction produce a $(k, \sqrt{k}, N)$-permutation selector of size $m = \tilde{O}(k)$? For such m, a random sequence of coupons from $\{0, 1, ..., k-1\}$ can be thought of as a "noisy" permutation. We would need to show that the probability that this random sequence does not contain an increasing sub-sequence of length $\sqrt{k}$ is exponentially small. This question is closely related to Ulam's Problem about the distribution of the longest increasing subsequence (LIS) in a random permutation. Ulam's Problem has been extensively studied, and it is known that for permutations of $0, 1, ..., k-1$ the expected length of LIS is $2\sqrt{k} + O(k^{1/6})$. (See [17], for example.) To our knowledge, however, the published concentration bounds are not sufficient for refining the probabilistic construction in the proof of Theorem 3 to yield a better bound.

References

1. Basagni, S., Bruschi, D., Chlamtac, I.: A mobility-transparent deterministic broadcast mechanism for ad hoc networks. IEEE/ACM Trans. Networking **7**(6), 799–807 (1999)
2. Chaudhuri, S., Radhakrishnan, J.: Deterministic restrictions in circuit complexity. In: Proceedings of the Twenty-Eighth Annual ACM Symposium on Theory of Computing, STOC 1996, pp. 30–36. Association for Computing Machinery, New York (1996)
3. Chlebus, B.S., Gasieniec, L., Gibbons, A., Pelc, A., Rytter, W.: Deterministic broadcasting in ad hoc radio networks. Distrib. Comput. **15**(1), 27–38 (2002)
4. Chrobak, M., Gasieniec, L., Rytter, W.: Fast broadcasting and gossiping in radio networks. J. Algorithms **43**(2), 177–189 (2002)

5. Clementi, A.E.F., Monti, A., Silvestri, R.: Distributed broadcast in radio networks of unknown topology. Theor. Comput. Sci. **302**(1–3), 337–364 (2003)
6. Czumaj, A., Davies, P.: Faster deterministic communication in radio networks. In: Proceedings of 43rd International Colloquium on Automata, Languages, and Programming (ICALP 2016), pp. 139:1–139:14 (2016)
7. De Bonis, A., Gąsieniec, L., Vaccaro, U.: Generalized framework for selectors with applications in optimal group testing. In: Baeten, J.C.M., Lenstra, J.K., Parrow, J., Woeginger, G.J. (eds.) ICALP 2003. LNCS, vol. 2719, pp. 81–96. Springer, Heidelberg (2003). https://doi.org/10.1007/3-540-45061-0_8
8. D'yachkov, A., Rykov, V.: Bounds on the length of disjunctive codes. Probl. Inf. Transm. **18**, 7 (1982)
9. Erdös, P., Frankl, P., Füredi, Z.: Families of finite sets in which no set is covered by the union of r others. Israel J. Math. **51**(1–2), 79–89 (1985)
10. Gasieniec, L., Radzik, T., Xin, Q.: Faster deterministic gossiping in directed ad hoc radio networks. In: Proceedings of Scandinavian Workshop on Algorithm Theory (SWAT 2004), pp. 397–407 (2004)
11. Hwang, F.K., Sos, V.T.: Non-adaptive hypergeometric group testing. Studia Scientiarum Mathematicarum Hungarica **22**, 257–263 (1987)
12. Kautz, W.H., Singleton, R.C.: Nonrandom binary superimposed codes. IEEE Trans. Inf. Theory **10**(4), 363–377 (1964)
13. Komlos, J., Greenberg, A.: An asymptotically fast nonadaptive algorithm for conflict resolution in multiple-access channels. IEEE Trans. Inf. Theory **31**(2), 302–306 (1985)
14. Liu, D., Prabhakaran, M.: On randomized broadcasting and gossiping in radio networks. In: Proceedings of 8th Annual International Conference on Computing and Combinatorics (COCOON 2002), pp. 340–349 (2002)
15. De Marco, G.: Distributed broadcast in unknown radio networks. SIAM J. Comput. **39**(6), 2162–2175 (2010)
16. Porat, E., Rothschild, A.: Explicit nonadaptive combinatorial group testing schemes. IEEE Trans. Inf. Theory **57**(12), 7982–7989 (2011)
17. Romik, D.: The Surprising Mathematics of Longest Increasing Subsequences. Cambridge University Press (2014)

Reconfigurable Routing in Data Center Networks

David C. Kutner[✉][iD] and Iain A. Stewart[iD]

Department of Computer Science, Durham University, Upper Mountjoy Campus, Stockton Road, Durham DH1 3LE, UK
{david.c.kutner,i.a.stewart}@durham.ac.uk

Abstract. A hybrid network is a static (electronic) network that is augmented with optical switches. The Reconfigurable Routing Problem (RRP) in hybrid networks is the problem of finding settings for the optical switches augmenting a static network so as to achieve optimal delivery of some given workload. The problem has previously been studied in various scenarios with both tractability and NP-hardness results obtained. However, the data center and interconnection networks to which the problem is most relevant are almost always such that the static network is highly structured (and often node-symmetric) whereas all previous results assume that the static network can be arbitrary (which makes existing computational hardness results less technologically relevant and also easier to obtain). In this paper, and for the first time, we prove various intractability results for RRP where the underlying static network is highly structured, for example consisting of a hypercube, and also extend some existing tractability results.

Keywords: algorithms · complexity · reconfigurable topologies · optical circuit switches · software-defined networking

1 Introduction

The rapid growth of cloud computing applications has induced demand for new technologies to optimize the performance of data center networks dealing with ever-larger workloads. The data center topology design problem (that of finding efficient data center topologies) has been studied extensively and resulted in myriad designs (see, e.g., [5]). Advances in hardware, such as optical switches reconfigurable in milli- to micro-seconds, have enabled the development of reconfigurable topologies (see, e.g., [14]). These topologies can adjust in response to demand (*demand-aware* reconfigurable topologies) or vary configurations over time according to a fixed protocol (*demand-oblivious* reconfigurable topologies; see, e.g., [2]). So-called *hybrid* data center networks are a combination of a static topology consisting of, for example, electrical switches, and a demand-aware reconfigurable topology implemented, for example, with optical circuit switches or free space optics (see, e.g., [4,11,15,19]). An intuitive example of a simple reconfigurable topology is illustrated in Fig. 1.

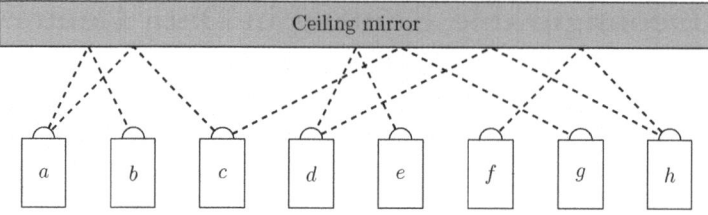

Servers with top-of-rack steerable free-space optics.

Fig. 1. Basic model of an optical wireless data-center network, as described in [4,15,19]. Practical timescales for reconfiguration vary from milliseconds [15] to microseconds or nanoseconds [4,19].

The hybrid network paradigm combines the robustness guarantees of static networks with the ability of demand-aware reconfigurable networks to serve large workloads at very low cost. Consider, for example, the hybrid network shown in Fig. 2, and the configuration shown in Fig. 3. In the (unaugmented) static network, there are two possible paths along which a message from node b to node d may be routed: $b \to f \to h \to e \to d$ or $b \to f \to e \to d$. In the hybrid network as configured in Fig. 3, the path $b \dashrightarrow a \to c \dashrightarrow d$ (among others) is an option[1].

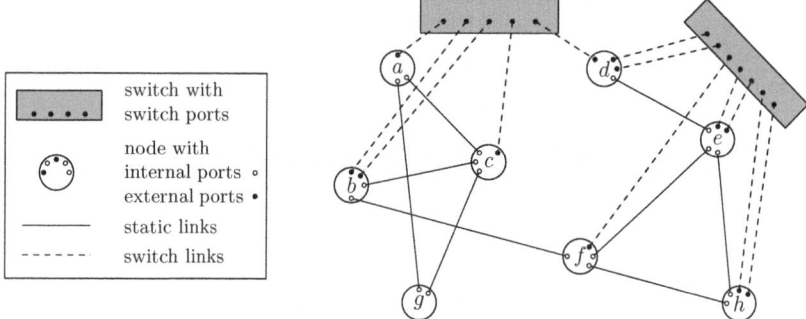

Fig. 2. A hybrid network.

Of particular interest to us is the question of how the reconfigurable (optical) portion of the network should be configured for some demand pattern, formalized by Foerster, Ghobadi and Schmid [9] as the RECONFIGURABLE ROUTING PROBLEM (RRP): in short, given a hybrid network (consisting of a static network and of some switches) and a workload, we wish to choose a *configuration* (setting of the switches) which results in an optimal delivery of the workload.

Crucially, existing hardness results are only valid when the static network is allowed to be arbitrary, which is almost never the case in practice where interconnection and data center network design is driven by symmetry, high connectivity,

---

[1] We denote by $u \dashrightarrow v$ the concatenation of a switch link from u to some switch, of the internal switch connection, and of a switch link to v from that switch.

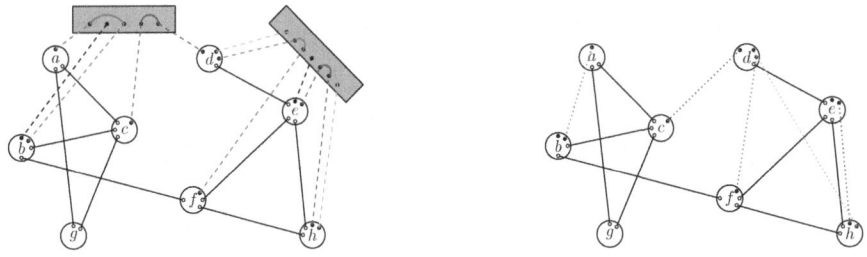

Fig. 3. An augmented network and its abstracted dynamic links.

recursive decomposition, and so forth. For example: the popular switch-centric data center network Fat-Tree [1] is derived from a folded Clos network; the server-centric data center network DCell [13] is recursively-structured whereby at each level, a graph-theoretic matching of servers is imposed; and the server-centric data center network BCube [12] is recursively-structured with a construction based around a generalized hypercube. (It should be noted that there do exist examples of unstructured data center networks, such as Jellyfish [17] and Xpander [18] which utilize the theory of random graphs.) Many (but not all) NP-complete problems become tractable when the input is restricted to the graphs providing the communications fabric for data center networks and other interconnection networks. For example, Hamiltonian paths are often trivial to find in many interconnection networks; indeed, no finite connected vertex-transitive graph *without* a Hamiltonian path is known to exist (the Lovász Conjecture contends there is no such graph - see Section 4 of [16]). This motivates our investigation into how the complexity of RRP changes when we restrict to more structured and realistic networks. The question of the complexity of RRP for specific network topologies was specifically identified as an area for future work in [8].

In this paper, we establish for the first time hardness results for RRP that apply to various specific families of highly structured static networks such as, for example, the hypercubes. Our constructions are (perhaps not surprisingly) of a much more involved nature than has hitherto been the case.

2 Problem Setting

The decision problem RECONFIGURABLE ROUTING PROBLEM considered in this paper is a proper restriction of that presented in prior work [8–10]. In this section, we provide technical detail to fully formalize our version of the problem, but also additionally provide sufficient framing to briefly review existing results and to identify the areas strengthened by our contribution.

We adopt the usual terminology of graph theory though we tend to use 'nodes' and 'links' when speaking about the components of reconfigurable networks and 'nodes' and 'edges' when dealing with (abstract) graphs. We denote the natural numbers by $\mathbb{N}$ (we include $0 \in \mathbb{N}$) and the non-negative rationals by $\mathbb{Q}_+$.

2.1 Hybrid Networks, (Re)configurations and (Segregated) Routing

A hybrid network $G(S)$ can be visualized as in Fig. 2, and consists of a static network G and some switches S augmenting it. A *static network* G can be abstracted as an undirected graph $G = (V, E)$ so that each *static link* $(u, v) \in E$ has some fixed *weight* $w \in \mathbb{Q}_+$ (reflecting a transmission cost) and is incident with *internal ports* of two distinct nodes of V. The number of internal ports of some node $v \in V$ is then exactly the degree of v in the abstracted graph G. We denote by S a set of *switches* augmenting the static network G with *switch links* joining *switch ports* of some switch to *external ports* of some of the nodes of V. Every switch link has weight 0 (we say more about switch link weights momentarily). Every switch $s \in S$ has at least two switch ports.

In general, the number of external ports of the nodes of a static network $G = (V, E)$ is variable, as is the number of switch ports of the switches of a hybrid network $G(S)$, and it may be the case that there is more than one switch link between a specific node and a specific switch. We assume that the switch links describe a bijection between the external ports and the switch ports; otherwise, there would be some unused ports, which we can safely ignore.

Given a hybrid network $G(S)$ and a switch $s \in S$, a *switch matching* N_s of s is a set of pairs of switch ports of s so that all switch ports involved are distinct. Each switch matching represents an internal setting of the switch and naturally yields a set of pairs of external ports of nodes where all such ports are distinct; we refer to a set of pairs of external ports obtained in this way as a *node matching* (note that this differs from the standard graph-theoretic notion of a matching). An illustration of a configured hybrid network is shown in Fig. 3: on the right side, switch matchings are represented as sets of arcs, and on the left side the corresponding node matching is shown as a set of dotted lines.

A *configuration* N is a set of switch matchings, one for each switch. A configuration straightforwardly encodes the corresponding node matchings. We say that (u, v) is a *dynamic link* in the configuration N (we sometimes write $(u, v) \in N$) if (u, v) appears in any node matching corresponding to N.

We allocate a fixed weight $\mu \in \mathbb{Q}_+$ to each internal port-to-port connection in a switch s. Although a dynamic link is an atomic entity, it can be visualized as consisting of a switch link followed by an internal port-to-port connection in s followed by another switch link. We denote by $G(N)$ the static network G augmented with the dynamic links (each of weight μ) resulting from the configuration N and we call $G(N)$ an *augmented network*. In the augmented network visualized in Fig. 3, for example: (a, b) is a dynamic link; (a, c) is a static link; and (e, h) is both a static link a dynamic link. Note that it is possible that an augmented network $G(N)$ is a multigraph.

The concepts defined above are driven by reconfigurable hardware technology such as optical switches, wireless (beamforming) and free-space optics, all of which establish port-to-port connections, i.e., switch matchings. The survey paper [11] provides some detail as regards the relationship between the emergent theoretical models and current opto-electronic technology.

2.2 Routing in Hybrid Networks

Consider again the example shown in Fig. 3. In the configuration shown, a message M from c to node e may be routed:

1. via static links only, along the path $\varphi_1 := c \to b \to f \to e$ with weight $3w$, or
2. via dynamic links only, along the path $\varphi_2 := c \dashrightarrow d \dashrightarrow h \dashrightarrow e$ with weight 3μ, or
3. via a combination of static and dynamic links, along the path $\varphi_3 := c \dashrightarrow d \to e$ with weight $\mu + w$.

Depending on the value of μ, any of the paths may minimize the cost to route M: if $\mu \geq 2w$ then φ_1 is optimal; if $\mu \leq \frac{w}{2}$ then φ_2 is optimal; and if $\mu \in [\frac{w}{2}, 2w]$ then φ_3 is an optimal. We may wish to bound the number of alternations allowed between optic and static links in any path a message takes; we capture this hardware requirement via a *segregation parameter* $\sigma \in \mathbb{N} \cup \{\infty\}$, as introduced in [10], that is the number of alternations between static and dynamic links. In the fully segregated case, $\sigma = 0$: messages may be routed either by static links only (as in φ_1) or by dynamic links only (as in φ_2). In the non-segregated case, $\sigma = \infty$ and there is no restriction on the number of alternations, so any path is admitted. Note φ_3 is admitted as a valid path to route M if and only if $\sigma \geq 1$.

Networks are expected to route many messages (of varying sizes) optimally at the same time. Given a hybrid network $G(S)$ we represent the set of all demands we must optimize for as a *workload (matrix)* D with entries $\{D[u,v] \in \mathbb{Q}_+ : u,v \in V\}$ providing the intended pairwise *node-to-node workloads* (each $D[u,u]$ is necessarily 0).

Given a configuration N and $u,v \in V$ for which $D[u,v] > 0$, we route the corresponding workload via a path in $G(N)$ from u to v in $G(N)$ so that this chosen *flow-path* $\varphi(u,v)$ has *workload cost* $D[u,v] \times wt_{G(N)}(\varphi(u,v))$, where the weight $wt_{G(N)}(\varphi(u,v))$ is the sum of the weights of the links of the flow-path $\varphi(u,v)$ (if $G(N)$ has both a static link (x,y) and a dynamic link (x,y) then we need to say which we are using in $\varphi(u,v)$). The *total workload cost* (of D under N) is defined as

$$\sum_{u,v \in V, D[u,v]>0} D[u,v] \times wt_{G(N)}(\varphi(u,v)).$$

Our aim will be to find a configuration N in some hybrid network $G(S)$ and flow-paths in $G(N)$ for which the total workload cost of some workload matrix D is minimized. In an unrestricted scenario, we would choose any flow-path $\varphi(u,v)$ to be a flow-path of minimum weight from u to v in $G(N)$, the weight of which we denote by $wt_{G(N)}(u,v)$. When $\sigma \neq \infty$ we must also ensure the flow-path has at most σ alternations. We also have the analogous concepts $wt_G(\varphi(u,v))$ and $wt_G(u,v)$ where we work entirely in the static network G. Note that we often describe D by a weighted digraph, which we usually call D', so that the node set is V and there is an edge (u,v) of weight $w > 0$ if, and only if, $D[u,v] = w$. We also refer to some $D[u,v] > 0$ as a *demand* (from u to v).

2.3 The Reconfigurable Routing Problem

We are now in a position to introduce our protagonist:

RECONFIGURABLE ROUTING PROBLEM (σ) (RRP(σ))
Input: $(G, S, \mu, w, D, \kappa)$: D is a workload matrix for the hybrid network $G(S)$ with static (resp. dynamic) links all of weight w (resp. μ).
Question: Does $G(S)$ admit some configuration N such that the total workload cost of D under N (where the number of alternations for any path is bounded by σ) is at most κ?

As previously alluded to, this setting is more expressive than we require for most of this paper, and more restrictive than the exact formalism considered in prior work [8–10]: in those works, w and μ are sometimes allowed to be functions of their endpoints rather than fixed constants. This provides much more expressivity; notably, their model loses no power when it is restricted to inputs where G is a complete graph and there is only one switch, since it is possible to simulate any other instance by assigning prohibitively large weights to any static edges and any pair of switch ports which should not be usable.

We now turn to the "realistic" networks we mentioned in our introduction. Henceforth unless otherwise specified, static link weights are all equal (and normalized to 1) and dynamic link weights are always some fixed constant $\mu \in \mathbb{Q}_+$. Also, there is a single switch and all nodes are connected to it with identical hardware. This is both practically relevant and intuitively realistic; see e.g. Figure 1. Then the set of switches S of the hybrid network consists of just one switch, which is fully described by the number of switch links each node in the hybrid network has, which we call Δ_S. This is closely related to the maximum reconfigurable degree Δ_R from [10], which is an upper bound on the number of external ports per node. The resulting restriction of RRP can be formalized as follows:

Δ_S-SWITCHED RRP (σ)
Input: (G, μ, D, κ): D is a workload matrix for the hybrid network $G(S)$ with static (resp. dynamic) links all have weight 1 (resp. μ) (where S consists of a single switch that every node in G is connected to exactly Δ_S times).
Question: Does $G(S)$ admit some configuration N such that the total workload cost of D under N (where the number of alternations for any path is bounded by σ) is at most κ?

---

3 Results

Table 1 shows a summary of hardness results from previous work as well as our three main intractability results. In general terms, we obtain NP-completeness

Table 1. Settings for some pre-existing hardness results for RRP. $|S|$ is the number of switches; Δ_R is the maximum number of external ports per node; σ is the segregation parameter; D is the workload matrix; n denotes the number of nodes in the instance.

Result	$|S|$	Δ_R	σ	D	link weights	notes
[8], Theorem 1	$\Theta(n)$ (or 1 †)	$\Theta(n)$	any $\sigma \geq 2$	sparse, all values 0 or 1	variable; $w \in [1, 100n^2]$ $\mu \in [1, 100n^2]$	Showed inapprox. within $\Omega(\log n)$
[9], Lemma 1	$\Theta(n)$		1		fixed; $w = \mu = 1$	All switches have 3 ports.
[9], Theorem 2						G has $\Theta(n)$ components
[10], Theorems 4.1, 4.2				dense, values in poly(n)		G is empty; there are no static links
Theorem 1		1	2	any $\sigma \geq 0$		fixed; $w = 1$ $\mu \in \Theta(\frac{1}{\text{poly}(n)})$	$G \in \mathcal{H}$, where $\mathcal{H}$ is any polynomial family of networks (incl. hypercubes, grids, cycles).
Theorem 2			3		sparse, values in poly(n)	fixed; $w = 1$ $\mu \in \Theta(\frac{1}{\log(n)})$	
Theorem 4			1	$\sigma = 3$		fixed; $w = 1$ any $\mu \in (0, 1)$	G is a hypercube

† By using variable μ with prohibitively large weights, it is possible to simulate many switches with just one.

for 2-SWITCHED RRP and 3-SWITCHED RRP on any fixed class of static networks of practical interest (defined more fully below) and for any value of σ. We then restrict our focus (and associated parameters) to the case where the static network is a hypercube when we establish the NP-completeness of 1-SWITCHED RRP$(\sigma = 3)$ in this setting; we conjecture that a similar construction can be used to establish hardness when $\sigma > 3$. We also, in Theorem 3, show that 1-SWITCHED RRP$(\sigma = 0)$ is solvable in polynomial time. The cases when $\sigma \in \{1, 2\}$ remain interesting open problems.

As is standard in NP-hardness proofs, we reduce from known NP-complete problems to instances of RRP; the challenge is that, due to the expansive scope of our theorems, we lose several "degrees of freedom" which are used for encoding hard instances in, e.g., [7–9]. Specifically, we may not make use of varying static or dynamic link weights to prohibit certain connections, nor encode any features of the input instance in the topology of the hybrid network $G(S)$. For example, in Lemma 1 [9], many small switches with two feasible configurations each are used to encode a truth assignment, and in Theorem 1 of [8] "bad" links are given weights of order $\Theta(n^2)$. Neither of these mechanisms can be leveraged to obtain hardness in our setting; in this sense, our hardness results are strictly stronger and also harder to obtain than those from [7–9]. We are constrained to choose a *size* for the network G, and then to encode the input instance in the demand matrix D.

Our first two results hold for a wide class of graph families, which may be of broader interest for the study of computational hardness in network problems. Rather than allowing arbitrary static networks in instances of RRP, we wish to force any such static network to come from a fixed family of networks where a *family of networks* $\mathcal{H}$ is an infinite sequence of networks $\{H_i : i \geq 0\}$ so that the size $|H_i|$ of any H_i is less than the size of H_{i+1}. However, we wish to control the sequence of network sizes. Consequently, we define a *polynomial family of networks* as being a family of networks $\mathcal{H} = \{H_i : i \geq 0\}$ where there exists a polynomial $p_\mathcal{H}(x)$ so that $|H_{i+1}| = p_\mathcal{H}(|H_i|)$, for each $i \geq 0$[2]. Note that given any $n \geq 0$, we can determine in time polynomial in n the smallest i such that $n \leq |H_i|$. As an example of a polynomial family of networks, consider the hypercubes; here, the polynomial $p_\mathcal{H}(x) = 2x$. Other examples include independent sets, complete graphs, cycles, complete binary trees and square grids, among many others. The sweeping generality of having a single construction which holds for any polynomial family $\mathcal{H}$ poses a challenge in our proofs of Theorems 1 and 2; we require that our constructed network $H(S)$ behaves identically when H is a connected (or even complete) graph and, at the opposite extreme, when H is disconnected (or even independent). For reasons of length, full proofs are deferred to the full version of this paper; we provide our construction for Theorem 1 in full, along with a sketch of the proof.

Theorem 1. *For any polynomial family of networks* $\mathcal{H} = \{H_i : i \geq 0\}$, *the problem* 2-SWITCHED RRP *restricted to instances* (H, μ, D, κ) *satisfying:*

- $H \in \mathcal{H}$ *has size* n
- *the workload matrix D is sparse and all values in it are polynomial in n*
- $\mu \in \Theta(\frac{1}{n})$ *is fixed for all dynamic links*

is NP-complete.

Proof. 2-SWITCHED RRP is straightforwardly in **NP** as a subproblem of RRP. We describe a polynomial-time reduction from the problem 3-MIN-BISECTION, which is known to be **NP**-complete [3] and is defined as follows:

3-MIN-BISECTION
Input: $(G = (V, E), k)$: G is a 3-regular graph on n vertices and $k \in \mathbb{N}$.
Question: Is there a partition of V into two disjoint subsets A and B, of equal size, so that the set of edges incident with both a node in A and a node in B has size at most k? Or: does G have *bisection width* at most k?

---

[2] Technically, we insist that there exists a polynomial Turing machine $\mathcal{M}$ which computes H_{i+1} on input H_i, for each $i \geq 0$, but this definition obfuscates the utility of this description.

Note that any 3-regular graph necessarily has an even number of nodes, and that we may assume that $k \leq \frac{n}{3} + 46$ as it was proven in [6] that every 3-regular graph has bisection width at most $\frac{n}{3} + 46$. Given an arbitrary instance $(G = (V, E), k)$ of size n of 3-MIN-BISECTION, we now build our instance (H, μ, D, κ).

We describe our workload matrix D via the weighted digraph $D' = (V', E')$, which has a directed edge (u, v) with weight w if, and only if, there is a node-to-node workload of w from u to v. Let $\bar{n}$ be the size of the network H_i where i is the smallest integer such that $n + 6n^2 + 2 \leq |H_i|$ and set $H = H_i$.

The node set V' is taken as a disjoint copy of the node set V of G, which we also refer to as V, together with the set of nodes $V_c = \{x_i, y_i : -\frac{L}{2} \leq i \leq \frac{L}{2}\}$, where $L = 3n^2$ (recall, n is even), and another set of nodes U of size $\bar{n} - (n + 6n^2 + 2)$; so, $|V'| = \bar{n}$. We call every node of V_c a *chain-node*. For ease of presentation, we denote the chain-nodes $x_{\frac{L}{2}}$ and $x_{-\frac{L}{2}}$ by x^+ and x^-, respectively, and we define the chain-nodes y^+ and y^- analogously. The (directed) edge set E' consists of $E_\alpha \cup E_\beta \cup E_1$ where:

- the set of *chain-edges* $E_\alpha = \{(x_i, x_{i+1}), (y_i, y_{i+1}) : 0 \leq i < \frac{L}{2}\} \cup \{(x_i, x_{i-1}), (y_i, y_{i-1}) : -\frac{L}{2} < i \leq 0\}$
- the set of *star-edges* $E_\beta = \{(x_0, v) : v \in V\} \cup \{(y_0, v) : v \in V\}$
- the set of *unit-edges* E_1 which is a copy of the edges E of G, but on our (copied) node set V and so that every edge is replaced by a directed edge of arbitrary orientation.

Note that the nodes of U are all isolated in D' and that $|V'| = \bar{n}$ (the nodes of U will play no role in the following construction). The workloads on the edges of E' are α, β or 1 depending upon whether the edge is a chain-edge from E_α, a star-edge from E_β or a unit-edge from E_1, respectively, where we define $\alpha = 24n^6$ and $\beta = 6n^3$. If the directed edge (u, v) has weight α (resp. β, 1) in D' then we say that (u, v) is an α-demand (resp. β-demand, 1-demand). The digraph D' can be visualized as in Fig. 4.

As stated earlier, our static network H is the network $H_i \in \mathcal{H}$ where $|H_i| = \bar{n}$. We refer to the node set of H as V' also and we refer to the subset of nodes within V' corresponding to V as V also. Since we are in the 2-switched setting, we have one switch s with $2|V'|$ ports so that every node of H is adjacent, via switch links, to exactly two ports of the switch. Hence, our switch set is $S = \{s\}$ and our hybrid network is $H(S)$. It is important to note that for any configuration N, any node of $H(N)$ can be adjacent to at most 2 other nodes via dynamic links (as $\Delta_S = 2$).

As can be seen, we have the graph $G = (V, E)$, the digraph $D' = (V', E')$ and the hybrid network $H(S)$ with node set V'. Although G, D' and $H(S)$ are disjoint in terms of node sets, we do not distinguish between, say, the node set V of G and the subset of nodes V of H.

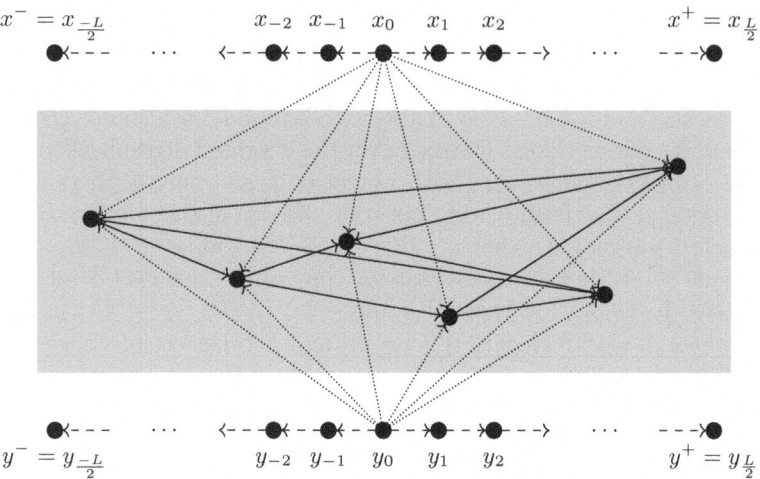

Fig. 4. The digraph D'. The nodes of V are in the grey rectangle, the nodes of V_c appear along the top and the bottom and the dashed (resp. dotted, solid) directed edges depict the chain-edges (resp. star-edges, unit-edges). The nodes of U are omitted.

We set the weight of any dynamic link as $\mu = \frac{1}{2L} = \frac{1}{6n^2}$ and the bound κ for the total workload cost as $\kappa = \kappa_\alpha + \kappa_\beta + \kappa_1$ where:

- $\kappa_\alpha = 24n^6$
- $\kappa_\beta = 3n^4 + \frac{n^3}{2} + n^2$
- $\kappa_1 = \frac{k}{2} + \frac{1}{8} - \frac{1}{4n} + \frac{k}{3n^2}$.

The values of κ_α, κ_β and κ_1 have the following significance.

- Suppose that for every chain-edge (u, v) of E_α, N contains the dynamic link joining u and v in $H(N)$ and the α-demand (u, v) is routed by the flow-path $u \dashrightarrow v$. Then the total workload cost of flow-paths serving α-demands is $2L\alpha\mu = 24n^6 = \kappa_\alpha$.
- Further, suppose that the dynamic links incident with nodes of V in $H(N)$ are chosen so that we have a path of dynamic links p_A from x^+ to either y^- or y^+, involving the subset of nodes $A \subseteq V$, and a path of dynamic links p_B from x^- to y^+ or y^-, respectively, involving the subset of nodes $B \subseteq V$, so that both p_A and p_B have length $\frac{n}{2} + 1$. That is, we choose the dynamic links so that they form a cycle C (of length $n + 2L + 2$) in $H(N)$ covering exactly the nodes of V and V_c. Suppose that for any star-edge (x_0, v) (resp. (y_0, v)) of E_β, we choose the flow-path in $H(N)$ serving this star-edge as consisting entirely of dynamic links resulting from the shortest path in our cycle C from x_0 to v (resp. y_0 to v). The total workload cost of flow-paths corresponding to the star-edges is

$$4\mu\beta \sum_{i=1}^{\frac{n}{2}} (\frac{L}{2} + i) = 3n^4 + \frac{n^3}{2} + n^2 = \kappa_\beta.$$

- Further, suppose we choose the flow-path in $H(N)$ serving the 1-demand (u, v) (in E_1) to be a path of dynamic links within the cycle C of shortest length. If u and v both lie on p_A or both lie on p_B then the workload cost of this flow-path is at most $\mu(\frac{n}{2} - 1) = \frac{1}{6n}(\frac{1}{2} - \frac{1}{n})$, and if one of u and v lies on p_A with the other node lying on p_B then the workload cost of this flow-path is at most $\mu(\frac{n}{2} + L + 1) = \frac{1}{2} + \frac{1}{12n} + \frac{1}{6n^2}$. If the width of the bisection of G formed by A and B is at most k then the total workload cost of flow-paths corresponding to the unit-edges is at most

$$(\frac{3n}{2} - k)\mu(\frac{n}{2} - 1) + k\mu(\frac{n}{2} + L + 1) = \frac{k}{2} + \frac{1}{8} - \frac{1}{4n} + \frac{k}{3n^2} = \kappa_1.$$

From above, we immediately obtain that if (G, k) is a yes-instance of 3-MIN-BISECTION then (H, μ, D, κ) is a yes-instance of 2-SWITCHED RRP.

It remains to show that if (H, μ, D, κ) is a yes-instance of 2-SWITCHED RRP, then (G, k) is a yes-instance of 3-MIN-BISECTION; this is much more technical. For reasons of length, we provide only a flavor of the full proof here. Our first step is to show that all chain-edges are realized as dynamic links (i.e. $E_\alpha \subseteq N$, abusing notation slightly), then that the set of dynamic links N forms a cycle C covering exactly the nodes of $V \cup V_c$. From there, we obtain that deleting V_c from C produces two paths on exactly $\frac{n}{2}$ nodes, and hence encodes a bisection A, B of G (the function of the β-demands is to force $|A| = |B|$). Lastly, applying our choice of κ_1 we obtain that there are at most k edges in G between A and B. So, if (H, μ, D, κ) is a yes-instance of 2-SWITCHED RRP then (G, k) is a yes-instance of 3-MIN-BISECTION. Our result follows as (H, μ, D, κ) can be constructed from (G, k) in time polynomial in n. □

This result significantly strengthens Theorems 4.1 and 4.2 from [10]: there, RRP($\Delta_R \geq 2, \sigma = 0$) is shown to be NP-complete when the static network is an independent set, and the proof does not enable us to restrict the workload matrix D meaningfully. The main weakness of Theorem 1 is its reliance on μ being a polynomial factor smaller than any static link weight. This is actually related to the fact that a connected 2-regular network, as is $G(N)$ when G is an independent set and $\Delta_S = 2$, has diameter linear in the number of nodes n. A network of maximum degree 3, on the other hand, may have diameter logarithmic in n (e.g., a complete binary tree has this property) and we indeed show NP-completeness of RRP($\Delta_S = 3$) when $\mu = \Theta(\frac{1}{\log n})$.

Theorem 2. *For any polynomial family of networks $\mathcal{H} = \{H_i : i \geq 0\}$, the problem 3-SWITCHED RRP restricted to instances (H, μ, D, κ) satisfying:*

- *$H \in \mathcal{H}$ has size n*
- *the workload matrix D is sparse and all values in it are polynomial in n*
- *$\mu \in \Theta(\frac{1}{\log(n)})$*

is NP-complete.

These results led us to consider the problem 2-SWITCHED RRP($\sigma = k$) for $k \geq 0$. By extending Theorem 3.1 from [10] (which establishes tractability in the case where $\sigma = 0$ and only paths using at most one dynamic link are admitted), we show that this restriction entails tractability when either $\sigma = 0$ or the static network is a complete graph, in contrast with our NP-completeness results.

Theorem 3. 1-SWITCHED RRP($\sigma = 0$) *is in* **P**.

Proof. Since each node is connected to the switch exactly once, no vertex is incident to two dynamic links under any configuration N, and hence no flow-path consists of two or more dynamic links. That is, the constraint on the number of dynamic links per flow-path is implicit in this setting, and tractability follows from Theorem 3.1 from [10]. □

Corollary 1. 1-SWITCHED RRP($\sigma = k$) *restricted to instances where the static network G is a complete graph is in* **P**, *for any* $k \in \mathbb{N} \cup \{\infty\}$.

Proof. If G is a complete graph (with all edge weights equal) then without loss under any configuration N, each demand $D[u,v]$ is routed via the flow-path $\varphi(u,v)$ of minimum weight, which is either a single static link from u to v with unit weight, or a single dynamic link from u to v with weight μ. It follows that setting $\sigma = 0$ introduces no new constraints, and then by Theorem 3 we have tractability. □

Corollary 1 rules out the possibility that 1-SWITCHED RRP might be NP-complete for any polynomial graph family $\mathcal{H}$ (since such a claim would extend to the family of complete graphs) unless **P** equals **NP**. This leaves open the practically relevant case where $\Delta_S = 1$ and $\sigma > 0$ for *specific* topologies. We consequently consider the scenario where the static network is a hypercube and the segregation parameter $\sigma = 3$.

Theorem 4. *For any fixed* $\mu \in (0,1)$, *the problem* 1-SWITCHED RRP*($\sigma = 3$) restricted to instances* (H, μ, D, κ) *satisfying:*

– $H \in \mathcal{Q}$, *where* $\mathcal{Q} := \{Q_d | d \in \mathbb{N}\}$ *is the family of hypercubes*
– *the workload matrix D is sparse and all values in it are polynomial in* n

is NP-complete.

We emphasize the relevance of the hypercube as a prototypical model of interconnection networks (see, e.g., [12]) and the fact that we obtain hardness here for any choice of fixed dynamic link weight μ.

4 Discussion and Future Work

Taken together, our results comprehensively establish the computational hardness of RRP in practically relevant settings. We establish that the problem remains intractable in several cases where the demand matrix is sparse, the hybrid network is highly structured (in fact node-symmetric) and the weights of links depend only on their medium. Furthermore, in Theorems 1, 2, and 4, the instrument used to "express" NP-completeness is the demand matrix D. In the real world, the computational workload for the network is generally expected to vary significantly with time, unlike the network's hardware, which (in addition to its structural properties already discussed) does not rapidly change. Our results are in this sense closely relevant to the hardness of the real world reconfigurable routing problem.

We take this opportunity to identify some specific questions we have left open, as well as several more general avenues for future work in this area. First, it would be interesting to study the restriction of the problem to cases where Δ_S is greater than 1 and μ is a fixed constant. Results in this setting would "bridge the gap" between Theorems 1 and 2, and Theorem 4. Analogously, there is a gap for 1-SWITCHED RRP on hypercubes between $\sigma = 0$ (which is solvable in polynomial time) and $\sigma = 3$ (which is an intractable case). The complexity of the problem with $\sigma = 1$ and $\sigma = 2$ remains open for hypercubes (note that results for arbitrary networks do exist when $\sigma = 2$, as shown in Table 1).

Secondly, the present work considers only exact computation. In [8] the authors establish inapproximability within $\Omega(\log n)$ for RRP in a more permissive setting (making use of variable link weights). However, the empty solution (there are no dynamic links and all demands are routed through the static network only) is a $\frac{\log n}{\mu}$-approximation for Δ_S-SWITCHED RRP on hypercubes. (This follows straightforwardly from hypercubes having logarithmic diameter.) It would be interesting to see what (in)approximability results can be derived in our model with fixed link weights, with and without restrictions to realistic topologies.

Lastly, parameterized algorithms may provide more fine-grained insights into the computational complexity of reconfigurable routing. Our Theorems 1 and 2 establish that structural parameters of the static network, such as treewidth, are insufficient to yield fixed-parameter tractable (fpt) algorithms (unless P=NP). However, it would be interesting to see whether it is possible to obtain an fpt algorithm by additionally parameterizing by the sum of the demand matrix D; some structural parameters for the digraph representation of the demands, D'; the dynamic link weight μ; or a combination of these.

References

1. Al-Fares, M., Loukissas, A., Vahdat, A.: A scalable, commodity data center network architecture. ACM SIGCOMM Comput. Commun. Rev. **38**, 63–74 (2008)
2. Avin, C., Schmid, S.: Toward demand-aware networking: a theory for self-adjusting networks. ACM SIGCOMM Comput. Commun. Rev. **48**, 31–40 (2019)
3. Berman, P., Karpinski, M.: Approximation hardness of bounded degree MIN-CSP and MIN-BISECTION. In: Proceedings of 29th International Colloquium on Automata, Languages and Programming (ICALP), pp. 623–632 (2002)
4. Chaintoutis, C., et al.: Free space intra-datacenter interconnects based on 2D optical beam steering enabled by photonic integrated circuits. Photonics **5**(3) (2018)

5. Chen, T., Gao, X., Guihai, C.: The features, hardware, and architectures of data center networks: a survey. J. Parallel Distrib. Comput. **96**, 45–74 (2016)
6. Clark, L.H., Entringer, R.C.: The bisection width of cubic graphs. Bull. Austral. Math. Soc. 389–396 (1988)
7. Fenz, T., Foerster, K.-T., Schmid, S., Villedieu, A.: Efficient non-segregated routing for reconfigurable demand-aware networks. In: Proceedings of IFIP Networking Conference, pp. 1–9. IEEE Press (2019)
8. Fenz, T., Foerster, K.-T., Schmid, S., Villedieu, A.: Efficient non-segregated routing for reconfigurable demand-aware networks. Comput. Commun. **164**, 138–147 (2020)
9. Foerster, K.-T., Ghobadi, M., Schmid, S.: Characterizing the algorithmic complexity of reconfigurable data center architectures. In: Proceedings of Symposium on Architectures for Networking and Communications Systems (ANCS), pp. 89–96. ACM Press (2018)
10. Foerster, K.-T., Pacut, M., Schmid, S.: On the complexity of non-segregated routing in reconfigurable data center architectures. ACM SIGCOMM Comput. Commun. Rev. **49**, 2–81 (2019)
11. Foerster, K.-T., Schmid, S.: Survey of reconfigurable data center networks: enablers, algorithms, complexity. ACM SIGACT News **50**, 62–79 (2019)
12. Guo, C., et al.: BCube: a high performance, server-centric network architecture for modular data centers. ACM SIGCOMM Comput. Commun. Rev. **39**, 63–74 (2009)
13. Guo, C., Wu, H., Tan, K., Shi, L., Zhang, Y., Lu, S.: DCell: a scalable and fault-tolerant network structure for data centers. In: Proceedings of ACM SIGCOMM Conference on Data Communication, pp. 75–86 (2008)
14. Hall, M.N., Foerster, K.-T., Schmid, S., Durairajan, R.: A survey of reconfigurable optical networks. Opt. Switch. Netw. **41**, 100621 (2021)
15. Hamedazimi, N., et al.: Firefly: a reconfigurable wireless data center fabric using free-space optics. In: Proceedings of the 2014 ACM Conference on SIGCOMM, SIGCOMM 2014, pp. 319–330. Association for Computing Machinery, New York (2014)
16. Pak, I., Radoičić, R.: Hamiltonian paths in cayley graphs. Discret. Math. **309**(17), 5501–5508 (2009). Generalisations of de Bruijn Cycles and Gray Codes/Graph Asymmetries/Hamiltonicity Problem for Vertex-Transitive (Cayley) Graphs
17. Singla, A., Hong, C.Y., Popa, L., Godfrey, P.B.: Jellyfish: networking data centers randomly. In: Proceedings of 9th USENIX Conference on Networked Systems Design and Implementation, pp. 225–238 (2012)
18. Valadarsky, A., Shahaf, G., Dinitz, M., Schapira, M.: Xpander: towards optimal-performance datacenters. In: Proceedings of 12th International Conference on Emerging Networking Experiments and Technologies, pp. 205–219 (2016)
19. Zhang, S., Xue, X., Tangdiongga, E., Calabretta, N.: Low-latency optical wireless data-center networks using nanoseconds semiconductor-based wavelength selectors and arrayed waveguide grating router. Photonics **9**(3) (2022)

The Threshold of Existence of δ-Temporal Cliques in Random Simple Temporal Graphs

George B. Mertzios[1](✉), Sotiris Nikoletseas[2], Christoforos Raptopoulos[3], and Paul G. Spirakis[4]

[1] Department of Computer Science, Durham University, Durham, UK
george.mertzios@durham.ac.uk
[2] Computer Engineering and Informatics Department, University of Patras, Patras, Greece
nikole@cti.gr
[3] Department of Mathematics, University of Patras, Patras, Greece
raptopox@upatras.gr
[4] Department of Computer Science, University of Liverpool, Liverpool, UK
p.spirakis@liverpool.ac.uk

Abstract. We consider random simple temporal graphs in which every edge of the complete graph K_n appears once within the time interval $[0,1]$ independently and uniformly at random. Our main result is a sharp threshold on the size of any maximum δ-clique (namely a clique with edges appearing at most δ apart within $[0,1]$) in random instances of this model, for any constant δ. In particular, using the probabilistic method, we prove that the size of a maximum δ-clique is approximately $\frac{2\log n}{\log \frac{1}{\delta}}$ with high probability (whp). We note that, even though the random simple temporal graph contains $\Theta(n^2)$ overlapping δ-windows, which (when viewed separately) correspond to different random instances of the Erdős-Rényi random graphs model, the size of the maximum δ-clique in the former model and the maximum clique size of the latter are approximately the same. Furthermore, we show that the minimum interval containing a δ-clique is $\delta - o(\delta)$ whp. We use this result to show that any polynomial time algorithm for δ-TEMPORAL CLIQUE is unlikely to have very large probability of success.

Keywords: Simple random temporal graph · δ-temporal clique · probabilistic method

---

G. B. Mertzios—Supported by the EPSRC grant EP/P020372/1.
C. Raptopoulos—Supported by the Hellenic Foundation for Research and Innovation (H.F.R.I.) under the "2nd Call for H.F.R.I. Research Projects to support Post-Doctoral Researchers" (Project Number: 704).
P. G. Spirakis—Supported by the EPSRC grant EP/P02002X/1.

1 Introduction

Dynamic network analysis, i.e. analysis of networks that change over time, is currently one of the most active topics of research in network science and theory. Many modern real-life networks are dynamic in nature, in the sense that the network structure undergoes discrete changes over time [21,25,27]. Here we deal with the discrete-time dynamicity of the network links (edges) over a fixed set of nodes (vertices), according to which edges appear in discrete times and are absent otherwise. This concept of dynamic network evolution is given by *temporal graphs* [18,22], which are also known by other names such as *evolving graphs* [5,13], or *time-varying graphs* [1].

Definition 1 (Temporal Graph). *A temporal graph is a pair* $\mathcal{G} = (G, \lambda)$, *where* $G = (V, E)$ *is an underlying (static) graph and* $\lambda : E \to 2^{\mathbb{N}}$ *is a time-labeling* function *which assigns to every edge of G a set of discrete-time labels. Whenever* $|\lambda(e)| \leq 1$ *for every* $e \in E$, $\mathcal{G}$ *is called a* simple *temporal graph.*

Our focus is on *simple* temporal graphs (in which edges appear only once), as, due to their conceptual simplicity, they offer a fundamental model for temporal graphs and they prove to be good prototypes for studying temporal computational problems. More specifically, we consider simple temporal graphs whose edge labels are chosen *uniformly at random* from a very large set of possible labels (e.g. the label of each edge is chosen uniformly at random within $[1, N]$ where $N \to \infty$). This can be equivalently modeled by choosing the time labels uniformly at random as real numbers in the interval $[0, 1]$, which leads to the following definition.

Definition 2 (Random Simple Temporal Graph). *A random simple temporal graph is a pair* $\mathcal{G} = (G, \lambda)$, *where* $G = (V, E)$ *is an underlying (static) graph and* $\{\lambda(e) : e \in E\}$ *is a set of independent random variables uniformly distributed within* $[0, 1]$.

Note that, in Definition 2, the probability that two edges lave equal labels is zero. For every $v \in V$ and every time slot t, we denote the *appearance of vertex v at time t* by the pair (v, t). For $Q \subseteq V$, the *restricted temporal graph* $(G, \lambda)|_Q$ is the temporal graph $(G[Q], \{\lambda(e) : e \in E(G[Q])\})$.

In the seminal paper of Casteigts, Raskin, Renken, and Zamaraev [9], the authors consider a related (essentially equivalent to ours) model of random simple temporal graphs based on random permutation of edges. They provide a thorough study of the temporal connectivity of such graphs and they provide sharp thresholds for temporal reachability. Their work motivated our research in this paper.

In many applications of temporal graphs, information can naturally only move along edges in a way that respects the ordering of their timestamps (i.e. time labels). That is, information can only flow along sequences of edges whose time labels are increasing (or non-decreasing). Motivated by this fact, most studies on temporal graphs have focused on "path-related" problems, such as e.g. temporal analogues of distance, diameter, reachability, exploration, and centrality [2,3,8,9,11,12,16,19,20,22,26,30]. In these problems, the most fundamental notion is that of a *temporal path* from a vertex u to a vertex v, which is a path from u to v such that the time labels of the edges are increasing (or at least non-decreasing) in the direction from u to v. To complement this direction, several attempts have been recently made to define meaningful "non-path" temporal graph problems which appropriately model specific applications. Some examples include temporal cliques, cluster editing, temporal vertex cover, temporal graph coloring, temporally transitive orientations of temporal graphs [4,6,10,14,15,17,23,24,28,29].

What is common to most of the path-related problems is that their extension from static to temporal graphs often follows easily and quite naturally from their static counterparts. For example, requiring a graph to be (temporally) connected results in requiring the existence of a (temporal) path among each pair of vertices. In the case of non-path related problems, the exact definition and its application is not so straightforward. For example, defining cliques in a temporal graph as the set of vertices that interact at least once in the lifetime of the graph would be a bit counter intuitive, as two vertices may just interact at the first time step and never again. To help with this problem, Viard et al. [28] introduced the idea of the *sliding time window* of some size δ, where they define a temporal clique as a set of vertices where in all δ consecutive time steps each pair of vertices interacts at least once. There is a natural motivation for this problem, namely to be able to find the contact patterns among high-school students. Following the idea of Viard et al. [28], many other problems on temporal graph were defined using sliding time windows. For an overview of recent works on sliding windows in temporal graphs, see [21].

In the next definition we introduce the notion of a δ-*temporal clique* in a random simple temporal graph, and the corresponding maximization problem.

Definition 3 (δ-TEMPORAL CLIQUE). *Let (G, λ) be a random simple temporal graph with n vertices, let $\delta \in [0, 1]$, and let $Q \subseteq V$ be a subset of vertices such that $G[Q]$ is a clique. The restricted temporal graph $(G, \lambda)|_Q$ is a δ-temporal clique, if $|\lambda(e) - \lambda(e')| \leq \delta$, for every two edges e, e' which have both their endpoints in Q.*

δ-TEMPORAL CLIQUE
Input: A simple temporal graph (G, λ).
Output: A δ-temporal clique Q of (G, λ) with maximum cardinality $|Q|$.

Our Contribution. In this paper, we consider simple random temporal graphs where the underlying (static) graph is the complete graph on n vertices, and we provide a sharp threshold on the size of maximum δ-cliques in random instances of this model, for any constant δ. In particular, using the probabilistic method, we prove that the size of a maximum δ-clique is approximately $\frac{2 \log n}{\log \frac{1}{\delta}}$ whp (Theorem 2). We note that, even though the random simple temporal graph contains

$\Theta(n^2)$ overlapping δ-windows, which (when viewed separately) correspond to different random instances of the Erdős-Rényi model $\mathcal{G}_{n,\delta}$ (in which edges appear independently with probability δ), the size of the maximum δ-clique and the maximum clique size of the latter are approximately the same [7]. Furthermore, we show that the minimum interval containing a δ-clique is $\delta - o(\delta)$ whp (Theorem 3). We use this result to show that any polynomial time algorithm for δ-TEMPORAL CLIQUE is unlikely to have very large probability of success (Theorem 4). Finally, we discuss some open problems related to the average case hardness of δ-TEMPORAL CLIQUE in the general case.

2 Existence of δ-TEMPORAL CLIQUE

We begin with a Lemma regarding the joint density function of the minimum and maximum label.

Lemma 1. *Let (G, λ) be a random simple temporal graph, where the underlying graph has $m = |E(G)| \geq 2$ edges. Let also $X \stackrel{def}{=} \min\{\lambda(e) : e \in E\}$ and $Y \stackrel{def}{=} \max\{\lambda(e) : e \in E\}$. Then the joint density function of X, Y is given by*

$$f_{X,Y}(x,y) = \begin{cases} m(m-1)(y-x)^{m-2}, & 0 \leq x \leq y \leq 1 \\ 0 & otherwise. \end{cases} \quad (1)$$

Proof. For $0 \leq x \leq y \leq 1$, we have that $\Pr(X \geq x, Y \leq y) = (y-x)^m$. Therefore, for any $0 \leq x \leq y \leq 1$, we have

$$f_{X,Y}(x,y) = -\frac{\partial^2 \Pr(X \geq x, Y \leq y)}{\partial x \partial y}$$
$$= -\frac{\partial^2 (y-x)^m}{\partial x \partial y} = m(m-1)(y-x)^{m-2}.$$

□

Similarly, we can prove the following:

Lemma 2. *Let (G, λ) be a random simple temporal graph. Let also $X \stackrel{def}{=} \min\{\lambda(e) : e \in E\}$. Then the density function of X is given by*

$$f_X(x) = m(1-x)^{m-1}, 0 \leq x \leq 1. \quad (2)$$

We now prove the following auxiliary Lemma, which gives an exact formula for the probability that a graph H appears as a subgraph within a δ-window.

Lemma 3. *Let (G, λ) be a random simple temporal graph. Let also $H = (V(H), E(H))$ be a (not necessarily induced) subgraph of G, with $h = |E(H)|$ edges. For any $\delta \in [0, 1]$, we have*

$$\Pr\left(|\lambda(e) - \lambda(e')| \leq \delta, \forall e, e' \in E(H)\right) = h\delta^{h-1}(1-\delta) + \delta^h. \quad (3)$$

Proof. We assume that $h > 0$ (since the case $h = 0$ is trivially handled), and fix $e_0 \in E(H)$. For any $\delta \in [0,1]$, we have

$$\Pr(|\lambda(e) - \lambda(e')| \leq \delta, \forall e, e' \in E(H), \text{ and } \lambda(e_0) < \lambda(e), \forall e \in E(H) \backslash e_0)$$

$$= \int_0^1 \Pr(\lambda(e) \in (x, \min\{x+\delta, 1\}], \forall e \in E(H) \backslash e_0 | \lambda(e_0) = x) \, dx$$

$$= \int_0^{1-\delta} \Pr(\lambda(e) \in (x, x+\delta], \forall e \in E(H) \backslash e_0 | \lambda(e_0) = x) \, dx$$

$$+ \int_{1-\delta}^1 \Pr(\lambda(e) \in (x, 1], \forall e \in E(H) \backslash e_0 | \lambda(e_0) = x) \, dx$$

$$= \int_0^{1-\delta} \delta^{h-1} dx + \int_{1-\delta}^1 (1-x)^{h-1} dx$$

$$= \delta^{h-1}(1-\delta) + \frac{1}{h}\delta^h.$$

The proof is completed by taking the union over all $e_0 \in E(H)$. $\square$

The following Theorem is a direct consequence of Lemma 3 (for $h = \binom{k}{2}$) and linearity of expectation.

Theorem 1. *Let (K_n, λ) be a random simple temporal graph where the underlying graph is the complete graph with n vertices. For any $\delta \in [0,1]$, and $k \in [n]$, the expected number of δ-temporal cliques of size k in (K_n, λ) is*

$$\binom{n}{k}\left(\binom{k}{2}\delta^{\binom{k}{2}-1}(1-\delta) + \delta^{\binom{k}{2}}\right).$$

By simple calculations and Theorem 1, we get the following:

Lemma 4 (First moment). *Let (K_n, λ) be a random simple temporal graph where the underlying graph is the complete graph with n vertices, and let $\delta \in (0,1)$ be a constant. For any integer $k \in [n]$, let $X^{(k)}$ denote the number of δ-temporal cliques of size k in (K_n, λ). Define $k_0 \stackrel{\text{def}}{=} \frac{2 \log n}{\log \frac{1}{\delta}}$. For any constant $\epsilon > 0$ that can be arbitrarily small, we have*

(i) $\mathbb{E}[X^{((1+\epsilon)k_0)}] \to 0$, *and*
(ii) $\mathbb{E}[X^{((1-\epsilon)k_0)}] \to \infty$,

as $n \to \infty$.

Proof. By Theorem 1, for any $\delta \in [0,1)$, the expected number of δ-temporal cliques of size k in (K_n, λ) is

$$\mathbb{E}[X^{(k)}] = \binom{n}{k}\left(\binom{k}{2}\delta^{\binom{k}{2}-1}(1-\delta) + \delta^{\binom{k}{2}}\right)$$

$$\leq \binom{n}{k}\binom{k}{2}\delta^{\binom{k}{2}-1} \leq \left(\frac{ne}{k}\right)^k k^2 \delta^{\binom{k}{2}-1}$$

$$= \exp\left\{k \ln n - \frac{k^2}{2}\ln\frac{1}{\delta} - \Theta(k \ln k)\right\}. \tag{4}$$

In particular, for any $k \geq (1+\epsilon)k_0$, by definition of k_0, the above exponent is at most $k\left(\ln n - (1+\epsilon)k_0 \frac{\ln\frac{1}{\delta}}{2}\right) = -\epsilon k \ln n$, which implies that the RHS of (4) goes to 0, for any $k \geq (1+\epsilon)k_0$, as $n \to \infty$. This proves part (i).

For part (ii), we note that similar calculations leading to (4) can also be used to prove the following lower bound (except for a different constant hidden in the Θ term in the exponent):

$$\mathbb{E}[X^{(k)}] \geq \left(\frac{n}{k}\right)^k \left(\frac{k}{2}\right)^2 \delta^{\binom{k}{2}-1}(1-\delta) = \exp\left\{k\ln n - \frac{k^2}{2}\ln\frac{1}{\delta} - \Theta(k\ln k)\right\}. \tag{5}$$

In particular, for any $k \leq (1-\epsilon)k_0$, the above exponent is at least $k\left(\ln n - (1-\epsilon)k_0\frac{\ln\frac{1}{\delta}}{2} - \Theta(\ln k_0)\right) = k(\epsilon\ln n - \Theta(\ln\ln n))$, by definition of k_0, which implies that the RHS of (5) goes to ∞, for any $k \leq (1-\epsilon)k_0$, as $n \to \infty$. □

The following lemma concerns the variance of the number of δ-temporal cliques.

Lemma 5 (Second moment). *Let (K_n, λ) be a random simple temporal graph where the underlying graph is the complete graph with n vertices, and let $\delta \in (0,1)$ be a constant. For any integer $k \in [n]$, let $X^{(k)}$ denote the number of δ-temporal cliques of size k in (K_n, λ). Define $k_0 \stackrel{\text{def}}{=} \frac{2\log n}{\log\frac{1}{\delta}}$. For any constant $\epsilon > 0$ that can be arbitrarily small, we have $\frac{\mathbb{E}\left[\left(X^{(k)}\right)^2\right]}{\mathbb{E}^2[X^{(k)}]} \to 1$, for any $k \leq (1-\epsilon)k_0$, as $n \to \infty$.*

Proof. Set $k = (1-\epsilon)k_0$, and note that, by part (ii) of Lemma 4, we have $\mathbb{E}[X^{(k)}] = \omega(1)$. Let $S_1, S_2, \ldots, S_{\binom{n}{k}}$ be an arbitrary enumeration of all cliques of size k in K_n. For any $i \in \{1, 2, \ldots, \binom{n}{k}\}$, denote by X_i the indicator random variable that is equal to 1 if S_i is a δ-temporal clique in (K_n, λ) and 0 otherwise. In particular, we have $X^{(k)} = \sum_{i=1}^{\binom{n}{k}} X_i$ and so $\left(X^{(k)}\right)^2 = \sum_{i,j} X_i X_j$. Taking expectations we get

$$\mathbb{E}\left[\left(X^{(k)}\right)^2\right] = \sum_{i,j} \mathbb{E}[X_i X_j]$$

$$= \sum_{t=0}^{k} \sum_{i,j:|S_i \cap S_j|=t} \mathbb{E}[X_i X_j]$$

$$= \sum_{t=0}^{k} \sum_{i,j:|S_i \cap S_j|=t} \mathbb{E}[X_i]\mathbb{E}[X_j | X_i = 1] \tag{6}$$

Observe that, by independence, the terms in the above sum corresponding to $t = 0$ are equal to $\sum_{i,j:|S_i \cap S_j|=\emptyset} \mathbb{E}[X_i]\mathbb{E}[X_j] = \binom{n}{k}\binom{n-k}{k}\left(\binom{k}{2}\delta^{\binom{k}{2}-1}(1-\delta) + \delta^{\binom{k}{2}}\right)^2$, where in the last equation we applied Lemma 3 with $h = \binom{k}{2}$. In particular, we have

$$\frac{\sum_{i,j:|S_i \cap S_j|=0} \mathbb{E}[X_i]\mathbb{E}[X_j]}{\mathbb{E}^2\left[X^{(k)}\right]} = \frac{\binom{n-k}{k}}{\binom{n}{k}} = \frac{(n-k)\cdots(n-2k+1)}{n\cdots(n-k+1)}$$
$$= \left(1 - \frac{k}{n}\right)\cdots\left(1 - \frac{k}{n-k+1}\right) = 1 - o(1), \quad (7)$$

where the last equation follows from the fact $k = o(n)$. Furthermore, it is easy to see that the terms in the sum of the RHS of (6) corresponding to $t = k$ is equal to $\mathbb{E}[X^{(k)}] = o(\mathbb{E}^2[X^{(k)}])$, since $k = (1-\epsilon)k_0$ and so $\mathbb{E}[X^{(k)}]$ goes to ∞ as $n \to \infty$. Therefore, by (6) and (7),

$$\frac{\mathbb{E}\left[\left(X^{(k)}\right)^2\right]}{\mathbb{E}^2\left[X^{(k)}\right]} = 1 + o(1) + \frac{\sum_{t=1}^{k-1}\sum_{i,j:|S_i \cap S_j|=t} \mathbb{E}[X_i]\mathbb{E}[X_j | X_i = 1]}{\mathbb{E}^2\left[X^{(k)}\right]}. \quad (8)$$

In view of the above, in what follows we will show that the sum in the RHS of the above equation is $o(1)$, which will prove the theorem. To this end, notice that $\mathbb{E}[X_j | X_i = 1]$ is equal to the probability that S_j is a δ-temporal clique given that S_i is a δ-temporal clique. By independence of label choices, when $|S_i \cap S_j| = t$ (i.e., S_i intersects with S_j on t vertices), $\mathbb{E}[X_j | X_i = 1]$ is upper bounded by the probability that all labels of edges that have both endpoints in S_j but not both endpoints in $S_i \cap S_j$ are at most δ apart. Therefore, by applying Lemma 3 with $h = \binom{k}{2} - \binom{t}{2}$, we get

$$\mathbb{E}[X_j | X_i = 1] \leq \left(\binom{k}{2} - \binom{t}{2}\right)\delta^{\binom{k}{2}-\binom{t}{2}-1}(1-\delta) + \delta^{\binom{k}{2}-\binom{t}{2}}$$
$$\leq \binom{k}{2}\delta^{\binom{k}{2}-\binom{t}{2}-1}. \quad (9)$$

Using the bound (9), and noting that $\mathbb{E}[X_i] = \binom{k}{2}\delta^{\binom{k}{2}-1}(1-\delta) + \delta^{\binom{k}{2}}$, for any $i \in \{1, 2, \ldots, \binom{n}{k}\}$, we get

$$\frac{\sum_{t=1}^{k-1}\sum_{i,j:|S_i\cap S_j|=t}\mathbb{E}[X_i]\mathbb{E}[X_j|X_i=1]}{\mathbb{E}^2\left[X^{(k)}\right]}$$

$$\leq \frac{\sum_{t=1}^{k-1}\sum_{i,j:|S_i\cap S_j|=t}\left(\binom{k}{2}\delta^{\binom{k}{2}-1}(1-\delta)+\delta^{\binom{k}{2}}\right)\binom{k}{2}\delta^{\binom{k}{2}-\binom{t}{2}-1}}{\binom{n}{k}^2\left(\binom{k}{2}\delta^{\binom{k}{2}-1}(1-\delta)+\delta^{\binom{k}{2}}\right)^2}$$

$$=\frac{\sum_{t=1}^{k-1}\binom{n}{k}\binom{k}{t}\binom{n-k}{k-t}\binom{k}{2}\delta^{\binom{k}{2}-\binom{t}{2}-1}}{\binom{n}{k}^2\left(\binom{k}{2}\delta^{\binom{k}{2}-1}(1-\delta)+\delta^{\binom{k}{2}}\right)}$$

$$\leq \sum_{t=1}^{k-1}\frac{\binom{k}{t}\binom{n-k}{k-t}\binom{k}{2}\delta^{\binom{k}{2}-\binom{t}{2}-1}}{\binom{n}{k}\binom{k}{2}\delta^{\binom{k}{2}-1}(1-\delta)}=\sum_{t=1}^{k-1}\frac{\binom{k}{t}\binom{n-k}{k-t}}{\binom{n}{k}\delta^{\binom{t}{2}}(1-\delta)}$$

$$\leq \sum_{t=1}^{k-1}\frac{\frac{k^t e^t}{t^t}\cdot\frac{n^{k-t}e^{k-t}}{(k-t)^{k-t}}}{\frac{n^k}{k^k}\delta^{\binom{t}{2}}(1-\delta)}=\sum_{t=1}^{k-1}\frac{k^{k+t}e^k}{t^t(k-t)^{k-t}n^t\delta^{\binom{t}{2}}(1-\delta)}. \quad (10)$$

By straightforward analysis on the function $g(t)=\frac{k^{k-t}}{t^t(k-t)^{k-t}}$, for $t\in[1,k-1]$, we get that it is strictly decreasing and so it is maximized at $t=1$, namely $\max\{g(t),1\leq t\leq k-1\}=g(1)=\left(1-\frac{1}{k}\right)^{k-1}\leq\frac{1}{e}$. Therefore, by (10),

$$\frac{\sum_{t=1}^{k-1}\sum_{i,j:|S_i\cap S_j|=t}\mathbb{E}[X_i]\mathbb{E}[X_j|X_i=1]}{\mathbb{E}^2\left[X^{(k)}\right]}\leq \sum_{t=1}^{k-1}\frac{1}{e(1-\delta)}\frac{k^{2t}e^k}{n^t\delta^{\binom{t}{2}}}$$

$$=\sum_{t=1}^{k-1}\frac{1}{e(1-\delta)}e^{2t\ln k+k-t\ln n+\frac{t(t-1)}{2}\ln\frac{1}{\delta}}$$

$$\leq \sum_{t=1}^{k-1}\frac{1}{e(1-\delta)}e^{2t\ln k+k-t\ln n+t\frac{k\ln\frac{1}{\delta}}{2}}$$

$$=\sum_{t=1}^{k-1}\frac{1}{e(1-\delta)}e^{2t\ln k+k-\epsilon t\ln n}=o(1),$$

where in the last equality we used the fact that $k=(1-\epsilon)\frac{2\ln n}{\ln\frac{1}{\delta}}$ and $\ln k=o(\ln n)$. This completes the proof. □

By the probabilistic method, combining Lemma 4 and Lemma 5, we get the following:

Theorem 2. *Let (K_n,λ) be a random simple temporal graph where the underlying graph is the complete graph with n vertices, and let $\delta\in(0,1)$ be a constant. Define $k_0\stackrel{def}{=}\frac{2\log n}{\log\frac{1}{\delta}}$. As $n\to\infty$ we have the following:*

(i) *With high probability, (K_n,λ) has no δ-temporal clique of size $(1+o(1))k_0$.*
(ii) *With high probability, (K_n,λ) contains a δ-temporal clique of size $(1-o(1))k_0$.*

Proof. Let $\epsilon > 0$ be an arbitrarily small constant. Let also $X^{(k)}$ denote the number of δ-temporal cliques of size k in (K_n, λ). By part (i) of Lemma 4 and Markov's inequality, we have that $\Pr(X^{((1+\epsilon)k_0)} > 0) \leq \mathbb{E}[X^{((1+\epsilon)k_0)}] = o(1)$, as $n \to \infty$, which proves the first part of the Theorem.

For the second part, we use the following well-known inequality $\Pr(X^{(k)} > 0) \geq \frac{\mathbb{E}^2[X^{(k)}]}{\mathbb{E}[(X^{(k)})^2]}$. In particular, for $k = (1-\epsilon)k_0$, by part (ii) of Lemma 5, we have that $\Pr(X^{((1-\epsilon)k_0)} > 0) \geq \frac{\mathbb{E}^2[X^{((1-\epsilon)k_0)}]}{\mathbb{E}[(X^{((1-\epsilon)k_0)})^2]} = 1 - o(1)$, as $n \to \infty$, which proves the second part of the Theorem. □

We note that the above Theorem implies the following:

Theorem 3. *Let (K_n, λ) be a random simple temporal graph where the underlying graph is the complete graph with n vertices, and let $\delta \in (0, 1)$ be a constant. Let also $k_0 = \frac{2 \log n}{\log \frac{1}{\delta}}$ and let Q be any δ-temporal clique of size at least $(1-o(1))k_0$. Define the interval $\Delta(Q) \stackrel{def}{=} [\min(\lambda(e) : e \in Q), \max(\lambda(e) : e \in Q)]$. Then $|\Delta(Q)| = \delta - o(\delta)$ whp.*

Proof. Since $|\Delta(Q)| \leq \delta$, by definition of a δ-temporal clique, we only need to prove that $|\Delta(Q)| \geq \delta - o(\delta)$. Suppose there is some $\delta' \leq \delta - \epsilon$, for some positive constant ϵ, such that $\Pr(\exists Q : \Delta(Q) \leq \delta') \geq \epsilon$. This would imply that Q is a δ'-temporal clique in (K_n, λ), of size $(1-o(1))k_0$. However, Theorem 2, suggests that the largest δ'-temporal clique in (K_n, λ) is at most $(1-o(1))\frac{2 \log n}{\log \frac{1}{\delta'}}$, which is much smaller than $(1-o(1))k_0$, leading to a contradiction. □

Note 1. The above proofs also work for smaller values of $\delta = o(1)$ (e.g. $\delta = \frac{1}{\log \log n}$), but not too small (e.g. if $\delta = O(1/n)$ the expected size of a δ-temporal clique becomes constant and concentration results do not hold).

3 Average Case Hardness Implications and Open Problems

The threshold given in Theorem 2 on the size of the maximum δ-clique reveals an interesting connection between simple random temporal graphs (K_n, λ) and Erdős-Rényi random graphs $\mathcal{G}_{n,\delta}$. On one hand, notice that, if we only consider edges with labels within a given δ-window, then the corresponding graph is an instance of $\mathcal{G}_{n,\delta}$, which has maximum clique size asymptotically equal to $k_0 \stackrel{def}{=} \frac{2 \log n}{\log \frac{1}{\delta}}$ whp. On the other hand, the random simple temporal graph contains $\Theta(n^2)$ different instances of $\mathcal{G}_{n,\delta}$, but the size of a maximum δ-clique size is asymptotically the same. One explanation why this happens is that the different instances of $\mathcal{G}_{n,\delta}$ contained in the random simple temporal graph are highly dependent, even if these correspond to disjoint δ-windows (indeed, edges with labels appearing in one window do not appear in the other and vice versa).

It is therefore interesting to ask whether we can use the above connection algorithmically. One direction is clearly easier than the other: If there is a polynomial time algorithm $\mathcal{A}_{ER}(\delta)$ that can find a clique of size $q = \Theta(k_0)$ in a random instance of $\mathcal{G}_{n,\delta}$ whp, then we can use this algorithm to find an asymptotically equally large δ-clique in a random instance of (K_n, λ) with the same probability of success. We note that, finding a clique of size asymptotically close to k_0 in $\mathcal{G}_{n,\delta}$ is believed to be hard in the average case and there is no known algorithm for this problem that runs in polynomial time in n.

For the other direction, we conjecture that the following reduction may be possible:

Conjecture 1. Suppose that, for any $\delta \in [0,1]$ there is a polynomial time algorithm $\mathcal{A}_{SRT}(\delta)$ that finds an $(1-o(1))$-approximation of a maximum δ-clique in a random instance of (K_n, λ) whp. Then $\mathcal{A}_{SRT}(\delta)$ can be used to design a polynomial time algorithm that finds an $(1-o(1))$-approximation of a maximum in $\mathcal{G}_{n,\delta}$ whp.

It is clear that the probability of success of $\mathcal{A}_{SRT}(\delta)$ in the above Conjecture cannot be equal to 1 unless $P = NP$. In the following Theorem we also prove that the probability of success is unlikely to be too large.

Theorem 4. *Suppose that, for any constant $\delta \in (0,1)$, the probability of success of algorithm $\mathcal{A}_{SRT}(\delta)$ is $1 - \exp(-\omega(n^2))$. Then $\mathcal{A}_{SRT}(\delta/2)$ can be used to find a clique of size $(1-o(1))k_0$ in $\mathcal{G}_{n,\delta}$ whp.*

Proof. Let $G_{n,\delta}$ be a random instance of the Erdős–Rényi random graphs model. Let $\mathcal{E}$ be the event that, for a random instance of the random simple temporal graph (K_n, λ), all edges of $G_{n,\delta}$ appear inside $[0, \delta/2]$, while all other edges appear inside $[\delta, 1]$. By definition we then have that

$$\Pr(\mathcal{E}) = \left(\frac{\delta}{2}\right)^{|E(G_{n,\delta})|} (1-\delta)^{\binom{n}{2} - |E(G_{n,\delta})|} \geq (\min\{\delta/2, 1-\delta\})^{n^2} \geq \left(\frac{\delta(1-\delta)}{2}\right)^{n^2}.$$

Furthermore, notice that, by Theorem 3, given $\mathcal{E}$, any maximum $\frac{\delta}{2}$-clique belongs to $G_{n,\delta}$ and thus lies within $[0, \frac{\delta}{2}]$ whp. Indeed, a maximum clique of $G_{n,\delta}$ has size asymptotically equal to k_0, and there is no $\frac{\delta}{2}$-clique of size $(1-o(1))k_0$ within $[\delta, 1]$, whp. In particular, denoting by $\mathcal{C}$ the event that the maximum $\frac{\delta}{2}$-clique lies within $[0, \delta/2]$, we have

$$\Pr(\mathcal{E} \cap \mathcal{C}) = \Pr(\mathcal{E})\Pr(\mathcal{C}|\mathcal{E}) \geq (1-o(1))\left(\frac{\delta(1-\delta)}{2}\right)^{n^2} = \exp(-\Theta(n^2)). \quad (11)$$

In view of the above, given $G_{n,\delta}$, we construct the input instance for $\mathcal{A}_{SRT}$ as follows: (a) select the labels of edges in $E(G_{n,\delta})$ uniformly at random within $[0, \delta/2]$ and (b) select the labels of all other edges independently, uniformly at random within $[\delta, 1]$.

Since the failure probability of $\mathcal{A}_{SRT}(\delta/2)$ is, by assumption, at most $\exp(-\omega(n^2))$ (which is asymptotically smaller than the lower bound given in

(11)), the algorithm may only fail to find a $\frac{\delta}{2}$-temporal clique of size $(1-o(1))k_0$ in a vanishing fraction of input instances $\mathcal{I}$ created. In particular, the $\frac{\delta}{2}$-temporal clique constructed by $\mathcal{A}_{SRT}(\delta/2)$ will be an $(1-o(1))k_0$ clique of $G_{n,\delta}$ whp, as needed. □

In view of the above proof, one possible approach for Conjecture 1 would be to examine the distribution of the minimum interval containing all labels of edges in a δ-clique found by $\mathcal{A}_{SRT}$ (namely $\Delta(Q) \stackrel{def}{=} [\min(\lambda(e) : e \in Q), \max(\lambda(e) : e \in Q)]$), when the input instance $\mathcal{I} = \mathcal{I}(G_{n,\delta})$ is constructed as follows: Given $G_{n,\delta}$, (1) select labels $\{\lambda(e) : e \in E(G_{n,\delta})\}$ independently, uniformly at random (i.u.a.r.) within $[0, \delta]$, and (2) select the rest of the labels $\{\lambda(e) : e \notin E(G_{n,\delta})\}$ i.u.a.r. from $[\delta, 1]$. In particular, we conjecture the following:

Conjecture 2. Let Q^* be the δ-clique constructed by algorithm $\mathcal{A}_{SRT}$, on instance $\mathcal{I}(G_{n,\delta})$. Then $\Delta(Q^*)$ is distributed almost uniformly at random within $[0, 1]$.

References

1. Aaron, E., Krizanc, D., Meyerson, E.: DMVP: foremost waypoint coverage of time-varying graphs. In: Proceedings of the 40th International Workshop on Graph-Theoretic Concepts in Computer Science (WG), pp. 29–41 (2014)
2. Akrida, E.C., Gasieniec, L., Mertzios, G.B., Spirakis, P.G.: Ephemeral networks with random availability of links: the case of fast networks. J. Parallel Distrib. Comput. **87**, 109–120 (2016)
3. Akrida, E.C., Gasieniec, L., Mertzios, G.B., Spirakis, P.G.: The complexity of optimal design of temporally connected graphs. Theory Comput. Syst. **61**(3), 907–944 (2017)
4. Akrida, E.C., Mertzios, G.B., Spirakis, P.G., Zamaraev, V.: Temporal vertex cover with a sliding time window. J. Comput. Syst. Sci. **107**, 108–123 (2020)
5. Anagnostopoulos, A., Lacki, J., Lattanzi, S., Leonardi, S., Mahdian, M.: Community detection on evolving graphs. In: Proceedings of the 30th Conference on Neural Information Processing Systems (NIPS), pp. 3522–3530 (2016)
6. Bentert, M., Himmel, A.-S., Molter, H., Morik, M., Niedermeier, R., Saitenmacher, R.: Listing all maximal k-plexes in temporal graphs. In: Proceedings of the 2018 IEEE/ACM International Conference on Advances in Social Networks Analysis and Mining (ASONAM), pp. 41–46 (2018)
7. Bollobás, B., Erdős, P.: Cliques in random graphs. Math. Proc. Camb. Phil. Soc. **80**, 419–427 (1976)
8. Casteigts, A., Himmel, A., Molter, H., Zschoche, P.: Finding temporal paths under waiting time constraints. Algorithmica **83**(9), 2754–2802 (2021)
9. Casteigts, A., Raskin, M., Renken, M., Zamaraev, V.: Sharp thresholds in random simple temporal graphs. In: Proceedings of the 62nd IEEE Annual Symposium on Foundations of Computer Science (FOCS), pp. 319–326 (2021)
10. Chen, J., Molter, H., Sorge, M., Suchý, O.: Cluster editing in multi-layer and temporal graphs. In: Proceedings of the 29th International Symposium on Algorithms and Computation (ISAAC), vol. 123, pp. 24:1–24:13 (2018)

11. Enright, J.A., Meeks, K., Mertzios, G.B., Zamaraev, V.: Deleting edges to restrict the size of an epidemic in temporal networks. J. Comput. Syst. Sci. **119**, 60–77 (2021)
12. Erlebach, T., Hoffmann, M., Kammer, F.: On temporal graph exploration. J. Comput. Syst. Sci. **119**, 1–18 (2021)
13. Ferreira, A.: Building a reference combinatorial model for MANETs. IEEE Netw. **18**(5), 24–29 (2004)
14. Ghosal, S., Ghosh, S.C.: Channel assignment in mobile networks based on geometric prediction and random coloring. In: Proceedings of the 40th IEEE Conference on Local Computer Networks (LCN), pp. 237–240 (2015)
15. Hamm, T., Klobas, N., Mertzios, G.B., Spirakis, P.G.: The complexity of temporal vertex cover in small-degree graphs. In: Proceedings of the 36th AAAI Conference on Artificial Intelligence (AAAI), pp. 10193–10201 (2022)
16. Heeger, K., Hermelin, D., Mertzios, G.B., Molter, H., Niedermeier, R., Shabtay, D.: Equitable scheduling on a single machine. In: Proceedings of the 35th AAAI Conference on Artificial Intelligence (AAAI), pp. 11818–11825 (2021)
17. Himmel, A., Molter, H., Niedermeier, R., Sorge, M.: Adapting the Bron-Kerbosch algorithm for enumerating maximal cliques in temporal graphs.Soc. Netw. Anal. Min. **7**(1), 35:1–35:16 (2017)
18. Kempe, D., Kleinberg, J.M., Kumar, A.: Connectivity and inference problems for temporal networks. In: Proceedings of the 32nd Annual ACM Symposium on Theory of Computing (STOC), pp. 504–513 (2000)
19. Klobas, N., Mertzios, G.B., Molter, H., Niedermeier, R., Zschoche, P.: Interference-free walks in time: temporally disjoint paths. Auton. Agents Multi-Agent Syst. **37**(1) (2023)
20. Klobas, N., Mertzios, G.B., Molter, H., Spirakis, P.G.: The complexity of computing optimum labelings for temporal connectivity. In: Proceedings of the 47th International Symposium on Mathematical Foundations of Computer Science (MFCS), pp. 62:1–62:15 (2022)
21. Klobas, N., Mertzios, G.B., Spirakis, P.G.: Sliding into the future: investigating sliding windows in temporal graphs. In: Proceedings of the 48th International Symposium on Mathematical Foundations of Computer Science (MFCS), pp. 5:1–5:12 (2023)
22. Mertzios, G.B., Michail, O., Spirakis, P.G.: Temporal network optimization subject to connectivity constraints. Algorithmica **81**(4), 1416–1449 (2019)
23. Mertzios, G.B., Molter, H., Renken, M., Spirakis, P.G., Zschoche, P.: The complexity of transitively orienting temporal graphs. In: Proceedings of the 46th International Symposium on Mathematical Foundations of Computer Science (MFCS), pp. 75:1–75:18 (2021)
24. Mertzios, G.B., Molter, H., Zamaraev, V.: Sliding window temporal graph coloring. J. Comput. Syst. Sci. **120**, 97–115 (2021)
25. Michail, O., Spirakis, P.: Elements of the theory of dynamic networks. Commun. ACM **61**(2), 72–72 (2018)
26. Michail, O., Spirakis, P.G.: Traveling salesman problems in temporal graphs. Theor. Comput. Sci. **634**, 1–23 (2016)
27. Santoro, N.: Computing in time-varying networks. In: Proceedings of the 13th International Symposium on Stabilization, Safety, and Security of Distributed Systems (SSS), p. 4 (2011)
28. Viard, T., Latapy, M., Magnien, C.: Computing maximal cliques in link streams. Theor. Comput. Sci. **609**, 245–252 (2016)

29. Yu, F., Bar-Noy, A., Basu, P., Ramanathan, R.: Algorithms for channel assignment in mobile wireless networks using temporal coloring. In: Proceedings of the 16th ACM International Conference on Modeling, Analysis & Simulation of Wireless and Mobile Systems (MSWiM), pp. 49–58 (2013)
30. Zschoche, P., Fluschnik, T., Molter, H., Niedermeier, R.: The complexity of finding small separators in temporal graphs. J. Comput. Syst. Sci. **107**, 72–92 (2020)

The Exact Spanning Ratio of the Parallelogram Delaunay Graph

Prosenjit Bose[1], Jean-Lou De Carufel[2], and Sandrine Njoo[2(✉)]

[1] Carleton University, Ottawa, Canada
[2] University of Ottawa, Ottawa, Canada
snjoo045@uottawa.ca

Abstract. Finding the exact spanning ratio of a Delaunay graph has been one of the longstanding open problems in Computational Geometry. Currently there are only four convex shapes for which the exact spanning ratio of their Delaunay graph is known: the equilateral triangle, the square, the regular hexagon and the rectangle. We add a fifth convex shape by proving the exact spanning ratio of the parallelogram Delaunay graph. The worst-case spanning ratio is *exactly*

$$\frac{\sqrt{2}\sqrt{1+A^2+2A\cos(\theta_0)}+(A+\cos(\theta_0))\sqrt{1+A^2+2A\cos(\theta_0)}}{\sin(\theta_0)},$$

where A is the aspect ratio and θ_0 is the non-obtuse angle of the parallelogram.

Keywords: Geometric Spanner · Delaunay Graph · Spanning Ratio

1 Introduction

Graphs are used to model many structures such as computer networks. If a graph G has a quadratic number of edges, reducing the complexity of this graph is desirable by approximating G with a spanning subgraph G' of linear complexity. However, G' should retain the characteristic properties of G. One measure of similarity between two graphs G and G' is its spanning ratio. A spanning subgraph G' is a c-spanner of G provided that the shortest path between any pair of vertices in G' is at most c times the length of the shortest path in G.

We focus on geometric graphs. A *geometric graph* is an undirected and weighted graph whose vertices are points in the plane and edges are segments joining pairs of vertices, where the weight of an edge is the Euclidean distance between its two endpoints. We study the spanning ratio of a family of geometric graphs referred to as *Generalized Delaunay Graphs*. Informally, a standard Delaunay graph of a planar point set $\mathcal{P}$ is a geometric graph whose vertex set is $\mathcal{P}$ and whose edge set consists of pairs of vertices x,y such that there exists a disk with x,y on its boundary with no points of $\mathcal{P}$ in its interior. A generalized Delaunay graph replaces this disk with homothets of a given convex shape. These graphs, while geometric in nature, are natural choices to construct lightweight, well-connected wireless networks in the real world.

Determining the exact spanning ratio of the Delaunay graph is a notoriously difficult problem. Dobkin et al. [8] were the first to show that the Delaunay graph has a spanning ratio of at most $\pi(1+\sqrt{5})/2 \approx 5.08$. This was later improved by Keil and Gutwin [9] who showed an upper bound of $4\pi/3\sqrt{3} \approx 2.42$. Currently, the best known upper bound of 1.998 was shown by Xia [12]. Chew [7] gave a lower bound of $\pi/2$ which was long believed to be optimal until Bose et al. [6] proved a lower bound of 1.5846. This was later improved to 1.5932 by Xia and Zhang [13]. A tight bound on the spanning ratio of the Delaunay graph remains elusive. For generalized Delaunay graphs, Bose et al. [3] showed that the Delaunay graph defined by the homothet of any convex shape C has a spanning ratio that is bounded by a constant times the ratio of the perimeter of C to its width. Moreover, Bose et al. [2] then showed that a Delaunay graph defined by any affine transformation C' of C is a constant spanner where the spanning ratio depends on the eigenvalues of the affine transformation. However, even if the spanning ratio for shape C is tight, the upper bound obtained on the spanning ratio for C' is not necessarily tight. Until recently, exact bounds on the spanning ratio of Delaunay graphs were known for only 3 shapes, namely equilateral triangles [7], squares [1] and regular hexagons [10].

The spanning ratio of empty rectangle Delaunay graphs was studied by Bose et al. [5] who showed a spanning ratio of $\sqrt{2}(2A+1)$, where A is the aspect ratio of the rectangle. This corroborates the intuition that long skinny rectangles have large spanning ratio. Recently, van Renssen et al. [11] improved this bound by generalizing Bonichon et al.'s result [1] to give a tight bound of $\sqrt{2}\sqrt{A^2+1+A\sqrt{1+A^2}}$ for empty rectangle Delaunay graphs. This is the fourth shape for which we now have an exact bound on the spanning ratio. Their result is a delicate case analysis where they study different cases depending on the aspect ratio of the empty rectangle and the slopes of the edges. Our main result is that we push the envelope further by proving a tight bound on the spanning ratio of Delaunay graphs defined by empty parallelograms. We generalize ideas from Bonichon et al. [1], van Renssen et al. [11] and Bose et al. [2]. The key idea was to find a way to change basis vectors without applying an affine transformation as in [2]. The generalization can be seen as follows: in Bonichon et al.'s approach, there is no degree of freedom in the shape defining the Delaunay graph since the aspect ratio of the square is fixed. In van Renssen et al.'s case, the shape has one degree of freedom, namely the aspect ratio. In our setting, the difficulty that arises is that our shapes have two degrees of freedom: the aspect ratio and the angle between adjacent sides of the parallelogram. We obtain an exact worst-case bound, and in fact, if we set the angle to $\pi/2$, we obtain van Renssen et al.'s result and in addition if we set the aspect ratio to 1, we obtain Bonichon et al.'s result.

Our Contributions. This paper further generalizes and extends the proof given by Bonichon et al. [1], and van Renssen et al. [11]. All together, we get an exact bound of

$$h(A, \theta_0) = \frac{\sqrt{2}\sqrt{1 + A^2 + 2A\cos(\theta_0)} + (A + \cos(\theta_0))\sqrt{1 + A^2 + 2A\cos(\theta_0)}}{\sin(\theta_0)}$$

on the spanning ratio of the parallelogram Delaunay graph, where A is the aspect ratio and θ_0 is the non-obtuse angle of the parallelogram.

We summarize our proof technique here. To obtain an upper bound on the spanning ratio, we proceed by induction on the rank of the distances between pairs of points. To go from a point a to a point b, we only consider the paths that use endpoints of segments that cross the line segment ab. If a point is above (resp. below) the line ab, we refer to that point as a high (resp. low) point. Moreover, we only consider the case where a is on the bottom left corner and b is on the rightmost side of the parallelogram.

To bound the length of the path from a to b, we break the path into three subpaths. The first part is bounded using the so-called *Crossing Lemma* (see below). The second part considers the length of the subpath where the points all have y-coordinates that are significantly different than that of b. On this path, the points are either all high points or all low points. The third part of the path is bounded using the induction hypothesis.

The Crossing Lemma is a crucial part in the proof. The goal of this lemma is to bound the length of the path from a until we reach a parallelogram with an edge between a high and a low point that is not *too steep*. Using an inductive argument, we use techniques such as bounding monotone paths using the L_1-norm as well as bounding edge lengths in terms of their horizontal component.

Preliminaries, Notations and Definitions. A Generalized Delaunay graph of a point set $\mathcal{P}$ is a geometric graph $(\mathcal{P}, E)$ where there is an edge between two vertices $u, v \in \mathcal{P}$ when there exists a homothet of a convex shape $\mathcal{C}$, with u and v on the boundary of $\mathcal{C}$ and no point of $\mathcal{P}$ in its interior. In this paper, we consider the Delaunay graph where the convex shape is a parallelogram P referred to as the *parallelogram Delaunay graph*. To avoid degeneracies, we assume the point set $\mathcal{P}$ is in *general position*: no three points lie on a common line and no four points lie on the boundary of a common homothet of P. Denote by ℓ and s the long and short side of P, respectively, where $\ell \geq s > 0$. We define the aspect ratio of P as $A := \frac{\ell}{s}$. For a point a in the plane, let x_a and y_a be the x- and y-coordinates of a, respectively. Observe that different parallelograms give different Delaunay graphs. Moreover, we emphasize the fact that rotations are *not* allowed, only scaled translate of P.

Without loss of generality, we assume that the long side is vertical and the short side has non negative slope. Let θ_0 be the non obtuse angle between the long and the short side of P. Note that any other orientation of the parallelogram can be seen as an isometry of the point set. The general position assumption we make on the point set $\mathcal{P}$ in this context is the following. We assume that no four vertices lie on the boundary of any scaled translate parallelogram of P and that no two vertices lie on a line parallel to the sides of P. This means that no two vertices lie on a vertical or a horizontal line. In general parallelogram Delaunay graphs are near-triangulations. A *near-triangulation* is a planar graph such that every bounded face is a triangle. As such, we denote them by $T_\mathcal{P}$ or simply T when the point set is clear from the context.

2 The Upper Bound

Since the parallelogram Delaunay graph of a point set is a near-triangulation, we denote it as T. In this section, we prove that the worst-case spanning ratio of T is at most $h(A, \theta_0)$. We obtain this result after a few preparatory lemmas and observations. Note that some proofs have been omitted due to space constraints, the full proofs can be found in [4].

Let a, b be any two vertices in T. Without loss of generality, assume $a = (0, 0)$ and $x_b > 0$. Let $d_2^T(a, b)$ be the length of the shortest path in T between a and b. We prove that $d_2^T(a, b)$ is at most $h(A, \theta_0) \, d_2(a, b)$ with equality occurring in the worst case, where $d_2(a, b)$ is the Euclidean distance from a to b. We denote the slope of the segment ab as $S := \frac{y_b}{x_b}$. Our proof considers four different scenarios, based on the value of S. Each scenario is illustrated in Fig. 1.

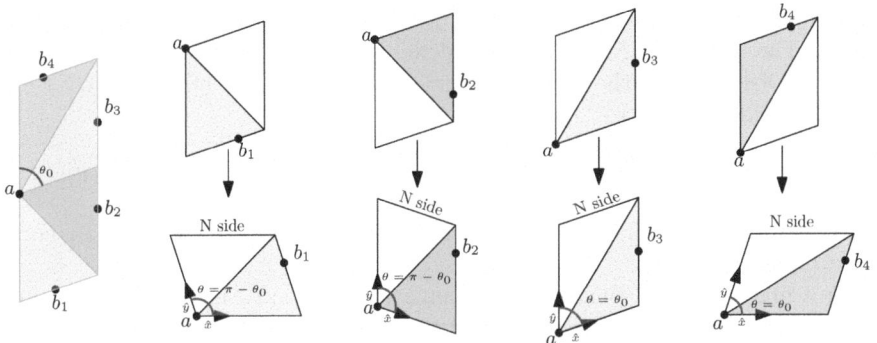

Fig. 1. The first row shows the four scenarios. The second row highlights the homothets of $\hat{P}$ (with a and b on its boundary) on which our analysis is based.

Scenario 1 A homothet of P with a on its top left corner and b on its lowest short side. Formally, the slope between a and b satisfies $S \in \left(-\infty, \frac{\cos(\theta_0) - A}{\sin(\theta_0)}\right]$. The usual basis $\{(1,0), (0,1)\}$. The usual basis $\{(1,0), (0,1)\}$ will be sent to $\hat{x} := (0, -1)$, $\hat{y} := (\sin(\theta_0), \cos(\theta_0))$ (observe that $\frac{1}{A}\hat{x}_b \geq \hat{y}_b$). The interior counterclockwise angle θ between $\hat{x}$ and $\hat{y}$ is then $\theta = \pi - \theta_0$.

Scenario 2 A homothet of P with a on its top left corner and b on its furthest long side. Formally, the slope between a and b satisfies $S \in \left(\frac{\cos(\theta_0) - A}{\sin(\theta_0)}, \frac{\cos(\theta_0)}{\sin(\theta_0)}\right]$. The usual basis $\{(1,0), (0,1)\}$ will be sent to $\hat{x} := (\sin(\theta_0), \cos(\theta_0))$, $\hat{y} := (0, -1)$ The interior counterclockwise angle θ between $\hat{x}$ and $\hat{y}$ is then $\theta = \pi - \theta_0$.

Scenario 3 A homothet of P with a on its bottom left corner and b on its furthest long side. Formally, the slope between a and b satisfies $S \in \left(\frac{\cos(\theta_0)}{\sin(\theta_0)}, \frac{\cos(\theta_0)+A}{\sin(\theta_0)} \right]$. The usual basis $\{(1,0),(0,1)\}$ will be sent to $\hat{x} := (\sin(\theta_0), \cos(\theta_0))$, $\hat{y} := (0,1)$. The interior counterclockwise angle θ between $\hat{x}$ and $\hat{y}$ is then $\theta = \theta_0$.

Scenario 4 A homothet of P with a on its bottom left corner and b on its highest short side. Formally, the slope between a and b satisfies $S \in \left(\frac{\cos(\theta_0)+A}{\sin(\theta_0)}, \infty \right)$. The usual basis $\{(1,0),(0,1)\}$ will be sent to $\hat{x} := (0,1)$, $\hat{y} := (\sin(\theta_0), \cos(\theta_0))$ The interior counterclockwise angle θ between $\hat{x}$ and $\hat{y}$ is then $\theta = \theta_0$.

In the first row of Fig. 1, we highlight the homothets of $\hat{P}$ (with a and b on the boundary) on which our analysis will be based. In the second row we show the homothets of $\hat{P}$ in the new basis $\{\hat{x}, \hat{y}\}$ for each scenario. Notice that $\hat{P}$ is an axis aligned rectangle in the $\{\hat{x}, \hat{y}\}$ basis. We define the W and E sides of $\hat{P}$ to be the two sides parallel to $\hat{y}$ with the W side having smaller $\hat{x}$-coordinate. Similarly, we define the N and S sides of $\hat{P}$ to be the two sides parallel to $\hat{x}$ with the N side having larger $\hat{y}$-coordinate. A point on the east edge of $\hat{P}$ is said to be *eastern*. The *directions* N, S, E, W are defined accordingly, refer to the last row of Fig. 1. Observe that the distance between the origin and any point $\alpha \hat{x} + \beta \hat{y}$ in all scenarios is equal to

$$\|\alpha \hat{x} + \beta \hat{y}\|_2 = \sqrt{\alpha^2 + \beta^2 - 2\alpha\beta \cos(\pi - \theta)} \leq \sqrt{\alpha^2 + \beta^2 + 2\alpha\beta |\cos(\theta)|}.$$

Moreover, observe that the L_1-norm in the usual basis is equal to the L_1-norm in the $\{\hat{x}, \hat{y}\}$-basis.

As a first step, we consider the triangles $T_1, T_2, ..., T_k$ intersecting the line segment ab ordered from a to b. We will show, in essence, that the shortest path between a and b in the graph induced by this collection of triangles is a spanning path whose spanning ratio is at most $h(A, \theta_0)$. Note that the triangulation of $\mathcal{P}$ may not contain its convex hull. As such, the sequence of triangles may not exist. If that is the case, consider the triangulation of a larger point set $\mathcal{P}' = \mathcal{P} \cup \{p_1, p_2, p_3, p_4\}$, where $\{p_1, p_2, p_3, p_4\}$ is defined as follows. The points in $\{p_1, p_2, p_3, p_4\}$ are the vertices of a homothet of P containing $\mathcal{P}$ such that the distance from any point in $\mathcal{P}$ to any point in $\{p_1, p_2, p_3, p_4\}$ is arbitrarily large. Adding these points guarantees that the larger triangulation contains all the edges of the convex hull of $\mathcal{P}'$. Moreover, all the edges of the triangulation of $\mathcal{P}'$ that are not in the triangulation of $\mathcal{P}$, by construction, are arbitrarily long. Therefore, these edges will not be used in any bounded path. In what follows, we bound the length of the shortest path between points in $\mathcal{P}$.

We will denote the triangle with vertices u, v and w by $\triangle uvw$. Note that with the additional four points, every face that intersects the line segment ab is bounded and therefore is a triangle. The boundary of each triangle intersects ab twice. Let h_i and l_i denote the endpoints of the edge in T_i intersecting line segment ab closest to b. Note that h_i is above ab and l_i is below ab (with respect to the $\{\hat{x}, \hat{y}\}$ basis[1]). Every pair of consecutive triangles along the line segment ab shares two vertices. As such, for all $1 \leq i < k$, either $l_i = l_{i+1}$ or $h_i = h_{i+1}$. We define $h_0 = l_0 = a$, and we let $l_k = h_k = b$.

For each triangle T_i (or $\hat{T}_i$ in the $\{\hat{x}, \hat{y}\}$ basis), there is a corresponding scaled translate P_i (or $\hat{P}_i$ in the $\{\hat{x}, \hat{y}\}$ basis) of P (or $\hat{P}$ in the $\{\hat{x}, \hat{y}\}$ basis). The parallelogram P_i contains no point of $\mathcal{P}$ in its interior and has the three vertices of T_i on its boundary. We define the parameter L as the positive slope of the diagonal of $\hat{P}$ expressed in the $\{\hat{x}, \hat{y}\}$ basis. The second row of Fig. 1 illustrates these diagonals[2]. If the long side of $\hat{P}$ is vertical, then $L = A$, as in Scenarios 2 and 3. Otherwise, $L = 1/A$, as in Scenarios 1 and 4.

For any point u, we denote $\hat{x}_u$ and $\hat{y}_u$ to be the coordinates of u in its $\{\hat{x}, \hat{y}\}$ coordinate system. In other words, $u = \hat{x}_u \hat{x} + \hat{y}_u \hat{y}$.

Definition 1. *A* gentle *edge (u, v) has the property that $|\hat{y}_v - \hat{y}_u| \leq L|\hat{x}_v - \hat{x}_u|$. Otherwise, the edge is* steep.

We next define the notion of an *inductive* parallelogram.

Definition 2. *If the edge (h_i, l_i) is gentle, then $\hat{P}_i$ is defined to be* inductive. *The point with the larger $\hat{x}$-coordinate among h_i and l_i is said to be the* inductive point *of $\hat{P}_i$, denoted by c.*

We use a potential to bound the spanning ratio. This potential is tied to a parallelogram. We highlight the exact relationship between the potential and the parallelogram below. Note that our potential is very similar to the potential introduced by Bonichon et al. [1] and also used by van Renssen et al. [11] who generalized it to account for the aspect ratio. We further modify this approach to account for the angle θ_0 in a parallelogram. Let $d_{\hat{P}_i}(h_i, l_i)$ be the length of the path when moving clockwise from h_i to l_i along the sides of $\hat{P}_i$.

Definition 3. *Parallelogram $\hat{P}_i$ has a* potential *if $d_2^T(a, h_i) + d_2^T(a, l_i) + d_{\hat{P}_i}(h_i, l_i) \leq (2 + 2L)\hat{x}_i$, where $\hat{x}_i$ is the $\hat{x}$-coordinate of the E side of $\hat{P}_i$.*

Next, we define $P(a, b)$ as the parallelogram $\{\alpha \hat{x} + \beta \hat{y} : \hat{x}_a \leq \alpha \leq \hat{x}_b, \hat{y}_a \leq \beta \leq \hat{y}_b\}$. Observe that in general, $P(a, b)$ is not a homothet of P or of $\hat{P}$. The following lemma describes how the potential of one parallelogram is related to the next. The proof of the following lemma has been omitted.

Lemma 1. *If (a, b) is not an edge in T and parallelogram $P(a, b)$ contains no point of $\mathcal{P}$ other than a and b, then $\hat{P}_1$ has a potential. Furthermore, if, for any $1 \leq i < k$, $\hat{P}_i$ has a potential but is not inductive, then $\hat{P}_{i+1}$ has a potential.*

We now use this notion of potential to prove an upper bound on the $\hat{x}$-distance between a and the inductive point of a parallelogram with potential.

---

[1] We do not use the notation $\hat{h}_i$ and $\hat{l}_i$ even though these two points are defined with respect to the $\{\hat{x}, \hat{y}\}$ basis. This would make expressions like $\hat{x}_{\hat{h}_i}$ too heavy.

[2] Note that the slope in the $\{\hat{x}, \hat{y}\}$ basis corresponds to the ratio of the sides of $\hat{P}$.

Lemma 2. *If parallelogram $\hat{P}_i$ has a potential and its inductive point c (either $c = h_i$ or $c = l_i$) lies on the E side of $\hat{P}_i$, then $d_2^T(a,c) \leq (1+L)\hat{x}_c$.*

Proof. Without loss of generality, assume $c = h_i$. Therefore, we have

$$\hat{x}_c = \hat{x}_{h_i} = \hat{x}_i \tag{1}$$

since h_i is eastern. Moreover, since $\hat{P}_i$ has a potential, we have (1) $d_2^T(a, h_i) \leq (1+L)\hat{x}_i = (1+L)\hat{x}_{h_i}$ or (2) $d_2^T(a, l_i) + d_{\hat{P}_i}(h_i, l_i) \leq (1+L)\hat{x}_i$. In the first case, we find $d_2^T(a, h_i) \leq (1+L)\hat{x}_i = (1+L)\hat{x}_c$ by (1). In the second case, since (l_i, h_i) is an edge in T, by the triangle inequality we get $d_2^T(a, h_i) \leq d_2^T(a, l_i) + d_2(l_i, h_i) \leq d_2^T(a, l_i) + d_{\hat{P}_i}(h_i, l_i) \leq (1+L)\hat{x}_i = (1+L)\hat{x}_c$ by (1). □

Definition 4. *Let $1 \leq j \leq k$. The* maximal high path ending at h_j *and the* maximal low path ending at l_j *are defined as follows:*
If h_j is eastern in $\hat{P}_j$, the maximal high path ending at h_j is simply h_j; otherwise, it is the path $h_i, h_{i+1}, ..., h_j$ such that $h_{i+1}, ..., h_j$ are not eastern in respectively, $\hat{P}_{i+1}, .., \hat{P}_j$ and either $i = 0$ or h_i is eastern in $\hat{P}_i$.
If l_j is eastern in $\hat{P}_j$, the maximal low path ending at l_j is simply l_j; otherwise, it is the path $l_i, l_{i+1}, ..., l_j$ such that $l_{i+1}, ..., l_j$ are not eastern in respectively, $\hat{P}_{i+1}, .., \hat{P}_j$ and either $i = 0$ or l_i is eastern in $\hat{P}_i$.

We now give upper bounds on the length of maximal high and low paths.

Lemma 3. *Suppose $h_i, h_{i+1}, ..., h_j$ is a maximal high path. Then we have $d_2^T(h_i, h_j) \leq (\hat{x}_{h_j} - \hat{x}_{h_i}) + (\hat{y}_{h_j} - \hat{y}_{h_i})$. On the other hand, the following inequality holds for a maximal low path $l_i, l_{i+1}, ..., l_j$: $d_2^T(l_i, l_j) \leq (\hat{x}_{l_j} - \hat{x}_{l_i}) + (\hat{y}_{l_i} - \hat{y}_{l_j})$.*

Proof. Although h_i may be E, we note that the remaining vertices of the maximal high path $h_{i+1}, .., h_j$ cannot be E. As such we have a succession of WN edges (by the general position assumption). As such, we have that $\hat{y}_{h_i} < \hat{y}_{h_{i+1}} < ... < \hat{y}_{h_j}$. By the triangle inequality, we have the following for all $i \leq k \leq j$: $d_2^T(h_k, h_{k+1}) \leq (\hat{x}_{h_{k+1}} - \hat{x}_{h_k}) + (\hat{y}_{h_{k+1}} - \hat{y}_{h_k})$. Therefore, we obtain $d_2^T(h_i, h_j) \leq \sum_{k=i}^{j} d_2^T(h_k, h_{k+1}) \leq \sum_{k=i}^{j}(\hat{x}_{h_{k+1}} - \hat{x}_{h_k}) + (\hat{y}_{h_{k+1}} - \hat{y}_{h_k}) \leq (\hat{x}_{h_j} - \hat{x}_{h_i}) + (\hat{y}_{h_j} - \hat{y}_{h_i})$. The bound on the length of the maximal low path can be shown using a symmetrical argument. □

Next we will prove the Crossing Lemma, which yields bounds on the distance in the triangulation from a to the first inductive point.

Lemma 4 *(Crossing Lemma). Assume $P(a,b)$ does not contain any other vertices of $\mathcal{P}$ and (a,b) is not an edge in the parallelogram Delaunay graph. Then in each case, we have the following:*

(1) If no parallelogram in $\hat{P}_1, \hat{P}_2, ..., \hat{P}_k$ is inductive then

$$d_2^T(a,b) \leq \left(L + \sqrt{1 + L^2 + 2L|\cos(\theta)|}\right)\hat{x}_b + \hat{y}_b$$

(2) Otherwise, let $\hat{P}_j$ be the first inductive parallelogram in the sequence $\hat{P}_1, \hat{P}_2, ..., \hat{P}_{k-1}$.
  (a) If $L = A$ (as in Scenarios 2 and 3) and h_j is the inductive point of $\hat{P}_j$ then, $d_2^T(a, h_j) + (\hat{y}_{h_j} - \hat{y}_b) \leq \left(A + \sqrt{1 + A^2 + 2A|\cos(\theta)|}\right) \hat{x}_{h_j}$.
  (b) If $L = A$ (as in Scenarios 2 and 3) and l_j is the inductive point of $\hat{P}_j$ then, $d_2^T(a, l_j) - \hat{y}_{l_j} \leq \left(A + \sqrt{1 + A^2 + 2A|\cos(\theta)|}\right) \hat{x}_{l_j}$.
  (c) If $L = 1/A$ (as in Scenarios 1 and 4) and h_j is the inductive point of $\hat{P}_j$ then, $d_2^T(a, h_j) + A(\hat{y}_{h_j} - \hat{y}_b) \leq \left(1 + \sqrt{1 + \frac{1}{A^2} + \frac{2|\cos(\theta)|}{A}}\right) \hat{x}_{h_j}$.
  (d) If $L = 1/A$ (as in Scenarios 1 and 4) and l_j is the inductive point of $\hat{P}_j$ then, $d_2^T(a, l_j) - A\hat{y}_{l_j} \leq \left(1 + \sqrt{1 + \frac{1}{A^2} + \frac{2|\cos(\theta)|}{A}}\right) \hat{x}_{l_j}$.

Proof.

(1) Suppose $P(a, b)$ is empty and there is no inductive parallelogram in the sequence $\hat{P}_1, \hat{P}_2, ..., \hat{P}_k$. Then by Lemma 1, $\hat{P}_k$ must have a potential since $\hat{P}_1$ has a potential. Next, b must lie on the E side of $\hat{P}_k$ by the general position assumption. Lemma 2 gives the following bound:

$$d_2^T(a, b) \leq (1+L)\hat{x}_k = (1+L)\hat{x}_b \leq \left(L + \sqrt{1 + L^2 + 2L|\cos(\theta)|}\right)\hat{x}_b + \hat{y}_b.$$

(2)(a) In this case, we are either in Scenario 2 or 3.

Suppose $\hat{P}_j$ is the first inductive parallelogram in $\hat{P}_1, \hat{P}_2, ..., \hat{P}_{k-1}$ and we assume that the inductive point of $\hat{P}_j$ is $c = h_j$.

By Lemma 1, every parallelogram $\hat{P}_i$ with $i \leq j$ has a potential. Note that in this case, l_j is to the left of h_j. Since the edge (l_j, h_j) is gentle it follows that the vertical distance between l_j and h_j can be bounded:

$$(\hat{y}_{h_j} - \hat{y}_{l_j}) \leq A(\hat{x}_{h_j} - \hat{x}_{l_j}) \iff (\hat{y}_{h_j} - \hat{y}_{l_j}) + A\hat{x}_{l_j} \leq A\hat{x}_{h_j}. \tag{2}$$

Moreover, we can bound the length of the edge (l_j, h_j) by

$$\begin{aligned} d_2(l_j, h_j) &\leq \sqrt{1 + A^2 - 2A\cos(\pi - \theta)}(\hat{x}_{h_j} - \hat{x}_{l_j}) \\ &\leq \sqrt{1 + A^2 + 2A|\cos(\theta)|}(\hat{x}_{h_j} - \hat{x}_{l_j}). \end{aligned} \tag{3}$$

Let $l_i, l_{i+1}, ..., l_{j-1} = l_j$ be the maximal low path ending at l_j. Note that by Lemma 3 we have

$$d_2^T(l_i, l_j) \leq (\hat{x}_{l_j} - \hat{x}_{l_i}) + (\hat{y}_{l_i} - \hat{y}_{l_j}). \tag{4}$$

Next, note that either $l_i = l_0 = a$ or l_i is an eastern point in $\hat{P}_i$ that has a potential and Lemma 2 applies. In this case we have that since l_i is eastern in $\hat{P}_i$ we have:

$$d_2^T(a, l_i) \leq (1+A)\hat{x}_i = (1+A)\hat{x}_{l_i} \tag{5}$$

Using inequalities (2), (3), (4) and (5), together with the triangle inequality, we get

$$d_2^T(a, h_j) + (\hat{y}_{h_j} - \hat{y}_b)$$
$$\leq d_2^T(a, l_i) + d_2^T(l_i, l_j) + d_2(l_j, h_j) + (\hat{y}_{h_j} - \hat{y}_b)$$
$$\leq (1+A)\hat{x}_{l_i} + (\hat{x}_{l_j} - \hat{x}_{l_i}) + (\hat{y}_{l_i} - \hat{y}_{l_j}) + \sqrt{1 + A^2 + 2A|\cos(\theta)|}(\hat{x}_{h_j} - \hat{x}_{l_j})$$
$$+ \hat{y}_{h_j} - \hat{y}_b$$
$$\leq A\hat{x}_{l_i} + \sqrt{1 + A^2 + 2A|\cos(\theta)|}\hat{x}_{h_j} + \hat{y}_{h_j} - \hat{y}_{l_j}$$
$$\leq \sqrt{1 + A^2 + 2A|\cos(\theta)|}\hat{x}_{h_j} + A\hat{x}_{l_j} + \hat{y}_{h_j} - \hat{y}_{l_j}$$
$$\leq \sqrt{1 + A^2 + 2A|\cos(\theta)|}\hat{x}_{h_j} + A\hat{x}_{h_j}$$
$$= \left(A + \sqrt{1 + A^2 + 2A|\cos(\theta)|}\right)\hat{x}_{h_j}.$$

The proofs for cases $(b), (c)$ and (d) have been omitted but follow a similar structure. □

The following lemma bounds the length of a path which consists of points whose $\hat{y}$-coordinates differ greatly from $\hat{y}_b$. Since the path is monotone in the $\hat{x}$-direction, we need to bound the path from the point of view of $\hat{y}$-direction to attain the upper bound on the spanning ratio.

Lemma 5. *Suppose that no vertices of $\mathcal{P}$ are in $P(a, b)$ and that (a, b) is not an edge. Let the coordinates of the inductive point c of $\hat{P}_i$ be such that $0 < L(\hat{x}_b - \hat{x}_c) < |\hat{y}_b - \hat{y}_c|$, for some $1 < i < k$.*

(i) If $c = h_i$, and thus $0 < L(\hat{x}_b - \hat{x}_c) < \hat{y}_c - \hat{y}_b$, then for the smallest $j > i$ such that $L(\hat{x}_b - \hat{x}_{h_j}) \geq \hat{y}_{h_j} - \hat{y}_b \geq 0$, all edges on the path $h_i, ..., h_j$ are NE edges.

(ii) If $c = l_i$, and thus $0 < L(\hat{x}_b - \hat{x}_c) < \hat{y}_b - \hat{y}_c$, then for the smallest $j > i$ such that $L(\hat{x}_b - \hat{x}_{l_j}) \geq \hat{y}_b - \hat{y}_{l_j} \geq 0$, all edges on the path $l_i, ..., l_j$ are SE edges.

Next we prove the main theorem of this section. Recall that in all scenarios, the $\{\hat{x}, \hat{y}\}$ basis was defined so that $L(\hat{x}_b - \hat{x}_a) > \hat{y}_b - \hat{y}_a$, i.e. $L\hat{x}_b \geq \hat{y}_b$. Moreover, recall that at the beginning of the section, we assumed, without loss of generality, that the long side of P is vertical and the short side of P has non-negative slope.

Let $\Delta_{\hat{x}}(a, b)$ (resp. $\Delta_{\hat{y}}(a, b)$) denote the $\hat{x}$-coordinate difference (resp. the $\hat{y}$-coordinate difference) between a and b. We now have all the ingredients needed to prove the main theorem.

Theorem 1. *Suppose a and b are vertices in the parallelogram Delaunay graph. When $A\Delta_{\hat{x}}(a, b) \geq \Delta_{\hat{y}}(a, b)$ (i.e. we are in Scenario 2 or 3), we have*

$$d_2^T(a, b) \leq \left(A + \sqrt{1 + A^2 + 2A|\cos(\theta)|}\right)\hat{x}_b + \hat{y}_b. \tag{6}$$

Else, (i.e. we are in Scenario 1 or 4), we have

$$d_2^T(a, b) \leq \left(1 + \sqrt{1 + \frac{1}{A^2} + \frac{2|\cos(\theta)|}{A}}\right)\hat{x}_b + A\hat{y}_b. \tag{7}$$

Proof. To prove Theorem 1 we use induction on pairs of vertices (a, b) ordered from closest to furthest in the following sense: the proximity of vertices a and b is associated with the size of the smallest scaled translate of $\hat{P}$ which contains a and b on its boundary. In this sense, the base case consists of pairs of vertices a, b which lie on the boundary of the smallest empty scaled translate of $\hat{P}$. Note that there cannot be any other vertices of $\mathcal{P}$ in such a scaled translate, otherwise a, b would not be the closest pair of points. Hence there is an edge between a, b. This satisfies the statement of the theorem for both cases. This concludes the base case.

Let a, b be two vertices in the parallelogram Delaunay graph. Now, suppose that the statement holds for any pair of vertices associated with a smaller parallelogram. We first investigate Case (1), where $P(a, b)$ is empty. Case (2), where $P(a, b)$ is not empty, will follow.

(1) Suppose $P(a, b)$ is empty. We will analyse two subcases, (i) Scenarios 2 and 3, and then (ii) Scenarios 1 and 4.

(i) Since we are in Scenario 2 or 3, we have $L = A$ and $A\hat{x}_b \geq \hat{y}_b$.

If the parallelogram Delaunay graph contains the edge (a, b), then the statement holds.

Next, assume that there is no inductive parallelogram in the sequence $\hat{P}_1, \hat{P}_2, ..., \hat{P}_k$, then by case (1) of Lemma 4 we have $d_2^T(a, b) \leq \left(A + \sqrt{1 + A^2 + 2A|\cos(\theta)|}\right) \hat{x}_b + \hat{y}_b$. Now we study the case where there exists an inductive parallelogram. Assume that $\hat{P}_i$ is the first inductive parallelogram. As in Lemma 4, we have two subcases to consider. First we will look at the case where h_i is the inductive point of $\hat{P}_i$, and the case where l_i is the inductive point will follow. Suppose for now that h_i is the inductive point of $\hat{P}_i$, then using case (2)(a) of Lemma 4, we have that $d_2^T(a, h_i) + (\hat{y}_{h_i} - \hat{y}_b) \leq \left(A + \sqrt{1 + A^2 + 2A|\cos(\theta)|}\right) \hat{x}_{h_i}$ which can be rearranged to obtain a bound on the distance between a and h_i:

$$d_2^T(a, h_i) \leq \left(A + \sqrt{1 + A^2 + 2A|\cos(\theta)|}\right) \hat{x}_{h_i} - (\hat{y}_{h_i} - \hat{y}_b). \tag{8}$$

As in Lemma 5, we suppose $j > i$ is minimal such that $A(\hat{x}_b - \hat{x}_{h_j}) \geq \hat{y}_{h_j} - \hat{y}_b \geq 0$ and h_j is on the E side of $\hat{P}_j$. Then since all edges on the path $h_i, ..., h_j$ are NE edges, we can bound their lengths using the triangle inequality. We get that

$$d_2^T(h_i, h_j) \leq (\hat{x}_{h_j} - \hat{x}_{h_i}) + (\hat{y}_{h_i} - \hat{y}_{h_j}). \tag{9}$$

Since the smallest scaled translate of $\hat{P}$ that has both h_j and b on its boundary is smaller than the scaled translate which has a and b on its boundary, we can use the induction hypothesis. Moreover we have $A(\hat{x}_b - \hat{x}_{h_j}) \geq \hat{y}_{h_j} - \hat{y}_b \geq 0$, hence we use inequality 6:

$$d_2^T(h_j, b) \leq \left(A + \sqrt{1 + A^2 + 2A|\cos(\theta)|}\right) (\hat{x}_b - \hat{x}_{h_j}) + (\hat{y}_{h_j} - \hat{y}_b). \tag{10}$$

Using inequalities (8), (9) and (10) as well as the triangle inequality we get that

$$d_2^T(a,b) \leq d_2^T(a,h_i) + d_2^T(h_i,h_j) + d_2^T(h_j,b)$$
$$\leq \left(A + \sqrt{1+A^2+2A|\cos(\theta)|}\right)\hat{x}_{h_i} - (\hat{y}_{h_i}-\hat{y}_b) + (\hat{x}_{h_j}-\hat{x}_{h_i})$$
$$+ (\hat{y}_{h_i}-\hat{y}_{h_j}) + \left(A+\sqrt{1+A^2+2A|\cos(\theta)|}\right)(\hat{x}_b-\hat{x}_{h_j}) + (\hat{y}_{h_j}-\hat{y}_b)$$
$$\leq \left(A + \sqrt{1+A^2+2A|\cos(\theta)|}\right)\hat{x}_b$$
$$< \left(A + \sqrt{1+A^2+2A|\cos(\theta)|}\right)\hat{x}_b + \hat{y}_b$$

This completes the proof for the case where the inductive point of $\hat{P}_i$ is h_i. The case where l_i is the inductive point of $\hat{P}_i$ has been omitted.
(ii) The proof when we are in Scenario 1 or 4 has been omitted.
(2) Assume $P(a,b)$ contains at least one vertex of $\mathcal{P}$. We distinguish (i) Scenarios 2 and 3 from (ii) Scenarios 1 and 4.
(i) Assume we are in Scenario 2 or 3. To simplify the proof, we partition $P(a,b)$ in three regions $\mathcal{A}$, $\mathcal{B}$ and $\mathcal{C}$. Intuitively, the regions are obtained by drawing the line through a and the line through b with the same slope as the positive diagonal of $\hat{P}$. The labelling of these regions $\mathcal{A}$, $\mathcal{B}$ and $\mathcal{C}$ is done from left to right (Refer to Fig. 2). More precisely, we have $\mathcal{A} = \{p \in P(a,b) : A(\hat{x}_p - \hat{x}_a) < \hat{y}_p - \hat{y}_a\}$, $\mathcal{B} = \{p \in P(a,b) : A(\hat{x}_p - \hat{x}_a) \geq \hat{y}_p - \hat{y}_a \land A(\hat{x}_b - \hat{x}_p) \geq \hat{y}_b - \hat{y}_p\}$, $\mathcal{C} = \{p \in P(a,b) : A(\hat{x}_b - \hat{x}_p) < \hat{y}_b - \hat{y}_p\}$.

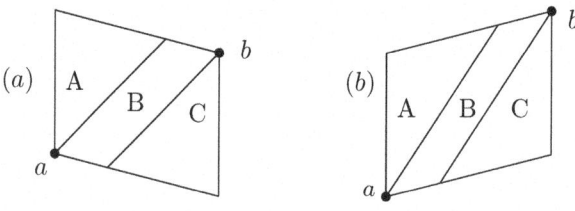

Fig. 2. Illustration of the three regions in $P(a,b)$. Scenario 2 is shown on the left (a), and Scenario 3 is shown on the right (b).

Observe that a point $p \in \mathcal{A}$ also satisfies $A(\hat{x}_b - \hat{x}_p) > \hat{y}_b - \hat{y}_p$. Moreover a point $p \in \mathcal{C}$ also satisfies $A(\hat{x}_p - \hat{x}_a) < \hat{y}_p - \hat{y}_a$.
When $p \in \mathcal{B}$, by definition we have that both $A(\hat{x}_p - \hat{x}_a) \geq \hat{y}_p - \hat{y}_a$ and $A(\hat{x}_b - \hat{x}_p) \geq \hat{y}_b - \hat{y}_p$ are satisfied. We can thus use inequality (6) on both pairs of vertices (a,p) and (p,b). We get

$$d_2^T(a,b) \le d_2^T(a,p) + d_2^T(p,b)$$
$$\le \left(A + \sqrt{1+A^2+2A|\cos(\theta)|}\right)(\hat{x}_p - \hat{x}_a) + (\hat{y}_p - \hat{y}_a)$$
$$+ \left(A + \sqrt{1+A^2+2A|\cos(\theta)|}\right)(\hat{x}_b - \hat{x}_p) + (\hat{y}_b - \hat{y}_p)$$
$$= \left(A + \sqrt{1+A^2+2A|\cos(\theta)|}\right)\hat{x}_b + \hat{y}_b.$$

Now we look at the case when there is no vertex in $\mathcal{B}$. Let $\hat{P}_a$ be the smallest homothet of $\hat{P}$ such that a is on its W side and there exists a vertex $p \in \mathcal{A}$ on its boundary. In an analogous fashion, we let $\hat{P}_b$ be the smallest homothet of $\hat{P}$ such that b is on its E side and there exists a vertex $q \in \mathcal{C}$ on its boundary. By assumption, there exists a vertex inside $P(a,b)$, thus either p or q exists. Assume for now that the vertex $p \in \mathcal{A}$ exists. The smallest scaled translate of $\hat{P}$ which has both p and b on its boundary is smaller than that of a and b. Moreover we that $A(\hat{x}_b - \hat{x}_p) > \hat{y}_b - \hat{y}_p$ hence we use inequality 6 to bound the length of the path between p and b. Therefore, we can apply the induction hypothesis on the pair (p,b). When (a,p) is an edge we have

$$d_2^T(a,b) \le d_2^T(a,p) + d_2^T(p,b) = d_2(a,p) + d_2^T(p,b)$$
$$\le (\hat{x}_p - \hat{x}_a) + (\hat{y}_p - \hat{y}_a) + \left(A + \sqrt{1+A^2+2A|\cos(\theta)|}\right)(\hat{x}_b - \hat{x}_p)$$
$$+ (\hat{y}_b - \hat{y}_p)$$
$$\le \left(A + \sqrt{1+A^2+2A|\cos(\theta)|}\right)\hat{x}_b + \hat{y}_b$$

The proof when a vertex q exists and (q,b) is an edge is similar.

If we suppose now that (a,p) is not an edge in the parallelogram Delaunay graph, then there exists at least one vertex in $\hat{P}_a \cap \mathcal{C}$. Let $p' \in \hat{P}_a \cap \mathcal{C}$ be the vertex closest to a, then we have that (a,p') is an edge. The smallest scaled translate of $\hat{P}$ which has both p' and b on its boundary is smaller than that of a and b. Moreover we have that $A(\hat{x}_b - \hat{x}_{p'}) < \hat{y}_b - \hat{y}_{p'}$ hence we use inequality 7 to bound the length of the path between p' and b.

$$d_2^T(p',b) \le A(\hat{x}_b - \hat{x}_{p'}) + \left(1 + \sqrt{1 + \frac{1}{A^2} + \frac{2|\cos(\theta)|}{A}}\right)(\hat{y}_b - \hat{y}_{p'}).$$

Since $p' \in \mathcal{C}$, we applied the induction hypothesis for instances of Scenarios 1 and 4 for the path from p' to b. This explains why we swapped the $\{\hat{x}, \hat{y}\}$ basis. We get

$$d_2^T(a,b) \leq d_2^T(a,p') + d_2^T(p',b)$$
$$= d_2(a,p') + d_2^T(p',b)$$
$$\leq (\hat{x}_{p'} - \hat{x}_a) + (\hat{y}_{p'} - \hat{y}_a) + A(\hat{x}_b - \hat{x}_{p'})$$
$$+ \left(1 + \sqrt{1 + \frac{1}{A^2} + \frac{2|\cos(\theta)|}{A}}\right)(\hat{y}_b - \hat{y}_{p'})$$
$$\leq A\hat{x}_b + \left(1 + \sqrt{1 + \frac{1}{A^2} + \frac{2|\cos(\theta)|}{A}}\right)\hat{y}_b$$

since $A \geq 1$.

Since we are in Scenario 2 or 3, $A\hat{x}_b \geq \hat{y}_b$ and we know that $1 + \sqrt{1 + \frac{1}{A^2} + \frac{2|\cos(\theta)|}{A}} > 1$, we have[3]

$$d_2^T(a,b) \leq A\hat{x}_b + \left(1 + \sqrt{1 + \frac{1}{A^2} + \frac{2|\cos(\theta)|}{A}}\right)\hat{y}_b$$
$$\leq \left(1 + \sqrt{1 + \frac{1}{A^2} + \frac{2|\cos(\theta)|}{A}}\right)A\hat{x}_b + \hat{y}_b$$
$$= \left(A + \sqrt{1 + A^2 + 2A|\cos(\theta)|}\right)\hat{x}_b + \hat{y}_b$$

This completes the proof when we are in Scenario 2 or 3.
(ii) The proof when we are in Scenario 1 or 4 has been omitted. □

We can now use the inequalities from Theorem 1 to bound the spanning ratio of the parallelogram Delaunay graph in the worst case. (The details have been omitted.) If we are in Scenario 2 or 3, we get

$$\frac{d_2^T(a,b)}{d_2(a,b)} \leq \frac{\left(A + \sqrt{1+A^2+2A|\cos(\theta)|}\right)\hat{x}_b + \hat{y}_b}{\sqrt{\hat{x}_b^2 + \hat{y}_b^2 - 2\hat{x}_b\hat{y}_b\cos(\pi-\theta)}} = \frac{A + \sqrt{1+A^2+2A|\cos(\theta)|} + \frac{\hat{y}_b}{\hat{x}_b}}{\sqrt{1 + (\frac{\hat{y}_b}{\hat{x}_b})^2 + 2\frac{\hat{y}_b}{\hat{x}_b}\cos(\theta)}}. \quad (11)$$

Let $f_{2,3}(\hat{y}_b/\hat{x}_b)$ be this function. However, if we are in Scenario 1 or 4 we get

$$\frac{d_2^T(a,b)}{d_2(a,b)} \leq \frac{\left(1 + \sqrt{1 + \frac{1}{A^2} + \frac{2|\cos(\theta)|}{A}}\right)\hat{x}_b + A\hat{y}_b}{\sqrt{\hat{x}_b^2 + \hat{y}_b^2 - 2\hat{x}_b\hat{y}_b\cos(\pi-\theta)}} = \frac{A + \sqrt{1+A^2+2A|\cos(\theta)|} + A^2\frac{\hat{y}_b}{\hat{x}_b}}{A\sqrt{1 + (\frac{\hat{y}_b}{\hat{x}_b})^2 + 2\frac{\hat{y}_b}{\hat{x}_b}\cos(\theta)}}. \quad (12)$$

Let $f_{1,4}(\hat{y}_b/\hat{x}_b)$ be this function.

The three candidate values for the maximum of $f_{2,3}(\hat{y}_b/\hat{x}_b)$ (resp. $f_{1,4}(\hat{y}_b/\hat{x}_b)$) are (1) $f_{2,3}(0)$ (resp. $f_{1,4}(0)$), (2) $\lim_{\hat{y}_b/\hat{x}_b \to \infty} f_{2,3}(\hat{y}_b/\hat{x}_b) = 1$

---

[3] From the fact that if $n > m > 0$ and $k > 1$ then $kn + m > km + n$ (Proof: $kn + m > km + n \iff k(n-m) + (m-n) > 0 \iff k(n-m) > (n-m)$ which is true for $k \geq 1$). In our case, we have that $n = A\hat{x}_b, m = \hat{y}_b$ and $k = 1 + \sqrt{1 + \frac{1}{A^2} + \frac{2|\cos(\theta)|}{A}}$.

(resp. $\lim_{\hat{y}_b/\hat{x}_b \to \infty} f_{1,4}(\hat{y}_b/\hat{x}_b) = A$) and (3) the value of $f_{2,3}$ (resp. $f_{1,4}$) when its derivative is 0, which we denote by $f_{2,3}^*$ (resp. $f_{1,4}^*$). We can show that $f_{2,3}(0) \geq f_{1,4}(0)$, $f_{2,3}^* \geq A$ and $f_{2,3}^* \geq f_{1,4}^*$. Hence, the maximum occurs in Scenario 2 or 3. Moreover, we can show that the maximum value of $f_{2,3}(\hat{y}_b/\hat{x}_b)$ is obtained when its derivative is 0, from which we get
$$\sqrt{2}\sqrt{1+A^2+A(|\cos(\theta)|-\cos(\theta))}+(A-\cos(\theta))\sqrt{1+A^2+2A|\cos(\theta)|}/\sin(\theta).$$
The worst case of this expression occurs when $\theta = \pi - \theta_0$, i.e., when we are in Scenario 2. This allows us to conclude with the following.

Theorem 2. *The spanning ratio of a parallelogram Delaunay graph is at most $h(A, \theta_0)$ (where $h(A, \theta_0)$ is defined in Sect. 1).*

3 The Lower Bound

Theorem 3. *There are parallelogram Delaunay graphs that have spanning ratio arbitrarily close to $h(A, \theta_0)$.*

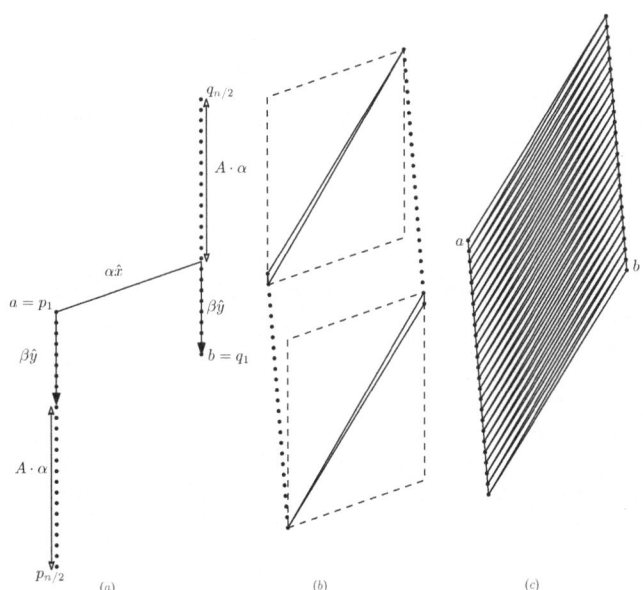

Fig. 3. Lower bound construction. Two triangles and their corresponding parallelograms are depicted.

Proof. Assume we are in Scenario 2 with $A \geq 1$, where $L = A$ and $\pi - \theta = \theta_0 \leq \frac{\pi}{2}$, the lower bound construction resembles that of Bonichon et al. [1]. Let a be the origin and let $b = \alpha\hat{x} + \beta\hat{y}$, with two vertical columns of equidistant vertices $p_1,..,p_{n/2}$ and $q_1,..,q_{n/2}$ with $p_1 = a, p_{n/2} = (\beta + \alpha A)\hat{y}, q_1 = b$ and $q_{n/2} = \alpha \hat{x} - \alpha A \hat{y}$. Move the vertices an arbitrary small distance in the horizontal direction, such that p_i lies to the left of p_{i+1} and q_i lies to the left of q_{i+1} for $1 \leq i \leq n/2$ (refer to Fig. 3. We analyze the length of one of the shortest paths between a and b, specifically the one via $p_{n/2}$. Since all perturbations can be made arbitrarily small, this path has length

$$(\beta + \alpha A) + \sqrt{\alpha^2 + (-\alpha A)^2 - 2\alpha(-\alpha A)\cos(\pi - \theta)} = \alpha(A + \sqrt{1 + A^2 + 2A\cos(\theta_0)}) + \beta.$$

The Euclidean distance between a and b is arbitrarily close to $\sqrt{\alpha^2 + \beta^2 - 2\alpha\beta\cos(\theta_0)}$. This implies that the spanning ratio is arbitrarily close to

$$\frac{\alpha(A + \sqrt{1 + A^2 + 2A|\cos(\theta_0)|}) + \beta}{\sqrt{\alpha^2 + \beta^2 - 2\alpha\beta\cos(\theta_0)}},$$

which matches $f_{2,3}(\beta/\alpha)$ defined at the end of the previous section. □

References

1. Bonichon, N., Gavoille, C., Hanusse, N., Perkovic, L.: Tight stretch factors for l_∞-Delaunay triangulations. Comput. Geom. **48**(3), 237–250 (2015)
2. Bose, P., Cano, P., Silveira, R.I.: Affine invariant triangulations. Comput. Aided Geom. Des. **91**, 102039 (2021)
3. Bose, P., Carmi, P., Collette, S., Smid, M.H.M.: On the stretch factor of convex Delaunay graphs. J. Comput. Geom. **1**(1), 41–56 (2010)
4. Bose, P., Carufel, J.L.D., Njoo, S.: The exact spanning ratio of the parallelogram Delaunay graph (2024). https://arxiv.org/abs/2312.14305
5. Bose, P., Carufel, J.D., van Renssen, A.: Constrained generalized Delaunay graphs are plane spanners. Comput. Geom. **74**, 50–65 (2018)
6. Bose, P., Devroye, L., Löffler, M., Snoeyink, J., Verma, V.: Almost all Delaunay triangulations have stretch factor greater than $\pi/2$. Comput. Geom. **44**(2), 121–127 (2011)
7. Chew, P.: There are planar graphs almost as good as the complete graph. J. Comput. Syst. Sci. **39**(2), 205–219 (1989)
8. Dobkin, D.P., Friedman, S.J., Supowit, K.J.: Delaunay graphs are almost as good as complete graphs. Discrete Comput. Geom. **5**(4), 399–407 (1990). https://doi.org/10.1007/BF02187801
9. Keil, J.M., Gutwin, C.A.: Classes of graphs which approximate the complete Euclidean graph. Discrete Comput. Geom. **7**(1), 13–28 (1992). https://doi.org/10.1007/BF02187821
10. Perkovic, L., Dennis, M., Türkoglu, D.: The stretch factor of hexagon-Delaunay triangulations. J. Comput. Geom. **12**(2), 86–125 (2021)
11. van Renssen, A., Sha, Y., Sun, Y., Wong, S.: The tight spanning ratio of the rectangle Delaunay triangulation. In: ESA. LIPIcs, vol. 274, pp. 99:1–99:15. Schloss Dagstuhl - Leibniz-Zentrum für Informatik (2023)
12. Xia, G.: The stretch factor of the Delaunay triangulation is less than 1.998. SIAM J. Comput. **42**(4), 1620–1659 (2013)
13. Xia, G., Zhang, L.: Toward the tight bound of the stretch factor of Delaunay triangulations. In: CCCG (2011)

A 1.5-Approximation Algorithm for Activating Two Disjoint st-Paths

Zeev Nutov[(✉)] and Dawod Kahba

The Open University of Israel, Ra'anana, Israel
nutov@openu.ac.il

Abstract. In the ACTIVATION k DISJOINT st-PATHS (ACTIVATION k-DP) problem we are given a graph $G = (V, E)$ with activation costs $\{c_{uv}^u, c_{uv}^v\}$ for every edge $uv \in E$, a source-sink pair $s, t \in V$, and an integer k. The goal is to compute an edge set $F \subseteq E$ of k internally node disjoint st-paths of minimum activation cost $\sum_{v \in V} \max_{uv \in F} c_{uv}^v$. The problem admits an easy 2-approximation algorithm. Alqahtani & Erlebach [1] claimed that ACTIVATION 2-DP admits a 1.5-approximation algorithm. The proof in [1] has an error, and we will show that the approximation ratio of their algorithm is at least 2. We will then give a different algorithm with approximation ratio 1.5.

1 Introduction

In network design problems one seeks a cheap subgraph that satisfies a prescribed property. A traditional setting is when each edge has a cost, and we want to minimize the cost of the subgraph. This setting does not capture many wireless networks scenarios, where a communication between two nodes depends on our "investment" in these nodes – like transmission energy and different types of equipment, and the cost incurred is a sum of these "investments". This motivates the type of problems we study here.

More formally, in **activation network design problems** we are given an undirected (multi-)graph $G = (V, E)$ where every edge $e = uv \in E$ has two (non-negative) **activation costs** $\{c_e^u, c_e^v\}$; here $e = uv \in E$ means that the edge e has ends u, v and belongs to E. An edge $e = uv \in E$ is **activated by a level assignment** $\{l_v : v \in V\}$ to the nodes if $l_u \geq c_e^u$ and $l_v \geq c_e^v$. The goal is to find a level assignment of minimum value $l(V) = \sum_{v \in V} l_v$, such that the activated edge set $F = \{e = uv \in E : c_e^u \leq l_u, c_e^v \leq l_v\}$ satisfies a prescribed property. Equivalently, the minimum value level assignment that activates an edge set $F \subseteq E$ is given by $\ell_F(v) = \max\{c_e^v : e \in \delta_F(v)\}$; here $\delta_F(v)$ denotes the set of edges in F incident to v, and a maximum taken over an empty set is assumed to be zero. We seek an edge set $F \subseteq E$ that satisfies the given property and minimizes $\ell_F(V) = \sum_{v \in V} \ell_F(v)$. Note that while we use l_v to denote a level assignment to a node v, we use a slightly different notation $\ell_F(v)$ for the function that evaluates the optimal assignment that activates a given edge set F.

© The Author(s), under exclusive license to Springer Nature Switzerland AG 2025
Q. Bramas et al. (Eds.): ALGOWIN 2024, LNCS 15026, pp. 159–172, 2025.
https://doi.org/10.1007/978-3-031-74580-5_12

Two types of activation costs were extensively studied in the literature, see a survey [14].

- **Node weights.** For all $v \in V$, c_e^v are identical for all edges incident to v. This is equivalent to having node weights w_v for all $v \in V$. The goal is to find a node subset $V' \subseteq V$ of minimum total weight $w(V') = \sum_{v \in V'} w_v$ such that the subgraph induced by V' satisfies the given property.
- **Power costs:** For all $e = uv \in E$, $c_e^u = c_e^v$. This is equivalent to having "power costs" $c_e = c_e^u = c_e^v$ for all $e = uv \in E$. The goal is to find an edge subset $F \subseteq E$ of minimum total power $\sum_{v \in V} \max\{c_e : e \in \delta_F(v)\}$ that satisfies the given property.

Node weighted problems include many fundamental problems such as SET COVER, NODE-WEIGHTED STEINER TREE, CONNECTED DOMINATING SET, and NODE WEIGHTED STEINER NETWORK c.f. [5,8,13,18]. Min-power problems were studied already in the 90's, c.f. [7,17,19,21], followed by many more. They were also widely studied in directed graphs, usually under the assumption that to activate an edge one needs to assign power only to its tail, while heads are assigned power zero, c.f. [6,7,12,14,20]. The undirected case has an additional requirement – we want the network to be bidirected, to allow a bidirectional communication. The general activation setting was suggested by Panigrahi [16] in 2011. Here we use a simpler but less general setting suggested in [9], which is equivalent to that of Panigrahi [16] for problems in which inclusion minimal feasible solutions have no parallel edges (but the input graph may have parallel edges).

In the traditional edge-costs scenario, a fundamental problem in network design is the SHORTEST st-PATH problem. A natural generalization and the simplest high connectivity network design problem is finding a set of k disjoint st-paths of minimum edge cost. Here the paths may be edge disjoint – the k EDGE DISJOINT st-PATHS problem, or internally (node) disjoint – the k DISJOINT st-PATHS problem. Both problems can be reduced to the MIN-COST k-FLOW problem, which has a polynomial time algorithm.

Similarly, one of the most fundamental problems in the activation setting is the ACTIVATION st-PATH problem. For the min-power version, a linear time reduction to the ordinary SHORTEST st-PATH problem is given by Althaus et al. [3]. Lando and Nutov [10] suggested a more general (but less efficient) "levels reduction" that converts several power problems into problems with node costs; this method extends also to the activation setting, see [14]. A fundamental generalization is activating a set of k internally disjoint or edge disjoint st-paths. Formally, the internally disjoint st-paths version is as follows.

ACTIVATION k DISJOINT st-PATHS (ACTIVATION k-DP)

Input: A multi-graph $G = (V, E)$ with activation costs $\{c_e^u, c_e^v\}$ for each uv-edge $e \in E$, $s, t \in V$, and an integer k.

Output: An edge set $F \subseteq E$ of k internally disjoint st-paths of minimum activation cost.

ACTIVATION k-DP admits an easy approximation ratio 2, c.f. [14, Corollary 15.4] and is polynomially solvable on bounded treewidth graphs [2]. NODE-WEIGHTED ACTIVATION k-DP admits a polynomial time algorithm, by a reduction to the ordinary MIN-COST k-DP. However, the complexity status of MIN-POWER k-DP is open even for unit power costs – it is not known whether the problem is in P or is NPC; this is so even for $k = 2$.

In the augmentation version of the problem – ACTIVATION k-DP AUGMENTATION, we are also given a subgraph $G_0 = (V, E_0)$ of G of activation cost zero that already contains $k - 1$ disjoint st-paths, and seek an augmenting edge set $F \subseteq E \setminus E_0$ such that $G_0 \cup F$ contains k disjoint st-paths. Specifically, we will consider the ACTIVATION 2-DP AUGMENTATION problem, where we want to augment an st-path P by an edge set $F \subseteq E \setminus P$ of minimum activation cost such that $P \cup F$ contains 2 disjoint st-paths. The following lemma was implicitly proved in [1].

Lemma 1 ([1]). *If* ACTIVATION 2-DP AUGMENTATION *admits a polynomial time algorithm then* ACTIVATION 2-DP *admits approximation ratio* 1.5.

The justification of Lemma 1 is as follows (see [1] for more details).

1. We may assume that we know the values $l_s = \ell_{F^*}(s)$ and $l_t = \ell_{F^*}(t)$ of some optimal solution F^* at s and t; there are at most $\deg_G(s) \cdot \deg_G(t) = O(m^2)$ choices, so we can try all choices and return the best outcome.
2. Remove edges $e = sv \in E$ with $c_e^s > l_s$ and edges $e = vt \in E$ with $c_e^t > l_t$. This gives an equivalent instance (for a correct choice of l_s, l_t).
3. Set $c_e^s = 0$ and $c_e^t = 0$ for every edge e incident to s and to t, respectively; this only shifts the optimal solution value by $l_s + l_t$.

Since the activation cost incurred at s and t is now zero, the cheaper among the two internally disjoint st-paths of F^* has activation cost at most $\frac{1}{2}$opt, where opt is the optimal solution value (to the modified problem). Thus if we compute an optimal st-path P (activation cost at most $\frac{1}{2}$opt) and an optimal augmenting edge set J (activation cost at most opt) such that $F = P \cup J$ has 2 internally-disjoint st-paths, then the overall activation cost of F will be at most $1.5 \cdot$ opt.

When the paths are required to be only edge disjoint we get the ACTIVATION k-EDP problem. This problem admits an easy approximation ratio $2k$. Lando & Nutov [10] improved the approximation ratio to k by showing that MIN-POWER k-EDP AUGMENTATION (the augmentation version of MIN-POWER k-EDP) admits a polynomial time algorithm. This algorithm extends to the activation case, see [14]. For simple graphs, MIN-POWER k-EDP admits approximation ratio $O(\sqrt{k})$ [15]. On the other hand [13] shows that ratio ρ for MIN-POWER k-EDP or NODE-WEIGHTED k-EDP with unit costs/weights implies ratio $1/2\rho^2$ for the DENSEST ℓ-SUBGRAPH problem, that currently has best known ratio $O(n^{-(1/4+\epsilon)})$ [4] and approximation threshold $\Omega\left(n^{-1/poly(\log \log n)}\right)$ [11].

Based on an idea of Srinivas & Modiano [20], Alqahtani & Erlebach [1] showed that ACTIVATION 2-EDP is not harder to approximate than ACTIVATION 2-DP.

Lemma 2 (Alqahtani & Erlebach [1]). *If* ACTIVATION 2-DP *admits approximation* ρ *then so does* ACTIVATION 2-EDP.

Alqahtani & Erlebach [1] claimed that ACTIVATION 2-DP AUGMENTATION admits a polynomial time algorithm, and thus (by Lemmas 1 and 2) both ACTIVATION 2-DP and ACTIVATION 2-EDP admit approximation ratio 1.5. In the next section we will give an example that the approximation ratio of the [1] algorithm for ACTIVATION 2-DP AUGMENTATION is not better than 2; the example and the mistake were confirmed by the authors of [1] in a personal communication. Then we will give a different polynomial algorithm for ACTIVATION 2-DP AUGMENTATION that is based on dynamic programming. Thus combining with Lemmas 1 and 2 we obtain the main result of this paper.

Theorem 1. ACTIVATION 2-DP AUGMENTATION *admits a polynomial time algorithm. Thus both* ACTIVATION 2-DP *and* ACTIVATION 2-EDP *admit approximation ratio* 1.5.

2 A Bad Example for the Alqahtani-Erlebach Algorithm

To illustrate the idea of the [1] algorithm, let us first describe a known algorithm for a particular case of the MIN-COST 2-EDP AUGMENTATION problem, where we seek to augment a Hamiltonian st-path P of cost 0 by an min-cost edge set F such that $P \cup F$ contains 2 edge disjoint st-paths. The algorithm reduces this problem to the ordinary MIN-COST st-PATH problem as follows, see Fig. 1(a, b).

Algorithm 1: HAMILTONIAN 2-EDP AUG$((V, E), c, P, \{s, t\})$

1 Construct an edge-weighted digraph D_P by directing P "backward" from t to s, and directing every edge not in P "forward" – from predecessor to successor in P.
2 Compute a shortest st-path P' in D_P.
3 Return the subset F of E that corresponds to the edges of $P' \setminus P$.

A slight modification of this algorithm works for ACTIVATION 2-EDP AUGMENTATION. For $v \in V$ let $L_v = \{c_{vu}^v : vu \in E\}$ be the set of possible **levels** at v. Apply the reduction in Algorithm 1, and then apply a step which we call **Levels Splitting**: for every pair (v, l) where $v \in V$ and $l \in L_v$ we add a node v_l of weight l, and put an edge from u_{l_i} to v_{l_j} if there is an edge $e = uv$ in D_P with $c_e^u \leq l_i$ and $c_e^v \leq l_j$. The reduction here is to the NODE-WEIGHTED st-PATH problem. The later problem can be easily reduced to the ordinary MIN-COST st-PATH problem by a step which we call **In-Out Splitting**: Replace each node $v \in V \setminus \{s, t\}$ by two nodes $v^{\text{in}}, v^{\text{out}}$ connected by the edge $v^{\text{in}} v^{\text{out}}$, and redirect every edge that enters v to enter v^{in} and every edge that leaves v to leave v^{out}, where we assume that $s^{\text{in}} = s^{\text{out}} = s$ and $t^{\text{in}} = t^{\text{out}} = t$. In this reduction the cost/weight of each edge $v^{\text{in}} v^{\text{out}}$ is the weight w_v of v, see Fig. 1(a, b, c). This is a particular case of the "Levels Reduction" of [10].

One can also solve the version when we have ordinary edge costs and require that $P \cup F$ contains 2 internally disjoint st-paths. For that, apply a standard reduction that converts edge connectivity into node connectivity, as follows

(i) After step 1 of Algorithm 1, add the In-Out Splitting step, where here the the cost of each edge $v^{in}v^{out}$ is 0.
(ii) Replace every edge $u^{out}v^{in} \notin P$ by the edge $u^{in}v^{out}$.

See Fig. 1(d), where after applying this reduction we switched between the names of $v^{in}v^{out}$, to be consistent with the [1] algorithm.

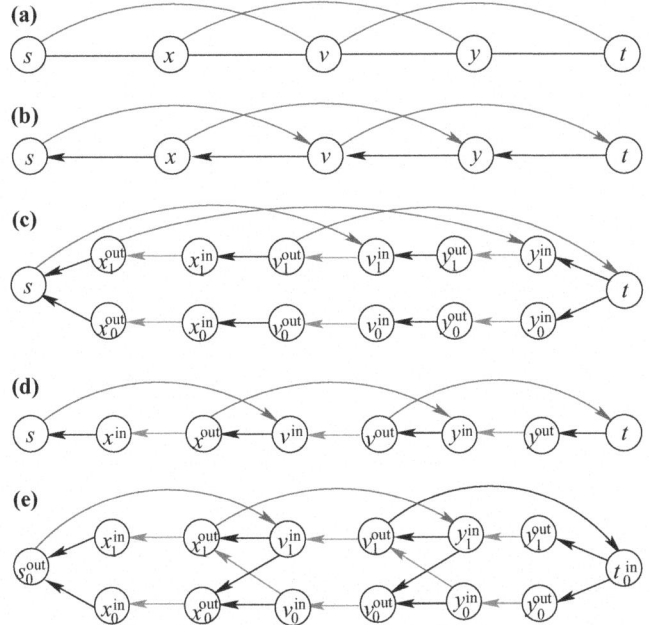

Fig. 1. Augmenting a Hamiltonian st-path to two edge/internally disjoint st-paths. Black edges have cost 0, blue and red edges have cost 1. (a) Problem instance. (b) Reducing MIN-COST 2-EDP AUGMENTATION to MIN-COST st-PATH. (c) Levels splitting, assuming that the activation costs of the blue edges in (a) are 1 at x, v, y and 0 at s, t. (d) Reducing MIN-COST 2-DP AUGMENTATION to MIN-COST st-PATH. (e) The reduction of [1]. (Color figure online)

The [1] algorithm attempts to combine the later reduction with the Levels Reduction in a sophisticated way. In the case when G has a zero cost Hamiltonian st-path P, $st \notin E$, $L = \{0,1\}$, $L_s = L_t = \{0\}$, and $c_{uv}^u = 1$ for all $e = uv \in E \setminus E(P)$ and $u \in V \setminus \{s,t\}$, the [1] algorithm reduces to the following, see Fig. 1(a, e).

1. Construct an edge-weighted directed graph D_P with nodes $s = s_0^{out}, t = t_0^{in}$ and 4 nodes $\{v_0^{in}, v_0^{out}, v_1^{in}, v_1^{out}\}$ for every $v \in V \setminus \{s,t\}$. The edge of D_P and their weights are:
   (i) For $v \in V \setminus \{s,t\}$: $\qquad w(v_a^{out} v_a^{in}) = 0 \quad a \in \{0,1\}$.
   (ii) For $uv \in P$: $\qquad w(v_b^{in} u_a^{out}) = a \quad a,b \in \{0,1\}$.
   For $uv \notin P$: $\qquad w(u_a^{out} v_b^{in}) = b \quad a,b \in \{0,1\}, \ u_a v_b \in E$.
2. Compute a cheapest st-path P' in D_P and return the subset of E that corresponds to P'.

Here for $e = uv \in E$ we write $u_a v_b \in E$ meaning that $c_e^a \leq a$ and $c_e^b \leq b$, namely, that uv can be activated by assigning a units to u and b units to v.

After the description of the algorithm, it was claimed in [1] that the cost of P' equals the activation cost of the subset of E that corresponds to P'. This is not correct, as shown by the following example. In the example in Fig. 1(d), the weight of P' is 2 while the optimal solution value is 3. Still, in this example the [1] algorithm computes an optimal solution. We give a more complicated example, which shows that the approximation ratio of this algorithm is no better than 2.

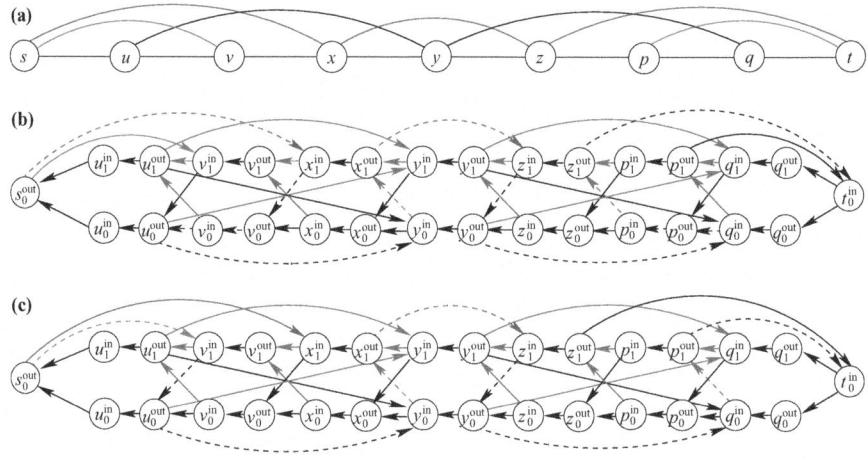

Fig. 2. Illustration to the [1] Algorithm. Black edges have weight/thresholds 0. (a) The input graph; colored edges have thresholds 0 at s,t and 1 otherwise. (b) The edge weighted directed graph D_P, w constructed in the AE reduction and the path (shown by dashed lines) in D_P of weight 4 that corresponds to the optimal solution $\{sx, xz, zt, uy, yq\}$. (c) The path (shown by dashed lines) in D_P of weight 4 that corresponds to the solution $\{sv, uy, xz, yq, pt\}$.

Consider the Fig. 2(a) graph with the st-path $s-u-v-x-y-z-p-q-t$. The optimal solution $\{sx, xz, zt, , uy, yq\}$ (the blue edges and the uy, yq edges) has value 2 (level assignment $l_x = l_z = 1$ and 0 otherwise); the $s_0^{out} t_0^{in}$-path in D_P of weight 4 that corresponds to this solution is (see Fig. 2(b)):

$s_0^{out} \to x_1^{in} \to v_0^{out} \to v_0^{in} \to u_0^{out} \to y_0^{in} \to x_1^{out} \to z_1^{in} \to y_0^{out} \to q_0^{in} \to p_0^{out} \to p_0^{in} \to z_1^{out} \to t_0^{in}$.

The solution $\{sv, uy, xz, yq, pt\}$ (the red edges and the uy, yq, xz edges) has value 4 (level assignment $l_v = l_x = l_z = l_p = 1$ and 0 otherwise); the $s_0^{out}t_0^{in}$-path in D_P of weight 4 that corresponds to this solution is (see Fig. 2(c)):

$s_0^{out} \to v_1^{in} \to u_0^{out} \to y_0^{in} \to x_1^{out} \to z_1^{in} \to y_0^{out} \to q_0^{in} \to p_1^{out} \to t_0^{in}$.

So in D_P, both paths have the same weight 4, but one path gives a solution of value 2 while the other of value 4.

3 Proof of Theorem 1

In this section we will prove Theorem 1 – that ACTIVATION 2-DP AUGMENTATION admits a polynomial time algorithm. The proof has two main ingredients:

1. A reduction to the case when P is a Hamiltonian path. For this, we will have to consider a slightly more general problem.
2. A dynamic programming polynomial time algorithm for instances when P is a Hamiltonian path. This is the hardest part, since decomposing a solution into two parts is highly non-trivial for (a generalization of) activation costs.

Recall that for $F \subseteq E$ and $v \in V$ we denote by $\ell_F(v) = \max_{e \in \delta_F(v)} c_e^v$ the activation cost incurred by F at v, and that for $S \subseteq V$ the activation cost incurred by F at nodes in S is

$$\ell_F(S) = \sum_{v \in S} \ell_F(v) = \sum_{v \in S} \max_{e \in \delta_F(v)} c_e^v . \quad (1)$$

For the proof of Theorem 1 it would be convenient to consider a more general problem where each edge $e = uv \in E$ has three costs $c_e^u, c(e), c_e^v$, where c_e^u, c_e^v are the activation costs of e and $c(e)$ is the ordinary "middle" cost of e. Then the activation cost of $F \subseteq E$ is denoted by $\tau(F)$ and defined to be the sum of the ordinary cost of F and the ordinary activation cost of F, namely:

$$\tau(F) = \ell_F(V) + c(F) = \sum_{v \in V} \max_{e \in \delta_F(v)} c_e^v + \sum_{e \in F} c(e) . \quad (2)$$

We now describe a method to convert an ACTIVATION 2-DP AUGMENTATION instance into an equivalent instance in which P is a Hamiltonian path but every edge has three costs as above. We call this problem 3-COST HAMILTONIAN ACTIVATION 2-DP AUGMENTATION. Formally, this problem is as follows.

3-COST HAMILTONIAN ACTIVATION 2-DP AUGMENTATION
Input: A multi-graph $G = (V, E)$ with activation costs $\{c_e^u, c_e, c_e^v\}$ for each uv-edge $e \in E$, $s, t \in V$, and a Hamiltonian st-path P edge disjoint to E.
Output: $F \subseteq E$ with $\tau(F)$ minimum such that $P \cup F$ contains 2 internally disjoint st-paths.

Let $\mathcal{I} = (G = (V, E), c, s, t, P)$ be an ACTIVATION 2-DP AUGMENTATION instance. Let us say that a uv-path Q in G is an **attachment path** if $u, v \in P$ but Q has no internal node in P. Note that any inclusion minimal edge set that contains 2 internally disjoint st-paths is a cycle. This implies that if F is an inclusion minimal solution to ACTIVATION 2-DP AUGMENTATION then $\deg_F(v) \in \{0, 2\}$ for every node $v \in V \setminus V(P)$, hence F partitions into attachment paths that are pairwise inner nodes disjoint. This enables us to apply a preprocessing similar to metric completion, and to construct an equivalent 3-COST HAMILTONIAN ACTIVATION 2-DP AUGMENTATION instance $\hat{\mathcal{I}} = (\hat{G} = (\hat{V}, \hat{E}), \hat{c}, s, t, P)$. For this, for every $u, v \in P$ and $(l_u, l_v) \in L_u \times L_v$ do the following.

1. Among all attachment uv-paths that have activation costs l_u at u and l_v at v (if any), compute the cheapest one $Q(l_u, l_v)$.
2. If $Q(l_u, l_v)$ exists, add a new "shortcut" edge $e = uv$ with activation costs $\hat{c}_e^u = l_u, \hat{c}_e^v = l_v$, and ordinary cost $\hat{c}_e = \ell_{Q(l_u, l_v)}(V) - (l_u + l_v)$ being the activation cost of $Q(l_u, l_v)$ on internal nodes of $Q(l_u, l_v)$.

After that, remove all nodes in $V \setminus V(P)$. Now P is a Hamiltonian path, and we get a 3-COST HAMILTONIAN ACTIVATION 2-DP AUGMENTATION instance $\hat{\mathcal{I}} = (\hat{G}, \hat{c}, s, t, P)$. It is easy to see that the instance $\hat{\mathcal{I}}$ can be constructed in polynomial time. Note that the instance $\mathcal{I}'$ may have many parallel edges, but this is allowed, also in the original instance $\mathcal{I}$ (Fig. 3).

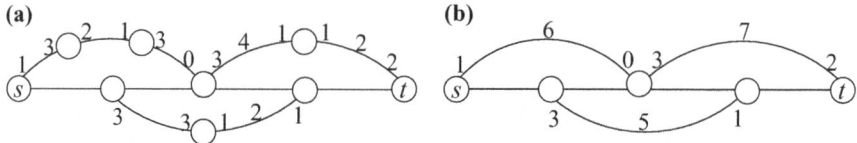

Fig. 3. Illustration of the reduction to 3-COST HAMILTONIAN ACTIVATION 2-DP AUGMENTATION. Zero middle costs are not shown. (a) ACTIVATION 2-DP AUGMENTATION feasible solution. (b) The "shortcut" solution. Note that both solutions have the same activation cost 28.

Now consider some inclusion minimal feasible solution F to $\mathcal{I}$. Replacing every attachment paths in F by a single edge as in step 2 above gives a feasible solution $\hat{F}$ to $\hat{\mathcal{I}}$ of value (activation cost) equal to that of F, since no two attachment paths in F share an inner node. Conversely, if $\hat{F}$ is a feasible $\hat{\mathcal{I}}$ solution, then replacing every edge in $\hat{F}$ by an appropriate path gives a feasible solution F to $\mathcal{I}$ of value at most that of $\hat{F}$; two such paths can share inner nodes but this may only decrease the activation cost of their union. Consequently, the new instance is equivalent to the original instance in the sense that every feasible solution to one of the instances can be converted to a feasible solution to the other instance of no greater value. We summarize this as follows.

Corollary 1. *If 3-COST HAMILTONIAN ACTIVATION 2-DP AUGMENTATION admits a polynomial time algorithm then so does ACTIVATION 2-DP AUGMENTATION.*

So from now and on our problem is 3-COST HAMILTONIAN ACTIVATION 2-DP AUGMENTATION. Let opt denote an optimal solution value for an instance of this problem. W.l.o.g. we will assume that $V = \{0, 1, \ldots, n\}$ and that $P = 0 - 1 - \cdots - n$ is a (Hamiltonian) $(0, n)$-path, and view each edge $ij \notin P$ as a directed edge (i, j) where $i < j$. Our goal is to find an edge set $F \subset E$ such that $P \cup F$ contains 2 internally disjoint $(0, n)$-paths and such that $\tau(F)$ is minimal.

Definition 1. *For $0 \leq i < j < n$ let $\mathcal{F}_{i,j}$ denote the family of all edge sets $F \subseteq E$ that satisfy the following two conditions.*

(i) F is an inclusion minimal edge set such that $P \cup F$ contains 2 internally disjoint $(j-1, n)$-paths.
(ii) No edge in F has an end strictly preceding i, namely, $x \geq i$ if $(x, y) \in F$.

One can easily see the following.

Proposition 1. $F \in \mathcal{F}_{0,j}$ *iff F is an inclusion minimal edge set such that $P \cup F$ has 2 internally disjoint $(j-1, n)$-paths. Hence* opt $= \min\{\tau(F) : F \in \mathcal{F}_{0,1}\}$.

We will need the following (essentially known) "recursive" property of the sets in $\mathcal{F}_{i,j}$, see Fig. 4(a).

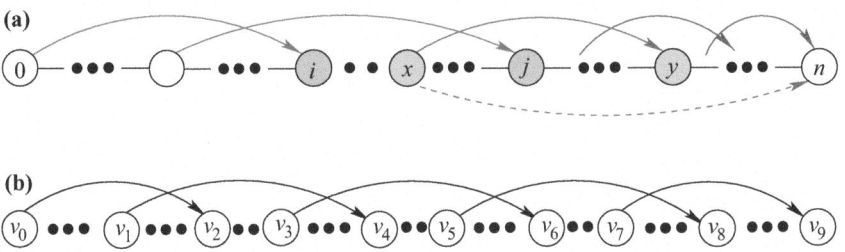

Fig. 4. Illustration to Lemma 3. Three dots between nodes indicates that these nodes are distinct, while if there are only two dots then the nodes may coincide.

Lemma 3. $F \in \mathcal{F}_{i,j}$ *if and only if there exists $i \leq x < j$ such that exactly one of the following holds, see Fig. 4(a).*

(i) $F = \{(x, n)\}$.
(ii) $F = \{(x, y)\} \cup F'$ for some $(x, y) \in E$ with $i \leq x < j < y < n$ and $F' \in \mathcal{F}_{j,y}$.

Proof. It is easy to see that if $|F| = 1$ then (i) must hold. Assume that $|F| \geq 2$. There is $(x, y) \in F$ with $x < j < y$ as otherwise $(P \cup F) \setminus \{j\}$ has no $(j-1, n)$-path. Let $F' = F \setminus \{(x, y)\}$. Then $P \cup F'$ contains 2 internally disjoint $(y-1, n)$-paths, as otherwise $(P \cup F) \setminus \{y\}$ has no $(j-1, n)$-path. Let x' be the lowest end of an edge in F', let $(x', y') \in F'$, and let $F'' = F \setminus \{(x', y')\}$. If $x' < j$ then $F' \in \mathcal{F}_{i,j}$ (if $y' \geq y$) or $F'' \in \mathcal{F}_{i,j}$ (if $y' \leq y$), contradicting the minimality of $\mathcal{F}$. If $x' \geq y$ then $(P \cup F) \setminus \{y\}$ has no $(j-1, n)$-path. This implies that $F' \in \mathcal{F}_{j,y}$, hence (ii) holds. □

Lemma 3 has the following (essentially known) consequence. Let F be an inclusion minimal feasible solution to our problem. Then the edges in F have an order $(v_0, v_2), (v_1, v_4), (v_3, v_6), \ldots, (v_{2q-1}, v_{2q+1})$ such that (see Fig. 4(b))

$$0 = v_0 < v_1 < v_2 \leq v_3 < v_4 \leq v_5 < \cdots \leq v_{2q-1} < v_{2q} < v_{2q+1} = n \ .$$

Note that in this node sequence some nodes may be identical (e.g., we may have $v_2 = v_3$), while the others are required to be distinct (e.g., $v_0 < v_1 < v_2$).

Recall the definition of the functions $\ell_F(S)$ in (1) and $\tau(F)$ in (2). For $(l_i, l_j) \in L_i \times L_j$ let us use the notation

$$E(l_i, l_j) = \{e \in E : \ell_e(i) \leq l_i, \ell_e(j) \leq l_j\} \ .$$

Let $0 \leq i < j < n$. For $F \subseteq E$ the (l_i, l_j)-**forced cost of** F is defined by

$$\alpha_F(l_i, l_j) = \begin{cases} c(F) + \ell_F(V \setminus \{i,j\}) + l_i + l_j & \text{if } F \subseteq E(l_i, l_j) \\ \infty & \text{otherwise} \end{cases}$$

Namely, assuming $F \subseteq E(l_i, l_j)$ we pay $\ell_F(v)$ at every node $v \in V \setminus \{i, j\}$, and in addition we "forcefully" pay l_i at i and l_j at j (even if F has no edge incident to i or to j). Note that

$$\alpha_F(l_i, l_j) = c(F) + \ell_F(V \setminus \{i,j\}) + l_i + l_j = \tau(F) + (l_i - \ell_F(i)) + (l_j - \ell_F(j)) \ .$$

This implies the following.

Corollary 2. $\alpha_F(l_i, l_j) \geq \tau(F)$ and an equality holds if and only if $\ell_F(i) = l_i$ and $\ell_F(j) = l_j$.

Let $f(l_i, l_j) = f(i, j, l_i, l_j)$ denote the minimal (l_i, l_j)-forced cost of an edge set $F \in \mathcal{F}_{i,j}$, namely

$$f(l_i, l_j) = f(i, j, l_i, l_j) = \min_{F \in \mathcal{F}_{i,j}} \alpha_F(l_i, l_j) \ . \tag{3}$$

Note that the definition of $f(l_i, l_j)$ depends on 4 parameters: the nodes i, j (as the minimum is taken over all $F \in \mathcal{F}_{i,j}$) and the activation values l_i, l_j that we "forcefully" assign to them; but to avoid a visual clutter we will use the abbreviated notation $f(l_i, l_j)$ for f, and also a similar abbreviated notation for functions derived from f. The number of possible values of $f(l_i, l_j) = f(i, j, l_i, l_j)$ is $O(|V|^2|L|^2)$ – there are $O(|V|^2)$ choices of i, j and at most $|L|^2$ choices of l_i, l_j. We will show how to compute all these values in polynomial time using dynamic programming. Specifically, we will get a recursive formula that enables us to compute each value either directly, or using previously computed values.

The next lemma shows how the function $f(l_i, l_j)$ is related to our problem.

Lemma 4. $\mathrm{opt} = \min_{l_0, l_1 \in L} f(l_0, l_1)$.

Proof. From the definition of $\mathcal{F}_{i,j}$ and Proposition 1 it follows that $\mathcal{F}_{0,1}$ is the set of all inclusion minimal feasible solutions. Let F^* be an inclusion minimal optimal solution and let $\hat{F}$ be the minimizer of (3). Then for any l_0, l_1 we have

$$f(l_0, l_1) = \alpha_{\hat{F}}(l_0, l_1) \geq \tau(\hat{F}) \geq \tau(F^*) = \mathsf{opt} \ .$$

Consequently, $\min_{l_0,l_1 \in L} f(l_0, l_1) \geq \mathsf{opt}$. On the other hand for $l_0 = \ell_{F^*}(0)$ and $l_1 = \ell_{F^*}(1)$ we have

$$f(l_0, l_1) = \alpha_{F^*}(l_0, l_1) = \tau(F^*) = \mathsf{opt} \ ,$$

by Corollary 2. This implies $\min_{l_0,l_1 \in L} f(l_0, l_1) \leq \mathsf{opt}$, concluding the proof. □

When $F = \{e\}$ is a single edge we will use the abbreviated notation $\alpha_e(l_i, l_j) = \alpha_{\{e\}}(l_i, l_j)$. For $(l_i, l_y) \in L_i \times L_y$ and an edge $e = (x, y) \in E(l_i, l_y)$ with $i \leq x < y$ let $\beta_e(l_i, l_y)$ be defined by

$$\beta_e(l_i, l_y) = \begin{cases} 0 & \text{if } x = i \\ \ell_e(x) & \text{if } x > i \end{cases}$$

We now define two functions that reflect the two different scenarios in Lemma 3.

$$g(l_i, l_j) = \min_e \{\alpha_e(l_i, l_j) : e = (x, n) \in E, i \leq x < j\}$$

$$h(l_i, l_j) = \min_{l_y, e} \{c(e) + l_i + \beta_e(l_i, l_y) + f(l_j, l_y) : e = (x, y) \in E(l_i, l_y), i \leq x < j < y\}$$

It is not hard to see that the function $g(l_i, l_j)$ is the minimal (l_i, l_j)-forced cost of a single edge set $e = (x, n)$ such that $\{e\} \in \mathcal{F}_{i,j}$. Thus if there exist a minimizer of (3) that is a single edge, then $f(l_i, l_j) = g(l_i, l_j)$.

We will show that the function $h(l_i, l_j)$ is the minimal (l_i, l_j)-forced cost of a non-singleton set $F \in \mathcal{F}_{i,j}$; note that by lemma 3 any such F is a union of some single edge $(x, y) \in F$ with $i \leq x < j < y < n$ and $F' \in \mathcal{F}_{j,y}$. We need the following lemma.

Lemma 5. *Let $F \in \mathcal{F}_{i,j}$ such that $F \subseteq E(l_i, l_j)$ and $|F| \geq 2$. Let $e = (x, y) \in F$ be the first edge of F as in Lemma 3, let $F' = F \setminus \{e\}$, and let $l_y = \ell_F(y)$. Then*

$$\alpha_F(l_i, l_j) = c(e) + l_i + \beta_e(l_i, l_y) + \alpha_{F'}(l_j, l_y) \ .$$

Proof. One can verify that for $l_y = \ell_F(y)$ we have $F' \subseteq E(l_j, l_y)$ and the following holds:

$$\ell_F(V \setminus \{i, j\}) = \beta_e(l_i, l_y) + \ell_{F'}(V \setminus \{j, y\}) + l_y \ .$$

From this and using that $c(F) = c(e) + c(F')$ we get

$$\begin{aligned}\alpha_F(l_i, l_j) &= c(F) + \ell_F(V \setminus \{i, j\}) + l_i + l_j \\ &= c(e) + l_i + \beta_e(l_i, l_y) + c(F') + \ell_{F'}(V \setminus \{j, y\}) + l_y + l_j \\ &= c(e) + l_i + \beta_e(l_i, l_y) + \alpha_{F'}(l_j, l_y) \ ,\end{aligned}$$

as required. □

Lemma 6. *Among all non-singleton sets in $\mathcal{F}_{i,j}$ let F^* have minimal (l_i, l_j)-forced cost. Then $h(l_i, l_j) = \alpha_{F^*}(l_i, l_j)$.*

Proof. We show that $\alpha_{F^*}(l_i, l_j) \geq h(l_i, l_j)$. Let $e = (x, y) \in F^*$ be the first edge of F^* as in Lemma 3(ii), let $F' = F \setminus \{e\}$, and let $l_y = \ell_{F^*}(y)$. Then $e \in E(l_i, l_y)$, hence by Lemma 5

$$\alpha_{F^*}(l_i, l_j) = c(e) + l_i + \beta_e(l_i, l_y) + \alpha_{F'}(l_j, l_y) \geq h(l_i, l_j) \ .$$

The inequality is since in the definition of $h(l_i, l_j)$ we minimize over $e = (x, y)$ and l_y.

We show that $\alpha_{F^*}(l_i, l_j) \leq h(l_i, l_j)$. Let $e = (x, y) \in E$ and l_y be the parameters for which the minimum in the definition of $h(l_i, l_j)$ is attained, and let $F' \in \mathcal{F}_{j,y}$ such that $f(l_j, l_y) = \alpha_{F'}(l_j, l_y)$. Let $F = F' \cup \{e\}$ and note that $F \in \mathcal{F}_{i,j}$ (by Lemma 3) and that $l_y = \ell_F(y)$ (by the definition of $h(l_i, l_j)$). Consequently,

$$\alpha_{F^*}(l_i, l_j) \leq \alpha_F(l_i, l_j) = c(e) + l_i + \beta_e(l_i, l_y) + f(l_j, l_y) = h(l_i, l_j)$$

The inequality is since F^* has minimal (l_i, l_j)-forced cost.

We showed that $\alpha_{F^*}(l_i, l_j) \geq h(l_i, l_j)$ and that $\alpha_{F^*}(l_i, l_j) \leq h(l_i, l_j)$, hence the proof is complete. □

Let F^* be the minimizer of (3). From Lemma 6 we have:

- If $|F^*| = 1$ then $f(l_i, l_j) = g(l_i, l_j)$.
- If $|F^*| \geq 2$ then $f(l_i, l_j) = h(l_i, l_j)$.

Therefore

$$f(l_i, l_j) = \min\{g(l_i, l_j), h(l_i, l_j)\} \qquad (4)$$

Note that the quantities $g(l_i, l_j)$ can be computed directly in polynomial time. The recurrence in (4) enables to compute values of $f(l_i, l_j)$, for all $0 \leq i < j \leq n - 1$ and $(l_i, l_j) \in L_i \times L_j$, in polynomial time. The number of such values is $O(n^2 |L|^2)$, concluding the proof of Theorem 1.

Let us illustrate the recursion by showing how the values of $f(l_i, l_j)$ are computed for $j = n - 1, n - 2$. Recall that the values of the function g are computed directly, without recursion and that

$$h(l_i, l_j) = \min_{l_y, e}\{c(e) + l_i + \beta_e(l_i, l_y) + f(l_j, l_y) : e = (x, y) \in E(l_i, l_y), i \leq x < j < y\}$$

For $j = n - 1$ we have $h(l_i, l_j) = \infty$, and thus:

$$f(l_i, l_{n-1}) = g(l_i, l_{n-1})$$

For $j = n - 2$, the only possible value of y is $y = n - 1$. For every $i \leq x < y = n - 1$ and $e = xy \in E$ we compute directly (without recursion) the values $\beta_e(l_i, l_y)$. Then

$$h(l_i, l_{n-2}) = \min_{l_y, e}\{c(e) + l_i + \beta_e(l_i, l_y) + f(l_j, l_y) : e = (x, y) \in E(l_i, l_y), i \leq x < j < y\}$$

$$= \min_{l_{n-1}, e}\left\{c(e) + l_i + \beta_e(l_i, l_{n-1}) + f(l_{n-2}, l_{n-1}) : \begin{array}{l} e = (x, n-1) \in E(l_i, l_{n-1}) \\ i \leq x < j < n - 1 \end{array}\right\}$$

Substituting the already computed value $f(l_{n-2}, l_{n-1}) = g(l_{n-2}, l_{n-1})$ enables to compute the minimum of the obtained expression, and thus also to compute $f(l_i, l_n - 2)$ via (4).

In a similar way we can compute $h(l_i, l_{n-3})$, then $f(l_i, l_{n-3})$, and so on.

4 Concluding Remarks

In this paper we developed a polynomial time algorithm for the ACTIVATION 2-DP AUGMENTATION problem. This implies approximation ratio 1.5 for ACTIVATION 2-DP and ACTIVATION 2-EDP, improving the trivial ratio of 2. We believe that our techniques may also enable to obtain a polynomial time algorithm for ACTIVATION 3-DP AUGMENTATION (increasing the number of st-paths from 2 to 3). If so then this would imply approximation ratio 11/6 for ACTIVATION 3-DP as follows. Similarly to the proof of Lemma 1, we may assume that $c_e^s = 0$ and $c_e^t = 0$ for every edge e incident to s and to t, respectively. Let F^* be an optimal solution and F_i^* the i paths of F^* of minimal activation cost, $i = 1, 2$; note that $\tau(F_i^*) \leq \frac{i}{3}\mathsf{opt}$.

1. Let P be an st-path of minimal activation cost. Then $\tau(P) \leq \tau(F_1^*) \leq \frac{1}{3}\mathsf{opt}$.
2. Let J be an optimal solution to ACTIVATION 2-DP AUGMENTATION with the path P. Then $\tau(P) \leq \tau(F_2^*) \leq \frac{2}{3}\mathsf{opt}$.
3. Finally, if J' is an optimal ACTIVATION 3-DP AUGMENTATION for $P \cup J$ then $\tau(J') \leq \mathsf{opt}$.

Consequently, the activation ciost of the solution $P \cup J \cup J'$ will be at most $\tau(P) + \tau(J) + \tau(J') \leq (1/3 + 2/3 + 1)\mathsf{opt} = 11/6 \cdot \mathsf{opt}$.

A major open problem in the field is to determine whether ACTIVATION 2-DP is NP-complete or can be solved in polynomial time. The problem is open even for power activation costs.

References

1. Alqahtani, H.M., Erlebach, T.: Approximation algorithms for disjoint st-paths with minimum activation cost. In: Spirakis, P.G., Serna, M. (eds.) CIAC 2013. LNCS, vol. 7878, pp. 1–12. Springer, Heidelberg (2013). https://doi.org/10.1007/978-3-642-38233-8_1
2. Alqahtani, H.M., Erlebach, T.: Minimum activation cost node-disjoint paths in graphs with bounded treewidth. In: Geffert, V., Preneel, B., Rovan, B., Štuller, J., Tjoa, A.M. (eds.) SOFSEM 2014. LNCS, vol. 8327, pp. 65–76. Springer, Cham (2014). https://doi.org/10.1007/978-3-319-04298-5_7
3. Althaus, E., Calinescu, G., Mandoiu, I., Prasad, S., Tchervenski, N., Zelikovsky, A.: Power efficient range assignment for symmetric connectivity in static ad-hoc wireless networks. Wireless Netw. **12**(3), 287–299 (2006)
4. Bhaskara, A., Charikar, M., Chlamtac, E., Feige, U., Vijayaraghavan, A.: Detecting high log-densities: an $O(n^{1/4})$ approximation for densest k-subgraph. In: STOC, pp. 201–210 (2010)

5. Guha, S., Khuller, S.: Approximation algorithms for connected dominating sets. Algorithmica **20**, 374–387 (1998)
6. Hajiaghayi, M., Kortsarz, G., Mirrokni, V., Nutov, Z.: Power optimization for connectivity problems. Math. Program. **110**(1), 195–208 (2007)
7. Kirousis, L.M., Kranakis, E., Krizanc, D., Pelc, A.: Power consumption in packet radio networks. Theoret. Comput. Sci. **243**(1–2), 289–305 (2000)
8. Klein, P., Ravi, R.: A nearly best-possible approximation algorithm for node-weighted Steiner trees. J. Algorithms **19**(1), 104–115 (1995)
9. Kortsarz, G., Nutov, Z., Shalom, E.: Approximating activation edge-cover and facility location problems. Theoret. Comput. Sci. **930**, 218–228 (2022)
10. Lando, Y., Nutov, Z.: On minimum power connectivity problems. J. Discrete Algorithms **8**(2), 164–173 (2010)
11. Manurangsi, P.: Almost-polynomial ratio ETH-hardness of approximating densest k-subgraph. In: STOC, pp. 954–961 (2017)
12. Nutov, Z.: Approximating minimum power covers of intersecting families and directed edge-connectivity problems. Theoret. Comput. Sci. **411**(26–28), 2502–2512 (2010)
13. Nutov, Z.: Approximating Steiner networks with node-weights. SIAM J. Comput. **39**(7), 3001–3022 (2010)
14. Nutov, Z.: Activation network design problems. In: Gonzalez, T.F., (ed.) Handbook on Approximation Algorithms and Metaheuristics, Second Edition, vol. 2, chapter 15. Chapman & Hall/CRC (2018)
15. Nutov, Z.: An $O(\sqrt{k})$-approximation algorithm for minimum power k edge disjoint st-paths. In: 19th Conference on Computability in Europe, CiE, pp. 287–296 (2023). To appear in Information Processing Letters
16. Panigrahi, D.: Survivable network design problems in wireless networks. In: SODA, pp. 1014–1027 (2011)
17. Rodoplu, V., Meng, T.H.: Minimum energy mobile wireless networks. In: IEEE International Conference on Communications (ICC), pp. 1633–1639 (1998)
18. Segev, A.: The node-weighted Steiner tree problem. Networks **17**, 1–17 (1987)
19. Singh, S., Raghavendra, C.S., Stepanek, J.: Power-aware broadcasting in mobile ad hoc networks. In: Proceedings of IEEE PIMRC (1999)
20. Srinivas, A., Modiano, E.H.: Finding minimum energy disjoint paths in wireless Ad-Hoc networks. Wireless Netw. **11**(4), 401–417 (2005)
21. Wieselthier, J.E., Nguyen, G.D., Ephremides, A.: On the construction of energy-efficient broadcast and multicast trees in wireless networks. In: Proceedings of IEEE INFOCOM, pp. 585–594 (2000)

Modular Population Protocols

Michael Raskin[✉][iD]

LaBRI, University of Bordeaux, CNRS UMR 5800, Bordeaux, France
mraskin@u-bordeaux.fr

Abstract. Population protocols are a model of distributed computation intended for the study of networks of independent computing agents with dynamic communication structure. Each agent has a finite number of states, and communication opportunities occur nondeterministically, allowing the agents involved to change their states based on each other's states. Population protocols are often studied in terms of reaching a consensus on whether the input configuration satisfied some predicate.

A desirable property of a computation model is modularity, the ability to combine existing simpler computations in a straightforward way. In the present paper we present a more general notion of functionality implemented by a population protocol in terms of multisets of inputs and outputs. This notion allows to design multiphase protocols as combinations of independently defined phases. The additional generality also increases the range of behaviours that can be captured in applications (e.g. maintaining the role distribution in a fleet of servers).

We show that composition of protocols can be performed in a uniform mechanical way, and that the expressive power is essentially semilinear, similar to the predicate expressive power in the original population protocol setting.

Keywords: Population protocols · Protocol verification · Modularity

1 Introduction

1.1 General Context of Population Protocols

Population protocols have been introduced in [2,3] as a restricted yet useful subclass of general distributed protocols. Each agent in a population protocol has a fixed amount of local storage, and an execution consists of selecting pairs of agents and letting them update their states based on an interaction. The choice of pairs is assumed to be performed by an adversary subject to a fairness condition. The fairness condition ensures that the adversary must allow the protocol to progress.

Typically, population protocols are studied from the point of view of recognising some properties of an input configuration. In this context population protocols and their subclasses have been studied, for example, from the point of view of expressive power [5], verification complexity [9,18,19], time to convergence [4,15], necessary state count [8], etc.

The original target application of population protocols and related models is modelling networks of restricted sensors, starting from the original paper [2] on population protocols. Of course, in the modern applications the cheapest microcontrollers typically have thousands of bits of volatile memory permitting the use of simpler and faster algorithms for recognising properties of an input configuration. So on the one hand, the original motivation for the restrictions in the population protocol model seems to have less relevance. On the other hand, verifying distributed systems benefits from access to a variety of restricted models with a wide range of trade-offs between the expressive power and verification complexity, as most problems are undecidable in the unrestricted case. Complex, unrestricted, and impossible to verify distributed deployments lead to undesirable and hard to predict and sometimes even diagnose situations such as so called gray failures [22] and similar.

From the theoretical point of view, population protocols provide a model of distributed computing with some of verification problems still decidable [17] although non-elementary [11]. This property puts them near the edge of decidability of verification, which is interesting on its own.

1.2 Composition

Unfortunately, as the standard approach considers protocols that compute predicates, composing protocols directly is limited to boolean combinations. Whenever a multiphase protocol needs to be constructed, the interaction between phases needs to be described and proven in an ad hoc way. We find it desirable to have better modularity in protocol design.

Naturally, for the composition to be useful, we need the protocols to achieve more complex output distributions than consensus. Moreover, some constructions in the literature [10,20] have more or less sub-protocols executed in parallel with different agents participating in different sub-protocols based on the output of yet another «previous» sub-protocol. From the other point of view, desirable behaviours of distributed systems go beyond consensus about a single property of initial configuration. For example, one might want to maintain task allocation across a fleet of servers. Task allocation usually depends on the server models, and servers are sometimes taken out of service for maintenance. From this point of view, we also find it interesting to study a more general notion of expressive power.

1.3 Related Work

Many approaches to composition of distributed protocols depend on a fixed communication structure [7], relatively rich local capabilities with infinite state space [25], or specific limits on how often each agents must be scheduled [12]. As there is no natural translation of such approaches to the model of population protocols, and the possibilities are less restricted in the richer models, we do not aim to classify such approaches.

Many composition methods rely on the notion of self-stabilisation introduced by Dijkstra [13], informally meaning that the agents will reach a correct (collective) configuration no matter what are their initial local states. Self-stabilising protocols compose naturally. Indeed, whatever effects on the consumer protocol happen because of the changes in the output of the producer protocol, the end results can be treated as the initial configuration before the self-stabilisation in the consumer protocol starts. This has been long used to design composition formalisms [14,21]. Self-stabilisation has been applied to population protocols [6]. There, a general definition of behaviours as sets of series of output configurations is used, and a subclass behaviours with eventually unchanging outputs is defined. However, self-stabilisation is a very restrictive requirement for a population protocol where each agent may talk to each other (i.e. the communication graph is a clique). It is shown [6] that one cannot do leader election in a self-stabilising way, and the same proof applies to reaching the consensus whether there is currently a leader.

Some papers on self-stabilisation use lemmas about composing completely generic behaviours [14], but this is done in a low-level way.

The limitations of self-stabilisation for population protocols are not shared by the protocols with stabilising inputs [1]. The idea is that each agent gets an input that can change finitely many times. The authors mention that this approach is useful for composition, but only study reaching consensus on the value of some predicates. Moreover, only a conference version of that article exists with proofs deferred to a full version that has never been finished, so for some statements it is unclear whether they should be considered proven.

One of the works on majority [20] explicitly describes the most complicated protocol via a sequential composition of protocols with eventually-stabilising inputs, while solving a problem that is impossible for general self-stabilising protocols. However, the proofs are specific to the protocols used and no general statement (nor a general definition) is given. In a sense, our approach is a broad and reusable generalisation of the approach there.

1.4 Contribution

In the present paper we introduce an alternative general notion of a protocol implementing an input-output specification. We consider each agent to have an input, and as usual there is an output function. An input-output specification is a relation between multisets of inputs and multisets of outputs, plus a compatibility relation between individual inputs and outputs. A protocol implements the specification, if in each fair execution from an input configuration there is a step after which the specification is always satisfied, both in terms of the multisets of inputs and outputs, and in terms of each agent's output being compatible with the input. The standard notion of computing predicates by stable consensus corresponds to a natural class of specifications where output is a single bit, only consensus output configurations are acceptable, and for each input configuration only one of the two consensus options is acceptable.

Additionally, we define computations with shutdown requests. We allow the scheduler to add new agents, or to tell existing agents to leave the computation. Each leaving agent can take some time to hand over the information, but must eventually terminate (in a fair execution). Once there is no turnover, an input-output specification must be eventually stably satisfied.

We show a natural completely mechanical way of combining two population protocols with shutdown requests implementing two relations to obtain a protocol with shutdown requests implementing the composition of these relations.

In terms of handling the inputs, we add the possibility of shutdown request to the approach of stabilising inputs. In terms of the specifications implemented, we study what multisets of outputs can get obtained from what multisets of inputs, while previous work for stabilising inputs only considered computing predicates.

The rest of the present paper is organised as follows. We start with presenting the standard definitions for population protocols, then in the next section we define our extension to the model to speak about specifications beyond predicate evaluation and provide some examples. In the section after that we define and construct sequential composition of protocols. We then proceed to characterise the expressive power of population protocols under our definition. The paper ends with a small conclusion with some future directions outlined.

Due to the space constraints, the proofs missing in the main text have been placed in the full version [24].

2 Basic Definitions

In this section we recall the standard definitions and facts related to population protocols. We use the definition where agents have identities for the purposes of analysis, but cannot distinguish each other. This will also be relevant in the generalisations. First we define the population protocols. We start by describing what information we need to specify a protocol.

Definition 1. *A <u>population protocol</u> is defined by a finite set of <u>states</u> Q and a <u>step relation</u> $Step \subset Q^2 \times Q^2$. When there is no ambiguity about the protocol, we abbreviate $((q_1, q_2), (q_1', q_2')) \in Step$ as $(q_1, q_2) \mapsto (q_1', q_2')$ and call the quadruple $(q_1, q_2) \mapsto (q_1', q_2')$ a <u>transition</u>.*

We use the following notation to work with function on agents.

Definition 2. *For a function f let $\mathrm{Dom}(f)$ denote the domain of the function.*

For a function f and $x \notin \mathrm{Dom}(f)$ let $f \cup \{x \mapsto y\}$ denote the function g defined on $\mathrm{Dom}(f) \cup \{x\}$ such that $g\,|_{\mathrm{Dom}(f)} = f$ and $g(x) = y$. For $u \in \mathrm{Dom}(f)$ let $f[u \mapsto v]$ denote the function h defined on $\mathrm{Dom}(f)$ such that $h\,|_{\mathrm{Dom}(f) \setminus \{u\}} = f\,|_{\mathrm{Dom}(f) \setminus \{u\}}$ and $h(u) = v$. For symmetry, if $w = f(u)$ let $f \setminus \{u \mapsto w\}$ denote restriction $f\,|_{\mathrm{Dom}(f) \setminus \{u\}}$.

Use of this notation implies an assertion of correctness, i.e. $x \notin \mathrm{Dom}(f)$, $u \in \mathrm{Dom}(f)$, and $w = f(u)$.

Definition 3. A <u>configuration</u> of a population protocol is a set A of agent identites, and a state function $C: A \to Q$, assigning states to agents. We identify the configuration with the state function as $A = \mathrm{Dom}(C)$. The <u>size</u> of a configuration C is the number of agents. An <u>execution</u> of a population protocol is a finite or infinite sequence $(C_0, C_1, \ldots)$ of configurations such that the set of agents is the same for each C_j, and for each j between 1 and the execution length we have some two agents a_1, a_2 that interact according to the rules, i.e. $C_j(a_1) = q_1$, $C_j(a_2) = q_2$, $C_{j+1} = C_j[a_1 \mapsto q_1'][a_2 \mapsto q_2']$ where $((q_1, q_2), (q_1', q_2')) \in Step$. In other words, we let two agents with states q_1 and q_2 interact in some way permitted by the Step relation.

Example 1. Consider the set of states $\{q_0, q_1, q_2, q_3\}$. The step relation is described by

$$(q_1, q_1) \mapsto (q_0, q_2),$$
$$(q_2, q_1) \mapsto (q_0, q_3),$$
$$(q_2, q_2) \mapsto (q_1, q_3),$$
$$(q_0, q_3) \mapsto (q_3, q_3),$$
$$(q_1, q_3) \mapsto (q_3, q_3),$$
$$(q_2, q_3) \mapsto (q_3, q_3).$$

Using agent identities 1, 2, and 3, and denoting a function from $1, 2, 3$ as a tuple, we can consider the following execution: $(q_1, q_1, q_1), (q_2, q_1, q_0), (q_0, q_3, q_0)$, $(q_3, q_3, q_0), (q_3, q_3, q_3)$. Here we use the first two steps, then twice the fourth step.

Remark 1. Note that all the configurations in an execution have the same size.

We often consider executions with the steps chosen by an adversary. However, we need to restrict adversary to ensure that some useful computation remains possible. To prevent the adversary from e.g. only letting one pair of agents to interact, we require the executions to be fair. The fairness condition can also be described by comparison with random choice of steps to perform: fairness is a combinatorial way to exclude a zero-probability set of bad executions.

Definition 4. Consider a population protocol $(Q, Step)$.

A configuration C' is <u>reachable</u> from configuration C iff there is a finite execution with the initial configuration C and the final configuration C'.

A finite execution is <u>fair</u> if it cannot be extended, i.e. it is not a prefix of any longer execution.

An infinite execution $C_0, C_1, \ldots$ is <u>fair</u> if for every configuration C' either C' is not reachable from some C_j (and all the following configurations), or C' occurs among C_j infinitely many times.

Example 2. The finite executions in the Example 1 are fair.

Remark 2. As long as the number of reachable configurations is finite, fairness implies that every set of configurations either becomes unreachable, or gets reached infinitely many times.

The most popular notion of expressive power for population protocols is computing predicates, defined in the following way.

Definition 5. *Consider a population protocol $(Q, Step)$ with additionally defined non-empty set of <u>input states</u> $I_s \subset Q$, output alphabet O and <u>output function</u> $o : Q \to O$.*

A state is <u>inhabited</u> in the configuration if there is at least one agent with this state. Considering a configuration as a function from agents to states, we can say that a state q is inhabited if $q \in \mathrm{Im}(C)$.

A configuration C is an <u>input configuration</u> if all the inhabited states are among the input states, $\mathrm{Im}(C) \subset I_s$.

A configuration C is a b-<u>consensus</u> for some $b \in O$ if the output function yields b for all the inhabited states, $\mathrm{Im}(o \circ C) = \{b\}$. A configuration is a <u>stable b-consensus</u> if it is a b-consensus together with all the configurations reachable from it. A configuration is called just a <u>consensus</u> or a <u>stable consensus</u> if it is a b-consensus (respectively stable b-consensus) for some b.

A protocol <u>computes</u> a function $\varphi : \mathbb{N}_s^I \to O$ iff for each input configuration C every fair execution with initial configuration C contains a stable $\varphi(C)$-consensus. We usually use the protocols computing predicates, which corresponds to $O = \{true, false\}$.

Example 3. If we define the set of input states $I_s = \{q_1\}$, output set $O = \{true, false\}$ and the output function $o(q){=}(q = q_3)$, the protocol in the example 1 computes the predicate $\varphi(C) = (C(q_1) \geq 3)$.

3 Model Extensions

In this section we describe our extensions.

Informally speaking, each agent knows its input (either a value or a shutdown request) as a part of the state, but the agent cannot change it. For convenience, all input state have the same «empty» internal component of the state. An agent whose input becomes a shutdown request and doesn't change should eventually change the internal component of the state to empty; agents with a shutdown request and empty internal component of the state do not participate in any interactions (and can be removed from the configuration). The scheduler can change the inputs and add agents in the input states, but only finitely many times.

A specification consists of two relations: the main relation on multisets of inputs and multisets of outputs; and a secondary relation on the input language and the output language. The first relation describes the global-level requirements, and the second describes compatibility of inputs and outputs (e.g. a server needs to have enough storage if it is a backup server). For every multiset of inputs there must be at least one acceptable multiset of input-output pairs (i.e. the task is never completely impossible). A protocol implements a specification (φ, ψ) if any finite sequence of scheduler actions from an input configuration followed by a fair execution without input changes or agent addition/removal eventually has a stable output for each agent and the multisets of inputs and outputs satisfy the relation φ, while each agent's input and output satisfy ψ. So we could say something like «the input being amount of storage for a server, we consider as many webservers as there are servers without sufficient storage for a database server, as many database servers as webservers, and the remaining servers as backup servers - and only servers with enough storage can be database servers or backup servers». Then after decommissioning some servers, deploying some new ones, and reconfiguring a few of the remaining ones, the fleet settles into a role assignment compliant with the policy. Formally, we also need some policy what to do when no servers have sufficient storage, accepting something that would be a misconfiguration otherwise.

Definition 6. *We use $\perp$ to denote lack of value (in the sense of a shutdown request or in the sense of the initial empty internal state).*

A protocol is <u>input-saving</u> if there is a set of input values I such that the set of states Q is the Cartesian product $(I \cup \{\perp\}) \times (Q_{int} \cup \{\perp\})$, the set of input states I_s is equal to $I \times \{\perp\}$, the output function on $(\perp, \perp)$ is equal to $\perp$, and the following conditions on the step relation hold:

1. *the first component of the state (the <u>input</u>) doesn't change;*
2. *if at least one agent has both components of the state equal to $\perp$, the states don't change at all (the agents don't interact while shut down).*

We call the first component of the state the <u>input</u>, and the second component of the state the <u>internal memory</u>.

A <u>reconfiguration</u> of an input-saving population protocol is one of the following changes to the configuration:

1. *removing an agent in the shutdown state $(\perp, \perp)$;*
2. *adding an agent in the shutdown state $(\perp, \perp)$;*
3. *changing an agent's input, i.e. replacing a state (i, q) with a state (i', q) that differs only in the first component.*

An <u>execution with reconfiguration</u> of an input-saving protocol is a finite or infinite sequence of steps and reconfigurations. An execution with reconfiguration is <u>fair</u> if it has a finite number of reconfigurations, and its suffix after the last reconfiguration is a fair execution.

An input-saving population protocol <u>respects shutdown requests</u>, if in each fair execution with reconfiguration after some time either all agents have the input $\perp$ or all the agents with the input $\perp$ are in the shutdown state $(\perp, \perp)$.

An input-saving population protocol <u>implements</u> a specification (φ, ψ) if the following conditions all hold:

1. *the protocol respects shutdown requests;*
2. *in each fair execution with reconfiguration each agent's output only changes a finite number of times;*
3. *φ is satisfied by the multiset of inputs and the multiset of outputs after stabilisation of outputs;*

4. for each agent, ψ is satisfied by the agent's input and output after stabilisation.

Remark 3. If we want an execution with reconfiguration to start with a non-empty configuration, we can instead use reconfiguration to add the necessary agents in the very beginning of the execution.

Remark 4. After the last reconfiguration in a fair execution with reconfigurations the number of reachable configurations becomes finite, so by fairness any set of configurations has to become unreachable or be reached infinitely many times.

Remark 5. When verifying a specific protocol, ψ is usually trivially ensured by the output function.

Example 4. Consider the following input-saving protocol.

The input language has two elements, «Yes» and «Maybe». The output language has three elements, «Yes» and «No», and $\bot$. The internal memory language has four elements «Me», «Yes», «No», and $\bot$.

The output function returns $\bot$ when the input is $\bot$, «Yes» when the input is «Yes» or the internal memory is «Yes», and «No» otherwise.

In a pattern form:

$$(\bot, *) \to \bot \tag{1}$$

$$(Yes, *) \to Yes \tag{2}$$

$$(Maybe, Yes) \to Yes \tag{3}$$

$$(Maybe, Me/No/\bot) \to No \tag{4}$$

The step function works as follows (right-hand-side $*$ keeps the value from the left-hand-side; same interactions are also possible in the reverse order).

$$(\bot, *), (Yes, *) \to (\bot, \bot), (Yes, Me) \tag{5}$$

$$(\bot, Me), (Maybe, *) \to (\bot, \bot), (Maybe, Me) \tag{6}$$

$$(\bot, Yes/No), (*, *) \to (\bot, \bot), (*, *) \tag{7}$$

$$(Yes, *), (Yes, *) \to (Yes, Me), (Yes, Me) \tag{8}$$

$$(Yes, *), (Maybe, *) \to (Yes, Me), (Maybe, Yes) \tag{9}$$

$$(Maybe, Me), (Maybe, *) \to (Maybe, Me), (Maybe, No) \tag{10}$$

$$(Maybe, \cancel{Me}), (Maybe, \cancel{Me}) \to (Maybe, *), (Maybe, *) \tag{11}$$

Here $\cancel{Me}$ means any value allowed in this position except Me.

Informally, internal memory «Me» is set by an own «Yes» input and gets replaced with «Yes» by observing another «Yes» input while not having a «Yes» input; it is also «handed over» before the shutdown; internal memory «Yes» is set by observing a «Yes» input of another agent and removed by observing a «Me» internal memory of an agent without «Yes» input.

We observe the following.

1. The protocol respects shutdown requests.
2. The protocol implements the specification «all inputs are "Maybe" and all outputs are "No", or there is a "Yes" input and all outputs are "Yes"»

The basic idea is that «Yes» in the memory appears when «Me» appears somewhere else, eventually all «Me» are for the same input, and «Me» with a given input spread either «Yes» or «No» output.

Leader election can be implemented in a similar way, and we provide the details in the full version. We only promise that eventually there will be a leader if after reconfigurations there are at least two non-shutdown agents.

Example 5. Consider the following protocol, parametrised by a positive integer m. The input language is $\{-m, -m+1, \ldots, m-1, m\}$. The output language is the same as the input language. The internal memory language is $\{-m, -m+1, \ldots, m-1, m\} \times \{-2m, -2m+1, \ldots, 2m-1, 2m\}$. We call the two sub-components of the internal memory «previous input» and «current balance».

We will call k-clamping of a number x the number x itself if it is at most k by absolute value (i.e. $|x| \leq k$) and k or $-k$ according to the sign of x otherwise (i.e. $k \cdot \operatorname{sign} x$). We write $\operatorname{clamp}_k x = \min(k, \max(-k, x))$.

The output function is the m-clamping of the current balance.

The step function is as follows.

First, for each of the agents we consider the current input i, the previous input p and the current balance b. We try to add the difference between the previous and the current input to the current balance and to the previous input, but make sure the values stay in the permitted range. More precisely, we consider $b' = \operatorname{clamp}_{2m}(b+i-p)$, $p' = p+b'-b$, and update the current balance to become b' and the previous input to become p'. (As p' is between p and i, it cannot cause range problems).

Then we consider the two updated current balances, $b'_1 \leq b'_2$ (possibly swapping the agents to ensure that the first balance is larger). We replace them with $b''_1 = \operatorname{clamp}_{2m}(b'_1 + b'_2)$ and $b''_2 = b'_1 + b'_2 - b''_1$.

Then if exactly one of the agents has the current input $\bot$ and the other agent has the current balance 0, we swap the current balances. Afterwards each agent with the current input $\bot$, the previous input 0, and the current balance 0 gets the internal memory set to $\bot$ to shut it down.

Observe that this protocol implements the specification that either there is at most one agent, or the following holds.

- Either there are no agents with a negative output or there are not agents with a positive output.
- The largest output by absolute value is the (clamped) sum of all the current inputs $\operatorname{clamp}_m \sum_j i_j$.

The basic idea is that the current balances cancel out when possible and accumulate otherwise, while the unused difference between current input and previous input in a stable situation can only be in the same direction as the sign of the global sum of inputs.

Remark 6. If we replace clamping with taking a remainder modulo m, and all the sums in the specification and the proof with sums modulo m, we obtain a very similar protocol for computing the sum of the inputs modulo m as the only non-zero agent output.

3.1 Parallel Composition

In this section we briefly mention the simpler composition methods for input-saving population protocols.

If we have two protocols with the same input language, we can take the Cartesian product of their output languages and internal memory languages, and execute the two protocols in parallel on the same population. For the internal memory we identify $(\bot, \bot)$ with $\bot$. Clearly, the product protocol will respect the shutdown requests if the original ones did. If the protocols implemented specifications (φ_1, ψ_1) and (φ_2, ψ_2), the product protocol will implement the specification that accepts a multiset of inputs and a multiset of outputs if replacing outputs with their first components makes φ_1 accept the pair of multisets and ψ_1 accept each agent's input-output pair, while replacing outputs with their second components satisfies φ_2 globally and ψ_2 locally.

It is possible that the protocols we wanted to combine had different inputs, and we want to combine the outputs in some way other than building a pair. For the output side, we can replace the output function with a composition of the old output function and an output-translating function. For the input side, given an input-translating function, we need to define the new transitions as the old transitions, where inputs are the images of the actual inputs. The specification will be composed with the translation functions in a natural way.

Example 6. We have a protocol (Example 4) to check whether any agent has input «Yes». If we want to verify that with the input language $\{0, 1, 2\}$ some agents have 0 and some agents have 1, we can ask each agent to participate in two independent copies of the «Yes»-checking protocol. One copy would interpret 0 as «Yes» (other inputs as «Maybe»), and the other copy would interpret 1 as «Yes». The output of naive Cartesian product protocol would be two «Yes»/«No»» values, but we use their conjunction as the top-level output.

4 Sequential Composition

In this section we show how to perform sequential composition, using the outputs of one protocol (producer) as input of the following one (consumer). This is similar to the general notion of a computational pipeline.

Definition 7. *Consider finite sets I, M, O (informally: global input, language in the middle, and global output, the protocols working from I to M and from M to O). Consider also finite sets Q_1 and Q_2 (to be used as internal memory* languages for the two protocols). Consider two input-saving population protocols $(I \times Q_1, Step_1, o_1)$ and $(M \times Q_2, Step_2, o_2)$ (the producer and the consumer protocols, correspondingly).

Then the <u>sequential composition</u> of these two protocols is the following input-saving population protocol. The input language is I. The output language is O. The internal memory language is $(Q_1 \times M \times Q_2)$; we identify $\perp$ with $(\perp, \perp, \perp)$ in the internal memory. The output function is $o(q_1, m, q_2) = o_2(q_2)$.

The step relation is defined by the following procedure. The procedure is deterministic if the two original protocols had functions as step relations. The procedure takes two states (saved input included), (i^1, q_1^1, m^1, q_2^1) and (i^2, q_1^2, m^2, q_2^2).

- We compute the new internal memory for the first (producer) protocol based on the global inputs and the old internal memory states. In other words, we non-deterministically pick an arbitrary fitting transition $(((i^1, q_1^1), (i^2, q_1^2)), ((i^1, q_1^{1'}), (i^2, q_1^{2'}))) \in Step_1$ if there is any, and otherwise we do nothing and take $(q_1^{1'}, q_1^{2'}) = (q_1^1, q_1^2)$. Note that the inputs cannot change during a step.
- We update the intermediate output-input as the output of the first (producer) protocol. In other words, we set $m^{1'} = o_1(i^1, q_1^{1'})$ and $m^{2'} = o_1(i^2, q_1^{2'})$.
- We compute the new internal memory for the second (consumer) protocol, based on the intermediate output-input as the input. In other words, we non-deterministically pick an arbitrary fitting transition $(((m^{1'}, q_2^1), (m^{2'}, q_2^2)), ((m^{1'}, q_2^{1'}), (m^{2'}, q_2^{2'}))) \in Step_2$ if there is any, and otherwise we do nothing and take $(q_2^{1'}, q_2^{2'}) = (q_2^1, q_2^2)$. Note that the input cannot change but we use its updated value.
- The new states are $(i^1, q_1^{1'}, m^{1'}, q_2^{1'})$ and $(i^2, q_1^{2'}, m^{2'}, q_2^{2'})$. (The input doesn't change, as required for an input-saving protocol).

We also want to combine specifications.

Definition 8. *The composition of relations $\varphi_1 \subseteq \mathcal{I} \times \mathcal{M}$ and $\varphi_2 \subseteq \mathcal{M} \times \mathcal{O}$, is the relation $\varphi \subseteq \mathcal{I} \times \mathcal{O} = \{(I, O) \mid \exists M : \varphi_1(I, M) \land \varphi_2(M, O)\}$. This is compatible with composition of relations as (multi-valued) functions.*

The composition of specifications composes the two components correspondingly.

Theorem 1. *Sequential composition of input-saving population protocols implementing two specifications implements the composition of the specifications as relations.*

The basic idea is that things that are allowed to happen during a fair execution with reconfigurations of the composition protocol correspond to things that are allowed to happen during each of the two protocols executed independently; and once things stabilise, we can recover the intermediate values from the intermediate output-input components of the internal memory.

5 Expressive Power

In this section we study which specifications can be implemented by input-saving population protocols. We show that these specifications are the semilinear (Presburger-definable) ones.

We use both equivalent definitions of these sets: they are definable as finite unions of linear sets, where a linear set is the set of points obtained from a base vector by repeated addition of the vectors from a fixed finite set of periods; and they are definable by boolean combination of equalities, inequalities, and fixed-modulo modular equalities of integer linear combinations of coordinates.

Strictly speaking, a protocol implementing a specification (φ, ψ) implements a disjunction $(\varphi \vee \varphi', \psi)$ for any relation φ'. We will call the former specification stronger than the latter. We will prove that for each specification implemented by a protocol there is a stronger semilinear specification implemented by some other protocol.

Definition 9. *A specification (φ, ψ) is <u>semilinear</u> if φ is semilinear when considered as a predicate on a tuple of multiplicities of possible input and output values.*

Theorem 2. *Every semilinear specification which can in principle be satisfied for each multiset of inputs is implemented by some input-saving population protocol.*

Here a specification (φ, ψ) can be satisfied for a multiset I of inputs if there exists a multiset P of pairs satisfying ψ, such that the multiset of the first components of all pairs in P is I, the multiset of the second components of pairs in P is some multiset O, and the multisets I and O of the first and the second components satisfy φ.

The basic (and very inefficient) idea is that we have already seen protocols that are enough to compute semilinear predicates, so we can guess the output assignment and verify that it is suitable.

Theorem 3. *Every specification implemented by an input-saving population protocol is weaker (accepts more multisets of input-output pairs) than some implementable semilinear specification.*

The basic idea is to consider two notions of reachability: with and without reconfiguration. Due to respect of shutdown request, execution with reconfiguration can always return to a configuration of size 1. Consider a bottom strongly connected component (BSCC) for reachability between size-1 configurations. Configurations of arbitrary size reachable from this BSCC via executions with reconfiguration have mutual reachability with this BSCC and thus form a semilinear set [23]. BSCCs of executions without reconfiguration form a semilinear set [16]; those of them that are reachable (with reconfiguration) from the chosen size-1 reconfiguration BSCC form a semilinear set as an intersection of two semilinear sets. It turns out that this set has to be allowed by the specification and also have at least one configuration for each multiset of inputs.

6 Conclusion and Future Directions

We have presented an extension of the population protocols model with a better support for modular design and synthesis of the protocols, as well as for a wider range of applications.

We have also established that the specifications that can be implemented this way are essentially the semilinear ones.

However, the constructions used are quite inefficient; it might be of interest to adapt to our model (and possibly extend beyond computing predicates) the existing fast and succinct protocols [10]. However, even a single-exponential-state-count polynomial-convergence-time construction for an arbitrary semilinear specification would be of interest.

Acknowledgements. I would like to thank Javier Esparza, Roland Guttenberg, Jérôme Leroux and Chana Weil-Kennedy for useful discussions. I am also grateful to the anonymous reviewers of this and previous versions for their valuable feedback and advice on presentation.

The project has been supported by a European Research Council (ERC) project under the European Union's Horizon 2020 research and innovation programme grant agreement No 787367 (PaVeS) This work has been supported by France National Research Agency (ANR) grant ANR-23-CE48-0005 (PaVeDyS).

Disclosure of Interests. The author(s) have no competing interests to declare that are relevant to the content of this article.

References

1. Angluin, D., Aspnes, J., Chan, M., Fischer, M.J., Jiang, H., Peralta, R.: Stably computable properties of network graphs. In: International Conference on Distributed Computing in Sensor Systems (2005). https://api.semanticscholar.org/CorpusID:16310485
2. Angluin, D., Aspnes, J., Diamadi, Z., Fischer, M.J., Peralta, R.: Computation in networks of passively mobile finite-state sensors. In: Chaudhuri, S., Kutten, S. (eds.) PODC, pp. 290–299. ACM (2004). https://doi.org/10.1145/1011767.1011810
3. Angluin, D., Aspnes, J., Diamadi, Z., Fischer, M.J., Peralta, R.: Computation in networks of passively mobile finite-state sensors. Distrib. Comput. **18**(4), 235–253 (2006)
4. Angluin, D., Aspnes, J., Eisenstat, D.: Fast computation by population protocols with a leader. In: Dolev, S. (ed.) In Distributed Computing: 20th International Symposium, DISC 2006. Lecture Notes in Computer Science, vol. 4167, pp. 61–75. Springer (2006)
5. Angluin, D., Aspnes, J., Eisenstat, D., Ruppert, E.: The computational power of population protocols. Distrib. Comput. **20**(4), 279–304 (2007). https://arxiv.org/abs/cs/0608084
6. Angluin, D., Aspnes, J., Fischer, M.J., Jiang, H.: Self-stabilizing population protocols. In: TAAS (2005). https://api.semanticscholar.org/CorpusID:63153

7. Austin, M.A., Johnson, J.: Compositional approach to distributed system behavior modeling and formal validation of infrastructure operations with finite state automata: application to viewpoint-driven verification of functionality in waterways. Syst. **6**, 2 (2018). https://api.semanticscholar.org/CorpusID:4786185
8. Blondin, M., Esparza, J., Genest, B., Helfrich, M., Jaax, S.: Succinct population protocols for Presburger arithmetic. In submission (2019). http://arxiv.org/abs/1910.04600
9. Blondin, M., Esparza, J., Jaax, S., Meyer, P.J.: Towards efficient verification of population protocols. In: Schiller, E.M., Schwarzmann, A.A. (eds.) PODC, pp. 423–430. ACM (2017)
10. Czerner, P., Guttenberg, R., Helfrich, M., Esparza, J.: Fast and succinct population protocols for Presburger arithmetic. J. Comput. Syst. Sci. **140**, 103481 (2024). https://doi.org/10.1016/j.jcss.2023.103481
11. Czerwiński, W., Lasota, S., Lazić, R., Leroux, J., Mazowiecki, F.: The reachability problem for Petri nets is not elementary. In: Proc. 51st Annual ACM SIGACT Symposium on Theory of Computing (STOC), pp. 24–33 (2019). https://doi.org/10.1145/3313276.3316369
12. Delporte-Gallet, C., Devismes, S., Fauconnier, H.: Robust stabilizing leader election. In: Safety-critical Systems Symposium (2007). https://api.semanticscholar.org/CorpusID:2179550
13. Dijkstra, E.W.: Self-stabilizing systems in spite of distributed control. Commun. ACM **17**, 643–644 (1974). https://api.semanticscholar.org/CorpusID:11101426
14. Dolev, S., Israeli, A., Moran, S.: Self-stabilization of dynamic systems assuming only read/write atomicity. Distrib. Comput. **7**(1), 3–16 (1993). https://doi.org/10.1007/BF02278851
15. Doty, D., Soloveichik, D.: Stable leader election in population protocols requires linear time. In: Moses, Y. (ed.) DISC. LNCS, vol. 9363, pp. 602–616. Springer, Cham (2015). https://arxiv.org/abs/1502.04246
16. Esparza, J., Ganty, P., Leroux, J., Majumdar, R.: Verification of population protocols. In: Aceto, L., de Frutos Escrig, D. (eds.) 26th International Conference on Concurrency Theory (CONCUR 2015). Leibniz International Proceedings in Informatics (LIPIcs), vol. 42, pp. 470–482. Schloss Dagstuhl–Leibniz-Zentrum fuer Informatik, Dagstuhl (2015). https://doi.org/10.4230/LIPIcs.CONCUR.2015.470, http://drops.dagstuhl.de/opus/volltexte/2015/5377
17. Esparza, J., Ganty, P., Leroux, J., Majumdar, R.: Model checking population protocols. In: Lal, A., Akshay, S., Saurabh, S., Sen, S. (eds.) 36th IARCS Annual Conference on Foundations of Software Technology and Theoretical Computer Science (FSTTCS 2016). Leibniz International Proceedings in Informatics (LIPIcs), vol. 65, pp. 27:1–27:14. Schloss Dagstuhl–Leibniz-Zentrum fuer Informatik, Dagstuhl (2016). https://doi.org/10.4230/LIPIcs.FSTTCS.2016.27, http://drops.dagstuhl.de/opus/volltexte/2016/6862
18. Esparza, J., Jaax, S., Raskin, M.A., Weil-Kennedy, C.: The complexity of verifying population protocols. Distrib. Comput. **34**(2), 133–177 (2021). https://doi.org/10.1007/s00446-021-00390-x
19. Esparza, J., Raskin, M., Weil-Kennedy, C.: Parameterized analysis of immediate observation petri nets (2019). http://arxiv.org/abs/1902.03025
20. Gasieniec, L., Hamilton, D.D., Martin, R., Spirakis, P.G., Stachowiak, G.: Deterministic population protocols for exact majority and plurality. In: Fatourou, P., Jiménez, E., Pedone, F. (eds.) 20th International Conference on Principles of Distributed Systems, OPODIS 2016, 13–16 December 2016, Madrid, Spain. LIPIcs,

vol. 70, pp. 14:1–14:14. Schloss Dagstuhl - Leibniz-Zentrum für Informatik (2016). https://doi.org/10.4230/LIPICS.OPODIS.2016.14
21. Gouda, M., Herman, T.: Adaptive programming. IEEE Trans. Software Eng. **17**(9), 911–921 (1991). https://doi.org/10.1109/32.92911
22. Huang, P., et al.: Gray failure. In: Proceedings of the 16th Workshop on Hot Topics in Operating Systems - HotOS 2017. ACM Press (2017). https://doi.org/10.1145/3102980.3103005
23. Leroux, J.: Vector addition system reversible reachability problem. Log. Methods Comput. Sci. **9**(1) (2013). https://doi.org/10.2168/LMCS-9(1:5)2013
24. Raskin, M.: Modular population protocols. CoRR (2024). https://arxiv.org/abs/2111.11983v3
25. Viroli, M., Audrito, G., Beal, J., Damiani, F., Pianini, D.: Engineering resilient collective adaptive systems by self-stabilisation. ACM Trans. Model. Comput. Simul. (TOMACS) **28**, 1–28 (2017). https://api.semanticscholar.org/CorpusID:4302945

Decreasing Verification Radius in Local Certification

Laurent Feuilloley[2], Jan Janoušek[1], Jan Matyáš Křišťan[1], and Josef Erik Sedláček[1(✉)]

[1] Faculty of Information Technology, CTU in Prague, Prague, Czech Republic
{kristja6,sedlajo5}@fit.cvut.cz
[2] CNRS, INSA Lyon, UCBL, LIRIS, UMR5205, 69622 Villeurbanne, France

Abstract. This paper deals with *local certification*, specifically locally checkable proofs: given a *graph property*, the task is to certify whether a graph satisfies the property. The verification of this certification needs to be done *locally* without the knowledge of the whole graph. More precisely, a distributed algorithm, called a *verifier*, is executed on each vertex. The verifier observes the local neighborhood up to a constant distance and either accepts or rejects.

We examine the trade-off between the visibility radius and the size of certificates. We describe a procedure that decreases the radius by encoding the neighbourhood of each vertex into its certificate. We also provide a corresponding lower bound on the required certificate size increase, showing that such an approach is close to optimal.

Keywords: Local certification · locally checkable proofs · proof-labeling schemes · graphs · distributed computing · self-stabilization

1 Introduction

The problem studied in this paper involves certifying a global graph property without having knowledge of the entire graph. In particular, we study the model of locally checkable proofs of Göös and Suomela [13].

In this model, a distributed algorithm called a *verifier* examines the local neighbourhood of each vertex up to some fixed distance, called the *radius*. On each vertex, the verifier either accepts if it cannot deny that the graph has the desired property, or rejects if it is certain that the property is not satisfied. The final decision about the property is then made as follows: If the verifier rejected on at least one vertex, the decision is that the property is not satisfied. If it accepts on all vertices, the decision is that the property holds.

To enhance the decision-making capabilities of the model, the vertices are equipped with unique identifiers and possibly more general labels. Furthermore, each vertex is given a *certificate*.

Certificates, are bit-strings that are used to help the verifier in deciding the answer about the property. The verifier reads the certificates in its local view as a part of its input. For each graph that satisfies the property, the verifier must accept for at least one assignment of certificates. If the graph does not satisfy the property, the verifier must reject every assignment of certificates.

The key notion of local certification is that of a *proof labeling scheme*, which is a pair $(f, \mathcal{A})$, where $\mathcal{A}$ is the verifier and f, often called a *prover*, gives each graph with the property an assignment of certificates that is accepted by $\mathcal{A}$.

An intuitive example of a problem requiring certificates is k-colorability, where k is a constant. Clearly, $\mathcal{O}(\log k)$ bits are enough, as the coloring can be provided in the certificates. If the graph is not k-colorable, then at least one vertex will be adjacent to a vertex with the same color (or use a color greater than k) and it would reject.

1.1 Previous Work

Similar models, related to the LOCAL model [17], have been studied under different names [13,15]. The name *local certification* is a general term used for the similar models [5].

The concept of local certification is relevant to self-stabilization [1,4], as it is a component of many self-stabilizing algorithms [15].

Since local certification has been introduced, lower bounds and upper bounds for the size of the certificates for many graph properties and problems have been proven [2,3,7,14]. Also, the strength of the model in general and under various restrictions was studied [10–12]. For a general survey see [5].

It has been previously shown how, and under which conditions, certificate size can be decreased at the cost of increasing the visibility radius [6,9,16]. We provide a similar result, showing how the visibility radius can be decreased at the cost of increasing the certificate size.

There is a subtle but crucial distinction between these two problems. While the previous results allow increasing the radius while decreasing the size of certificates in the general case, the implied inverse procedure of decreasing the radius and increasing the certificate size works only for the very particular type of proof labeling schemes that result from the original procedure. The novelty of our results lies in allowing the decrease of the radius of *any* proof labeling schemes.

1.2 Our Contribution

We show a general procedure for decreasing the radius of a proof labeling scheme at the expense of increasing the size of its certificates. We also provide a corresponding lower bound on the necessary certificate size increase.

Consider the following motivation for this result. Given a network, it may be needed to check that it satisfies a given property, such as absence of a cycle. Communication between nodes of the network may be bounded by distance, which corresponds to the visibility radius of the verifier. Under these conditions, proof labeling schemes provide a template for verifying properties of this network.

Our procedure then allows to decrease the communication distance at the cost of increasing the memory and computational requirements of each node.

In Sect. 3 we formally describe the procedure. Given a proof labeling scheme $(f, \mathcal{A})$ with radius r certifying some property $\mathcal{P}$, we show how to construct a proof labeling scheme with radius $(r - \delta)$ certifying $\mathcal{P}$ with size bounded by $\mathcal{O}((\Delta - 1)^\delta(\Delta \log(n) + s(n) + \ell(n)))$, where Δ is the maximum degree of the certified graph, s is the certificate size of $(f, \mathcal{A})$, and ℓ is the size of labels on the vertices of the input graph. In Sect. 4, we show that the increase by a factor of $C \cdot \Delta^{\delta-1}$ is necessary for some graph properties, while in Sect. 5 we prove that in some cases the multiplicative logarithmic terms can be replaced by an additive one.

2 Preliminaries

All the graphs are assumed to be undirected and simple with possible labels. We also assume that all graphs are connected, as two different connected components have no way to interact with each other. Formally $G = (V, E, L)$ where $L: V \to \{0,1\}^*$. The vertices are assumed to have assigned integer *identifiers*, formally for a graph on n vertices, we assume that $V = \{1, \ldots, n\}$.

Neighbours of a vertex v are denoted as $N_G(v)$, if G is clear from the context, $N(v)$ is used. Distance between two vertices u, v is denoted as $d_G(u, v)$, and the subscript is omitted if G is clear from the context. We denote the set of vertices within distance r from v as $V[v, r]$, also called the r-local neighbourhood of v.

A *graph property* is formally a set of graphs that is closed under isomorphism, that is, its membership does not depend on the choice of identifiers. Note that it may depend on the labels of the graph. A *certificate assignment* P for G is a function $P: V(G) \to \{0,1\}^*$ that associates with each vertex a *certificate*. We say that P has size s if $|P(v)| \leq s(n)$ for every v. A *verifier* is a function that takes as an input a graph G, its certificate assignment P and $v \in V(G)$ and outputs either 0 or 1. In this case, we say that the verifier is invoked on v.

We denote the induced subgraph $G[V[v,r]]$ as $G[v,r]$ and the restriction of P to $V[v,r]$ is denoted as $P[v,r]$, that is $P[v,r]: V[v,r] \to \{0,1\}^*$. A verifier $\mathcal{A}$ is *r-local* if $\mathcal{A}(G, P, v) = \mathcal{A}(G[v,r], P[v,r], v)$ for all G, P, and v.

An r-local *proof labeling scheme* certifying a property of labeled graphs $\mathcal{P}$ is a pair $(f, \mathcal{A})$, where $\mathcal{A}$ is an r-local verifier and f, called the *prover*, assigns to each $G \in \mathcal{P}$ a certificate assignment P such that the following properties hold.

- *Completeness*: If $G \in \mathcal{P}$, then $\mathcal{A}(G[v,r], P[v,r], v) = 1$ for all v, where $P = f(G)$.
- *Soundness*: If $G \notin \mathcal{P}$, then for every certificate assignment P', there is v such that $\mathcal{A}(G[v,r], P'[v,r], v) = 0$.

We say that $(f, \mathcal{A})$ has size $s : \mathbb{N} \to \mathbb{N}$ if $|f(G)(v)| \leq s(|V(G)|)$ for all $G \in \mathcal{P}$ and all $v \in V(G)$.

3 Decreasing the Radius of a Proof Labeling Scheme

The goal of this section is to show that given an r-local proof labeling scheme $(f_r, \mathcal{A}_r)$ certifying property $\mathcal{P}$, we can construct an $(r - \delta)$-local proof labeling scheme $(f, \mathcal{A})$ certifying $\mathcal{P}$ for any $\delta < r$ at the cost of increasing the certificate size by a certain amount. The increase of the certificate size can be expressed as a function of the size of the input graph and its maximum degree. The result is precisely formulated as follows.

Theorem 1. *Given an r-local proof labeling scheme $(f_r, \mathcal{A}_r)$ of size s certifying a graph property $\mathcal{P}$, for every $\delta < r$, we can construct an $(r - \delta)$-local proof labeling scheme certifying $\mathcal{P}$ with certificates of size*

$$\mathcal{O}((\Delta - 1)^\delta (\Delta \log(n) + s(n) + \ell(n)))$$

where $\ell(n)$ is the maximum size of a label and $\Delta \geq 3$ is the maximum degree of the input graph.

Note that in the case of $\Delta = 2$, the maximum size of a δ-neighborhood of a vertex grows only linearly with δ and we may obtain the bound on certificate size of $\mathcal{O}(\delta(\Delta \log(n) + s(n) + \ell(n)))$.

3.1 Overview of the Proof Technique

When the verifier $\mathcal{A}_r$ is invoked on v, it is given $G[v, r]$ and $P[v, r]$ on its input. If we want to reduce that information to $G[v, r - \delta], P[v, r - \delta]$, a first step can be to *move* the now missing information into the certificates. The first obstacle comes from the fact that information in the certificates may not be true (as opposed to $G[v, r]$ provided on the input) and must be verified.

3.2 Encoding Neighborhood into Certificates

The essential idea is simple, we have each vertex hold its distance δ neighborhood in its certificate. This allows other vertices within distance $r - \delta$ to gain information about the entire distance r neighborhood and feed this information to the original r-local verifier.

Instead of having each vertex explicitly encode its δ neighborbood, we define the notion of *packets*, which are then *broadcast* into the extended neighborhood. The effect is the same as encoding the δ neighborhood in the certificate, and the notion allows us to break down the verification into simple checks and the proof of correctness into simple observations.

Definition 1. *We say that (D, L, C, ω, d) is a packet, if*

- *D is a set of vertices,*
- *$L, C \in \{0, 1\}^*$,*
- *ω is the identifier of so-called origin vertex,*

– and $d \in \{0, \ldots, \delta\}$.

Note that a packet can be easily encoded and decoded into a binary string. Furthermore, it is easy to locally check that the individual elements of the packet correspond to the definition and have the correct types.

Intuitively, D, L, and C are used to carry the local information around ω. In particular, D will be the identifiers of $N(v)$, L will be the label on v, and C is a certificate on v eventually passed on to $\mathcal{A}_r$. We use d to keep the distance of the packet from ω to ensure the correct distribution of the packet among other vertices.

The origin of a packet p is denoted as $\omega(p)$, a similar notation is used with the other components of the packet. Given a certificate assignment $P: V(G) \to \{0,1\}^*$ and $v \in V$, $\texttt{pts}(P, v)$ denotes the set of packets encoded in $P(v)$ (if $P(v)$ is not a valid encoding of packets then $\texttt{pts}(P, v) = \emptyset$). We define $\texttt{has-pt}(P, v, x)$ as true if and only if there is $p \in \texttt{pts}(P, v)$ such that $\omega(p) = x$ and if true, we denote such packet p as $\texttt{pt}(P, v, x)$.

Definition 2. *We say that packet $p = (D, L, C, \omega, d)$ is* well-formed *if and only if $D = N_G(\omega)$ and L is the label on ω.*

Now, we show how well-formed packets can be used to reconstruct the neighborhood. Let $\mathcal{B}$ be a set of packets and $\omega(\mathcal{B}) := \{\omega(p) \mid p \in \mathcal{B}\}$. Let $G(\mathcal{B}) := (\omega(\mathcal{B}), E(\mathcal{B}), L(\mathcal{B}))$, where $E(\mathcal{B}) := \{\{x, y\} \mid x, y \in \omega(\mathcal{B})$ and $\exists p \in \mathcal{B}$ such that $\omega(p) = x$ and $y \in D(p)\}$ and $L(\mathcal{B})(v) = L(p)$ such that $\omega(p) = v$.

Observation 1. *Let $\mathcal{B}$ be a set of well-formed packets such that $\omega(\mathcal{B}) = V[v, r]$. Then $G(\mathcal{B}) = G[v, r]$.*

Proof. For each $\{x, y\} \in E(G[v, r])$, there is $p \in \mathcal{B}$ with $\omega(p) = x$ and $y \in D(p) = N(x)$ as p is well-formed. On the other hand, for each p with $\omega(p) = x$ and $y \in D(p)$, there is $\{x, y\} \in E(G[v, r])$ if also $y \in V[v, r]$. □

Similarly, we can reconstruct the encoded certificate assignment, we define $\mathcal{C}(\mathcal{B}) : \omega(\mathcal{B}) \to \{0,1\}^*$ so that $\mathcal{C}(\mathcal{B})(v) = C(p)$ where $p \in \mathcal{B}$ such that $\omega(p) = v$.

3.3 Constructing the $(r - \delta)$-Local Verifier

Recall that we are given an r-local proof labeling scheme $(f_r, \mathcal{A}_r)$ certifying the property of labeled graphs $\mathcal{P}$. We now define the $(r - \delta)$-local verifier. The main task of the verifier is to ensure that all packets are distributed as needed and all are well-formed, that is they can be used to reconstruct wider neighbourhoods.

Let $\mathcal{B}[P, u, r - \delta] := \bigcup_{v \in V[u, r-\delta]} \texttt{pts}(P, v)$, that is $\mathcal{B}[P, u, r - \delta]$ is the set of all packets that are visible from u to distance $r - \delta$ and are encoded in P. We define $\mathcal{A}$ so that $\mathcal{A}(G[v, r - \delta], P[v, r - \delta], v) = 1$ if and only if the following conditions are all satisfied:

Condition B1: For each x, there is at most one $p \in \texttt{pts}(P, v)$ such that $\omega(p) = x$,

Condition B2: $(N(v), L(v), C', v, 0) \in \text{pts}(P, v)$ for some $C' \in \{0,1\}^*$,
Condition B3: if $\text{has-pt}(P, v, u)$ and $v \neq u$ then $1 \leq d(\text{pt}(P, v, u)) = 1 + \min\{d(\text{pt}(P, x, u)) \mid \text{has-pt}(P, x, u) \text{ and } x \in N(v)\}$,
Condition B4: $\text{has-pt}(P, v, u)$ for $v \neq u$ if and only if there is $x \in N(v)$ and $p' = \text{pt}(P, x, u)$ such that $d(p') < \delta$,
Condition B5: for every $p = \text{pt}(P, v, u) \in \text{pts}(P, v)$ and every existing $p' = \text{pt}(P, x, u)$ such that $x \in N(v)$, it holds $D(p) = D(p'), L(p) = L(p'), C(p) = C(p')$,
Condition B6: let $G' = G(\mathcal{B}[P, v, r - \delta])$ and $P' = C(\mathcal{B}[P, v, r - \delta])$, then $\mathcal{A}_r(G'[v, r], P'[v, r], v) = 1$.

Note that each condition requires information only about neighbours within distance at most $r - \delta$ and hence can be locally verified. Condition B1 makes the reasoning easier, as we can assume that at most one packet from an originating vertex is present in the certificate. Condition B2 ensures that every vertex has a well-formed packet originating from the vertex itself. Condition B3 allows us to inductively prove that each packet correctly holds its distance from its originating vertex. Condition B4 ensures that a packet originating from a vertex is distributed to vertices within a distance δ from it. Condition B5 ensures that the packet is correctly *copied* from one vertex to another. Condition B6 ensures that the original verifier accepts the described graph and certificate assignment.

Now, we can establish properties of the encoded packets, given that the verifier accepts them. To make the notation shorter, we denote $\mathcal{A}(G[v, r-\delta], P[v, r-\delta], v)$ as $\mathcal{A}(v)$. First, we establish that the encoded distances are equal to the actual distances in the graph.

The following lemmas follow from the definitions of the six Conditions. The reasoning is straightforward, so we have omitted the proofs in this version of the paper due to limited space. They are provided in the full version available on arXiv [8].

Lemma 1. *If $\mathcal{A}(v) = 1$ for all v, then $d(\boldsymbol{pt}(P, u, v)) = d_G(u, v)$ for all $u, v \in V$ such that $\boldsymbol{has\text{-}pt}(P, u, v)$.*

Next, we establish that the local information of each vertex is indeed distributed into its δ neighborhood, given that the verifier accepts the certificates.

Lemma 2. *If $\mathcal{A}(v) = 1$ for all v, then for every $u, x \in V$ it holds $\boldsymbol{has\text{-}pt}(P, u, x)$ if and only if $u \in V[x, \delta]$.*

We now show that all packets with the same origin must hold the same local information.

Lemma 3. *If $\mathcal{A}(v) = 1$ for all v, then $C(\boldsymbol{pt}(P, v, x)) = C(\boldsymbol{pt}(P, u, x))$ for all v, u, x such that $\boldsymbol{has\text{-}pt}(P, v, x)$ and $\boldsymbol{has\text{-}pt}(P, u, x)$.*

Next, we show that the information carried by the packets must be well-formed.

Lemma 4. *If $\mathcal{A}(v) = 1$ for all v, then $\mathtt{pt}(P, v, x)$ is well-formed for every v, x such that $\mathtt{has\text{-}pt}(P, v, x)$.*

It remains to establish that each vertex has access to enough packets to compute its distance r neighborhood.

Lemma 5. *If $\mathcal{A}(v) = 1$ for all v, then for every $u \in V$ it holds $V[u, r] \subseteq \omega(\mathcal{B}[P, u, r - \delta])$.*

Next, we establish that if the original r-local verifier $\mathcal{A}_r$ accepts based on both the local information and the information in packets, the graph indeed satisfies the property $\mathcal{P}$.

Lemma 6. *If $\mathcal{A}(v) = 1$ for all v, then $G \in \mathcal{P}$.*

Finally, we are ready to prove the main theorem.

Proof (Theorem 1). It follows from Lemma 6 that $\mathcal{A}$ accepts G only if $G \in \mathcal{P}$. It remains to show that any $G \in \mathcal{P}$ has a certificate assignment accepted by $\mathcal{A}$, with each certificate of size at most $\mathcal{O}((\Delta - 1)^\delta (\Delta \log(n) + s(n) + \ell(n)))$.

Given $G \in \mathcal{P}$, we construct P so that for each u, $P(u)$ is an encoding of packets with one packet for each vertex $x \in V[u, \delta]$. A packet $p_x = (D, L, C, \omega, d)$ for vertex u is constructed by setting $D := N_G(x)$, $L := L_G(x)$, $C := f_r(G)(x)$, $\omega := x$, and $d := d_G(x, u)$. It remains to check that the verifier returns 1 on each vertex.

Note that Conditions B1, B2, B3, B4, and B5 hold from the construction. Finally, note that by Observation 1, we have

$$\mathcal{A}_r(G(\mathcal{B}[P, v, r - \delta])[v, r], C(\mathcal{B}[P, v, r - \delta])[v, r], v) = \mathcal{A}_r(G[v, r], f_r(G)[v, r]) = 1$$

for each v and hence Condition B6 holds. Thus, the certificate assignment P is accepted by $\mathcal{A}$.

Now, we proceed to bound the maximum size of a certificate assigned by P. Assuming we encode a set of vertices as a set of their identifiers, each of size $\mathcal{O}(\log(n))$, the size of encoding of (D, L, C, ω, d) is bounded by $\mathcal{O}(\Delta(n) \log(n) + \ell(n) + s(n))$. We have $|\mathtt{pts}(P, v)| = |V[v, \delta]| \leq (\Delta(\Delta - 1)^\delta - 2)/(\Delta - 2)$ for $\Delta \geq 3$ and for all v, thus the size of encoding of $P(v)$ is bounded by $\mathcal{O}((\Delta - 1)^\delta (\Delta \log(n) + s(n) + \ell(n)))$.

In the case of $\Delta = 2$, we have $|V[v, \delta]| = 2\delta + 1$ and then the size of encoding of $P(v)$ if bounded by $\mathcal{O}(\delta(\Delta \log(n) + s(n) + \ell(n)))$. □

4 Lower Bound on the Increase of Certificate Size

This section aims to show that there are proof labeling schemes for which the radius can be decreased by δ only if we also increase the certificate size by $C(\Delta - 1)^{\delta - 1}$, where C is a fixed constant. We present a property of labeled graphs, for which we also provide a proof labeling scheme and both an upper

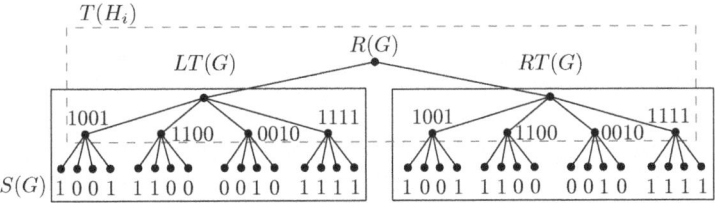

Fig. 1. An example of a graph with property $\mathcal{P}_\Delta$ with $\Delta = 5$. Here, $R(G)$ is the root, $LT(G)$ and $RT(G)$ are the left and right subtrees, $S(G)$ is the binary sequence in the leaves, and the red strings are certificates. The subgraph $T(H_i)$ is used in the proof of Lemma 8 and corresponds to $r = 2$. (Color figure online)

and a lower bound on its size. Later, we describe a property of graphs without labels utilizing very similar idea.

Let $\Delta \geq 3$, then we define $\mathcal{P}_\Delta$ so that a labeled $G \in \mathcal{P}_\Delta$ if and only if it satisfies all of the following three properties. For an example of a graph with the property, see Fig. 1.

Property 1 (Tree structure). G has a single vertex of degree 2, denoted as $R(G)$ (or just R, when a concrete G is irrelevant or clear from the context), which is adjacent to two complete $(\Delta - 1)$-nary trees of the same size.

Property 2 (Label structure). For every vertex v except for the root $R(G)$, the label $L(v)$ encodes an integer $a \in \{1, 2, \ldots, \Delta - 1\}$ that uniquely defines its order among its siblings. Additionally, if $deg(v) = 1$, then $L(v)$ also encodes one bit $b \in \{0, 1\}$. Therefore, on leaves $L(v)$ encodes a pair (a, b). For $L(R(G))$, the label is empty.

This allows us to naturally define the *left* and *right* subtrees of G, i.e. the subtrees rooted on the first and second child of $R(G)$ respectively. We denote those as $LT(G)$ and $RT(G)$. Furthermore, it allows us to order the leaves of G. We denote as $S(v)$ the binary string created by taking the values of b on all leaves in their natural order in the subtree rooted at v. We define $S(G) = S(R(G))$.

Property 3 (String structure). $S(G) = XX$ for some binary string X, i.e. $S(G)$ is a result of concatenating a string X with itself once.

Now we describe a proof labeling scheme of $\mathcal{P}_\Delta$. The following lemma provides an upper bound on the optimal certificate size for a given radius. This is then used together with a corresponding lower bound, to show a lower bound on the necessary increase of the certificate size of $\mathcal{P}_\Delta$ when decreasing the radius.

Lemma 7. *Graph property $\mathcal{P}_\Delta$ has an r-local proof labeling scheme of size $C \cdot n/(\Delta - 1)^{r-1}$ for every $r \geq 1$ and a fixed C.*

Proof. We will show how to certify the Properties 1, 2, and 3. To certify Property 1, each vertex can be given in its certificates the identifier of the root (the vertex of degree 2), its distance from the root, and the depth of the tree. It is well known that distances are enough to certify the acyclicity of a graph and described for instance in [5]. To verify the depth of the whole tree, it suffices to ensure that each certificate has the same value of this depth and on leaves, this depth is verified to be equal to the distance from the root.

To certify Property 2, it suffices to check the structure of each label. Checking the uniqueness of a among siblings can be verified by each parent.

To certify Property 3, each vertex v holds $S(v)$ in its certificate. This is again trivial to verify on a leaf and for any other v, assuming that all children c_i hold correct $S(c_i)$, it suffices to check that $S(v)$ is their concatenation.

Now the key idea of reducing the size of certificates is to encode the value of $S(v)$ only in the vertices with $d(v, R) \geq r$. Certificates of the vertices with $d(v, R) < r$ are left empty. Note that the number of leaves of the subtree of v with $d(v, R) = k$ is at most $n/(2(\Delta - 1)^{k-1})$ as there are $(2(\Delta - 1)^{k-1})$ vertices with distance k from R. Hence, we can encode $S(v)$ using at most $\mathcal{O}(n)/(\Delta - 1)^{k-1}$ bits. Now, R may compute $S(G)$ as the concatenation of $S(v)$ for all v with $d(v, R) = r$ and check that it satisfies Property 3.

The rest of the properties require only $\mathcal{O}(\log(n))$ bits in certificates, thus there is an r-local proof labeling scheme that certifies $\mathcal{P}_\Delta$ with certificates of size at most $C \cdot n/(\Delta - 1)^{r-1}$ for some fixed C and large enough n. □

Now, we show a lower bound on the required certificate size to locally certify $\mathcal{P}_\Delta$.

Lemma 8. *For all r-local proof labeling schemes certifying $\mathcal{P}_\Delta$ of size s, it holds*

$$s(n) \geq \frac{n \cdot \varepsilon}{12(\Delta - 1)^r}$$

for a large enough n and all $\varepsilon < 1$.

Proof. The idea of the proof is inspired by the proof of Theorem 6.1 of Göös and Suomela [13]. Following their approach, we will show that for every supposed proof labeling scheme of size less than $(n \cdot \varepsilon)/(12(\Delta - 1)^r)$, we can construct an instance not in $\mathcal{P}_\Delta$ which the verifier would necessarily accept.

Suppose there exists an r-local proof labeling scheme $(\mathcal{A}, f)$ certifying $\mathcal{P}_\Delta$ such that for every n' there exists $n \geq n'$ such that $s(n) < (n \cdot \varepsilon)/(12(\Delta - 1)^r)$. For an instance $H_i \in \mathcal{P}_\Delta$, let $T(H_i)$ denote $V[R(H_i), r]$. Let $H_j \in \mathcal{P}_\Delta$ and let $\sim$ be a binary relation on $\mathcal{P}_\Delta$ defined so that $H_i \sim H_j$ if and only if $f(H_i)[T(H_i)] = f(H_j)[T(H_j)]$ and $H_i[T(H_i)] = H_j[T(H_j)]$, that is both the subgraphs on $T(H_i)$, $T(H_j)$, and their certificates as assigned by f are the same. The equality of induced subgraphs here means the equality of the identifiers, the labels, and the edges. Note that $\sim$ is an equivalence. See again Fig. 1 for an illustration.

Let $\mathcal{P}_\Delta[n]$ be the set of instances in $\mathcal{P}_\Delta$ on n vertices and with a fixed identifier assignment, meaning the identifier of a vertex with a given position in the tree is the same in all the instances.

Claim. For all n', there exists $n \geq n'$ and $H_1, H_2 \in \mathcal{P}_\Delta[n]$ such that $H_1 \sim H_2$ and $S(H_1) \neq S(H_2)$.

Proof. We will show that for large enough n, the number of possible binary sequences in the leaves of instances in $\mathcal{P}_\Delta[n]$ is greater than the number of equivalence classes of $\sim$ when restricted to $\mathcal{P}_\Delta[n]$.

By the assumption, each vertex has less than $(n \cdot \varepsilon)/(12(\Delta-1)^r)$ certificate bits, thus for an instance $H_i \in \mathcal{P}_\Delta[n]$, there are at most $2^{(n\cdot\varepsilon)/(12(\Delta-1)^r)\cdot|T(H_i)|}$ different certificate assignments on $T(H_i)$, and at most $(\Delta-1)^{|T(H_i)|}$ different assignments of labels on $T(H_i)$. The rest of the structure on $T(H_i)$, including the identifiers is fixed by the fact that $H_i \in \mathcal{P}_\Delta[n]$.

Furthermore, observe that $|T(H_i)| = 1 + 2\sum_{i=0}^{r-1}(\Delta-1)^i \leq 3(\Delta-1)^r$ as $\Delta \geq 3$. In total, we have that $\sim$ has on $\mathcal{P}_\Delta[n]$ at most $2^{(n\cdot\varepsilon)/4} \cdot (\Delta-1)^{3(\Delta-1)^r}$ different equivalence classes.

On the other hand, each instance has at least $n/4$ leaves in the left subtree and thus there are at least $2^{n/4}$ different possible binary strings in the left subtree. It remains to observe that

$$2^{(n\cdot\varepsilon)/4} \cdot (\Delta-1)^{3(\Delta-1)^r} < 2^{n/4}$$

for large enough n. Therefore by the pigeonhole principle, there are $H_1, H_2 \in \mathcal{P}_\Delta[n]$ such that $S(H_1) \neq S(H_2)$ and $H_1 \sim H_2$. □

Now, we take $H_1, H_2 \in \mathcal{P}_\Delta[n]$ such that $H_1 \sim H_2$ and $S(H_1) \neq S(H_2)$ and construct $H' = (V', E', L')$ by starting with $H_1[T(H_1)] = H_2[T(H_2)]$ and completing the left subtree by $LT(H_1)$ and the right subtree by $RT(H_2)$. Formally, let $L_S(G)$ be the neighbour of $R(G)$ in $LT(G)$ and $R_S(G)$ the neighbour in $RT(G)$. Then

$$V' = V(LT(H_1)) \cup V(RT(H_2)) \cup \{R(H_1)\}$$
$$E' = E(LT(H_1)) \cup E(RT(H_2)) \cup \{R(H'), L_S(H_1)\} \cup \{R(H'), R_S(H_2)\}).$$

Observe that the identifier assignment of H' is the same as those of H_1 and H_2, hence by construction, we have that H' satisfies Properties 1 and 2 and the verifier can not reject H' on their basis. Furthermore, observe that $H' \notin \mathcal{P}_\Delta$ as the string in the leaves does not satisfy Property 3.

Now, we choose the certificate assignment on H' as

$$P(v) = \begin{cases} f(H_1)(v) & \text{if } v \in LT(H') \cup \{R(H')\} \\ f(H_2)(v) & \text{otherwise} \end{cases}$$

Recall that f is the prover of the proof labeling scheme of $\mathcal{P}_\Delta$.

Claim. For all $v \in V(H')$ it holds $\mathcal{A}[H'[v,r], P[v,r]] = 1$.

Proof. First, recall that $T(H') = T(H_1) = T(H_2)$, and by construction of P, we also have $P[T(H')] = f(H_1)[T(H_1)] = f(H_2)[T(H_2)]$. Observe that if $v \in LT(H') \cup \{R(H')\}$, we have $H'[v,r] = H_1[v,r]$ and $P[v,r] = f(H_1)[v,r]$ and thus $\mathcal{A}[H'[v,r], P[v,r]] = 1$. Similarly, if $v \in RT(H')$, we have $H'[v,r] = H_2[v,r]$ and $P[v,r] = f(H_2)[v,r]$ and thus $\mathcal{A}[H'[v,r], P[v,r]] = 1$. □

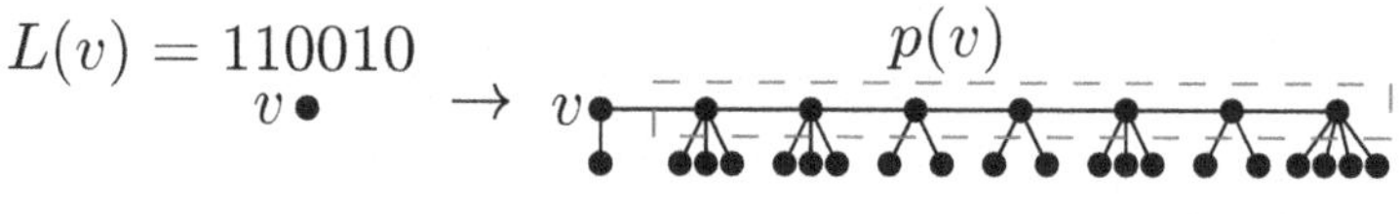

$$L(v) = 110010$$
$$v \bullet \quad \to \quad v$$

Fig. 2. An example of a vertex v in a graph $G \in \mathcal{P}^l$ and the same vertex in $g(G)$

Hence, there is an instance $H' \notin \mathcal{P}_\Delta$ which is accepted by $\mathcal{A}$, contradicting the assumption that $(f, \mathcal{A})$ certifies $\mathcal{P}_\Delta$. This finishes the proof. □

Similar approach can be used in a graph property without labels. The idea behind it is to encode the labels using some subgraphs.

We denote the optimal certificate size of an r-local proof labeling scheme for a property $\mathcal{P}$ as $s^*(\mathcal{P}, r, n)$. An r-local proof labeling scheme has optimal certificate size s if there is no other r-local proof labeling scheme of size s' such that there is n with $s'(n) < s(n)$.

Lemma 9. *For every property $\mathcal{P}^l$ with r-local proof labeling scheme of at most polynomial and at least logarithmic size, there exists a property $\mathcal{P}^u$ with no labels, except for unique identifiers, such that*

$$s^*(\mathcal{P}^l, r, n) \leq c_1 s^*(\mathcal{P}^u, r, n) \leq c_2 s^*(\mathcal{P}^l, r, n),$$

for every r and every large enough n, and where c_1, c_2 are fixed positive constants.

The result is not surprising and the idea of the proof is simple but technical, therefore we decided to omit the proof here. It is available in the full version [8]. An example of the encoding of a label into a subgraph can be seen in the Fig. 2. A single leaf vertex and a path $p(v)$ is attached to each vertex v. The i-th vertex of $p(v)$ has 2 or 3 leaf neighbours depending on the i-th bit of $L(v)$. The last vertex represents the end of the string. We then assume that we are provided with a proof labeling scheme for the unlabeled property and make the decision based on this scheme.

Now, we are ready to prove there are proof labeling schemes, such that the increase of certificate size by $C(\Delta-1)^{\delta-1}$ is necessary when decreasing the radius by δ.

Theorem 2. *There is an r-local proof labeling scheme, certifying a property without labels, of size s_r such that after decreasing its radius by δ, it holds for any possible resulting $r - \delta$-local proof labeling schema of size $s_{r-\delta}$ and every large enough n*

$$s_{r-\delta}(n) \geq s_r(n) \cdot C(\Delta - 1)^{\delta-1}$$

where Δ is the maximum degree of the input graph and C is a fixed constant.

Proof. Consider the property $\mathcal{P}_\Delta$. By Lemma 7, it can be certified by an r-local proof labeling schema of size s_r with $s_r(n) \leq C' \cdot n/(\Delta-1)^{r-1}$ for every large enough n. By Lemma 8, we have

$$s_{r-\delta}(n) \geq (n \cdot \varepsilon)/(12(\Delta-1)^{r-\delta}) \geq \frac{\varepsilon}{12\,C'} \cdot s_r(n) \cdot (\Delta-1)^{r-1-(r-\delta)} =$$
$$= s_r(n) \cdot C(\Delta-1)^{\delta-1}$$

for every large enough n and a fixed C.

By Lemma 9, for any r and $\mathcal{P}_\Delta$, there exists a property $\mathcal{P}^u$ with optimal certificate size s_r^u of an r-local proof labeling scheme such that: $C_1 s_r^u(n) \geq s_r(n) \geq C_2 s_r^u(n)$. Applied on both s_r and $s_{r-\delta}$, we obtain

$$C_1 s_{r-\delta}^u(n) \geq s_{r-\delta}(n) \geq s_r(n) C(\Delta - 1)^{\delta - 1} \geq s_r^u(n) C_2 \cdot C(\Delta - 1)^{\delta - 1}.$$

□

5 Saving on the Log Factors on Paths

In Sect. 4, we proved that in general when reducing the verification radius, a blow-up of the certificate size is necessary. Roughly, the size of the certificates for radius 1 needs to be multiplied by the size of the ball of radius d, compared with certificates for radius d. In the expression of Theorem 1, there are two additional terms: one related to the input labeling (which seems difficult to remove), and one related to identifiers, of the form "size of the ball" multiplied by $O(\log n)$. In this section, we show that when the graph is a path, this last term can be replaced by a simple additive $O(\log n)$. In other words, it is not always necessary to encode locally all the identifiers of the ball at distance d.

Theorem 3. *Consider a property $\mathcal{P}$ on paths. If there exists a proof-labeling scheme at distance d for $\mathcal{P}$ using certificates of size $s(n)$, then there exists a proof-labeling scheme at distance 1, with certificates of size $O((2d+1)s(n) + \log n)$.*

Note that without additional work, Theorem 1 gives size $O((2d+1)s(n) + (2d+1)\log n)$ (forgetting about input labels).

The full proof is omitted in this version and can be found in the full version [8]; here, we only provide the intuition. In the general approach to reduce the verification radius, we need to write the identifiers of all the nodes of the ball at distance d in the new certificates (in addition to the old certificates and the inputs). This is because otherwise the new verifier would not be able to safely simulate the old verifier. Now, if we imagine that the identifier assignment is fixed, and not adversarial, we could go without that: a node would only check its own identifier and deduce safely the identifiers of its neighbors (forgetting about symmetry issues). What we prove is that if the graph is a path, then the prover can give and certify a new identifier assignment, 1, 2, 3, ..., and give certificates related to this virtual assignment. And then the verifier can check that it would accept in the virtual identifier assignment, which is enough to prove the correctness of the input graph. This requires the prover to give only one identifier in the new certificates (the one of the node at hand) and not all the identifiers of the ball, which makes the multiplicative $O(\log n)$ become an additive $O(\log n)$. We refer the reader to the appendix for discussion of this "virtual identifier" technique, which, as far as we know, has never been used.

6 Conclusion

There are several remaining interesting open questions regarding the role of radius in local certification. An open question is the price of reducing radius considering some other family of graphs than bounded degree graphs. An example of such a family may be planar graphs (degeneracy).

Another question to consider is the price of decreasing radius depending on the properties being certified. While our approach works in general, there may be more efficient certification methods for specific properties.

Acknowledgment. This work was supported by the Grant Agency of the Czech Technical University in Prague, grant No. SGS23/205/OHK3/3T/18.

References

1. Altisen, K., Devismes, S., Dubois, S., Petit, F.: Introduction to Distributed Self-Stabilizing Algorithms. Synthesis Lectures on Distributed Computing Theory. Morgan & Claypool Publishers (2019). https://doi.org/10.2200/S00908ED1V01Y201903DCT015
2. Ardévol Martínez, V., Caoduro, M., Feuilloley, L., Narboni, J., Pournajafi, P., Raymond, J.-F.: Lower bound for constant-size local certification. In: International Symposium on Stabilizing, Safety, and Security of Distributed Systems, pp. 239–253. Springer (2022)
3. Censor-Hillel, K., Paz, A., Perry, M.: Approximate proof-labeling schemes. Theor. Comput. Sci. **811**, 112–124 (2020)
4. Dolev, S.: Self-Stabilization. MIT Press (2000). http://www.cs.bgu.ac.il/%7Edolev/book/book.html
5. Feuilloley, L.: Introduction to local certification. Discrete Math. Theor. Comput. Sci. **23** (2021). (Distributed Computing and Networking)
6. Feuilloley, L., Fraigniaud, P., Hirvonen, J., Paz, A., Perry, M.: Redundancy in distributed proofs. Distrib. Comput. **34**(2), 113–132 (2021). https://doi.org/10.1007/S00446-020-00386-Z
7. Feuilloley, L., Fraigniaud, P., Montealegre, P., Rapaport, I., Rémila, É., Todinca, I.: Local certification of graphs with bounded genus. Discrete Appl. Math. **325**, 9–36 (2023). https://www.sciencedirect.com/science/article/pii/S0166218X22003833. https://doi.org/10.1016/j.dam.2022.10.004
8. Feuilloley, L., Janoušek, J., Křišťan, J.M., Sedláček, J.E.: Decreasing verification radius in local certification. arXiv preprint https://arxiv.org/abs/2408.10757 (2024)
9. Fischer, O., Oshman, R., Shamir, D.: Explicit space-time tradeoffs for proof labeling schemes in graphs with small separators. In: 25th International Conference on Principles of Distributed Systems (OPODIS 2021). Schloss Dagstuhl-Leibniz-Zentrum für Informatik (2022)
10. Fraigniaud, P., Göös, M., Korman, A., Suomela, J.: What can be decided locally without identifiers? In: Proceedings of the 2013 ACM Symposium on Principles of Distributed Computing, pp. 157–165 (2013)
11. Fraigniaud, P., Hirvonen, J., Suomela, J.: Node labels in local decision. Theor. Comput. Sci. **751**, 61–73 (2018)

12. Fraigniaud, P., Korman, A., Peleg, D.: Towards a complexity theory for local distributed computing. J. ACM (JACM) **60**(5), 1–26 (2013)
13. Göös, M., Suomela, J.: Locally checkable proofs in distributed computing. Theory Comput. **12**(1), 1–33 (2016)
14. Korman, A., Kutten, S.: Distributed verification of minimum spanning trees. In: Proceedings of the Twenty-Fifth Annual ACM Symposium on Principles of Distributed Computing, PODC 2006. Association for Computing Machinery, New York (2006). https://doi.org/10.1145/1146381.1146389
15. Korman, A., Kutten, S., Peleg, D.: Proof labeling schemes. Distrib. Comput. **22**(4), 215–233 (2010). https://doi.org/10.1007/S00446-010-0095-3
16. Ostrovsky, R., Perry, M., Rosenbaum, W.: Space-time tradeoffs for distributed verification. In: Das, S., Tixeuil, S. (eds.) Structural Information and Communication Complexity, pp. 53–70. Springer, Cham (2017)
17. Peleg, D.: Distributed Computing: A Locality-Sensitive Approach. SIAM (2000)

Author Index

A
Adamson, Duncan 1
Almalki, Nada 16

B
Banerjee, Rik 31
Bose, Prosenjit 144
Busson, Anthony 46

C
Chrobak, Marek 106

D
De Carufel, Jean-Lou 144

F
Feldmann, Sarah 61
Feuilloley, Laurent 188
Flaherty, Nathan 1

G
Gupta, Siddharth 16, 76

J
Janoušek, Jan 188
Jawhar, Khaled 91

K
Kahba, Dawod 159
Kranakis, Evangelos 91
Křišťan, Jan Matyáš 188
Kumar, Manish 31
Kuschner, Jordan 106
Kutner, David C. 117

M
Marin, Malory 46
Mertzios, George B. 131
Michail, Othon 16, 76
Molla, Anisur Rahaman 31

N
Nikoletseas, Sotiris 131
Njoo, Sandrine 144
Nutov, Zeev 159

P
Padalkin, Andreas 76
Potapov, Igor 1

R
Raptopoulos, Christoforos 131
Raskin, Michael 173

S
Schürenberg, Torben 61
Sedláček, Josef Erik 188
Shashwat, Yugarshi 106
Spirakis, Paul G. 1, 131
Stewart, Iain A. 117

V
van Kreveld, Marc 76

W
Watrigant, Rémi 46

Y
Yadav, Sarthak 106

SPRINGER NATURE

GPSR Compliance

The European Union's (EU) General Product Safety Regulation (GPSR) is a set of rules that requires consumer products to be safe and our obligations to ensure this.

If you have any concerns about our products, you can contact us on ProductSafety@springernature.com

In case Publisher is established outside the EU, the EU authorized representative is:

Springer Nature Customer Service Center GmbH
Europaplatz 3
69115 Heidelberg, Germany

The manufacturer's authorised representative in the EU is Springer Nature Customer Service Centre GmbH, Europaplatz 3, 69115 Heidelberg, Germany. If you have any concerns regarding our products, please contact ProductSafety@springernature.com

Printed and bound by CPI Group (UK) Ltd, Croydon, CR0 4YY

26/03/2026

02078935-0005